THE UNDERWATER WELDER

BY JEFF LEMIRE

TOP SHELF PRODUCTIONS
ATLANTA / PORTLAND

ISBN 978-1-60309-074-2. The Underwater Welder © 2012 Jeff Lemire. Lettering: Steve Wands. Cover design: Jeff Lemire, Chris Ross, and Brett Warnock.

Published by: Top Shelf Productions, PO Box 1282, Marietta, GA 30061-1282, USA. Publishers: Brett Warnock and Chris Staros.

Edited by Chris Staros. Top Shelf Productions® and the Top Shelf logo are registered trademarks of Top Shelf Productions, Inc. All Rights Reserved.

No part of this publication may be reproduced without permission, except for small excerpts for purposes of review.

Visit our online catalog at www.topshelfcomix.com. First printing, August 2012.

Printed in Canada.

FOR GUS.

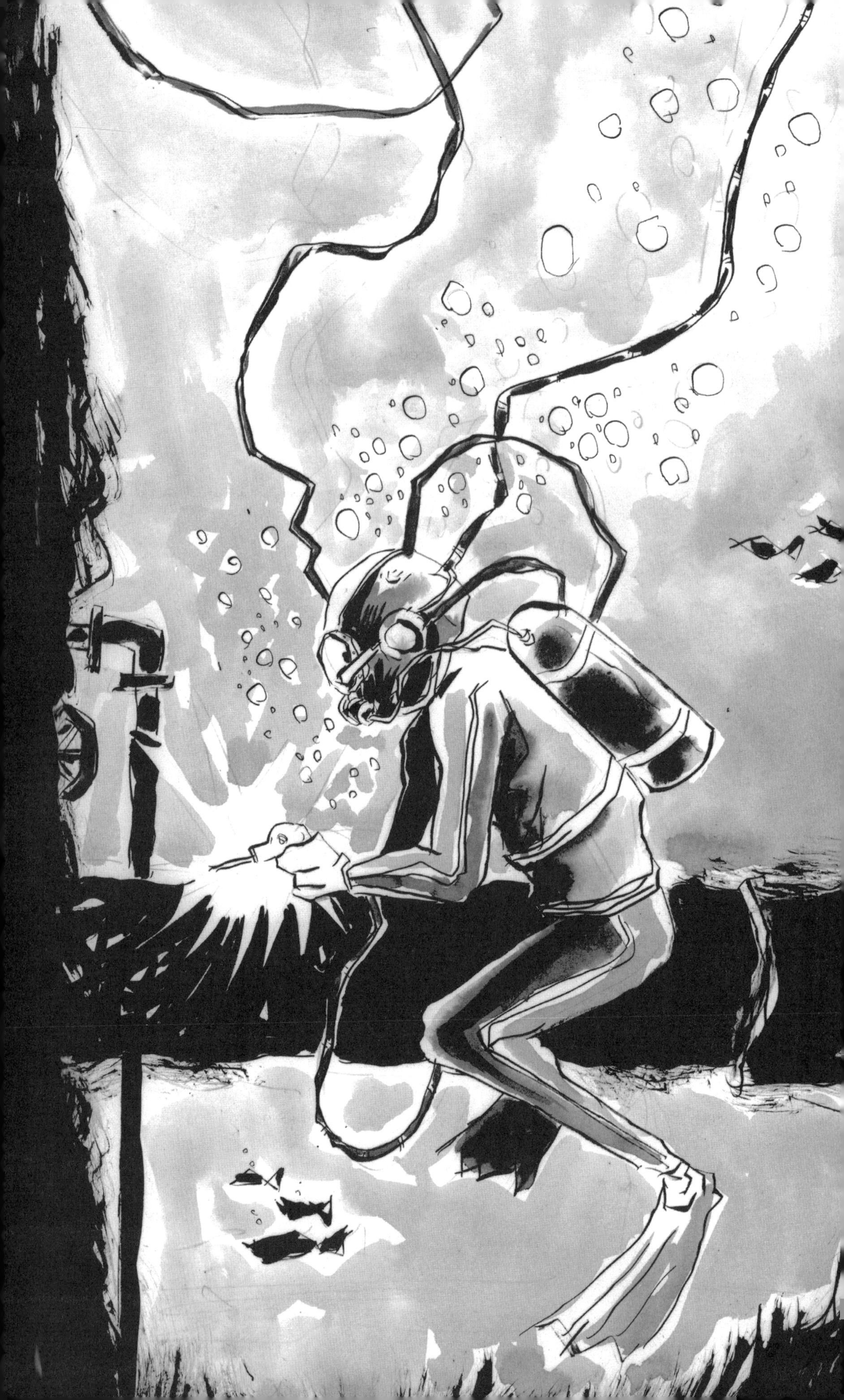

INTRODUCTION

You guys like *The Twilight Zone?*

Yeah, of course you do. Because you read cool graphic novels like the one you're currently holding in your hands. And because *The Twilight Zone* is undeniably awesome.

Well, ladies and gentlemen, you are about to read the most spectacular episode of *The Twilight Zone* that was never produced.

The Underwater Welder is written and illustrated by the staggeringly talented Jeff Lemire. I am deeply threatened by Jeff's creativity, a fact mitigated only partially by the fact that he is Canadian and thus, inherently non-threatening.

But I digress.

So. Why do I compare this incredible piece of work to *The Twilight Zone?* Well, all classic episodes combined several key ingredients, all of which are brilliantly demonstrated within these pages. First and foremost, they were strange and creepy. *Underwater Welder?* Big-time strange and creepy.

Secondly, *Zone* stories featured deeply flawed and profoundly real characters...people who often made mistakes and were now suffering for them. And folks?

Just wait until you meet Jack.

Finally, and most importantly, there had to be some sort of broader theme...a lesson to be learned without being overtly preachy. And at the core of this message, which was often received too late, damning the hero to his or her own private hell, there was always a beating heart. There was emotion. We cared.

As I promised Jeff I would not get overly sentimental (like I said, he's Canadian), I will leave it at this—I really, really care about the people in this story. A lot. And I can pretty much guarantee you will too. So, my fellow divers, allow me to do my best Serling impression before you dive into the cold waters before you.

Ahem...

Picure if you will, a man named Jack. Occupation: Underwater Welder. Tomorrow, it will be Halloween, and while the children in white sheets roam the streets, Jack will be haunted by a different kind of ghost entirely. Because down there, in the vastness of the ocean, deep below where even the light of a blowtorch is swallowed up in the darkness, there is a doorway. And on the other side? Memories, just as dark...and the cold, wet embrace of the Twilight Zone.

Damon Lindelof
February, 2012

Damon Lindelof is the co-creator and executive producer of the ABC series *LOST*. He is also known for his work on the recent *Star Trek* film, its sequel, and Ridley Scott's *Prometheus*

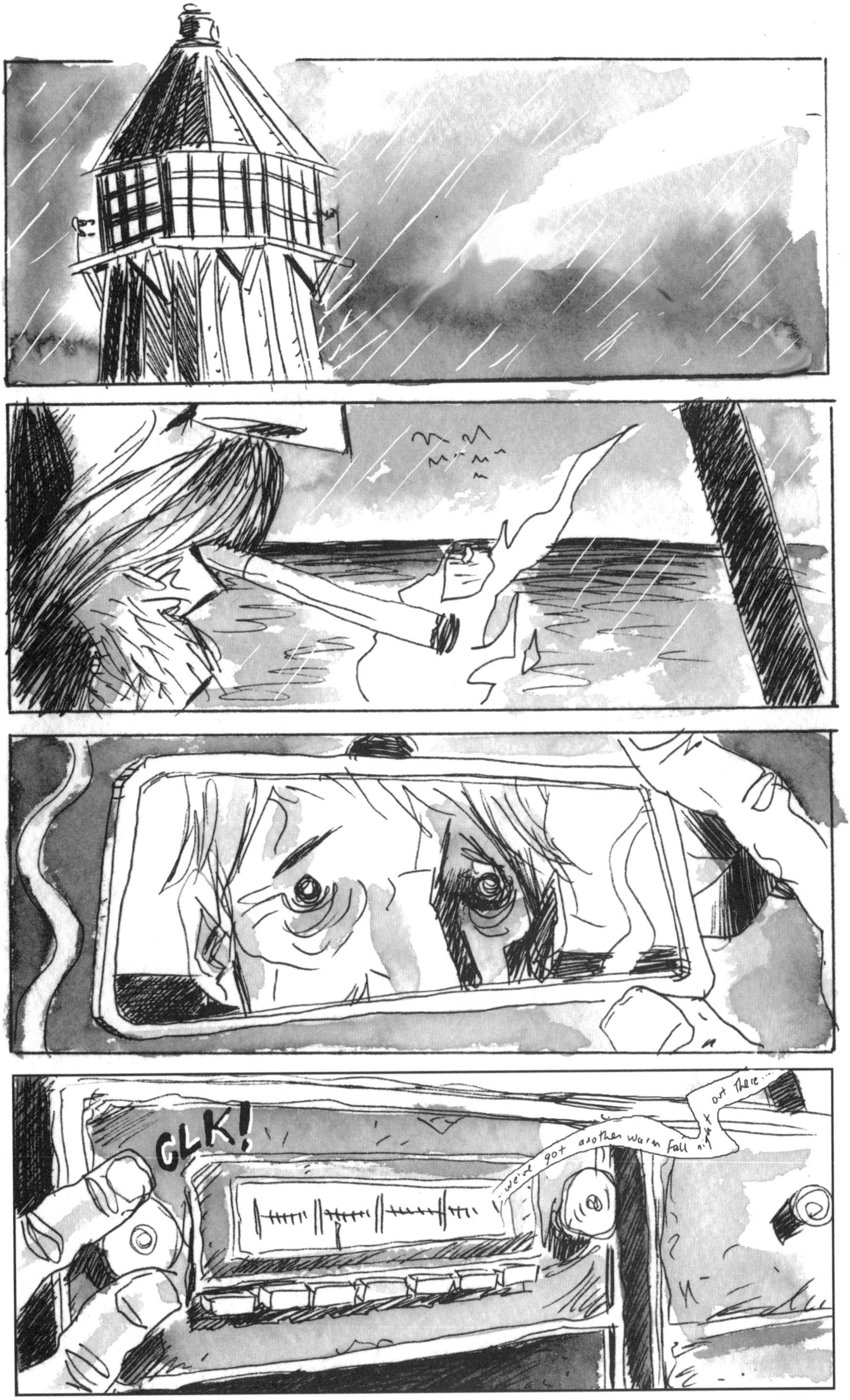
CLK!
...we've got another warm fall night out there....

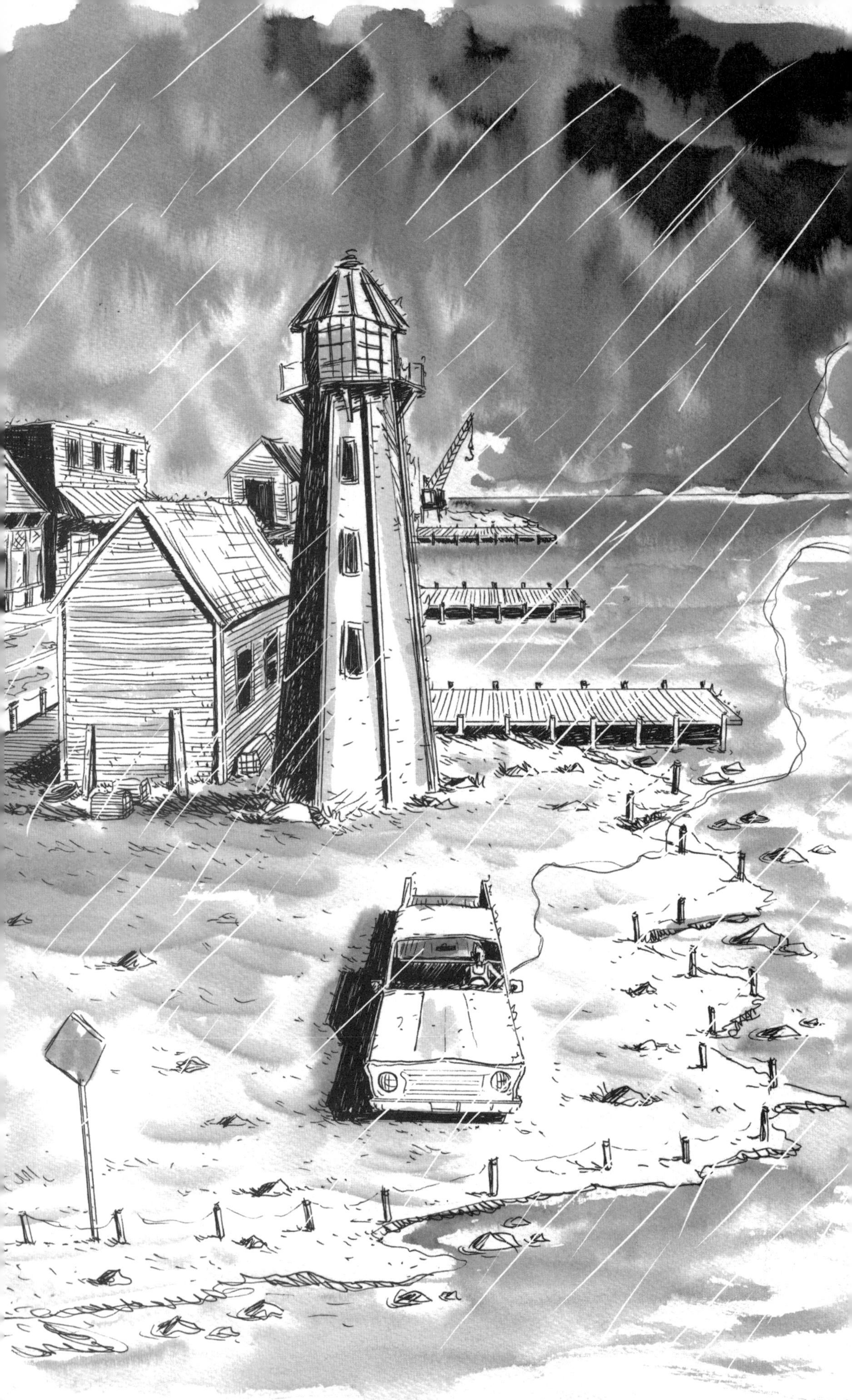

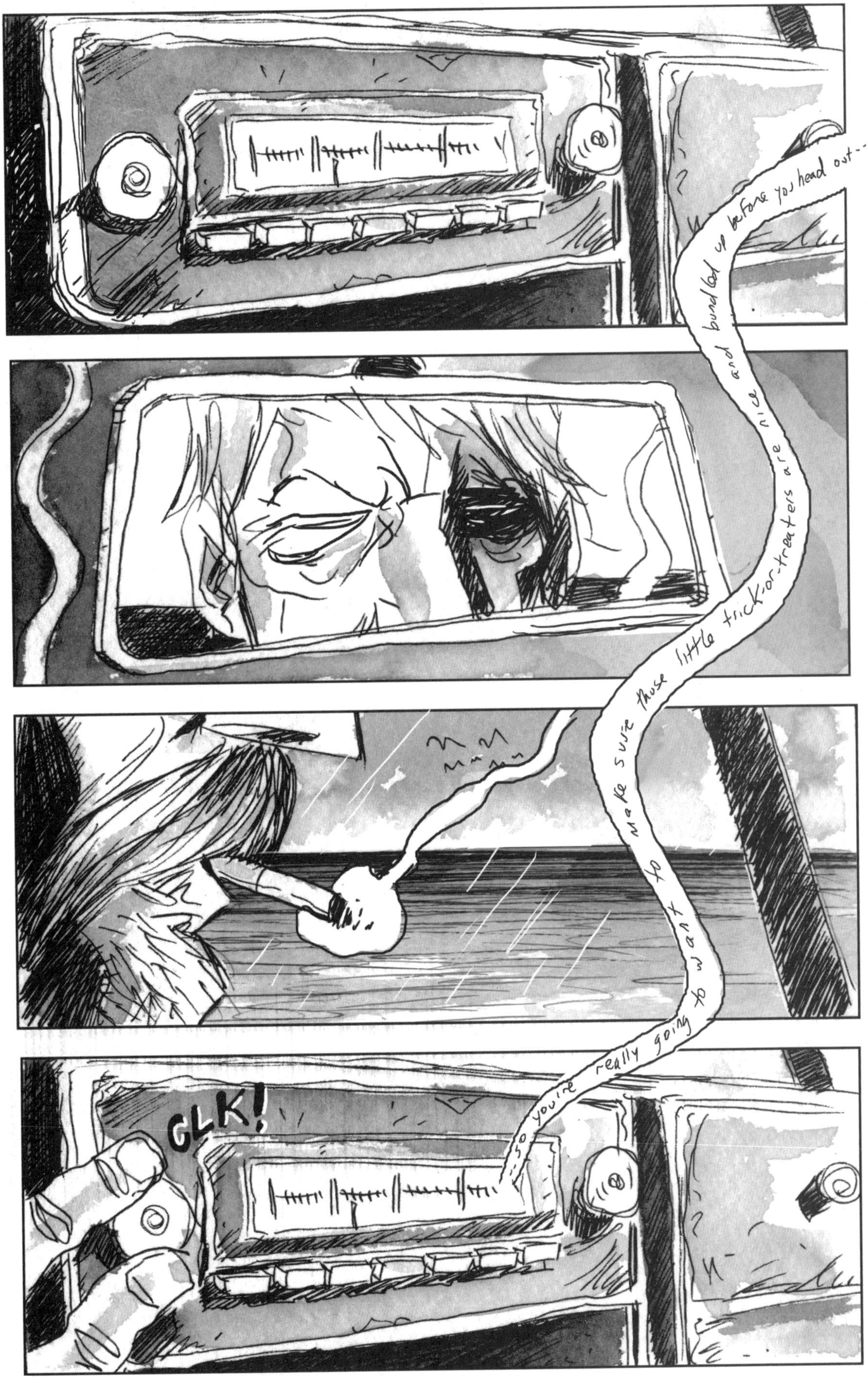

...so you're really going to want to make sure those little trick-or-treaters are nice and bundled up before you head out...
CLK!

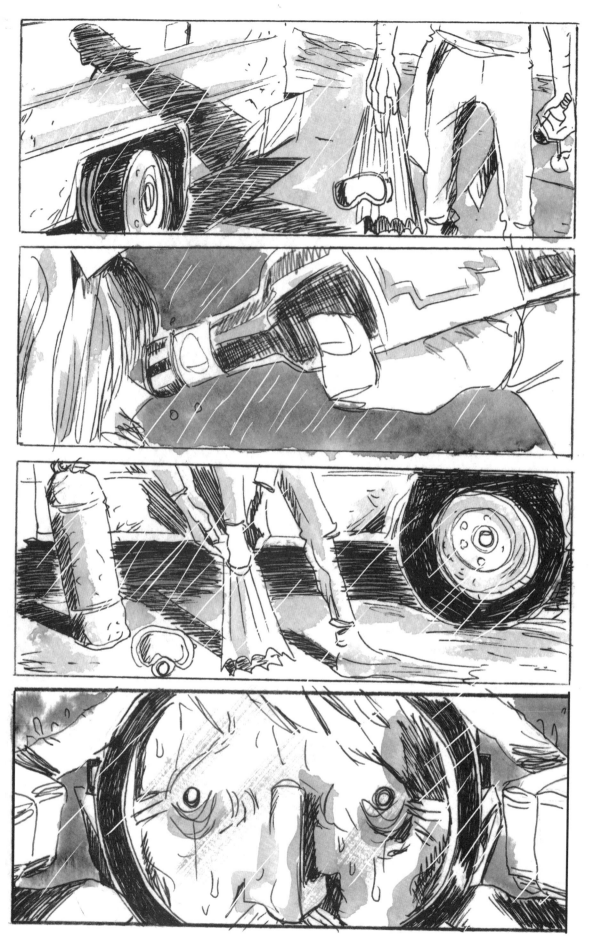

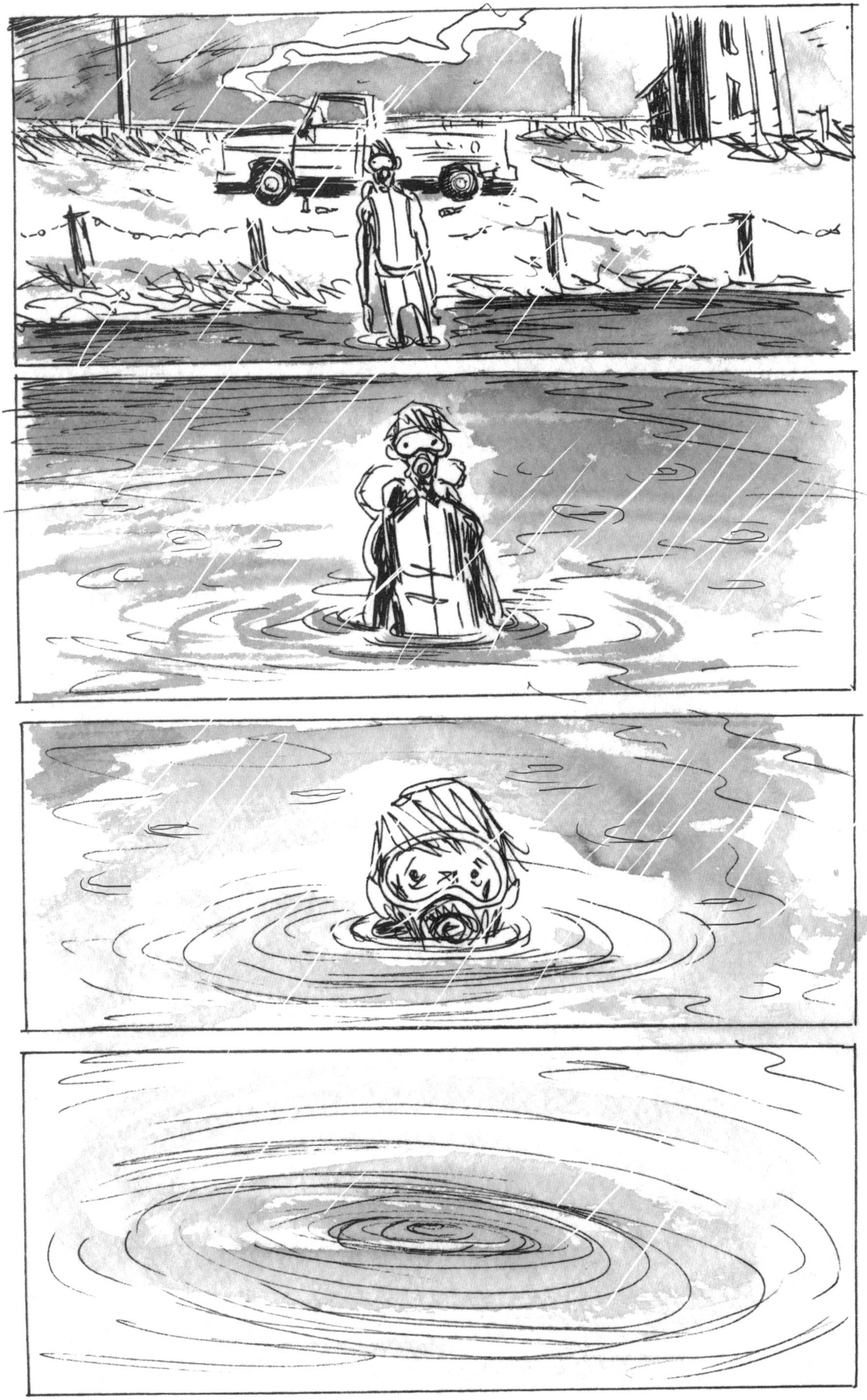

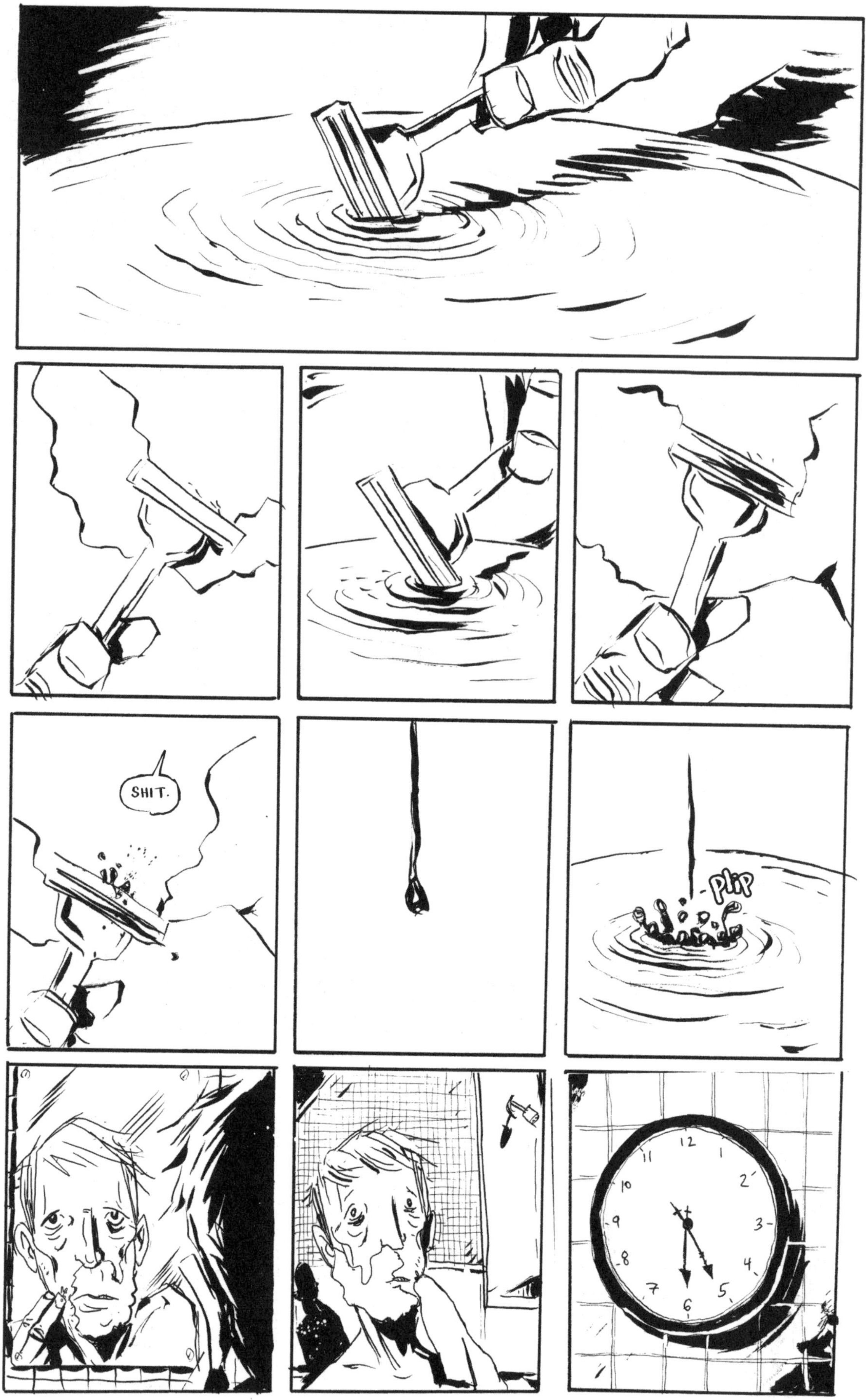
SHIT.
PLIP

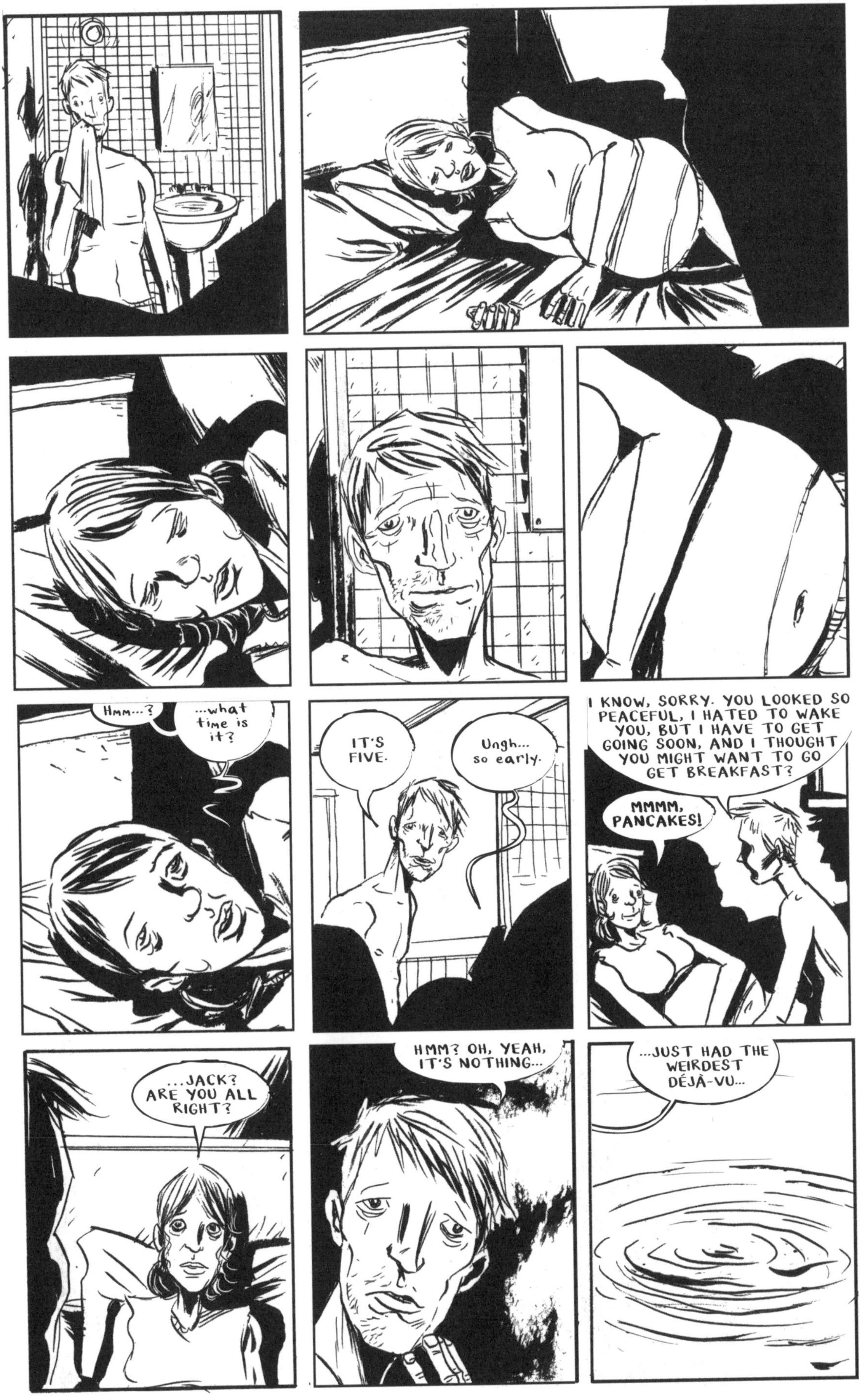
Hmm...?
...what time is it?
IT'S FIVE.
Ungh... so early.
I KNOW, SORRY. YOU LOOKED SO PEACEFUL, I HATED TO WAKE YOU, BUT I HAVE TO GET GOING SOON, AND I THOUGHT YOU MIGHT WANT TO GO GET BREAKFAST?
MMMM, PANCAKES!
...JACK? ARE YOU ALL RIGHT?
HMM? OH, YEAH, IT'S NOTHING...
...JUST HAD THE WEIRDEST DÉJÀ-VU...

1. MYSTERIES OF THE DEEP

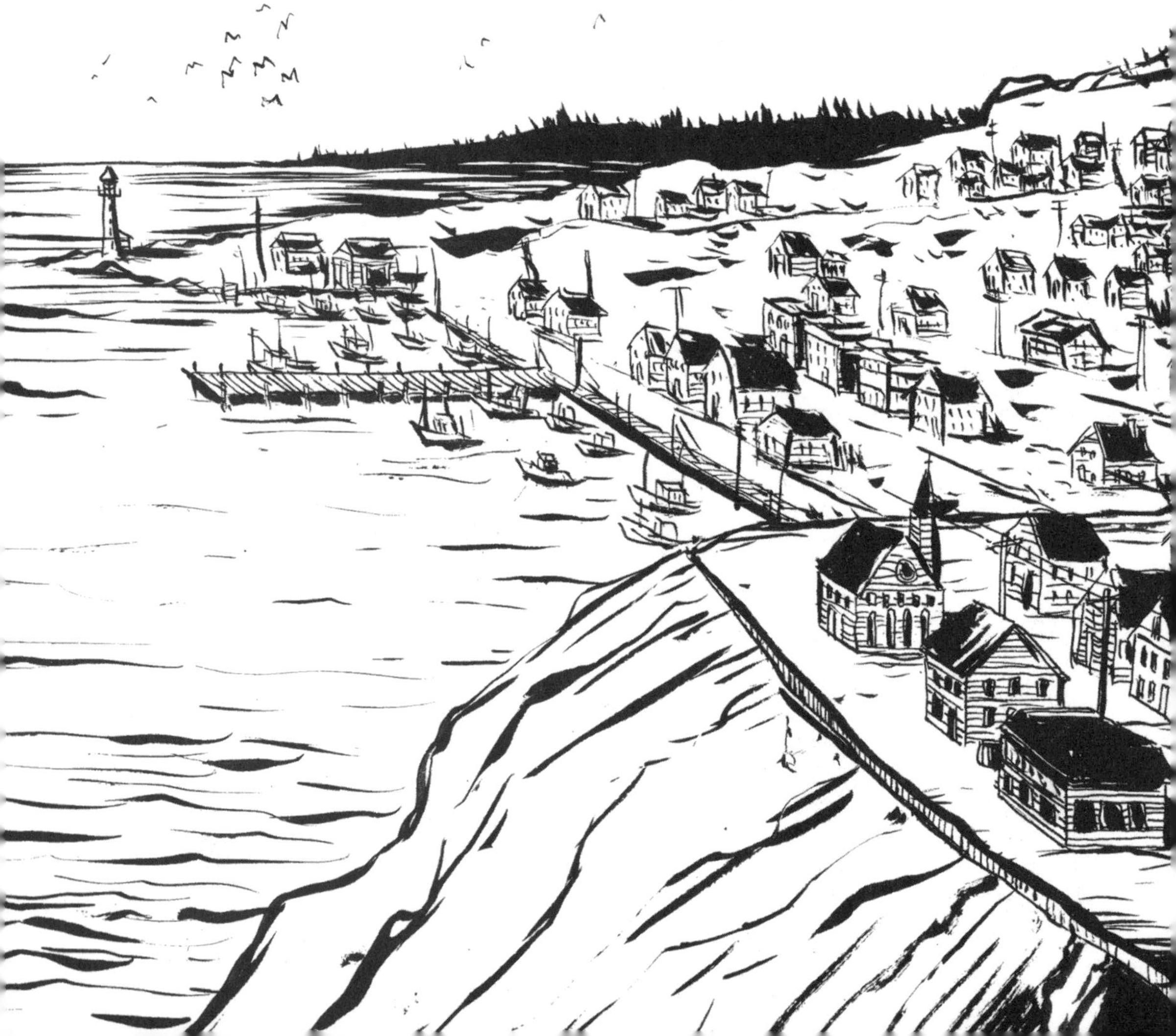

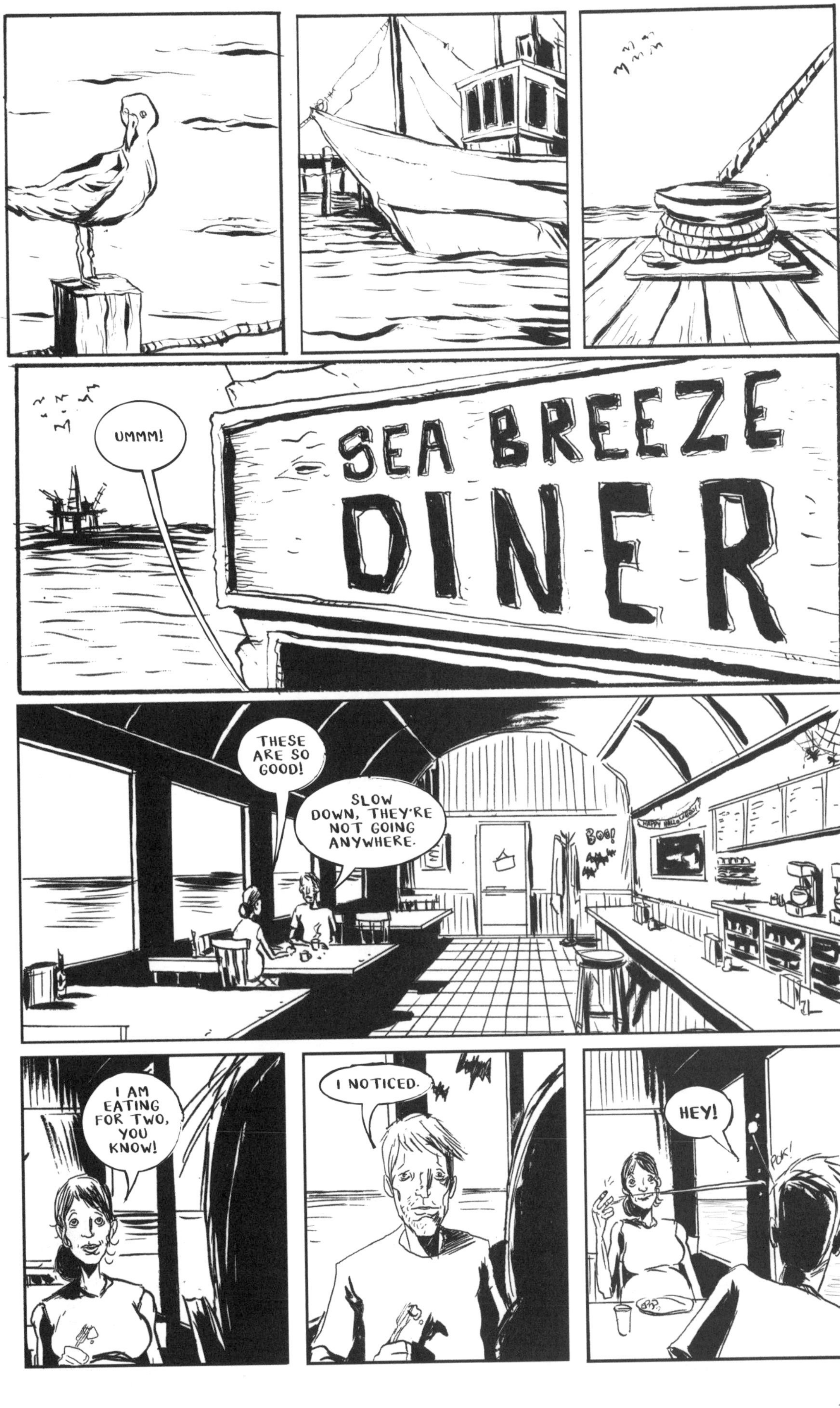
SEA BREEZE DINER
UMMM!
THESE ARE SO GOOD!
SLOW DOWN, THEY'RE NOT GOING ANYWHERE.
BOO!
I AM EATING FOR TWO, YOU KNOW!
I NOTICED.
HEY!
POK!

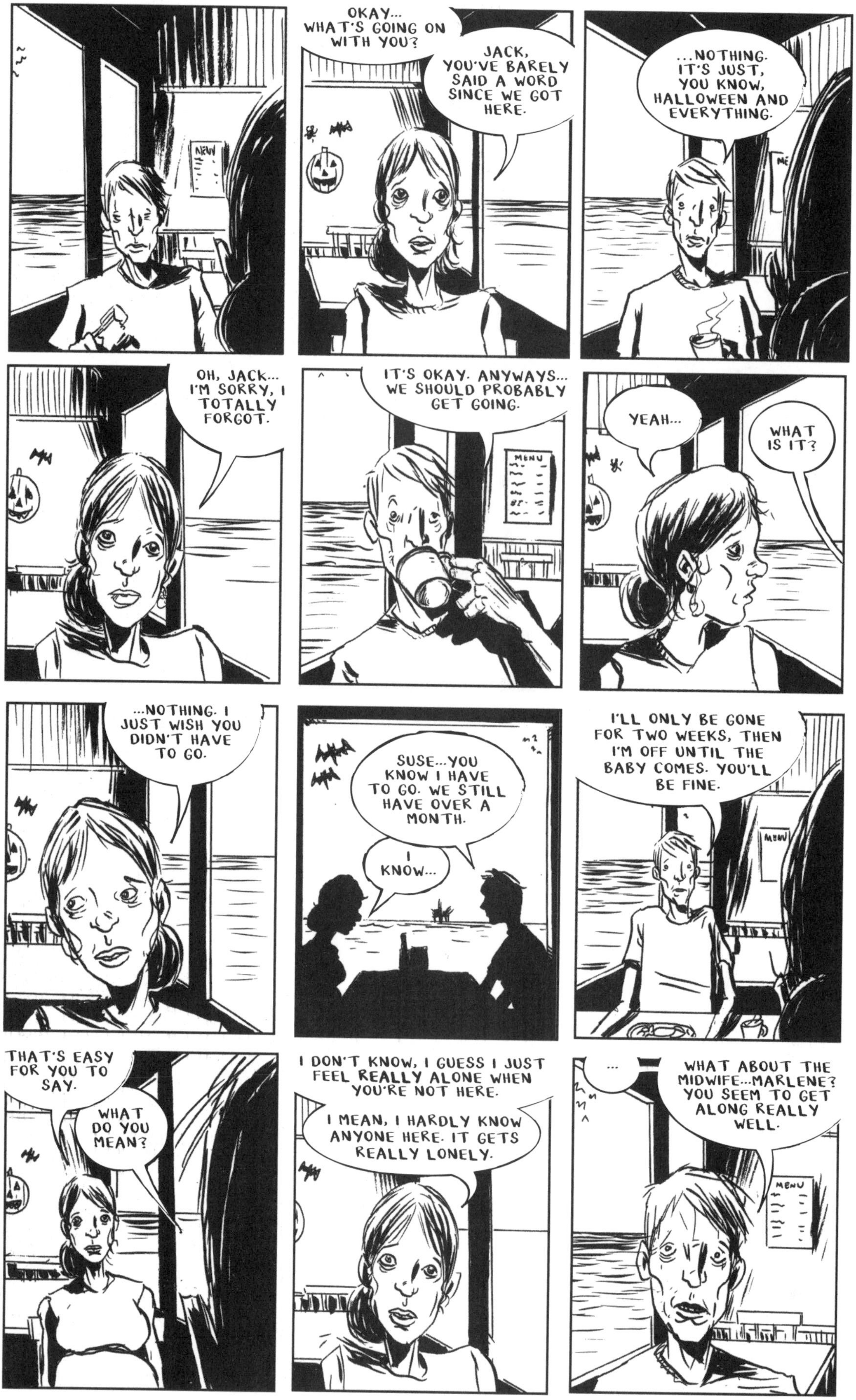

OKAY... WHAT'S GOING ON WITH YOU?
JACK, YOU'VE BARELY SAID A WORD SINCE WE GOT HERE.
...NOTHING. IT'S JUST, YOU KNOW, HALLOWEEN AND EVERYTHING.
OH, JACK... I'M SORRY, I TOTALLY FORGOT.
IT'S OKAY. ANYWAYS... WE SHOULD PROBABLY GET GOING.
YEAH...
WHAT IS IT?
...NOTHING. I JUST WISH YOU DIDN'T HAVE TO GO.
SUSE...YOU KNOW I HAVE TO GO. WE STILL HAVE OVER A MONTH.
I KNOW...
I'LL ONLY BE GONE FOR TWO WEEKS, THEN I'M OFF UNTIL THE BABY COMES. YOU'LL BE FINE.
THAT'S EASY FOR YOU TO SAY.
WHAT DO YOU MEAN?
I DON'T KNOW, I GUESS I JUST FEEL REALLY ALONE WHEN YOU'RE NOT HERE.
I MEAN, I HARDLY KNOW ANYONE HERE. IT GETS REALLY LONELY.
...
WHAT ABOUT THE MIDWIFE...MARLENE? YOU SEEM TO GET ALONG REALLY WELL.

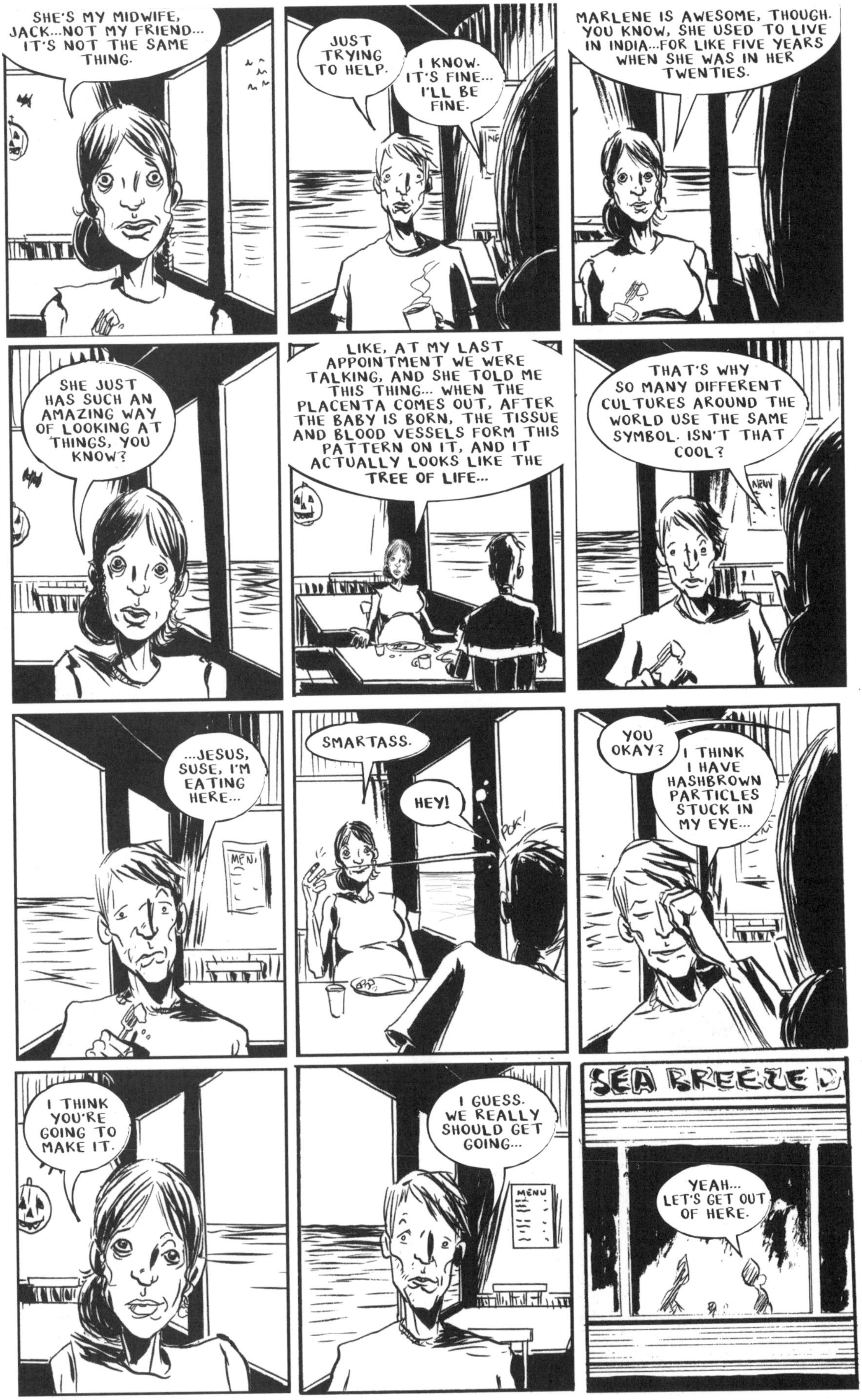
SHE'S MY MIDWIFE, JACK...NOT MY FRIEND... IT'S NOT THE SAME THING.
JUST TRYING TO HELP.
I KNOW. IT'S FINE... I'LL BE FINE.
MARLENE IS AWESOME, THOUGH. YOU KNOW, SHE USED TO LIVE IN INDIA...FOR LIKE FIVE YEARS WHEN SHE WAS IN HER TWENTIES.
SHE JUST HAS SUCH AN AMAZING WAY OF LOOKING AT THINGS, YOU KNOW?
LIKE, AT MY LAST APPOINTMENT WE WERE TALKING, AND SHE TOLD ME THIS THING... WHEN THE PLACENTA COMES OUT, AFTER THE BABY IS BORN, THE TISSUE AND BLOOD VESSELS FORM THIS PATTERN ON IT, AND IT ACTUALLY LOOKS LIKE THE TREE OF LIFE...
THAT'S WHY SO MANY DIFFERENT CULTURES AROUND THE WORLD USE THE SAME SYMBOL. ISN'T THAT COOL?
...JESUS, SUSE, I'M EATING HERE...
MENU
SMARTASS.
HEY!
POK!
YOU OKAY?
I THINK I HAVE HASHBROWN PARTICLES STUCK IN MY EYE...
I THINK YOU'RE GOING TO MAKE IT.
I GUESS. WE REALLY SHOULD GET GOING...
MENU
SEA BREEZE
YEAH... LET'S GET OUT OF HERE.

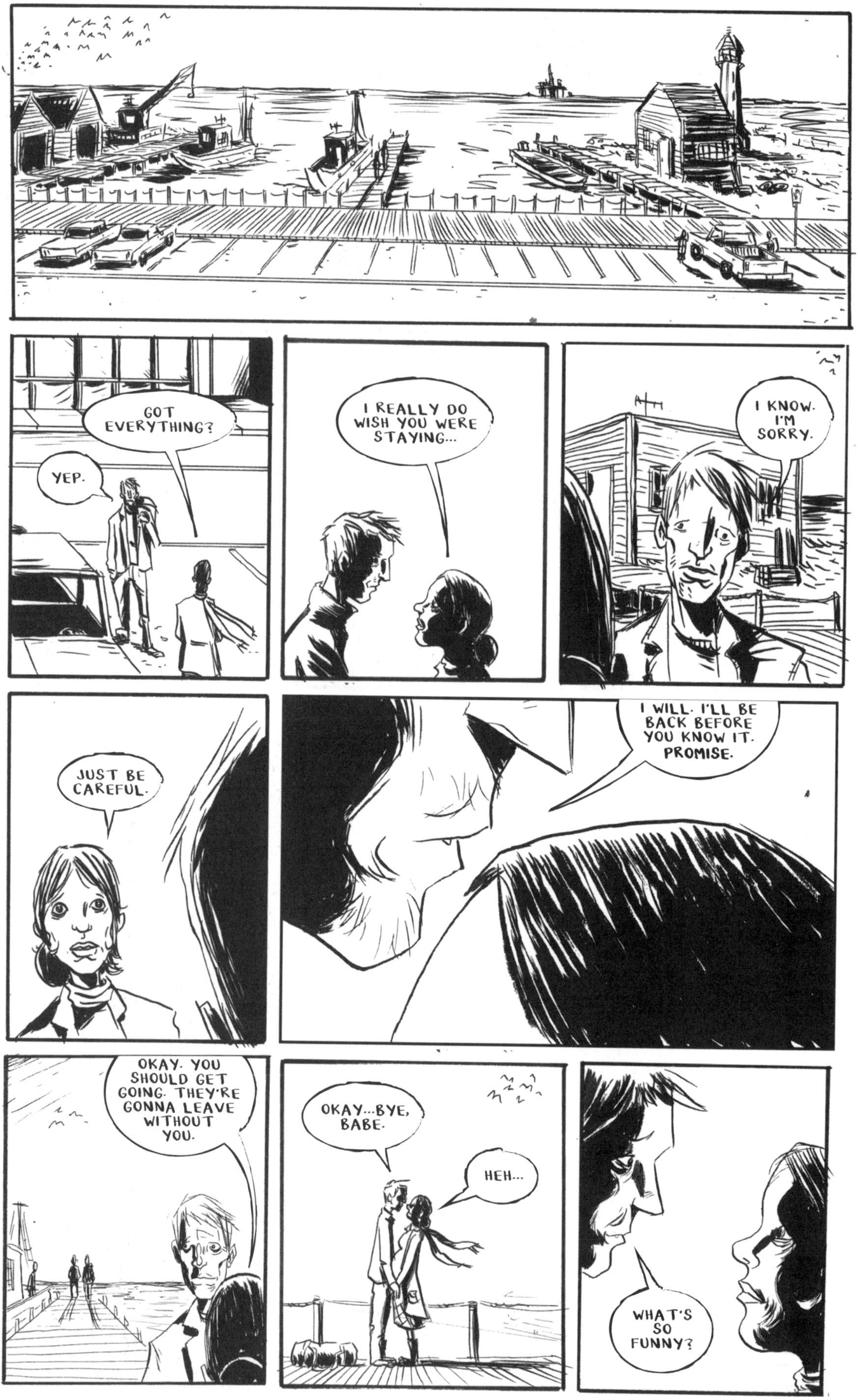
GOT EVERYTHING?
YEP.
I REALLY DO WISH YOU WERE STAYING...
I KNOW. I'M SORRY.
JUST BE CAREFUL.
I WILL. I'LL BE BACK BEFORE YOU KNOW IT. PROMISE.
OKAY. YOU SHOULD GET GOING. THEY'RE GONNA LEAVE WITHOUT YOU.
OKAY...BYE, BABE.
HEH...
WHAT'S SO FUNNY?

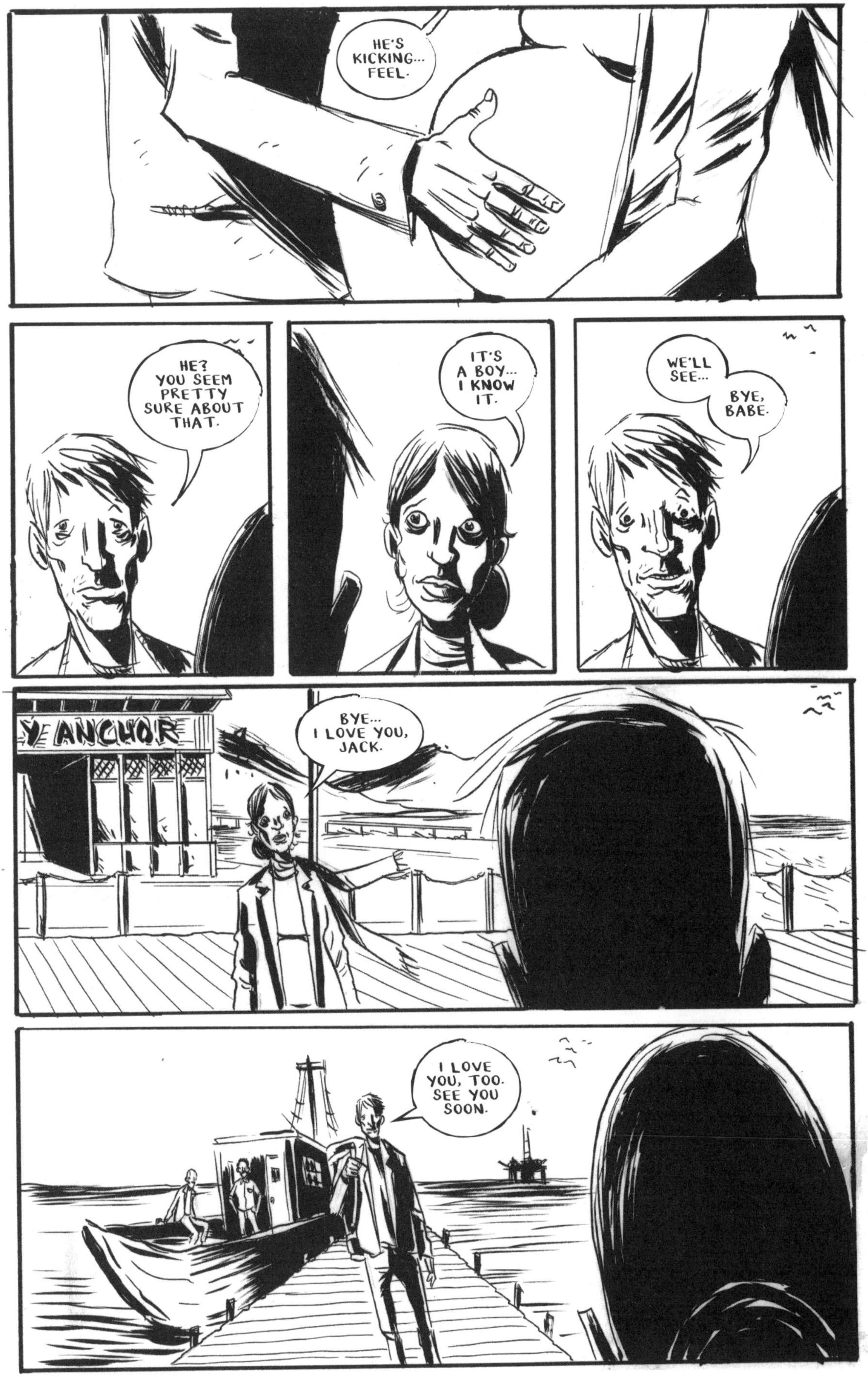
HE'S KICKING... FEEL.
HE? YOU SEEM PRETTY SURE ABOUT THAT.
IT'S A BOY... I KNOW IT.
WE'LL SEE...
BYE, BABE.
Y ANCHOR
BYE... I LOVE YOU, JACK.
I LOVE YOU, TOO. SEE YOU SOON.

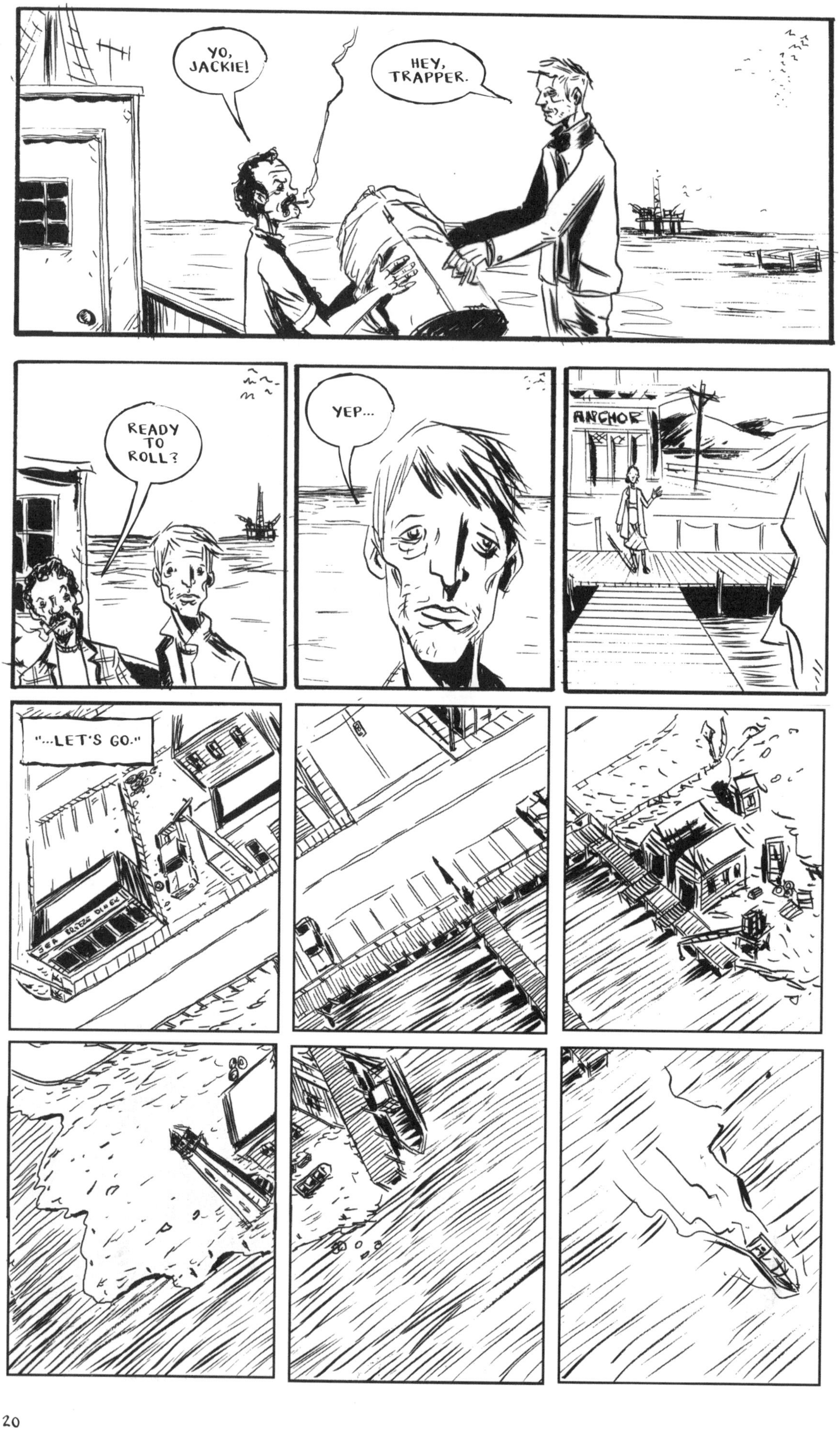
YO, JACKIE!
HEY, TRAPPER.
READY TO ROLL?
YEP...
ANCHOR
"...LET'S GO."

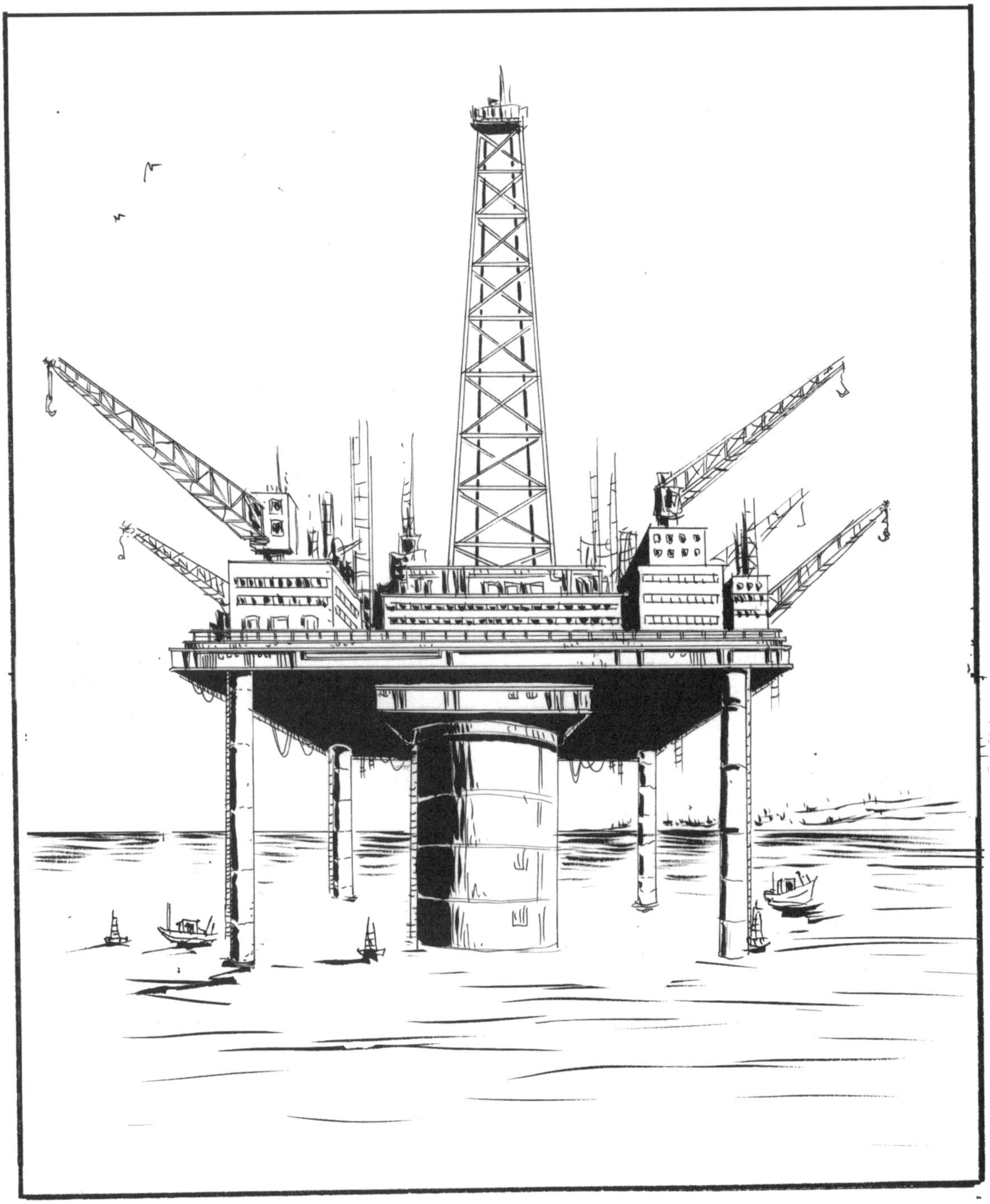

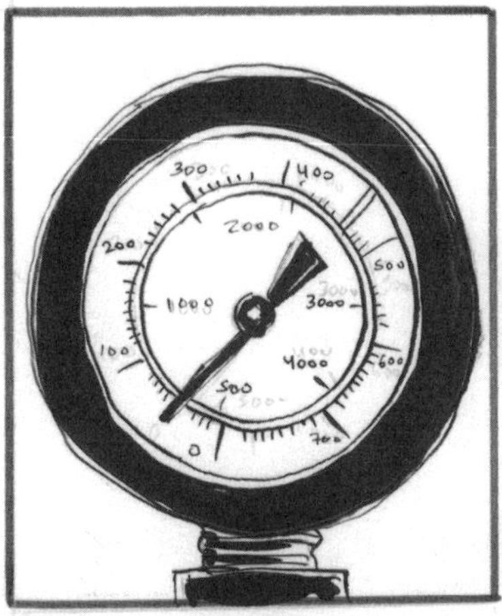
300
400
2000
200
500
1000
3000
100
4000
600
500
0
700

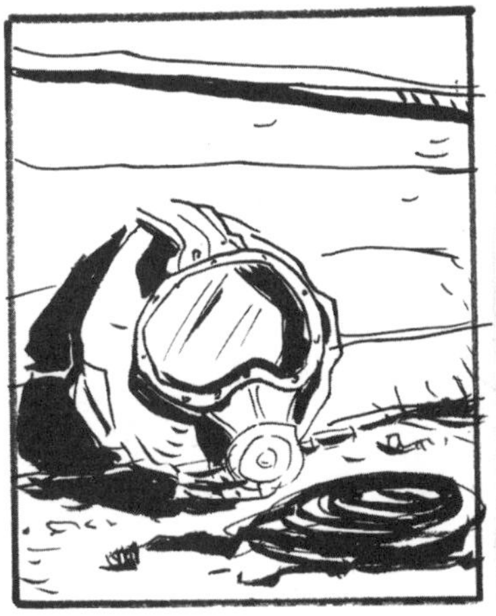

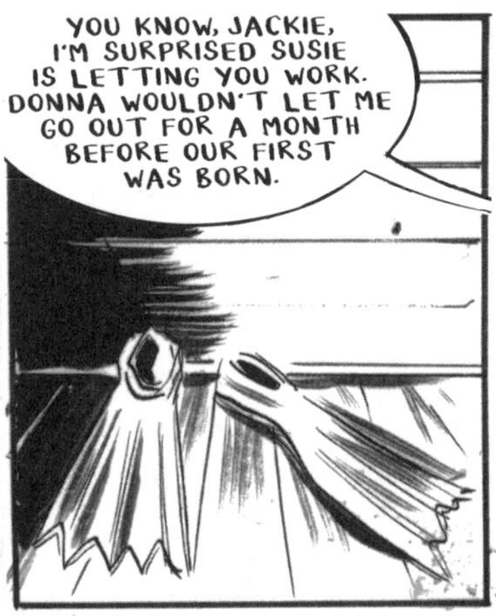
YOU KNOW, JACKIE, I'M SURPRISED SUSIE IS LETTING YOU WORK. DONNA WOULDN'T LET ME GO OUT FOR A MONTH BEFORE OUR FIRST WAS BORN.

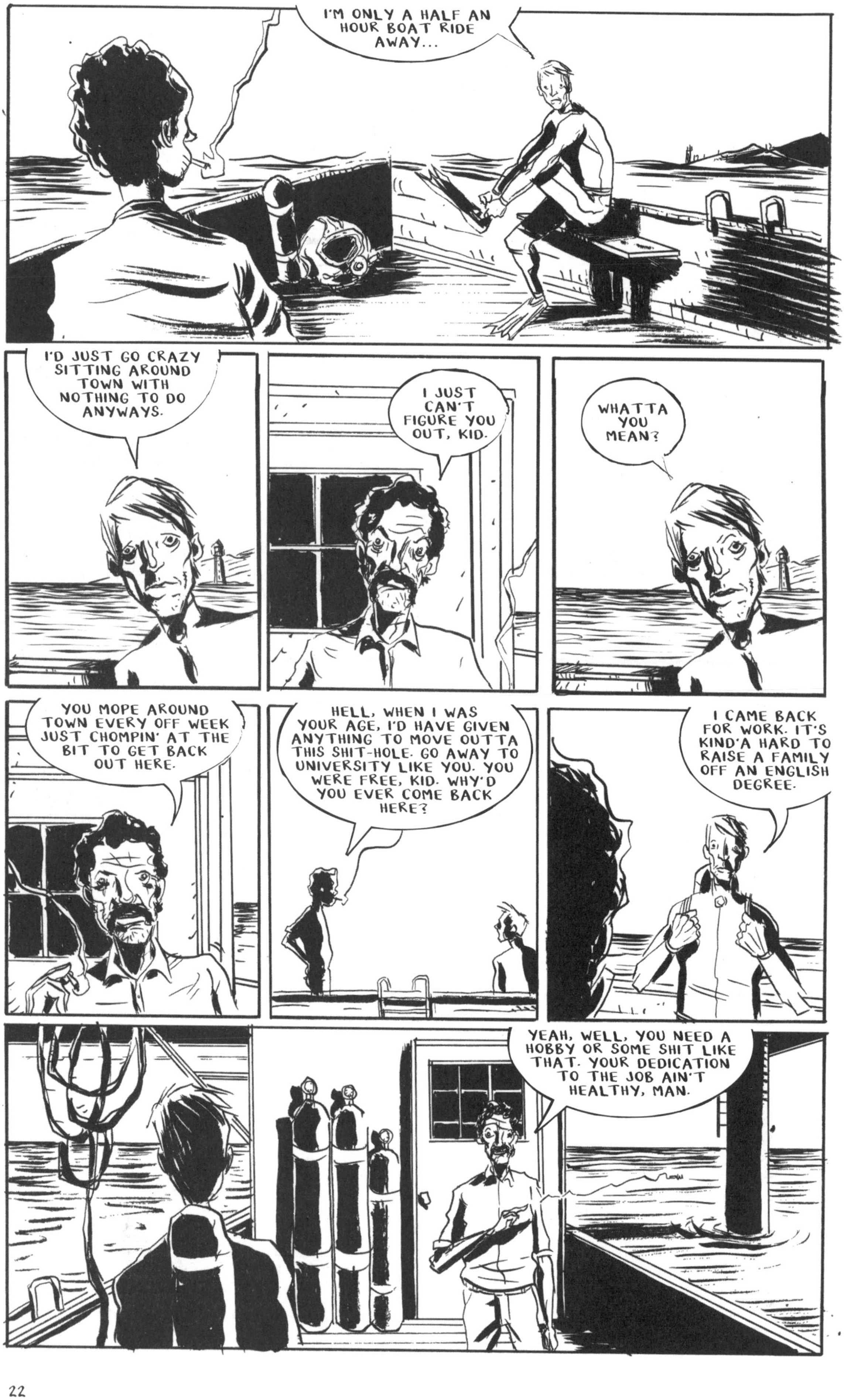
I'M ONLY A HALF AN HOUR BOAT RIDE AWAY...
I'D JUST GO CRAZY SITTING AROUND TOWN WITH NOTHING TO DO ANYWAYS.
I JUST CAN'T FIGURE YOU OUT, KID.
WHATTA YOU MEAN?
YOU MOPE AROUND TOWN EVERY OFF WEEK JUST CHOMPIN' AT THE BIT TO GET BACK OUT HERE.
HELL, WHEN I WAS YOUR AGE, I'D HAVE GIVEN ANYTHING TO MOVE OUTTA THIS SHIT-HOLE. GO AWAY TO UNIVERSITY LIKE YOU. YOU WERE FREE, KID. WHY'D YOU EVER COME BACK HERE?
I CAME BACK FOR WORK. IT'S KIND'A HARD TO RAISE A FAMILY OFF AN ENGLISH DEGREE.
YEAH, WELL, YOU NEED A HOBBY OR SOME SHIT LIKE THAT. YOUR DEDICATION TO THE JOB AIN'T HEALTHY, MAN.

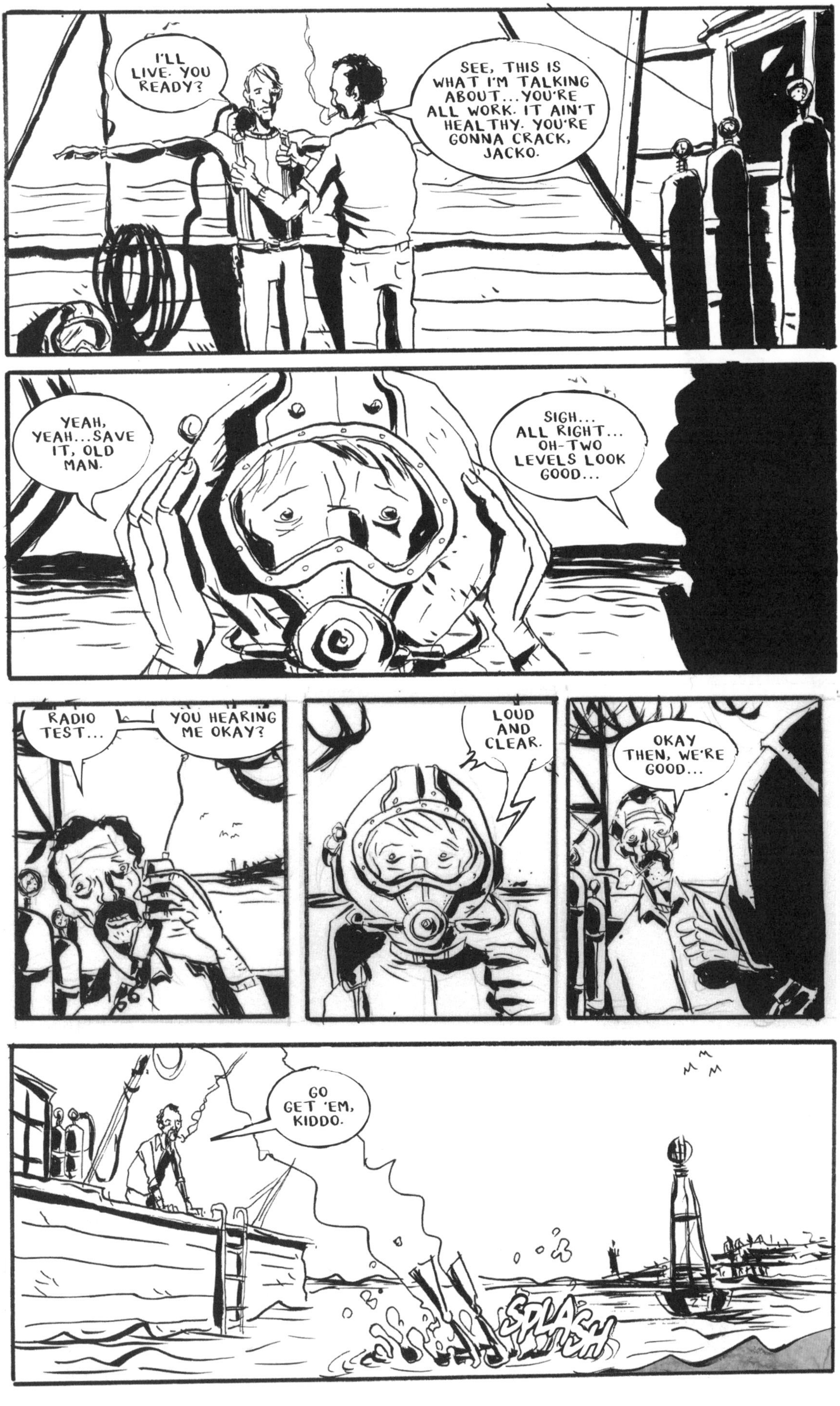
I'LL LIVE. YOU READY?
SEE, THIS IS WHAT I'M TALKING ABOUT... YOU'RE ALL WORK. IT AIN'T HEALTHY. YOU'RE GONNA CRACK, JACKO.
YEAH, YEAH... SAVE IT, OLD MAN.
SIGH... ALL RIGHT... OH-TWO LEVELS LOOK GOOD...
RADIO TEST...
YOU HEARING ME OKAY?
LOUD AND CLEAR.
OKAY THEN, WE'RE GOOD...
GO GET 'EM, KIDDO.
SPLASH

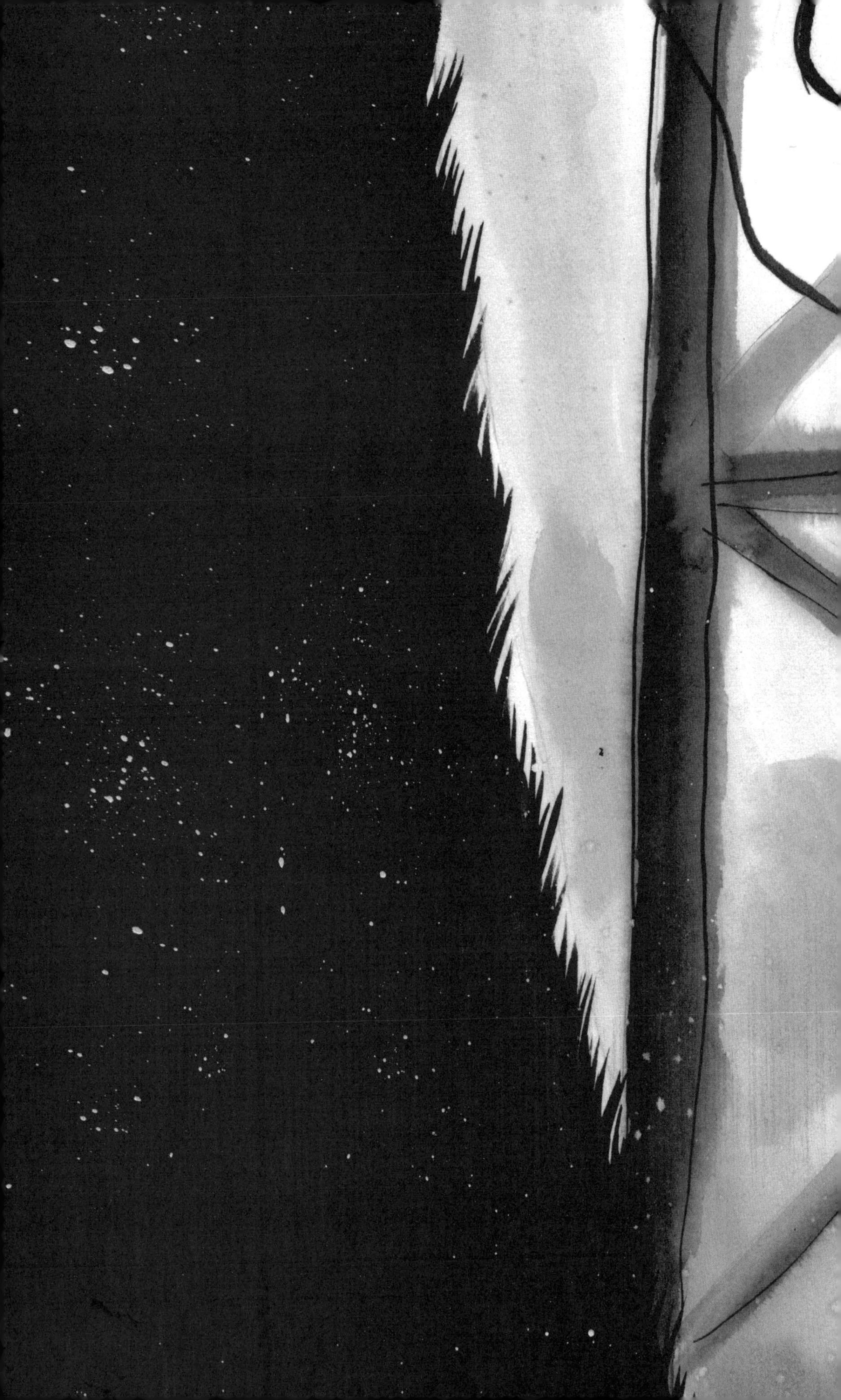

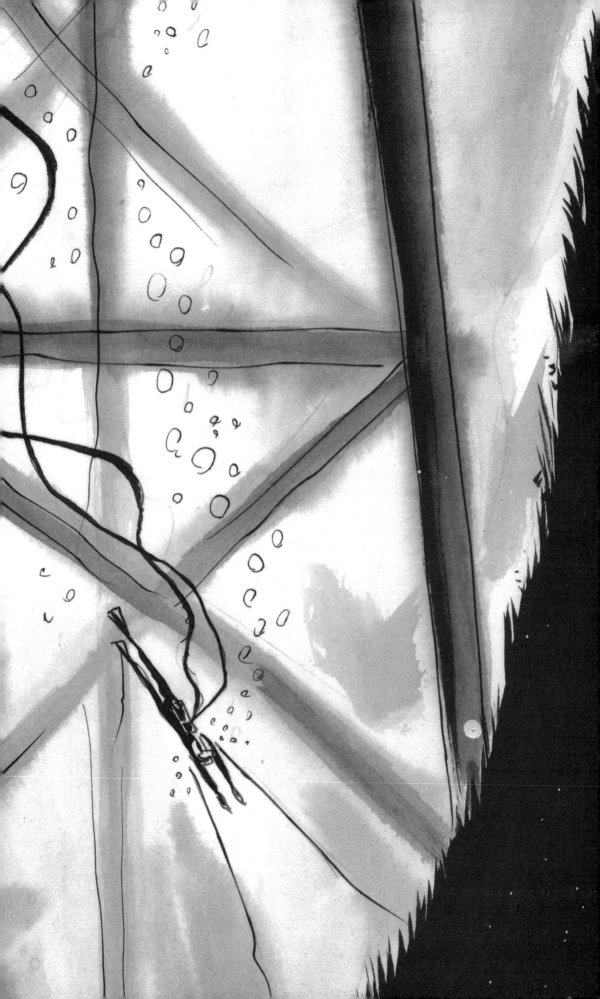

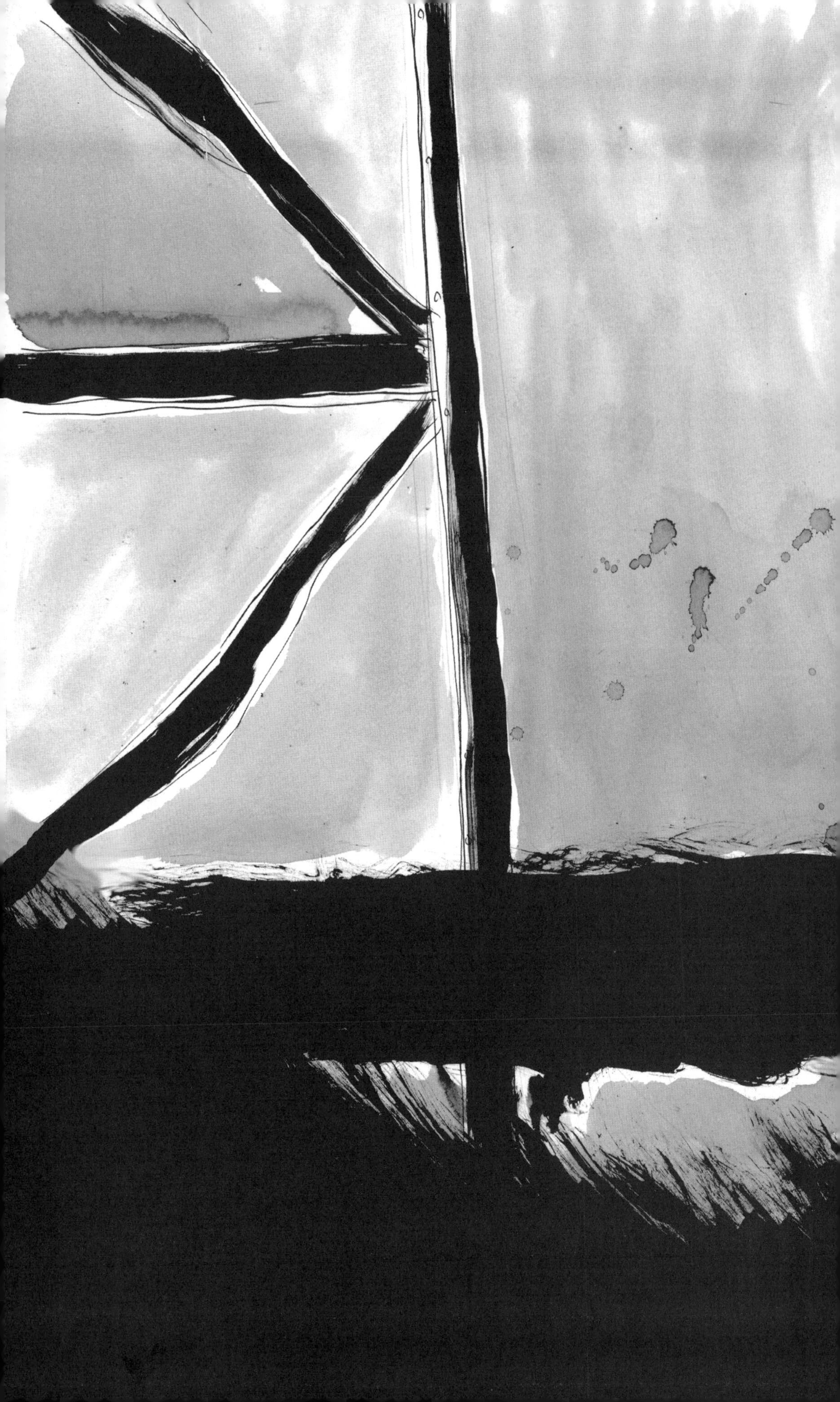

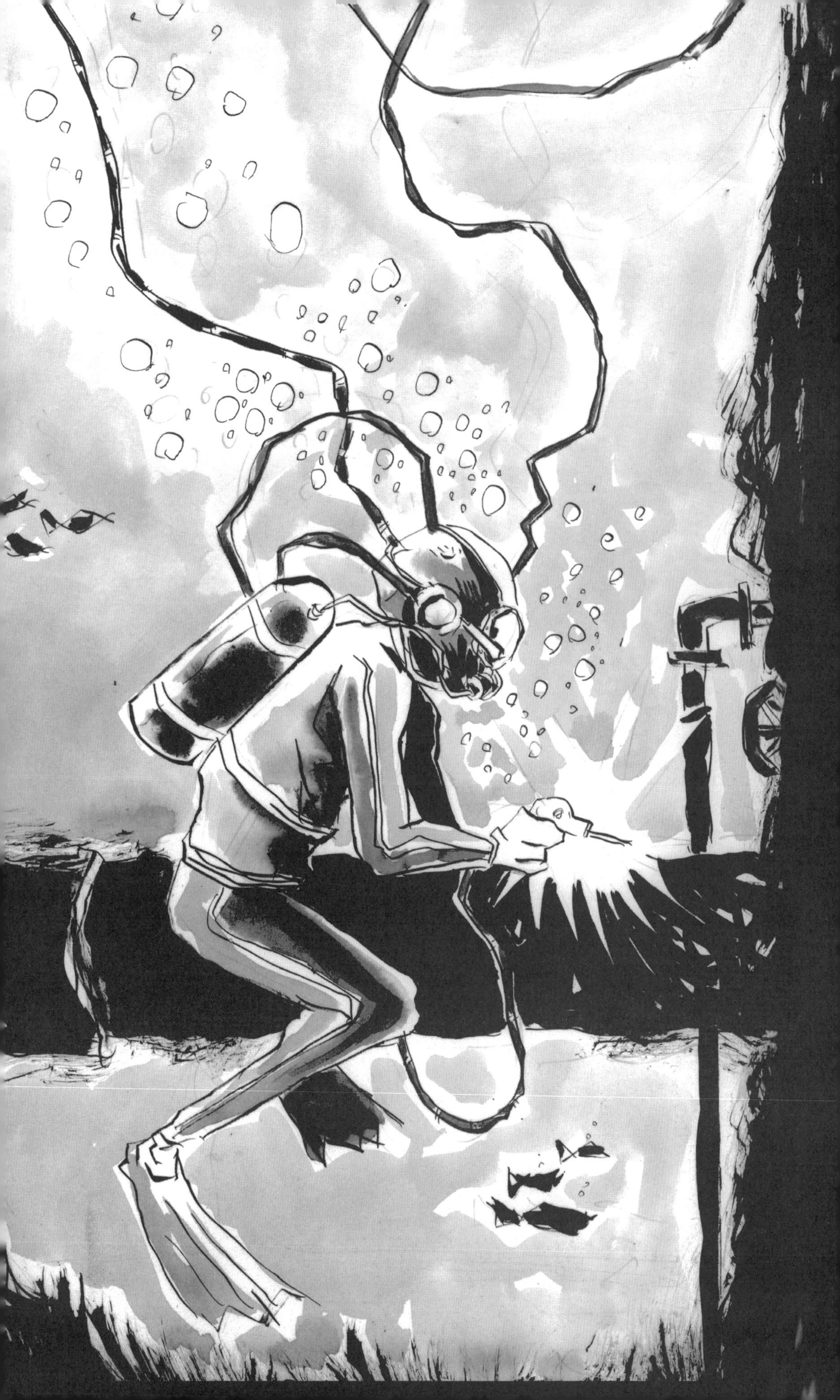

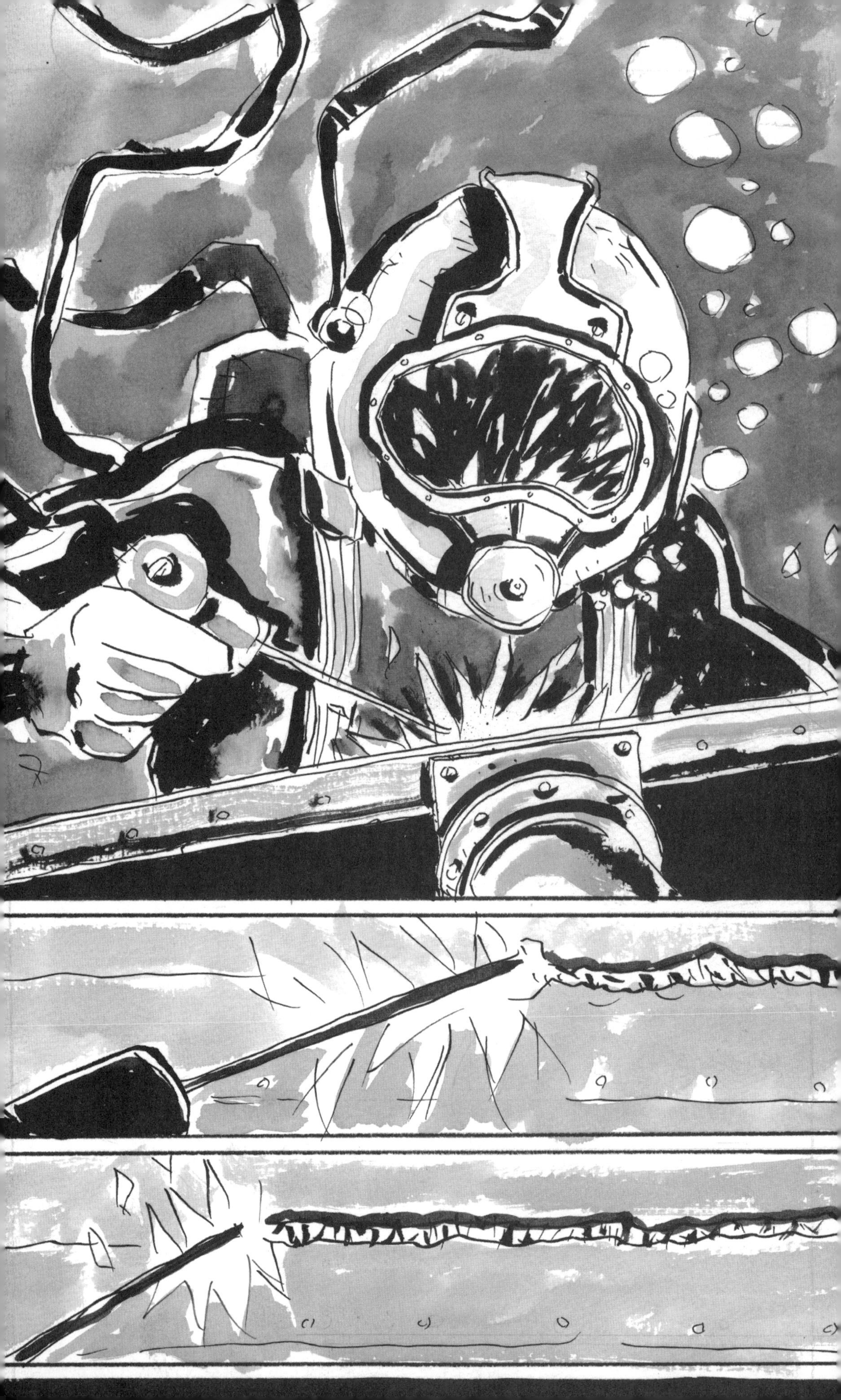

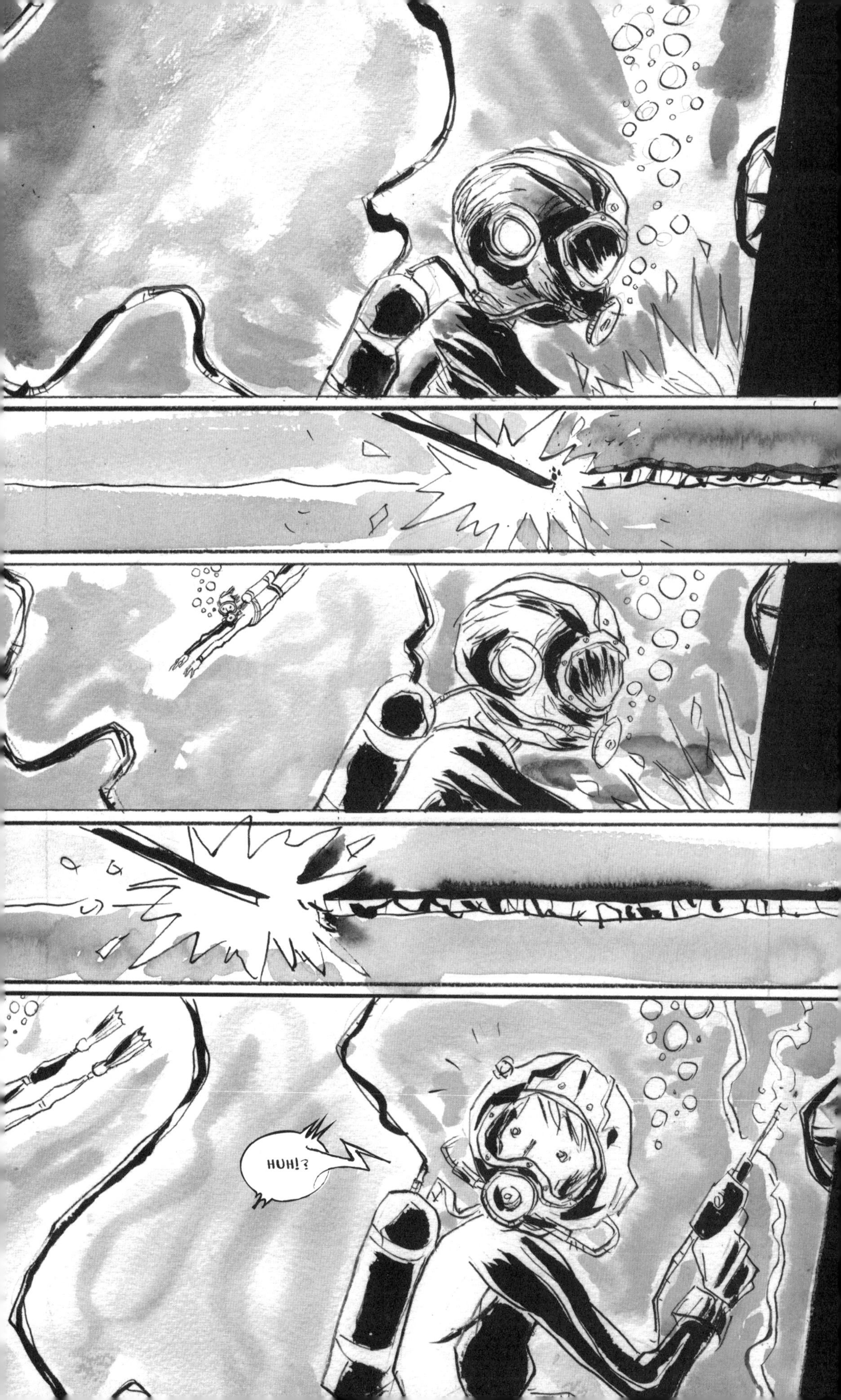
HUH!?

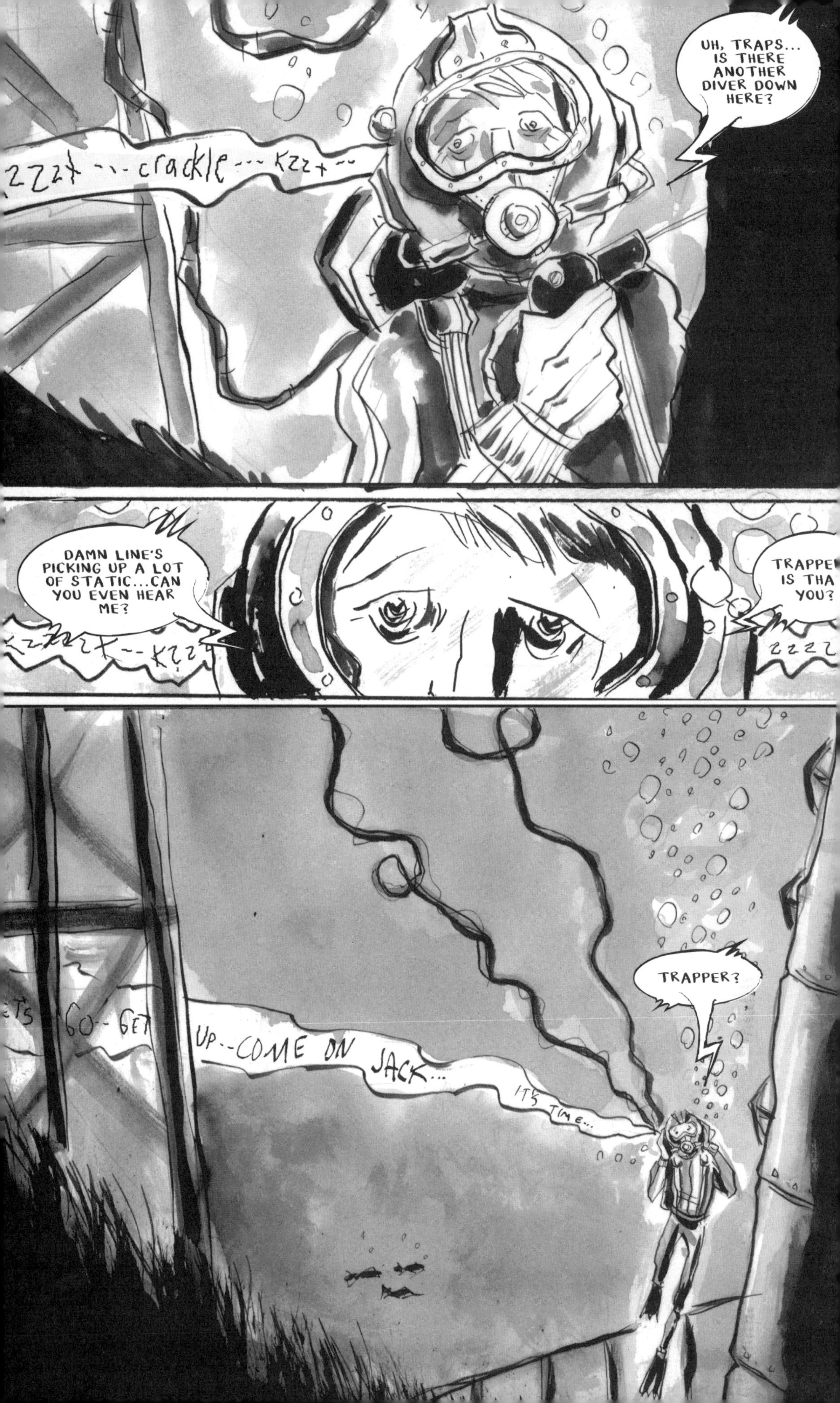
UH, TRAPS... IS THERE ANOTHER DIVER DOWN HERE?
ZZZT --- crackle --- kzzt --
DAMN LINE'S PICKING UP A LOT OF STATIC...CAN YOU EVEN HEAR ME?
TRAPPE IS THA YOU?
TRAPPER?
GO--GET UP--COME ON JACK... IT'S TIME...

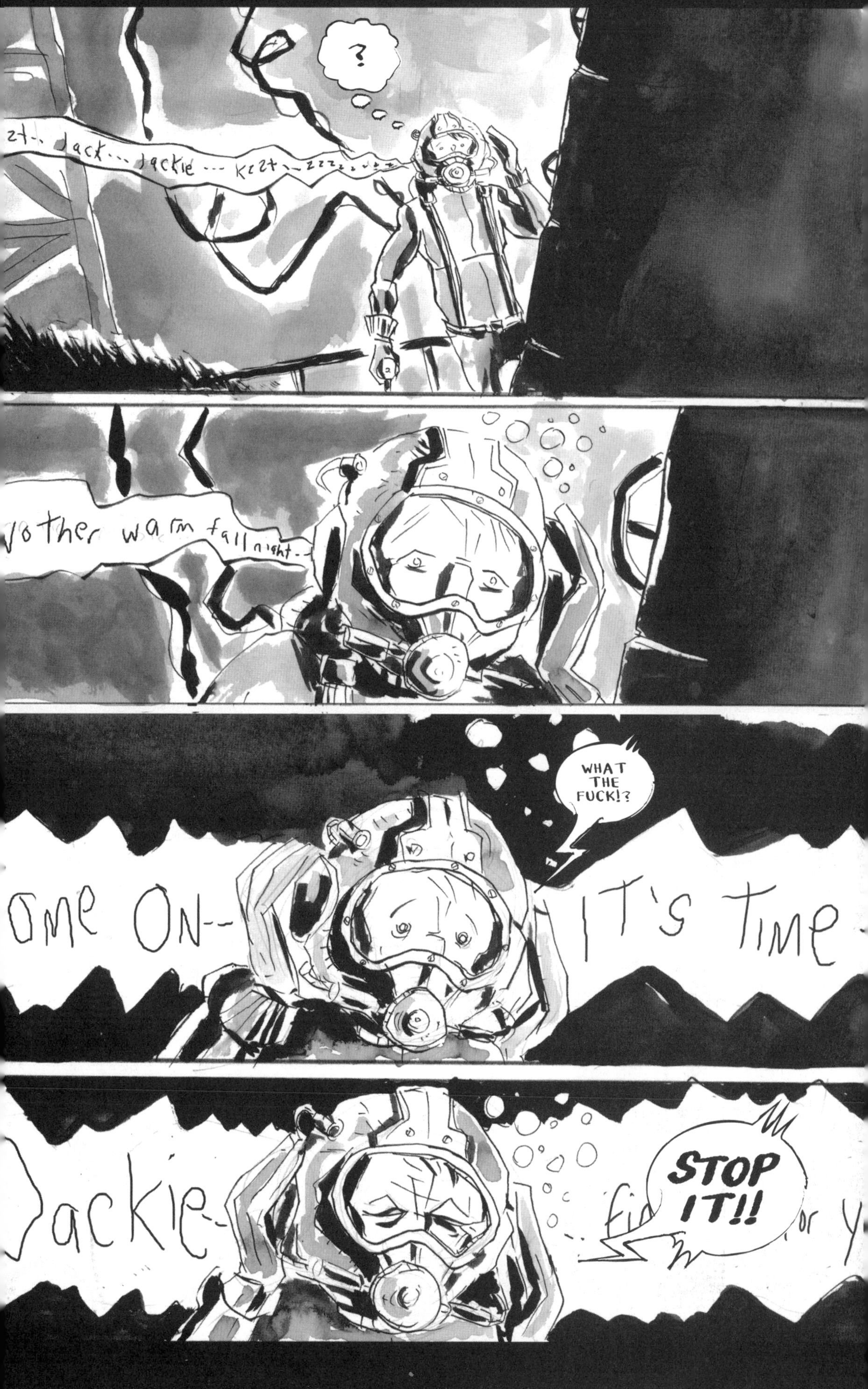
?
zt-- Jack--- Jackie --- kzzt--zzzz
other warm fall night--
ome On--
WHAT THE FUCK!?
IT's Time
Jackie--
STOP IT!!

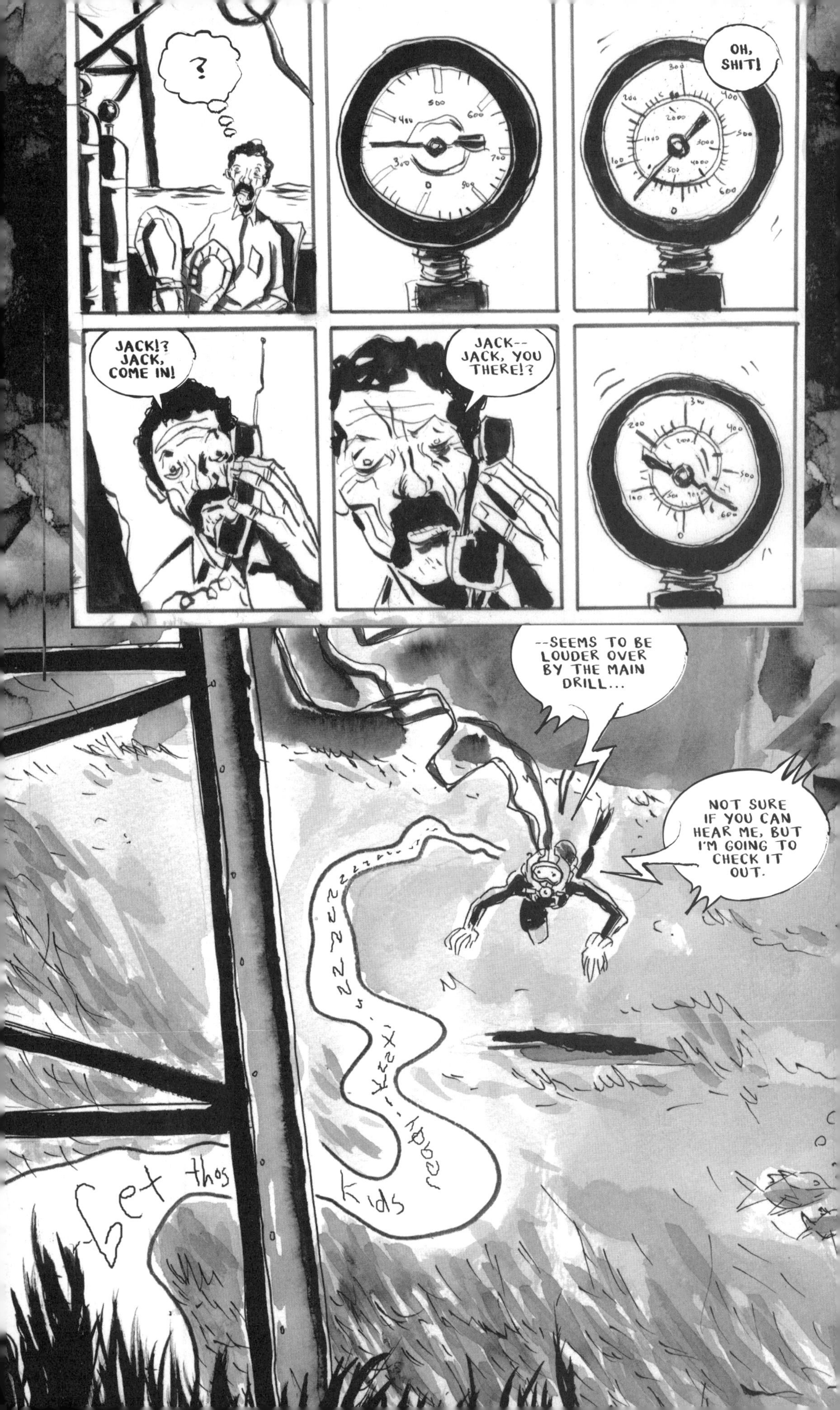
?
OH, SHIT!
JACK!? JACK, COME IN!
JACK-- JACK, YOU THERE!?
--SEEMS TO BE LOUDER OVER BY THE MAIN DRILL...
NOT SURE IF YOU CAN HEAR ME, BUT I'M GOING TO CHECK IT OUT.
Get thos
kids
ready

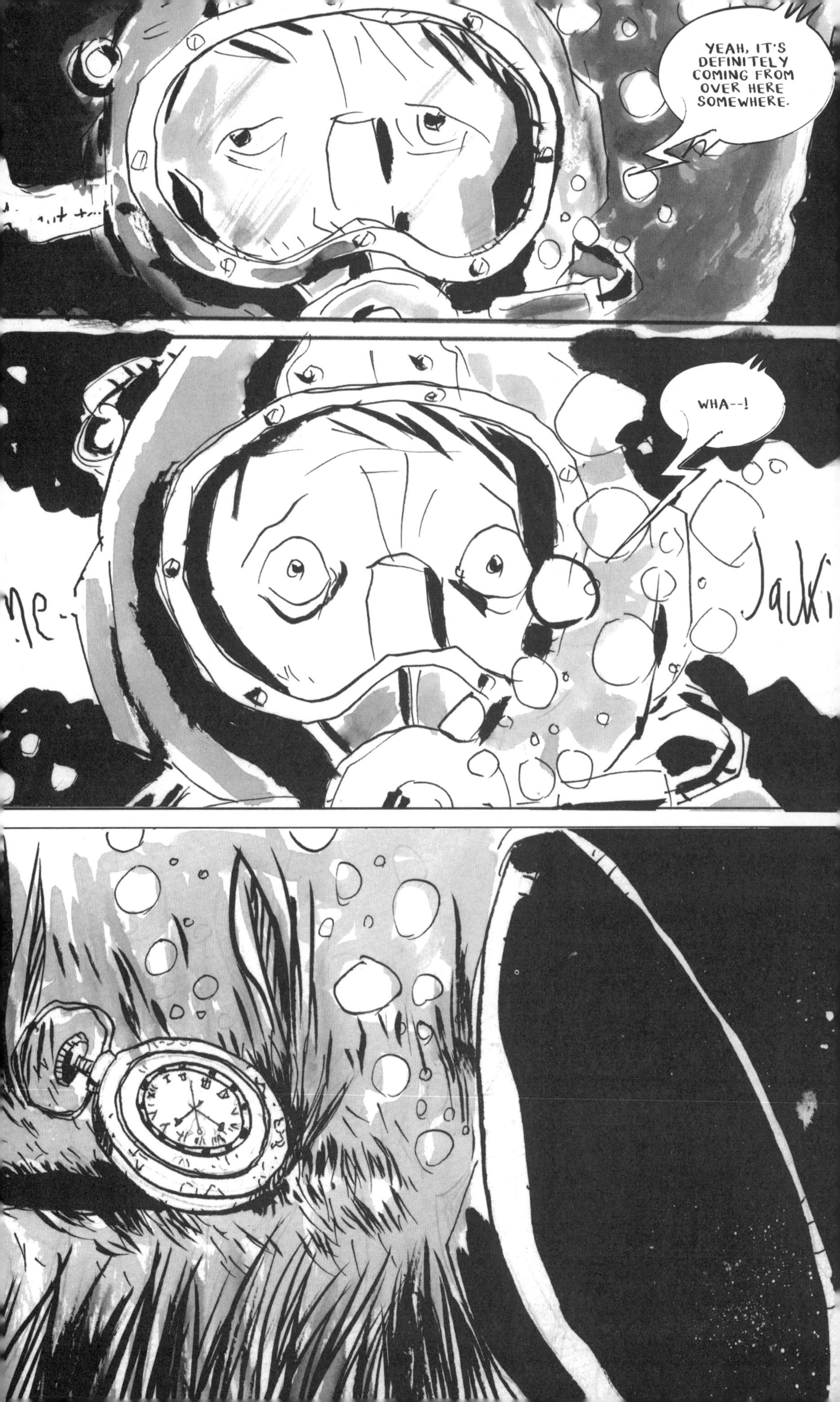
YEAH, IT'S DEFINITELY COMING FROM OVER HERE SOMEWHERE.
WHA--!

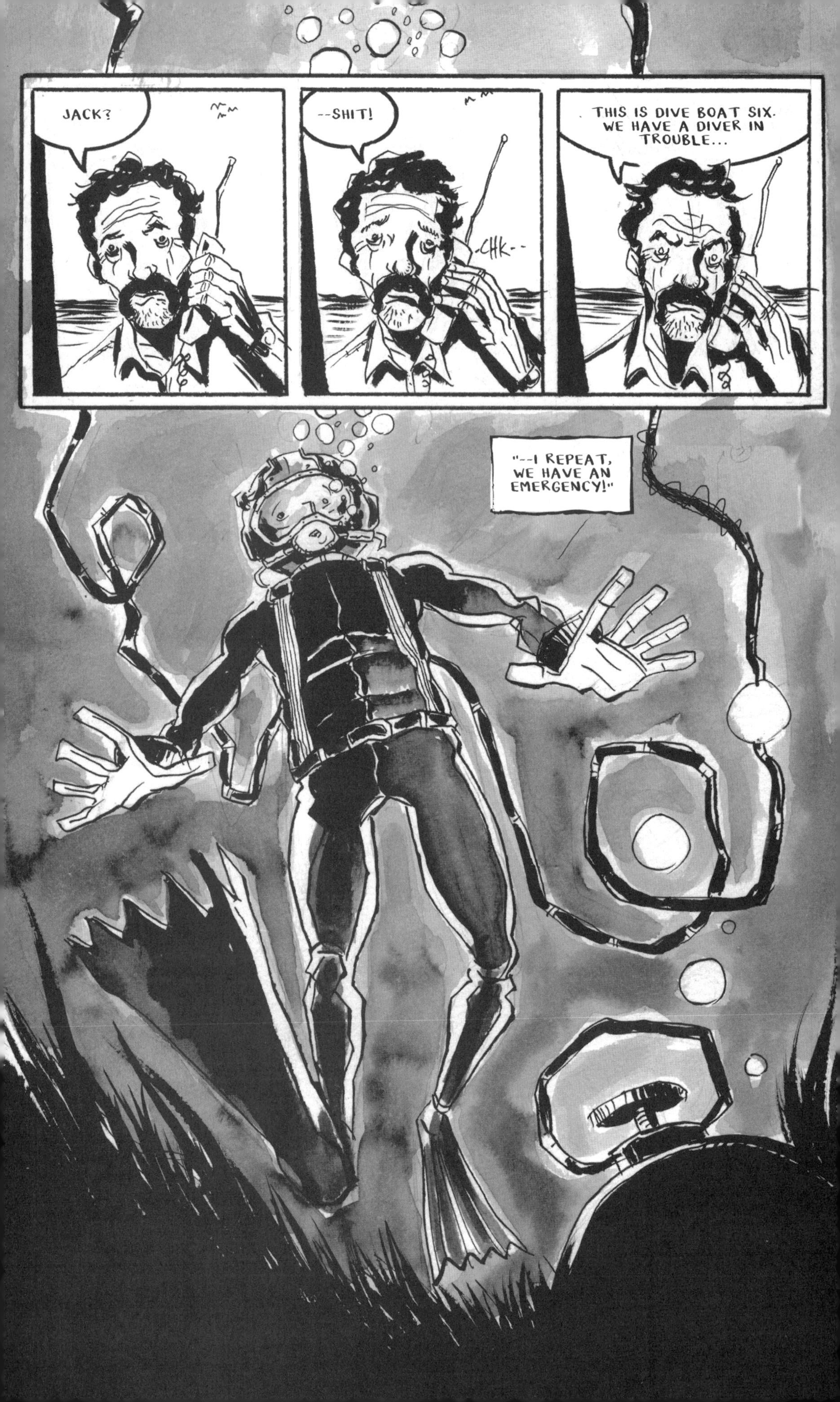
JACK?
--SHIT!
-CHK--
THIS IS DIVE BOAT SIX. WE HAVE A DIVER IN TROUBLE...
"--I REPEAT, WE HAVE AN EMERGENCY!"

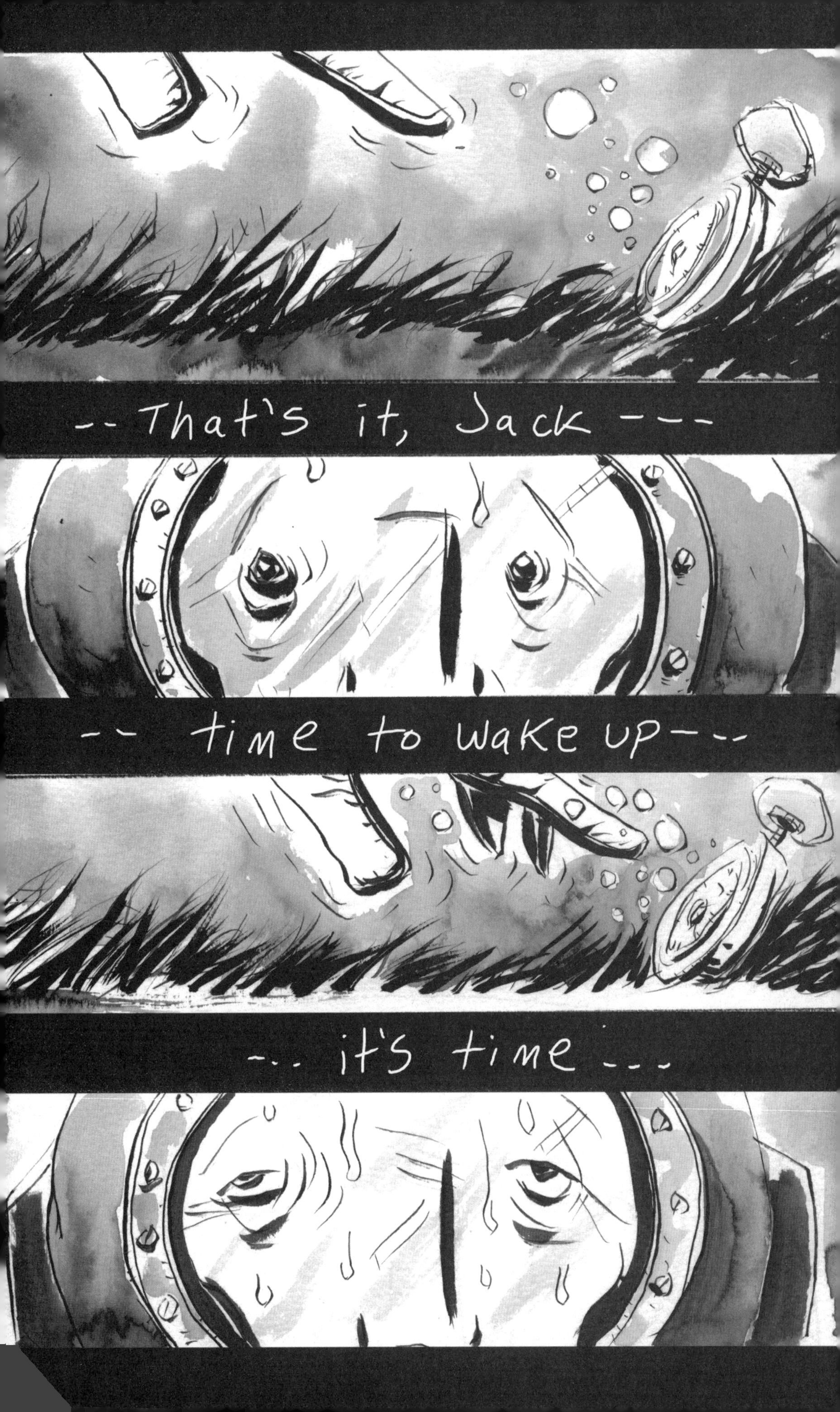
-- That's it, Jack ---
-- time to wake up---
-.. it's time ...

--Jack?

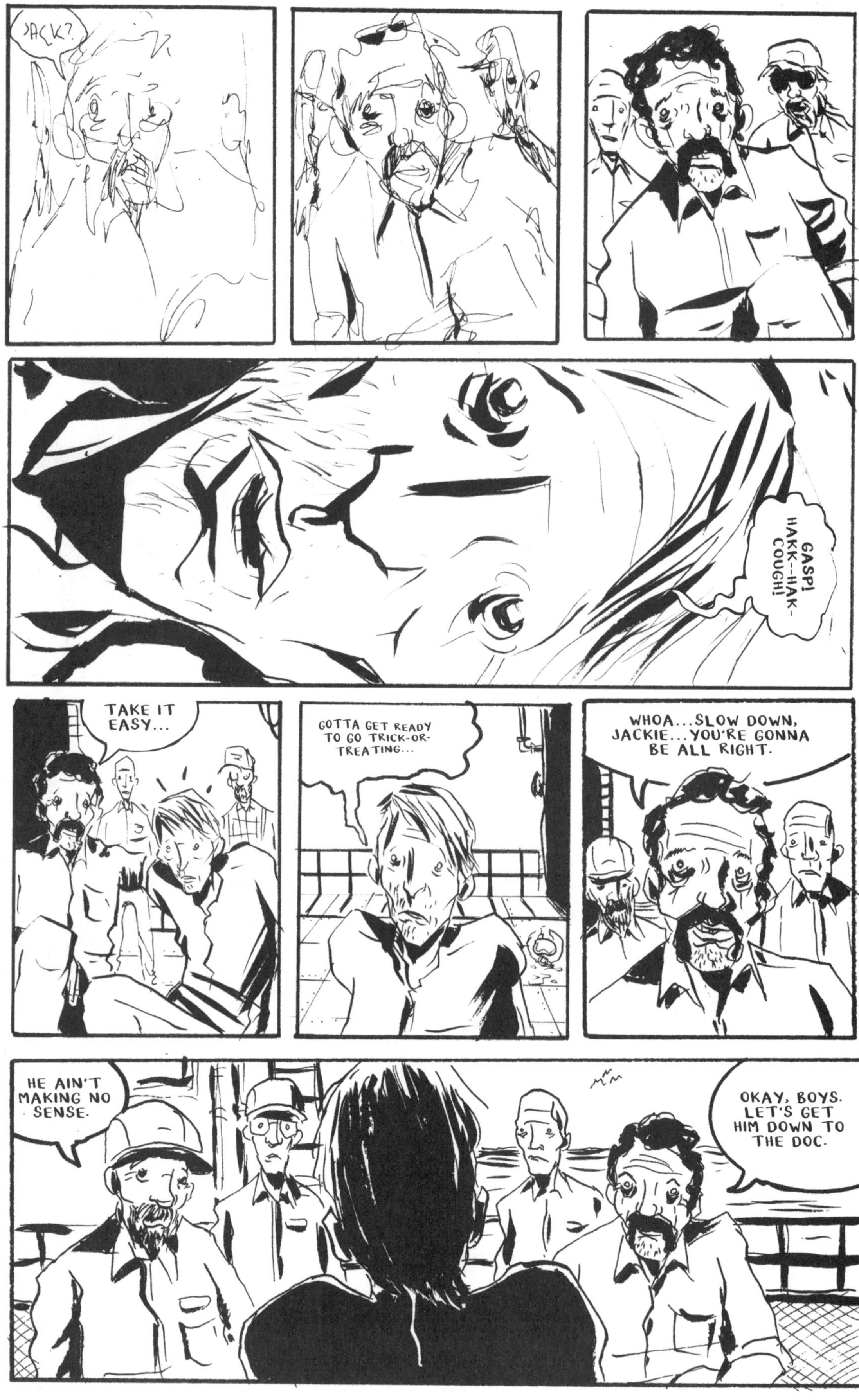
JACK?
GASP! HAKK--HAK-COUGH!
TAKE IT EASY...
GOTTA GET READY TO GO TRICK-OR-TREATING...
WHOA...SLOW DOWN, JACKIE...YOU'RE GONNA BE ALL RIGHT.
HE AIN'T MAKING NO SENSE.
OKAY, BOYS. LET'S GET HIM DOWN TO THE DOC.

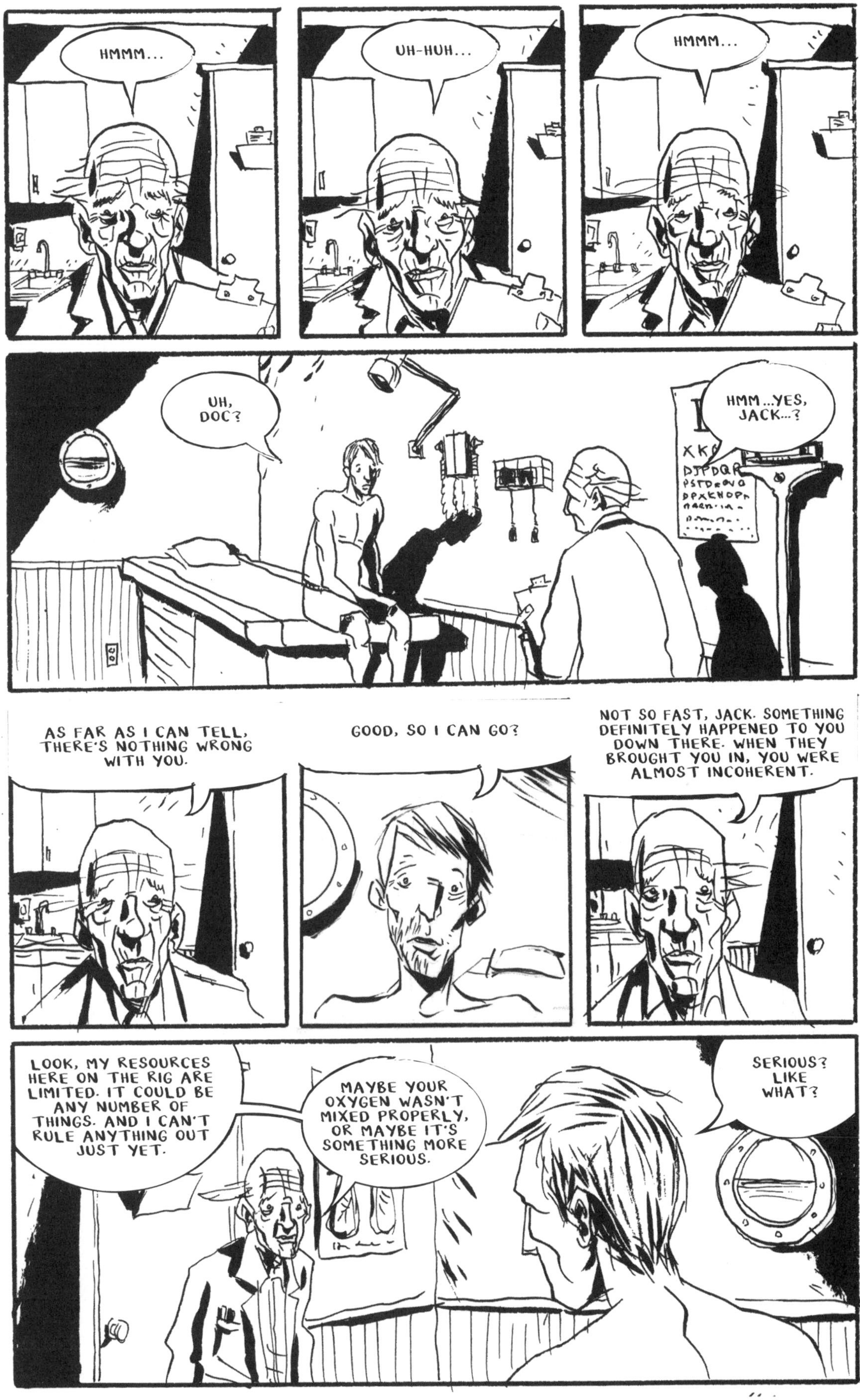
HMMM...
UH-HUH...
HMMM...
UH, DOC?
HMM...YES, JACK...?
AS FAR AS I CAN TELL, THERE'S NOTHING WRONG WITH YOU.
GOOD, SO I CAN GO?
NOT SO FAST, JACK. SOMETHING DEFINITELY HAPPENED TO YOU DOWN THERE. WHEN THEY BROUGHT YOU IN, YOU WERE ALMOST INCOHERENT.
LOOK, MY RESOURCES HERE ON THE RIG ARE LIMITED. IT COULD BE ANY NUMBER OF THINGS. AND I CAN'T RULE ANYTHING OUT JUST YET.
MAYBE YOUR OXYGEN WASN'T MIXED PROPERLY, OR MAYBE IT'S SOMETHING MORE SERIOUS.
SERIOUS? LIKE WHAT?

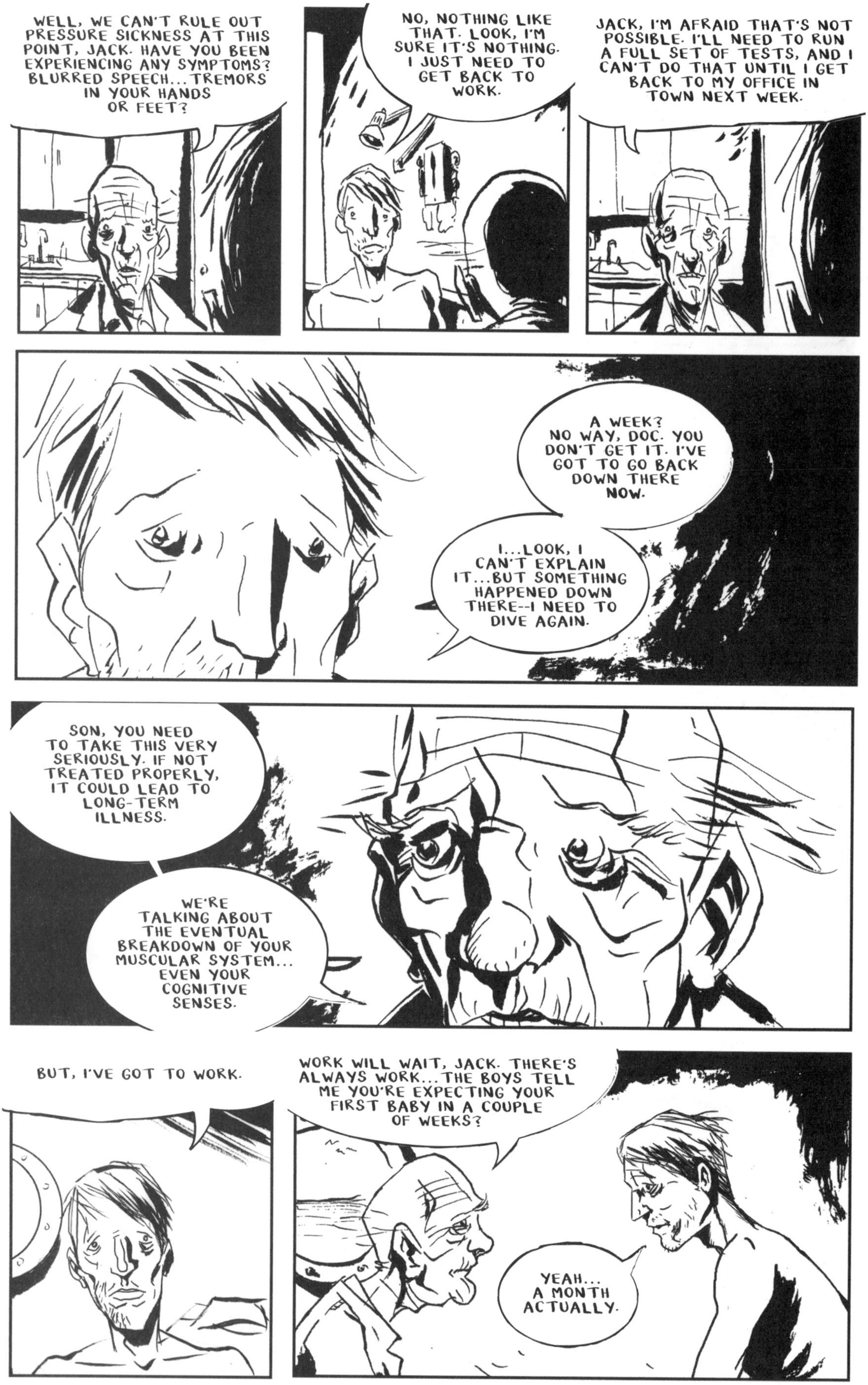
WELL, WE CAN'T RULE OUT PRESSURE SICKNESS AT THIS POINT, JACK. HAVE YOU BEEN EXPERIENCING ANY SYMPTOMS? BLURRED SPEECH... TREMORS IN YOUR HANDS OR FEET?
NO, NOTHING LIKE THAT. LOOK, I'M SURE IT'S NOTHING. I JUST NEED TO GET BACK TO WORK.
JACK, I'M AFRAID THAT'S NOT POSSIBLE. I'LL NEED TO RUN A FULL SET OF TESTS, AND I CAN'T DO THAT UNTIL I GET BACK TO MY OFFICE IN TOWN NEXT WEEK.
A WEEK? NO WAY, DOC. YOU DON'T GET IT. I'VE GOT TO GO BACK DOWN THERE NOW.
I...LOOK, I CAN'T EXPLAIN IT...BUT SOMETHING HAPPENED DOWN THERE--I NEED TO DIVE AGAIN.
SON, YOU NEED TO TAKE THIS VERY SERIOUSLY. IF NOT TREATED PROPERLY, IT COULD LEAD TO LONG-TERM ILLNESS.
WE'RE TALKING ABOUT THE EVENTUAL BREAKDOWN OF YOUR MUSCULAR SYSTEM... EVEN YOUR COGNITIVE SENSES.
BUT, I'VE GOT TO WORK.
WORK WILL WAIT, JACK. THERE'S ALWAYS WORK... THE BOYS TELL ME YOU'RE EXPECTING YOUR FIRST BABY IN A COUPLE OF WEEKS?
YEAH... A MONTH ACTUALLY.

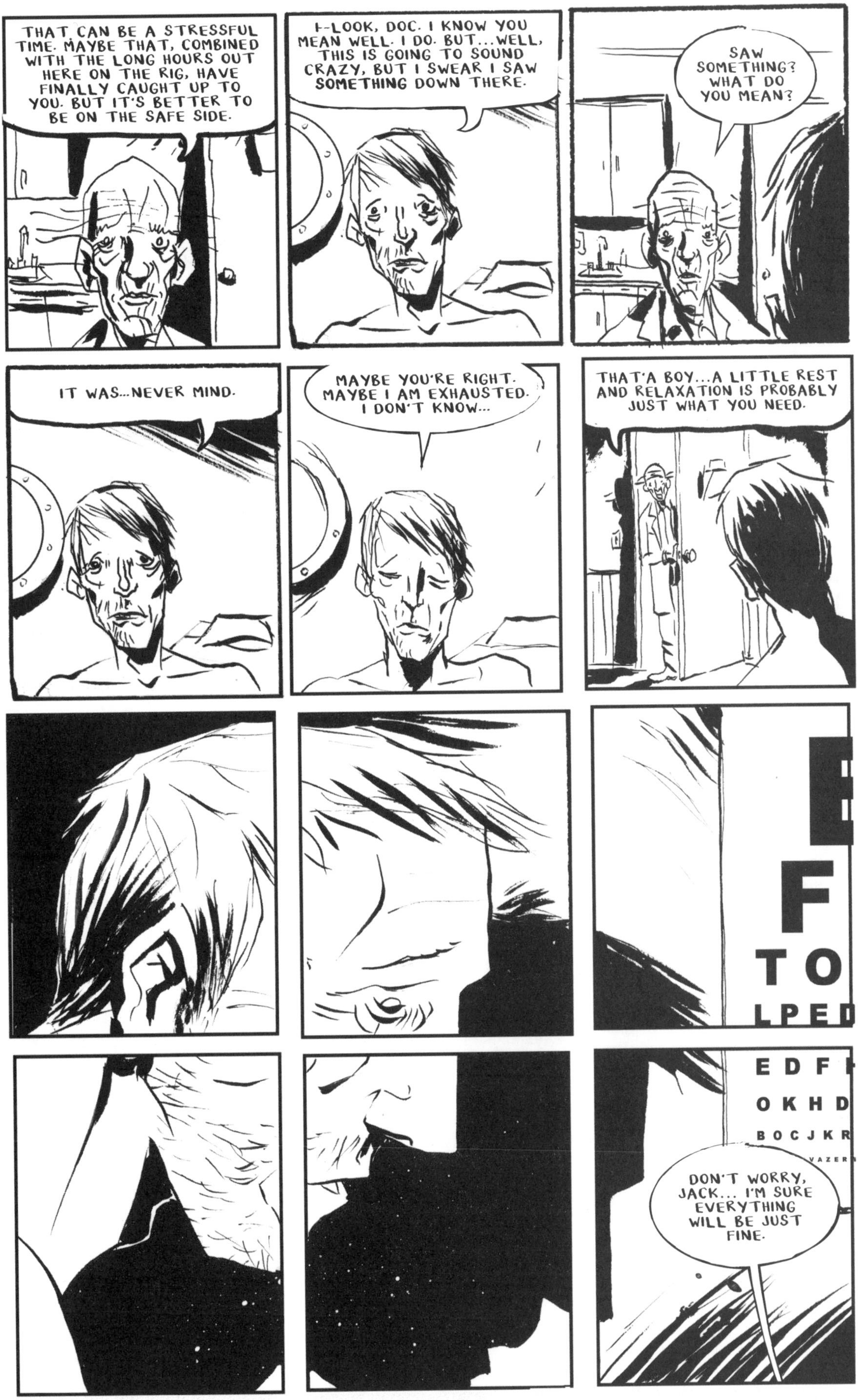
THAT CAN BE A STRESSFUL TIME. MAYBE THAT, COMBINED WITH THE LONG HOURS OUT HERE ON THE RIG, HAVE FINALLY CAUGHT UP TO YOU. BUT IT'S BETTER TO BE ON THE SAFE SIDE.
I-LOOK, DOC. I KNOW YOU MEAN WELL. I DO. BUT... WELL, THIS IS GOING TO SOUND CRAZY, BUT I SWEAR I SAW SOMETHING DOWN THERE.
SAW SOMETHING? WHAT DO YOU MEAN?
IT WAS... NEVER MIND.
MAYBE YOU'RE RIGHT. MAYBE I AM EXHAUSTED. I DON'T KNOW...
THAT'A BOY... A LITTLE REST AND RELAXATION IS PROBABLY JUST WHAT YOU NEED.
E
F
TO
LPED
EDF
OKHD
BOCJKR
DON'T WORRY, JACK... I'M SURE EVERYTHING WILL BE JUST FINE.

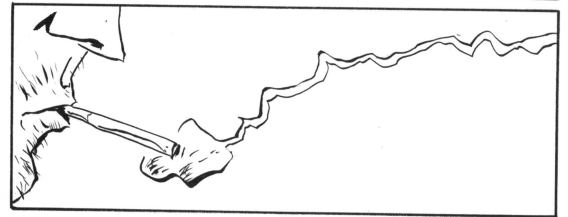

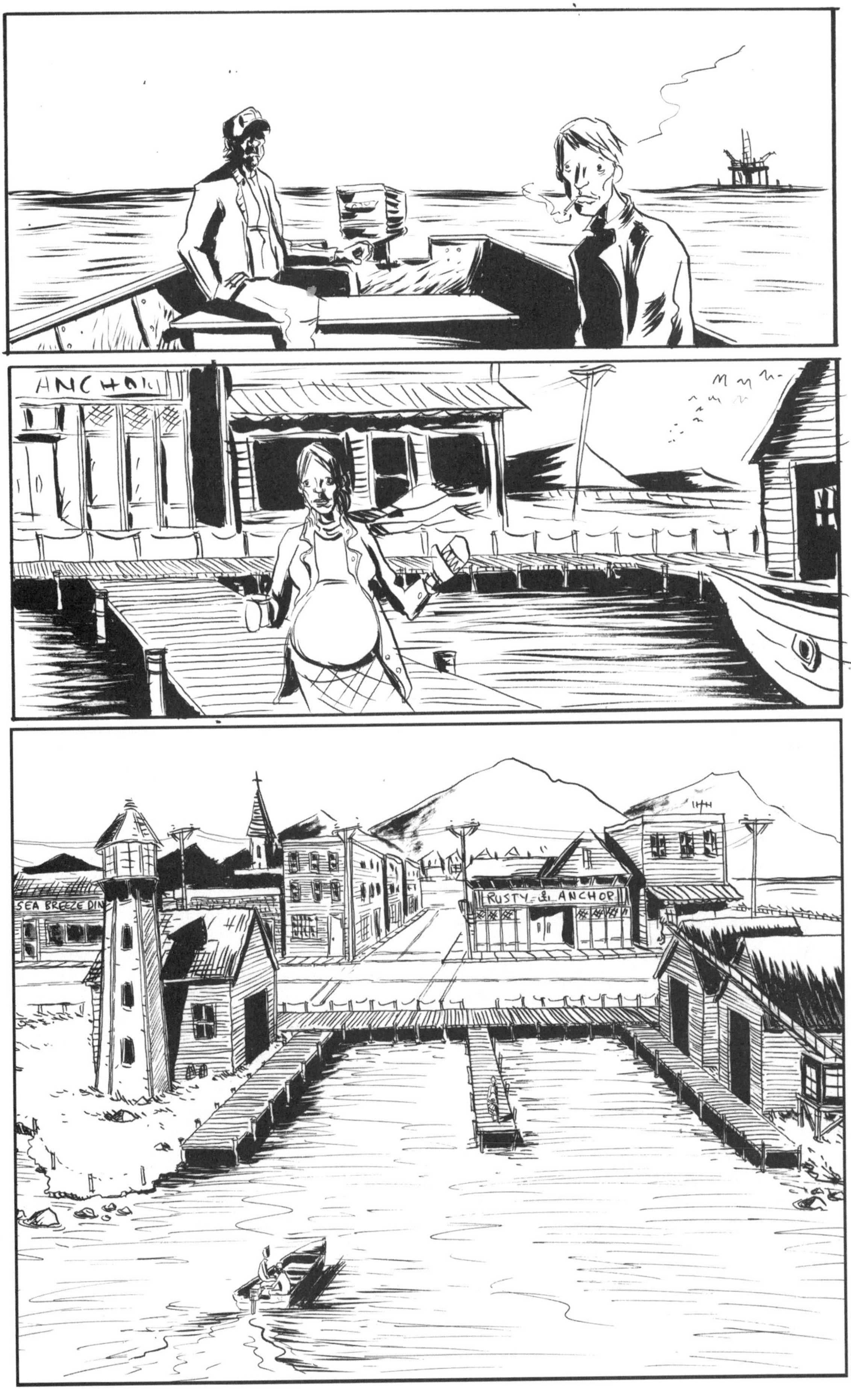
SEA BREEZE DIN
RUSTY ANCHOR

2. SHORE LEAVE

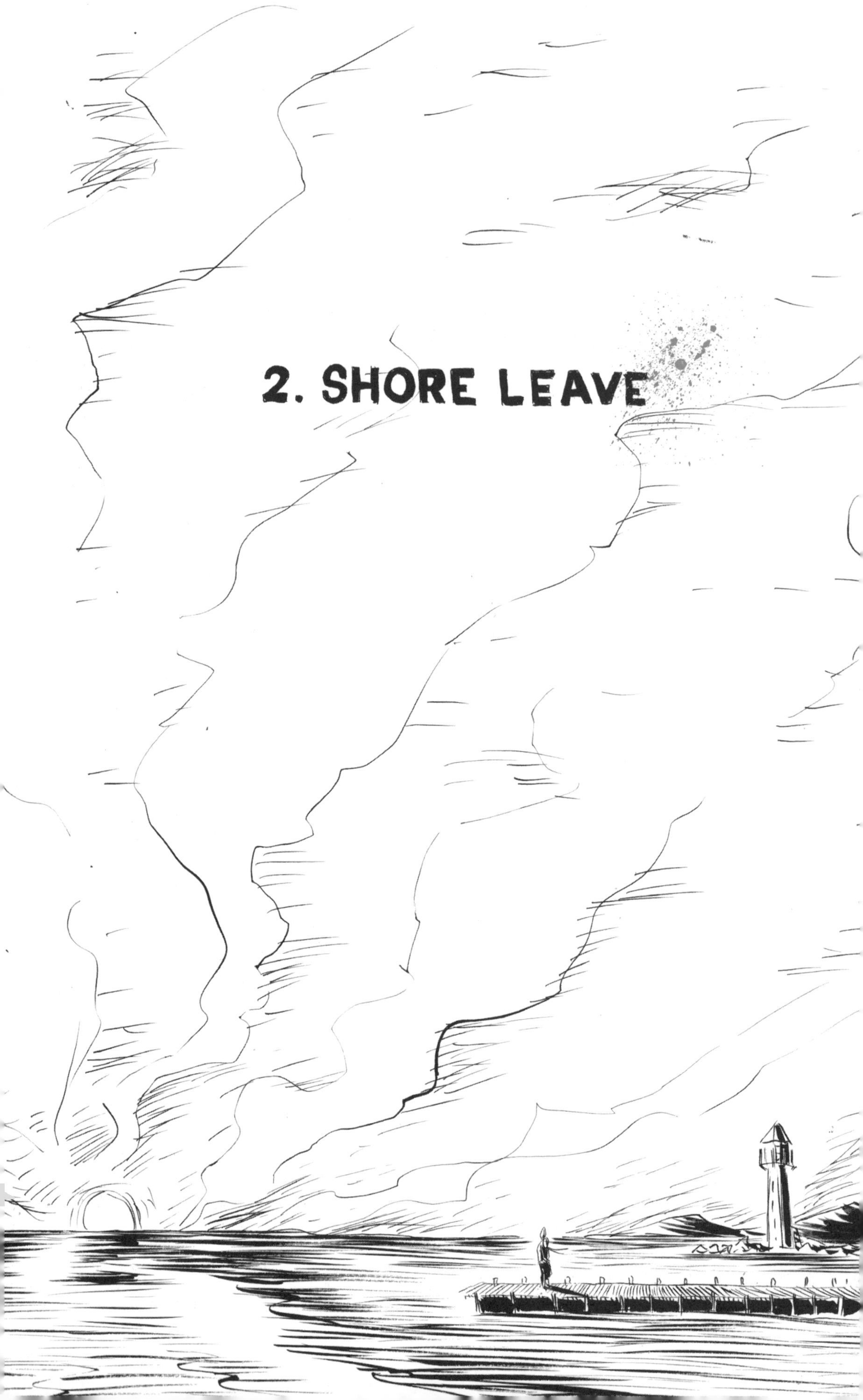

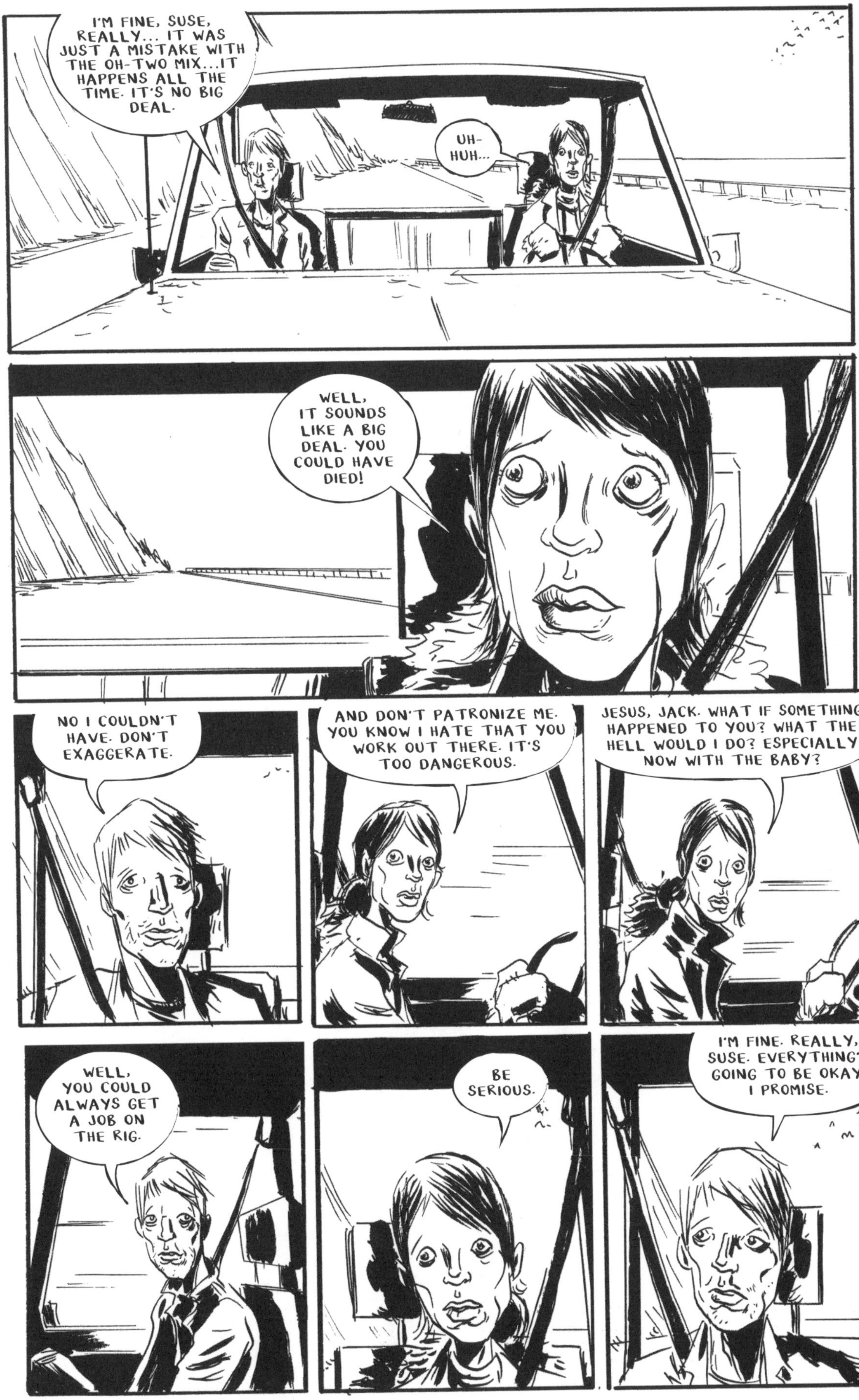
I'M FINE, SUSE, REALLY... IT WAS JUST A MISTAKE WITH THE OH-TWO MIX...IT HAPPENS ALL THE TIME. IT'S NO BIG DEAL.
UH-HUH...
WELL, IT SOUNDS LIKE A BIG DEAL. YOU COULD HAVE DIED!
NO I COULDN'T HAVE. DON'T EXAGGERATE.
AND DON'T PATRONIZE ME. YOU KNOW I HATE THAT YOU WORK OUT THERE. IT'S TOO DANGEROUS.
JESUS, JACK. WHAT IF SOMETHING HAPPENED TO YOU? WHAT THE HELL WOULD I DO? ESPECIALLY NOW WITH THE BABY?
WELL, YOU COULD ALWAYS GET A JOB ON THE RIG.
BE SERIOUS.
I'M FINE. REALLY, SUSE. EVERYTHING'S GOING TO BE OKAY. I PROMISE.

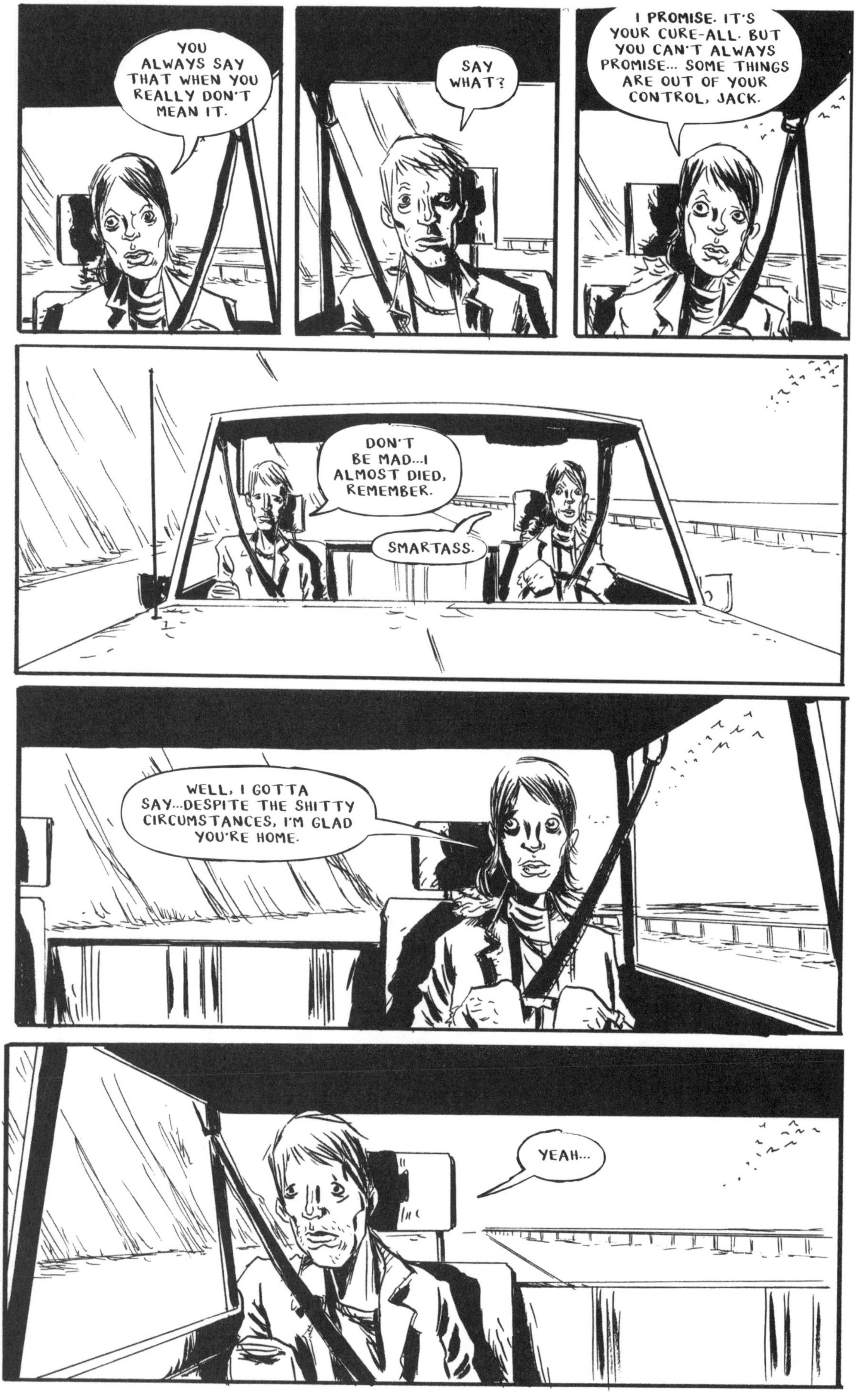
YOU ALWAYS SAY THAT WHEN YOU REALLY DON'T MEAN IT.
SAY WHAT?
I PROMISE. IT'S YOUR CURE-ALL. BUT YOU CAN'T ALWAYS PROMISE... SOME THINGS ARE OUT OF YOUR CONTROL, JACK.
DON'T BE MAD...I ALMOST DIED, REMEMBER.
SMARTASS.
WELL, I GOTTA SAY...DESPITE THE SHITTY CIRCUMSTANCES, I'M GLAD YOU'RE HOME.
YEAH...

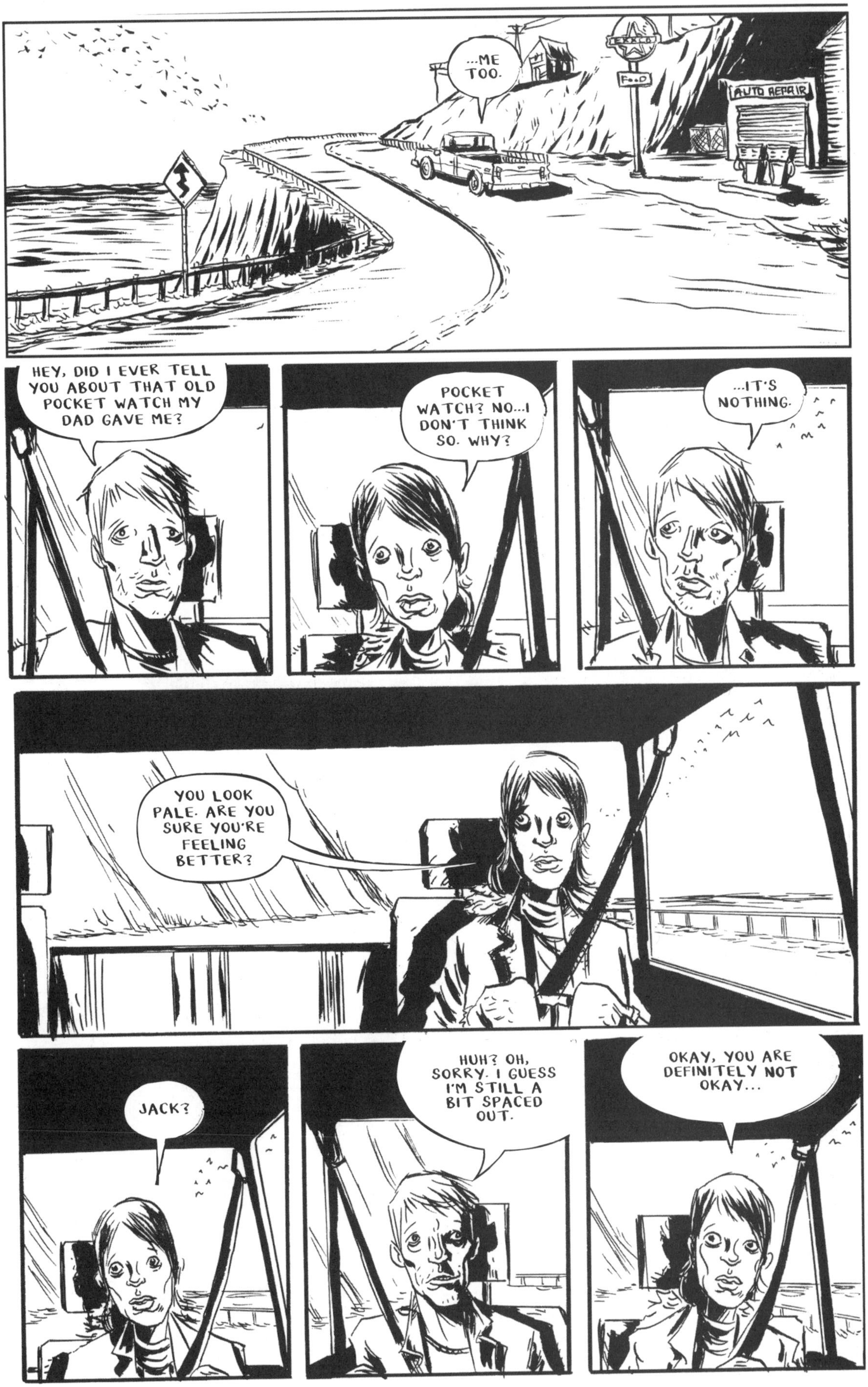

...ME TOO.
EXXO
FOOD
AUTO REPAIR
HEY, DID I EVER TELL YOU ABOUT THAT OLD POCKET WATCH MY DAD GAVE ME?
POCKET WATCH? NO...I DON'T THINK SO. WHY?
...IT'S NOTHING.
YOU LOOK PALE. ARE YOU SURE YOU'RE FEELING BETTER?
JACK?
HUH? OH, SORRY. I GUESS I'M STILL A BIT SPACED OUT.
OKAY, YOU ARE DEFINITELY NOT OKAY...

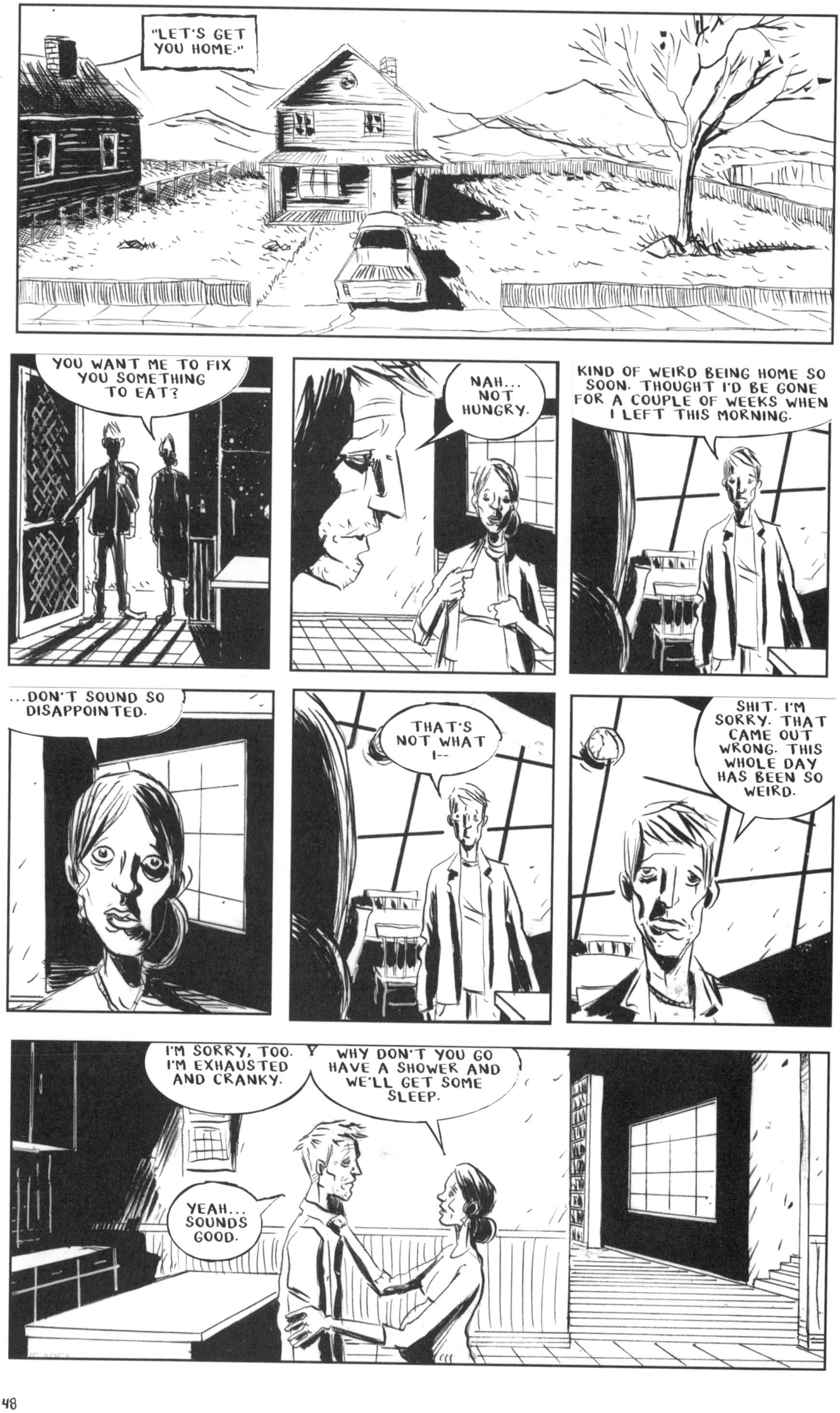
"LET'S GET YOU HOME."
YOU WANT ME TO FIX YOU SOMETHING TO EAT?
NAH... NOT HUNGRY.
KIND OF WEIRD BEING HOME SO SOON. THOUGHT I'D BE GONE FOR A COUPLE OF WEEKS WHEN I LEFT THIS MORNING.
...DON'T SOUND SO DISAPPOINTED.
THAT'S NOT WHAT I--
SHIT. I'M SORRY. THAT CAME OUT WRONG. THIS WHOLE DAY HAS BEEN SO WEIRD.
I'M SORRY, TOO. I'M EXHAUSTED AND CRANKY.
WHY DON'T YOU GO HAVE A SHOWER AND WE'LL GET SOME SLEEP.
YEAH... SOUNDS GOOD.

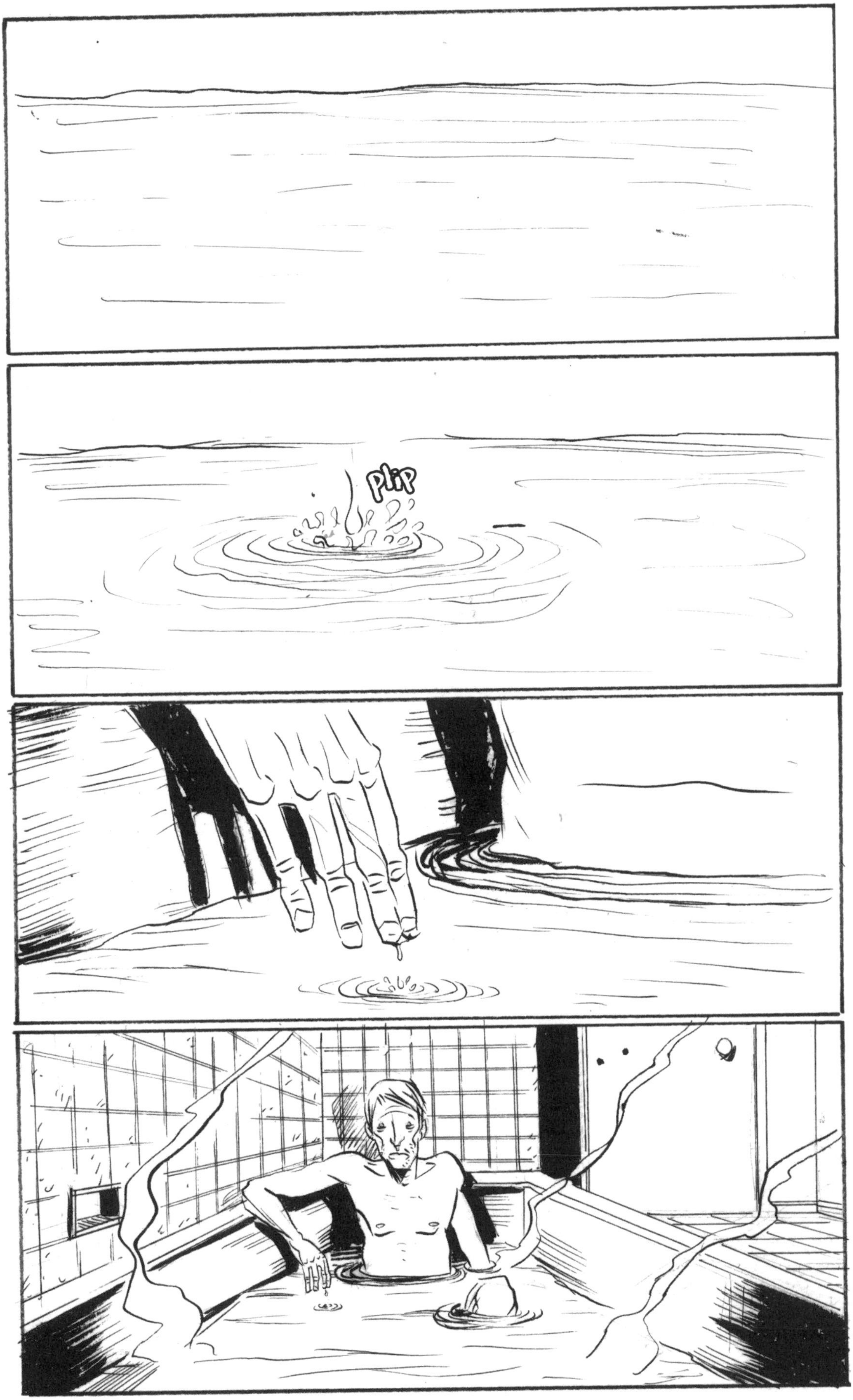
plip

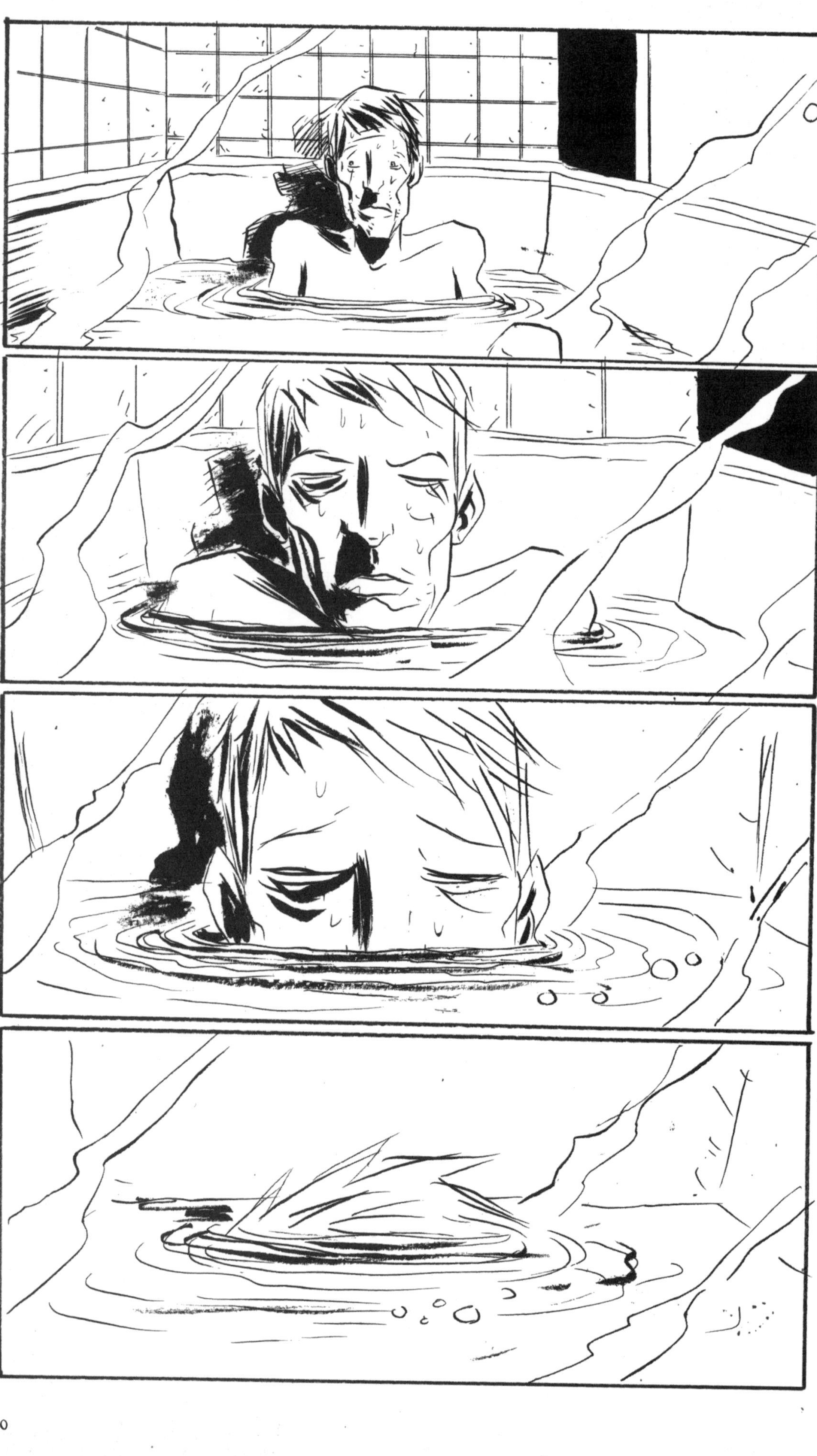

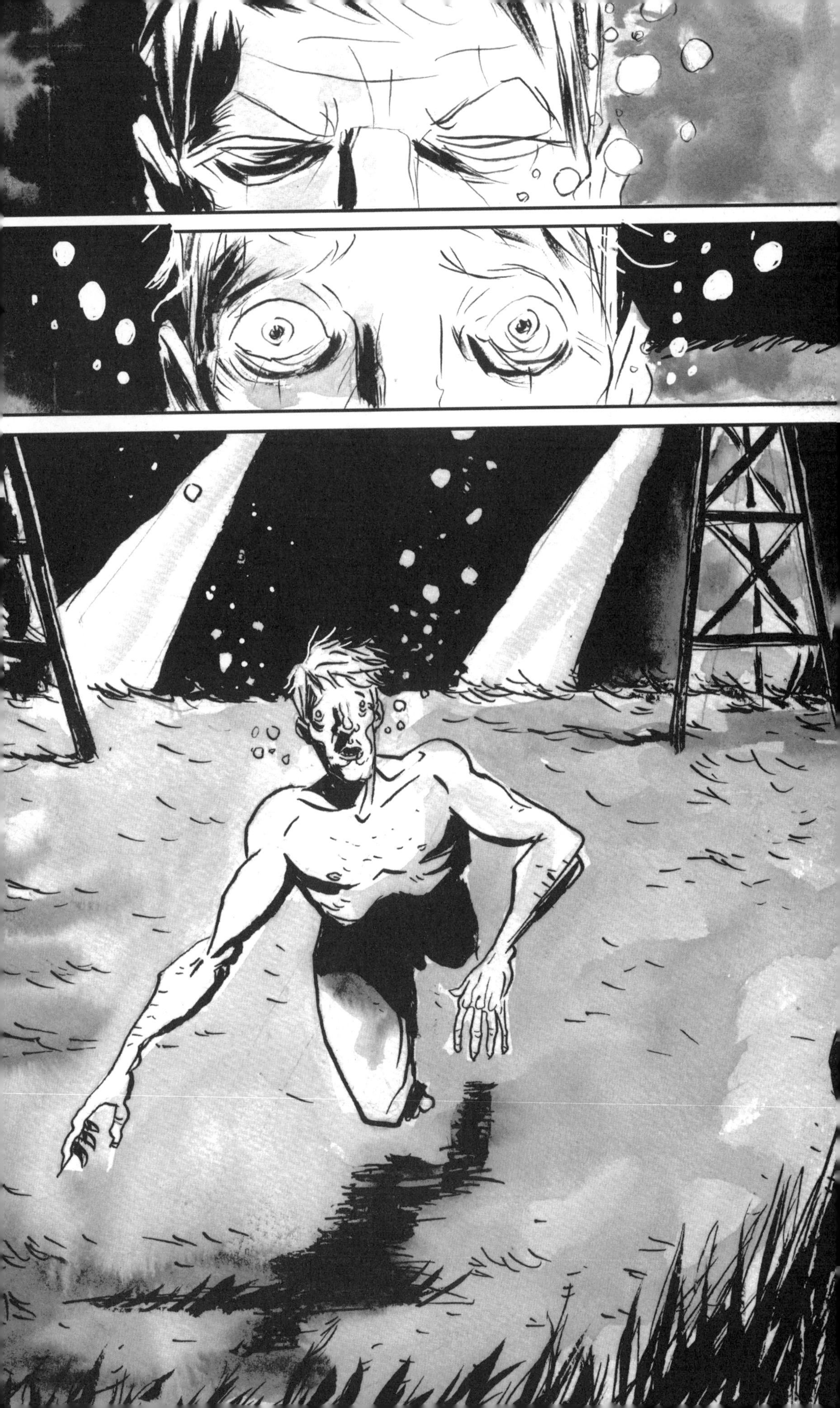

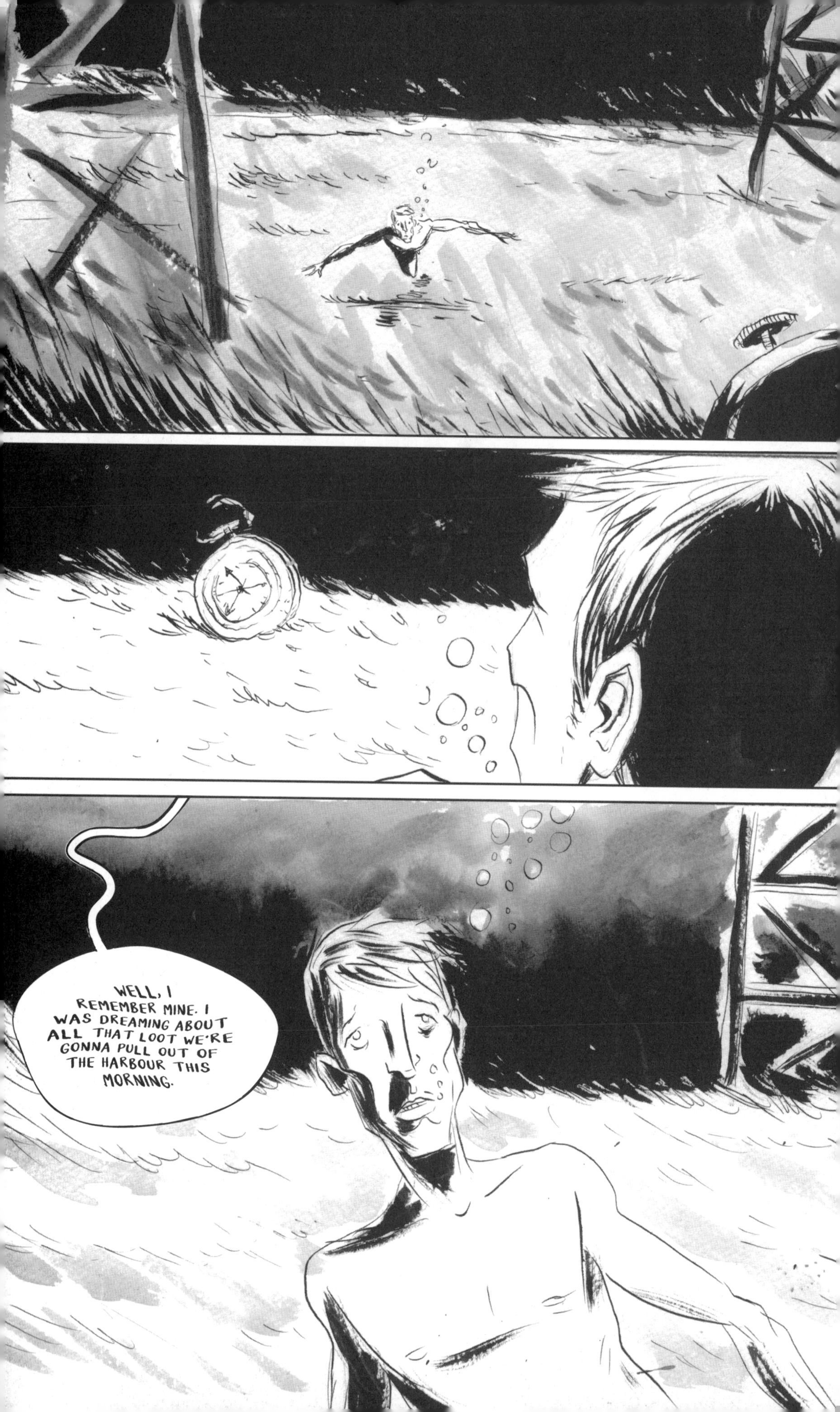
WELL, I REMEMBER MINE. I WAS DREAMING ABOUT ALL THAT LOOT WE'RE GONNA PULL OUT OF THE HARBOUR THIS MORNING.

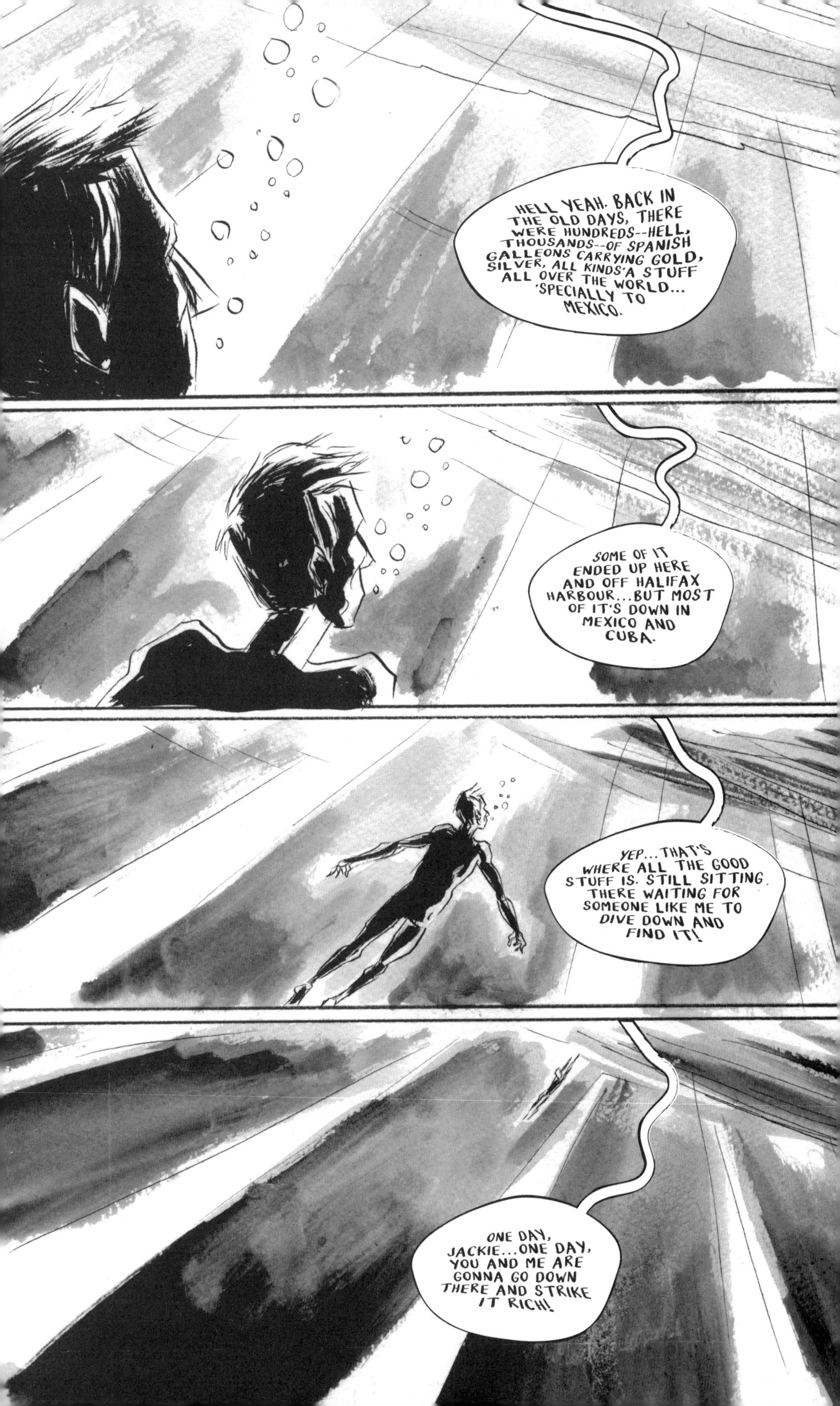
HELL YEAH. BACK IN THE OLD DAYS, THERE WERE HUNDREDS--HELL, THOUSANDS--OF SPANISH GALLEONS CARRYING GOLD, SILVER, ALL KINDS'A STUFF ALL OVER THE WORLD... 'SPECIALLY TO MEXICO.
SOME OF IT ENDED UP HERE AND OFF HALIFAX HARBOUR...BUT MOST OF IT'S DOWN IN MEXICO AND CUBA.
YEP... THAT'S WHERE ALL THE GOOD STUFF IS. STILL SITTING THERE WAITING FOR SOMEONE LIKE ME TO DIVE DOWN AND FIND IT!
ONE DAY, JACKIE...ONE DAY, YOU AND ME ARE GONNA GO DOWN THERE AND STRIKE IT RICH!

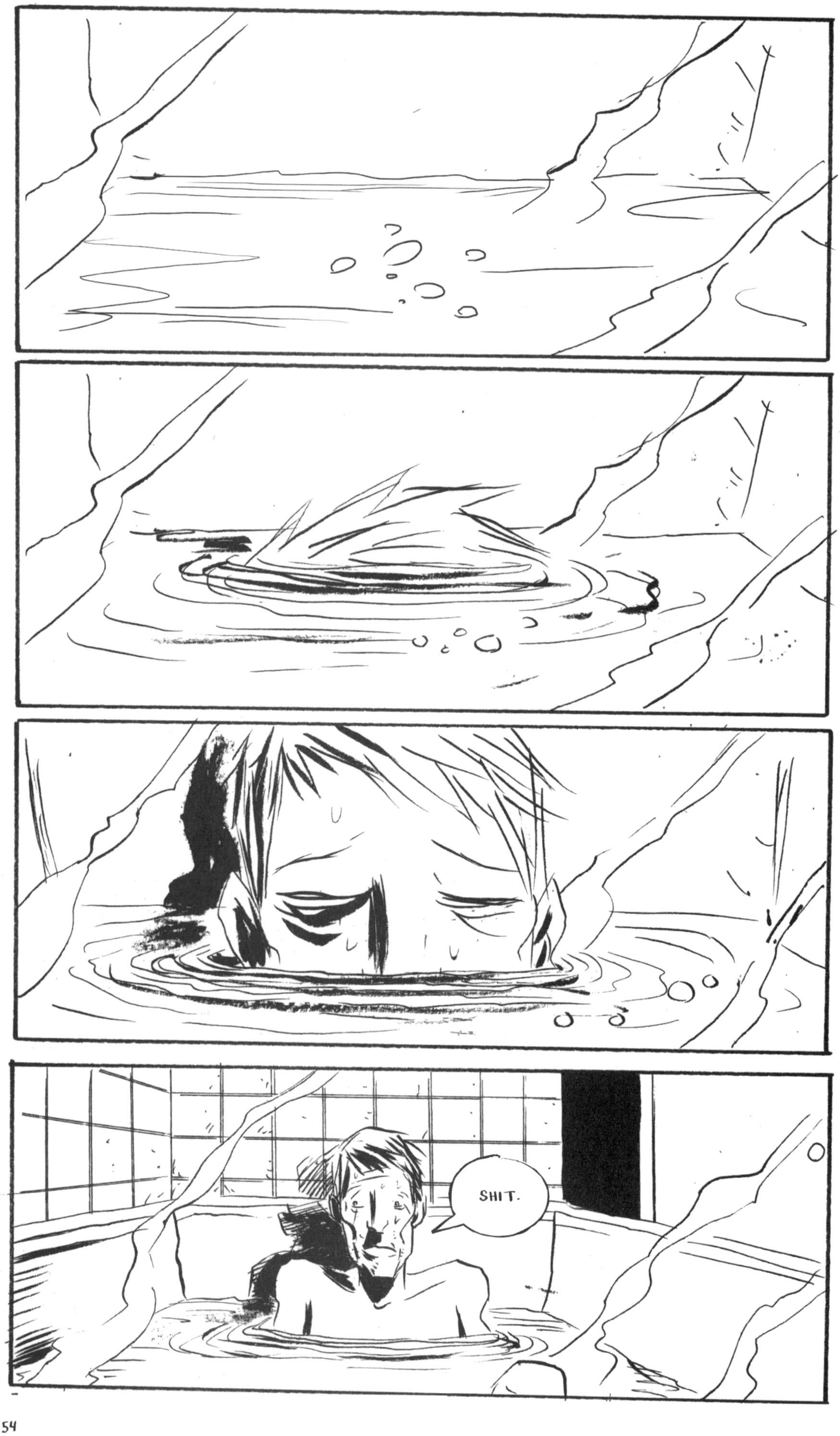
SHIT.

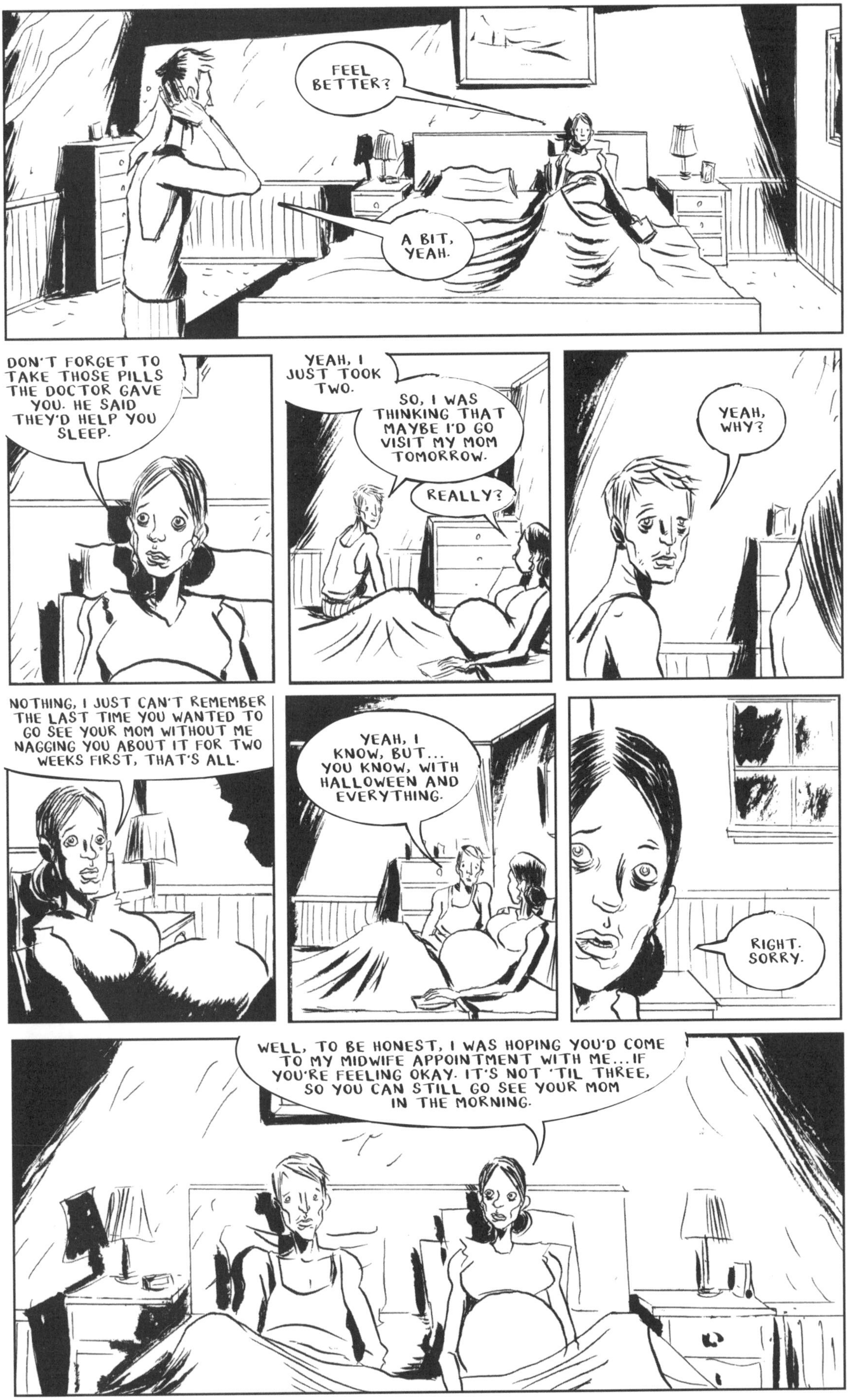
FEEL BETTER?
A BIT, YEAH.
DON'T FORGET TO TAKE THOSE PILLS THE DOCTOR GAVE YOU. HE SAID THEY'D HELP YOU SLEEP.
YEAH, I JUST TOOK TWO.
SO, I WAS THINKING THAT MAYBE I'D GO VISIT MY MOM TOMORROW.
REALLY?
YEAH, WHY?
NOTHING, I JUST CAN'T REMEMBER THE LAST TIME YOU WANTED TO GO SEE YOUR MOM WITHOUT ME NAGGING YOU ABOUT IT FOR TWO WEEKS FIRST, THAT'S ALL.
YEAH, I KNOW, BUT... YOU KNOW, WITH HALLOWEEN AND EVERYTHING.
RIGHT. SORRY.
WELL, TO BE HONEST, I WAS HOPING YOU'D COME TO MY MIDWIFE APPOINTMENT WITH ME... IF YOU'RE FEELING OKAY. IT'S NOT 'TIL THREE, SO YOU CAN STILL GO SEE YOUR MOM IN THE MORNING.

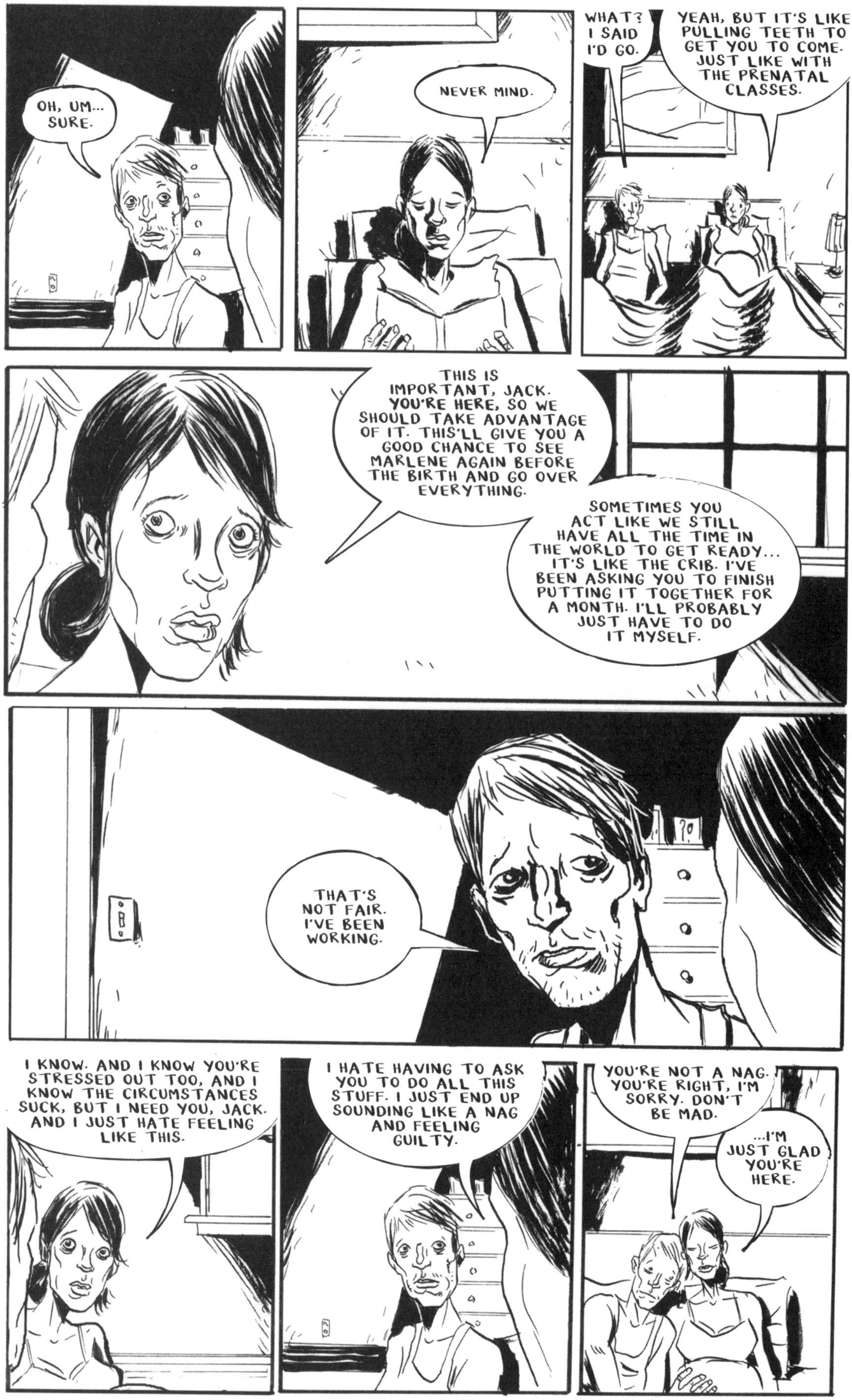

OH, UM... SURE.
NEVER MIND.
WHAT? I SAID I'D GO.
YEAH, BUT IT'S LIKE PULLING TEETH TO GET YOU TO COME. JUST LIKE WITH THE PRENATAL CLASSES.
THIS IS IMPORTANT, JACK. YOU'RE HERE, SO WE SHOULD TAKE ADVANTAGE OF IT. THIS'LL GIVE YOU A GOOD CHANCE TO SEE MARLENE AGAIN BEFORE THE BIRTH AND GO OVER EVERYTHING.
SOMETIMES YOU ACT LIKE WE STILL HAVE ALL THE TIME IN THE WORLD TO GET READY... IT'S LIKE THE CRIB. I'VE BEEN ASKING YOU TO FINISH PUTTING IT TOGETHER FOR A MONTH. I'LL PROBABLY JUST HAVE TO DO IT MYSELF.
THAT'S NOT FAIR. I'VE BEEN WORKING.
I KNOW. AND I KNOW YOU'RE STRESSED OUT TOO, AND I KNOW THE CIRCUMSTANCES SUCK, BUT I NEED YOU, JACK. AND I JUST HATE FEELING LIKE THIS.
I HATE HAVING TO ASK YOU TO DO ALL THIS STUFF. I JUST END UP SOUNDING LIKE A NAG AND FEELING GUILTY.
YOU'RE NOT A NAG. YOU'RE RIGHT, I'M SORRY. DON'T BE MAD.
...I'M JUST GLAD YOU'RE HERE.

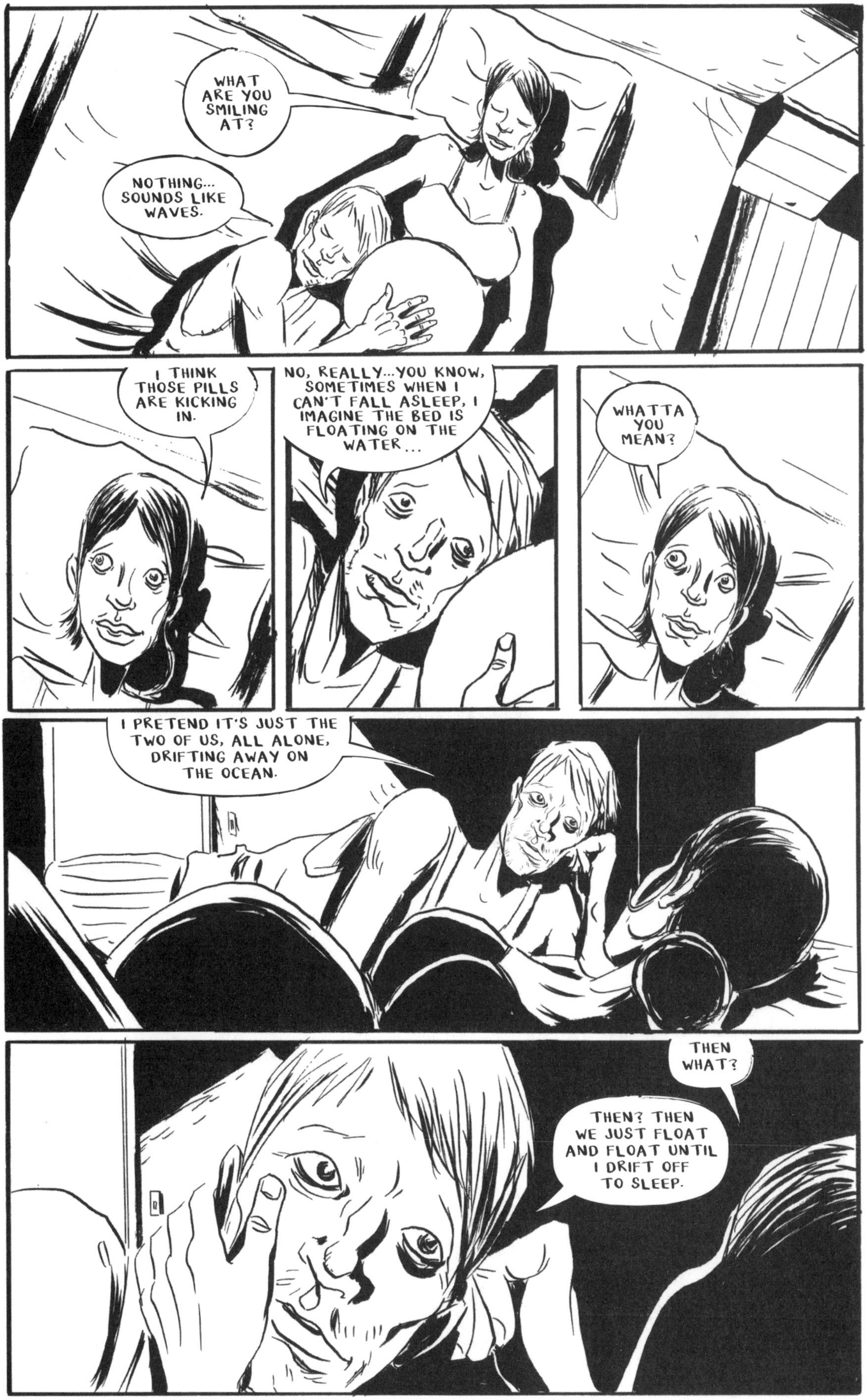
WHAT ARE YOU SMILING AT?
NOTHING... SOUNDS LIKE WAVES.
I THINK THOSE PILLS ARE KICKING IN.
NO, REALLY...YOU KNOW, SOMETIMES WHEN I CAN'T FALL ASLEEP, I IMAGINE THE BED IS FLOATING ON THE WATER...
WHATTA YOU MEAN?
I PRETEND IT'S JUST THE TWO OF US, ALL ALONE, DRIFTING AWAY ON THE OCEAN.
THEN WHAT?
THEN? THEN WE JUST FLOAT AND FLOAT UNTIL I DRIFT OFF TO SLEEP.

58

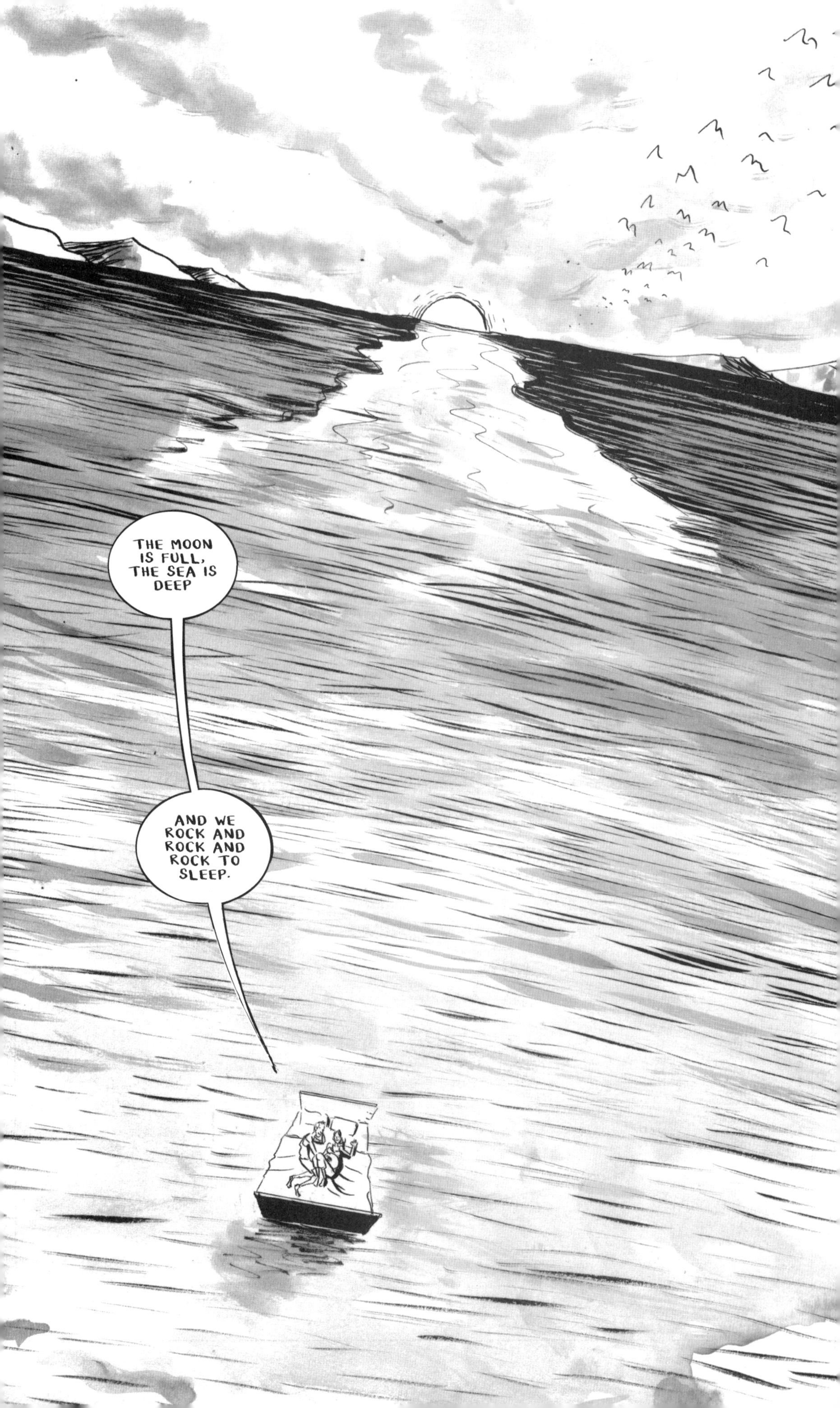
THE MOON IS FULL, THE SEA IS DEEP
AND WE ROCK AND ROCK AND ROCK TO SLEEP.

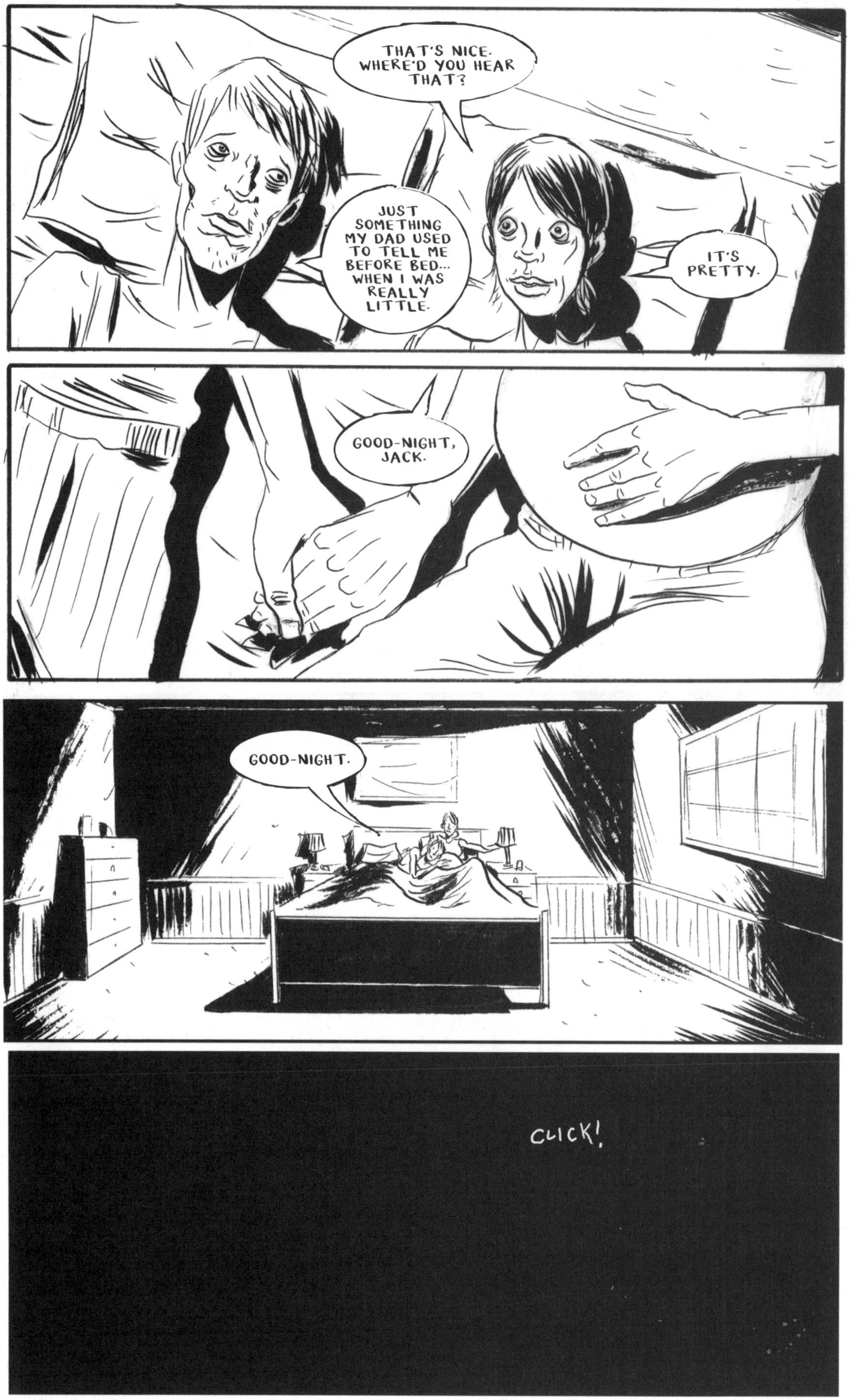
THAT'S NICE. WHERE'D YOU HEAR THAT?
JUST SOMETHING MY DAD USED TO TELL ME BEFORE BED... WHEN I WAS REALLY LITTLE.
IT'S PRETTY.
GOOD-NIGHT, JACK.
GOOD-NIGHT.
CLICK!

Jack?

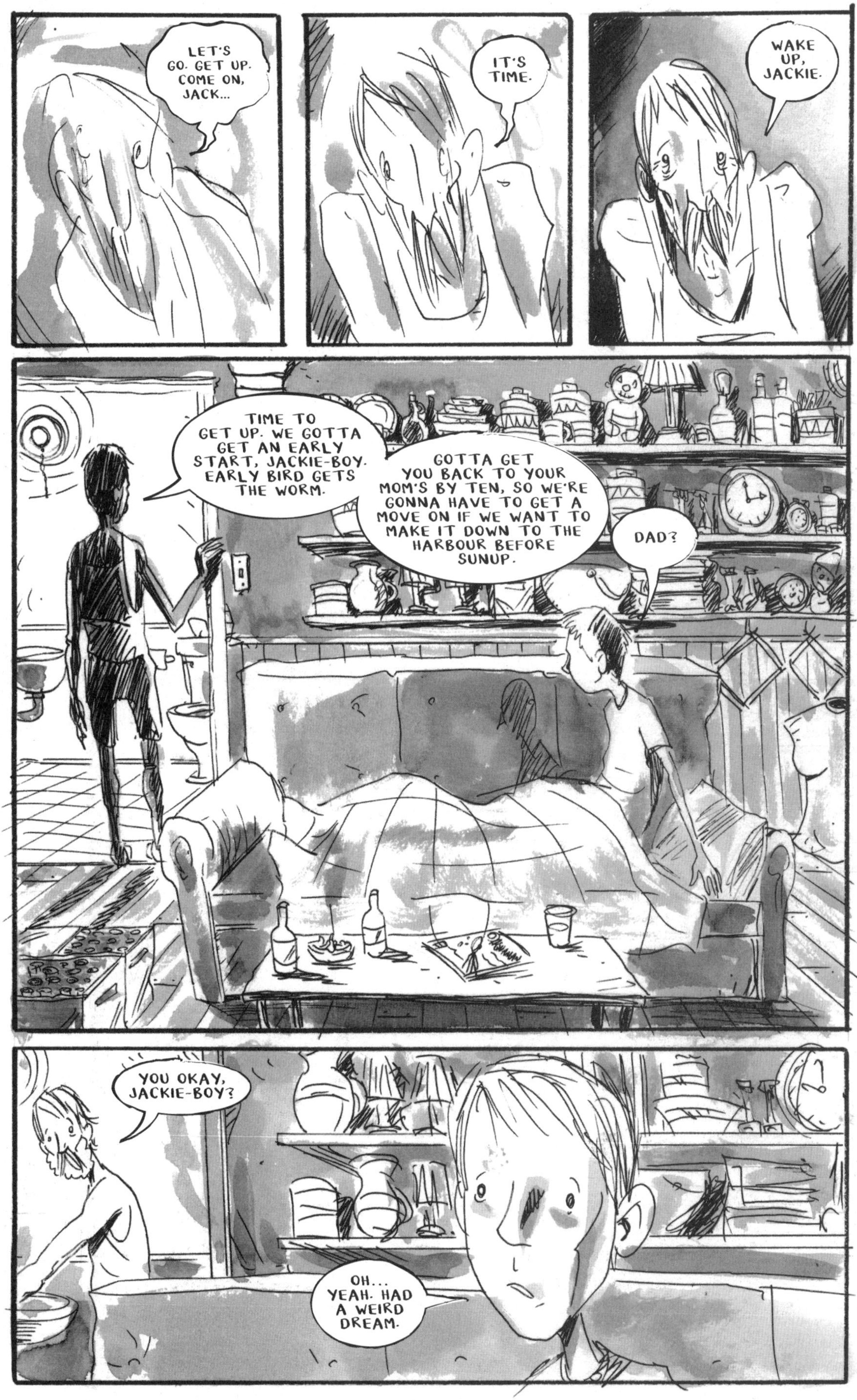
LET'S GO. GET UP. COME ON, JACK...
IT'S TIME.
WAKE UP, JACKIE.
TIME TO GET UP. WE GOTTA GET AN EARLY START, JACKIE-BOY. EARLY BIRD GETS THE WORM.
GOTTA GET YOU BACK TO YOUR MOM'S BY TEN, SO WE'RE GONNA HAVE TO GET A MOVE ON IF WE WANT TO MAKE IT DOWN TO THE HARBOUR BEFORE SUNUP.
DAD?
YOU OKAY, JACKIE-BOY?
OH... YEAH. HAD A WEIRD DREAM.

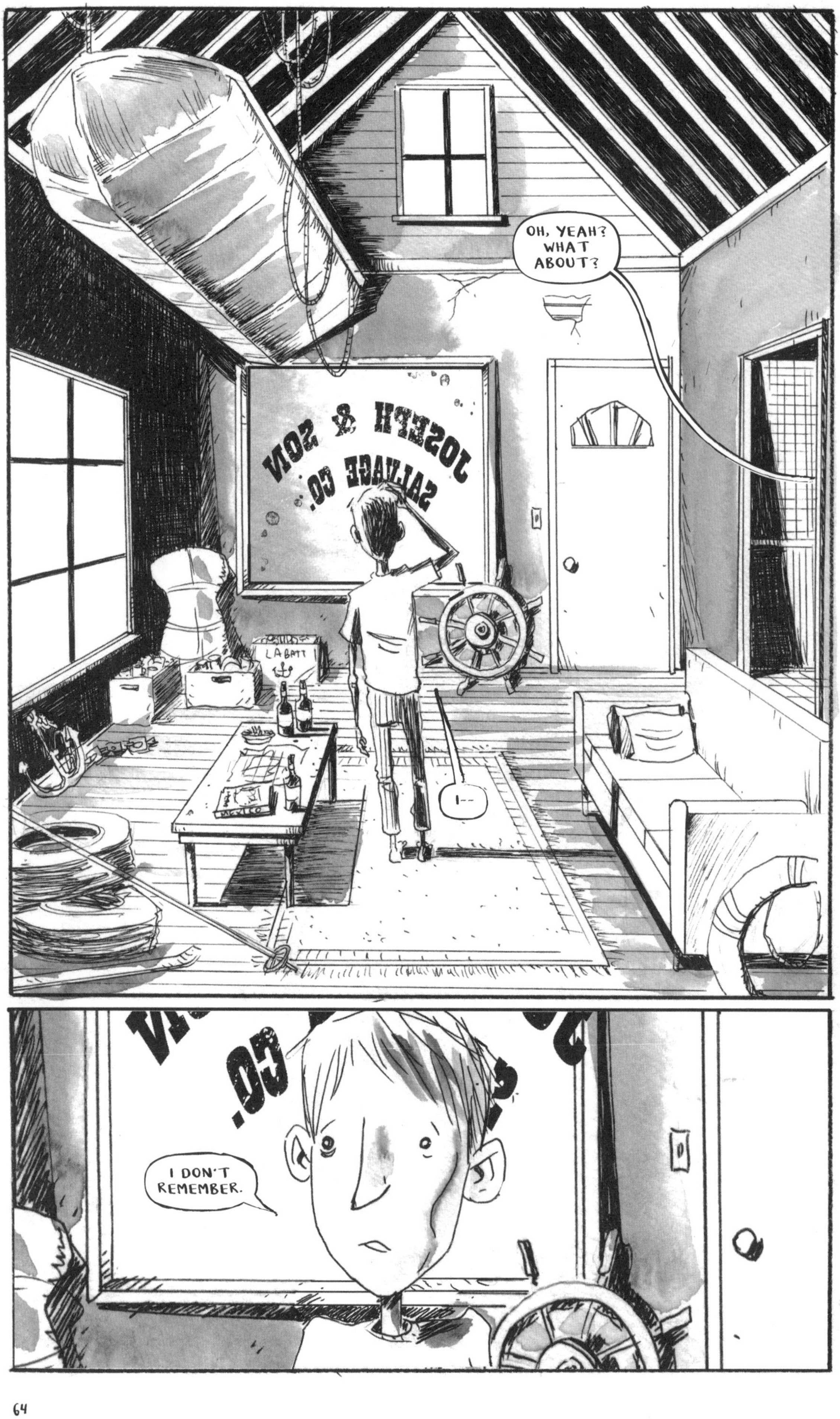
OH, YEAH? WHAT ABOUT?
I--
LABATT
I DON'T REMEMBER.

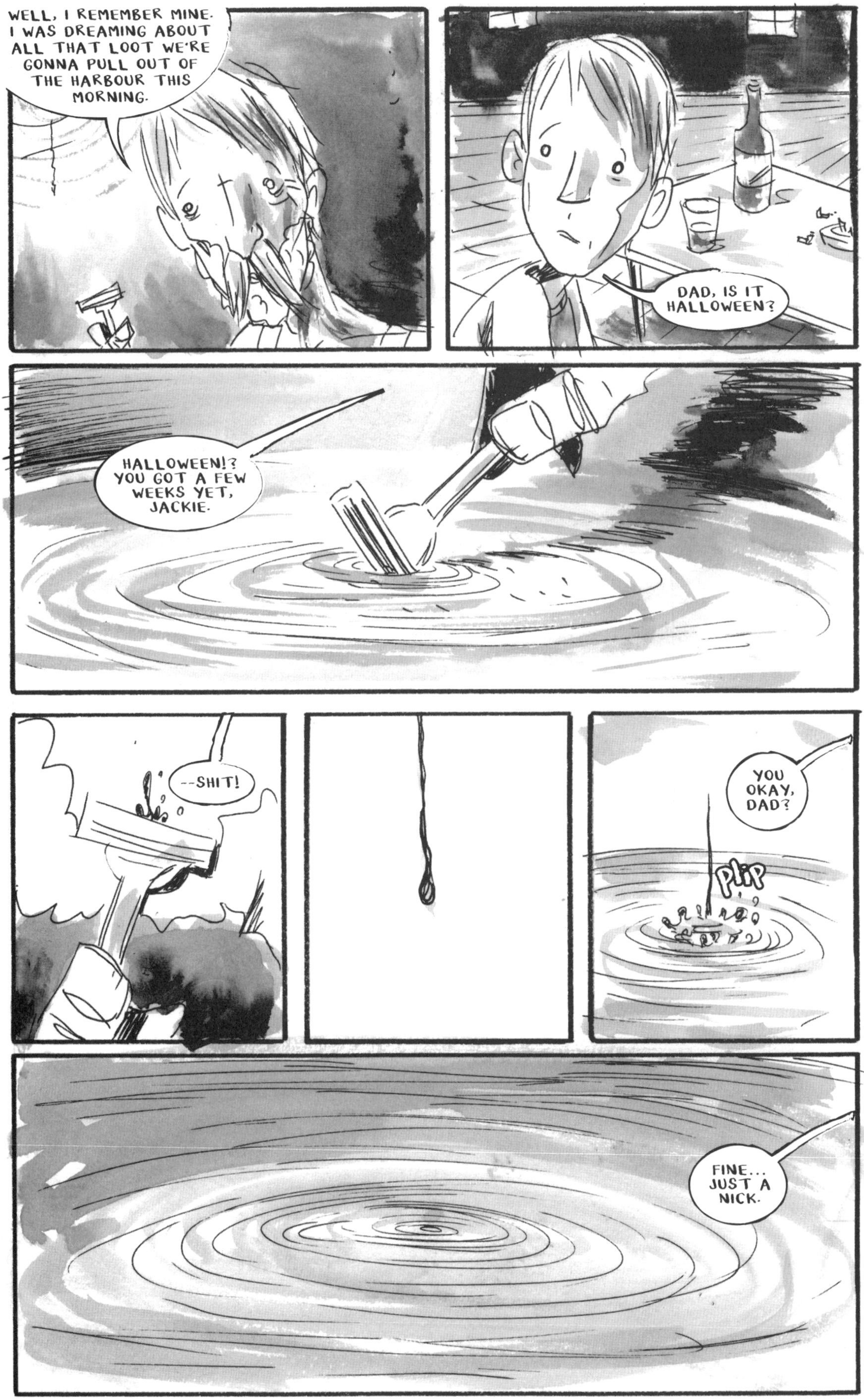
WELL, I REMEMBER MINE. I WAS DREAMING ABOUT ALL THAT LOOT WE'RE GONNA PULL OUT OF THE HARBOUR THIS MORNING.
DAD, IS IT HALLOWEEN?
HALLOWEEN!? YOU GOT A FEW WEEKS YET, JACKIE.
--SHIT!
YOU OKAY, DAD?
PLIP
FINE... JUST A NICK.

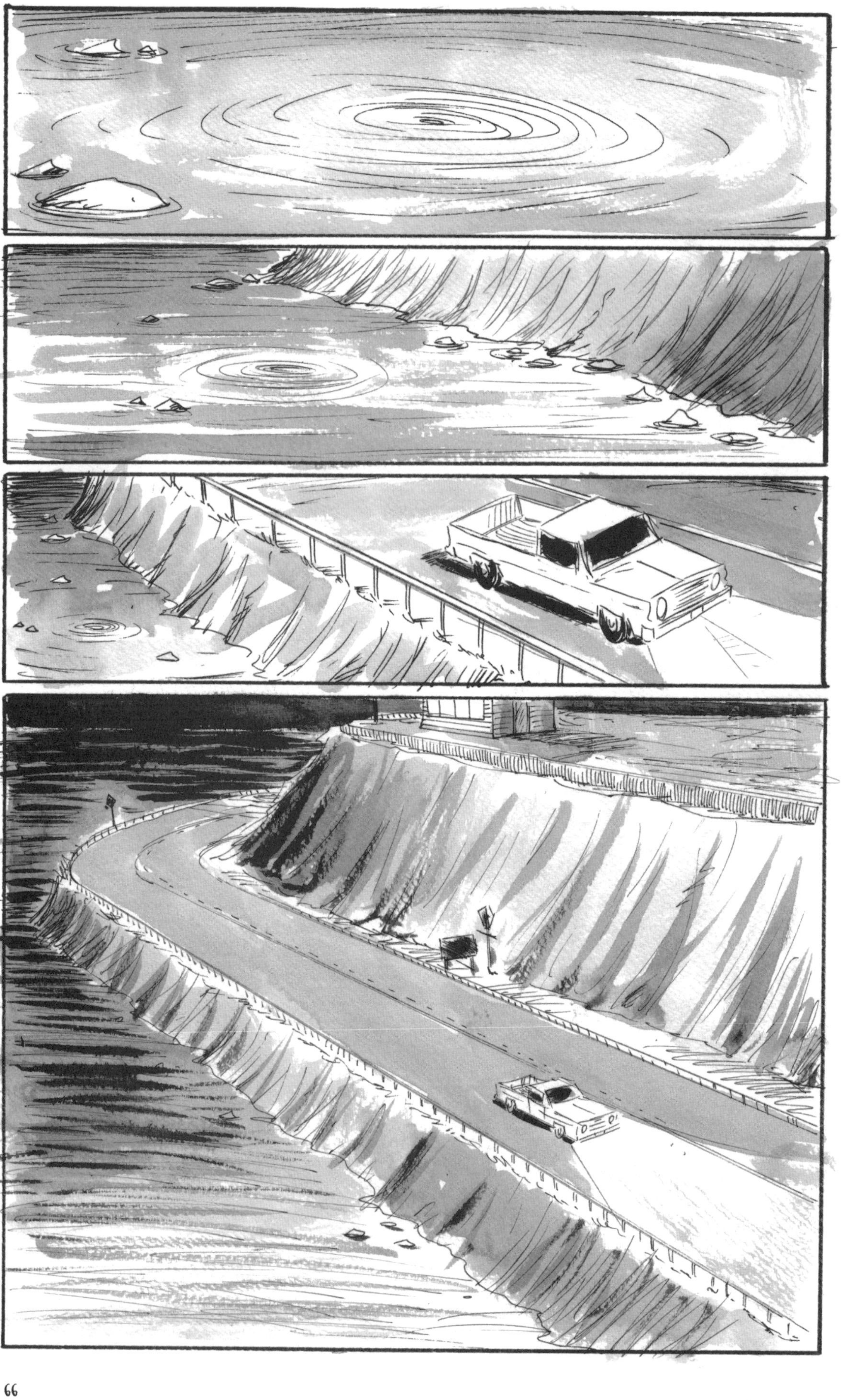

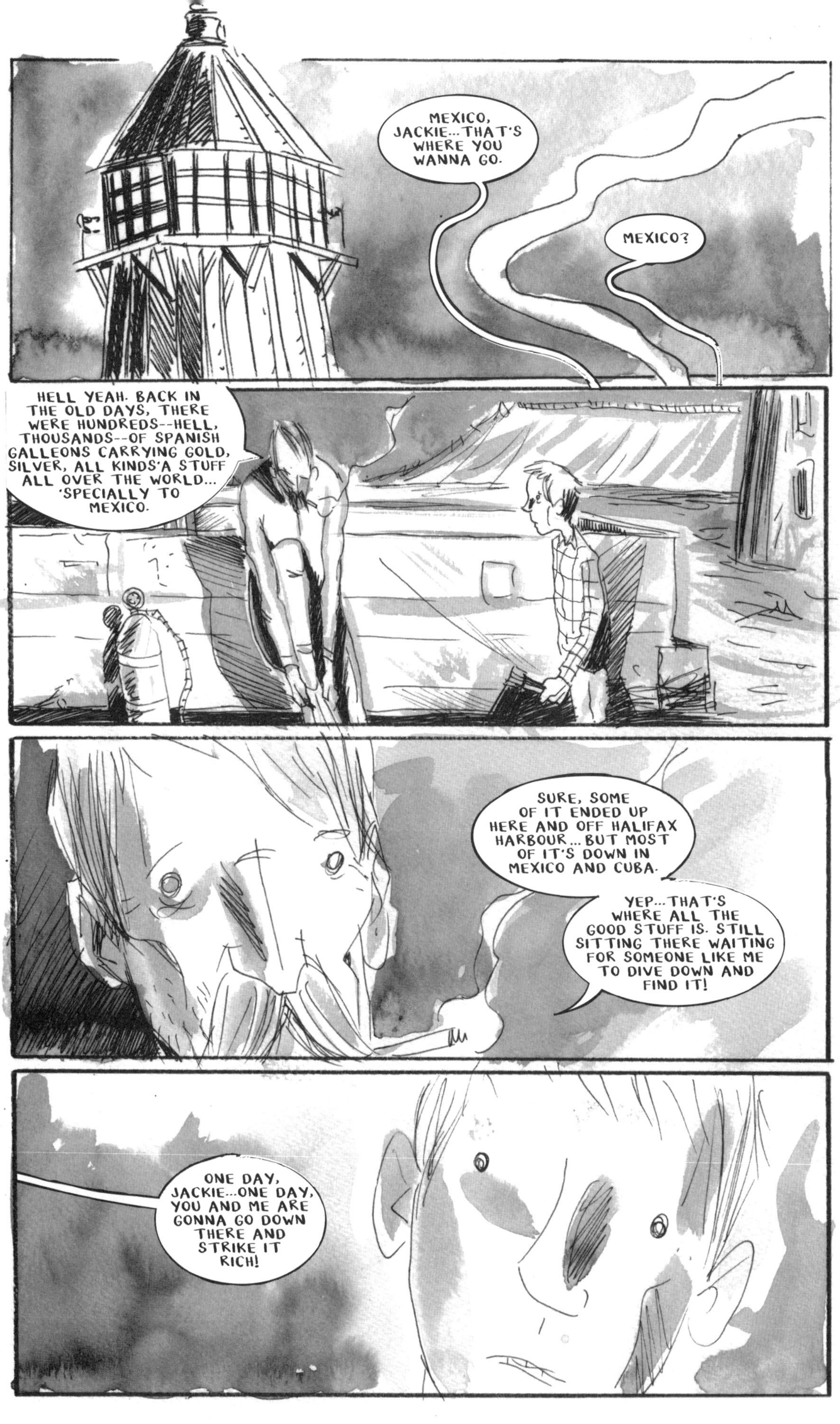
MEXICO, JACKIE...THAT'S WHERE YOU WANNA GO.
MEXICO?
HELL YEAH. BACK IN THE OLD DAYS, THERE WERE HUNDREDS--HELL, THOUSANDS--OF SPANISH GALLEONS CARRYING GOLD, SILVER, ALL KINDS'A STUFF ALL OVER THE WORLD... 'SPECIALLY TO MEXICO.
SURE, SOME OF IT ENDED UP HERE AND OFF HALIFAX HARBOUR... BUT MOST OF IT'S DOWN IN MEXICO AND CUBA.
YEP...THAT'S WHERE ALL THE GOOD STUFF IS. STILL SITTING THERE WAITING FOR SOMEONE LIKE ME TO DIVE DOWN AND FIND IT!
ONE DAY, JACKIE...ONE DAY, YOU AND ME ARE GONNA GO DOWN THERE AND STRIKE IT RICH!

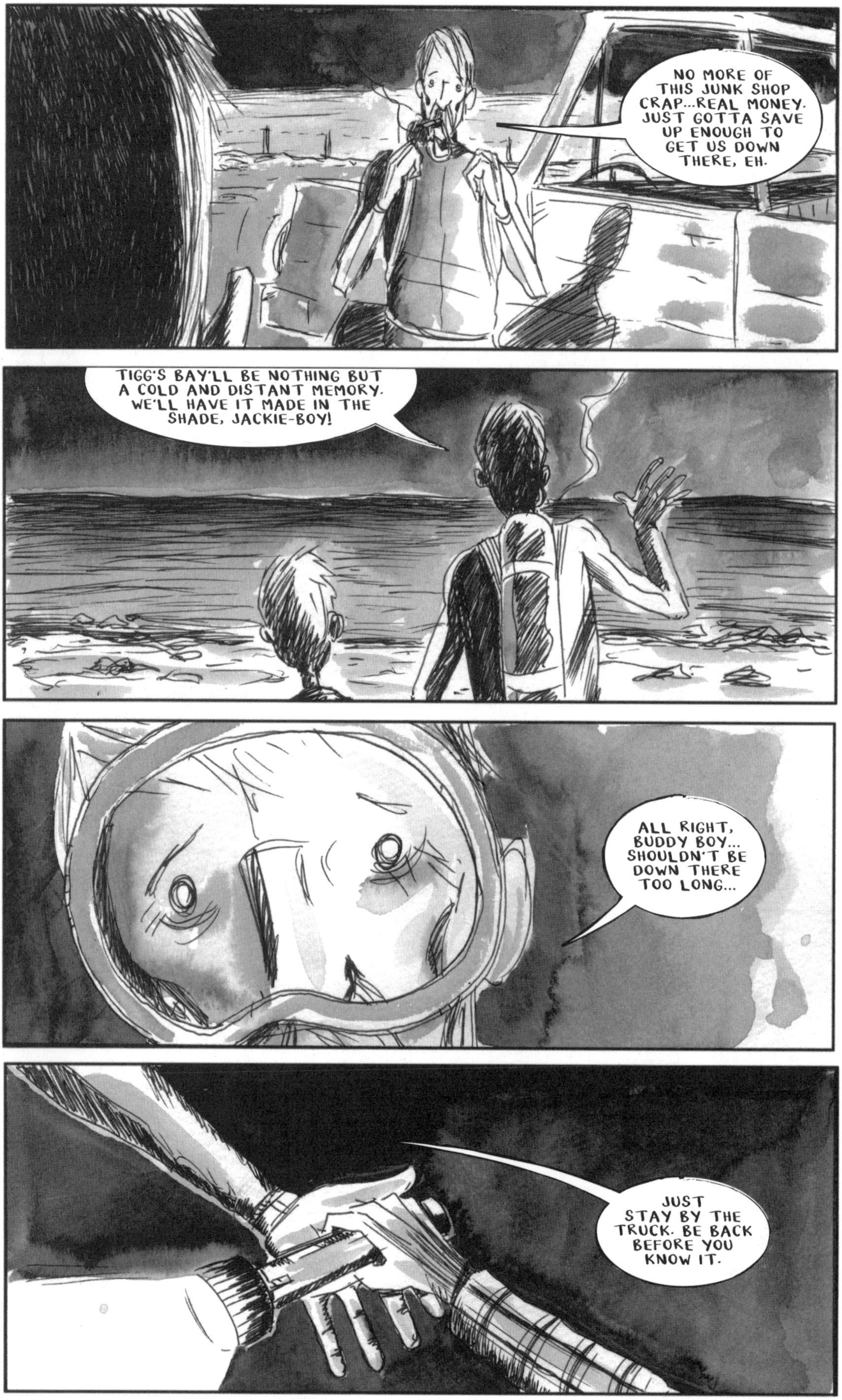
NO MORE OF THIS JUNK SHOP CRAP...REAL MONEY. JUST GOTTA SAVE UP ENOUGH TO GET US DOWN THERE, EH.
TIGG'S BAY'LL BE NOTHING BUT A COLD AND DISTANT MEMORY. WE'LL HAVE IT MADE IN THE SHADE, JACKIE-BOY!
ALL RIGHT, BUDDY BOY... SHOULDN'T BE DOWN THERE TOO LONG...
JUST STAY BY THE TRUCK. BE BACK BEFORE YOU KNOW IT.

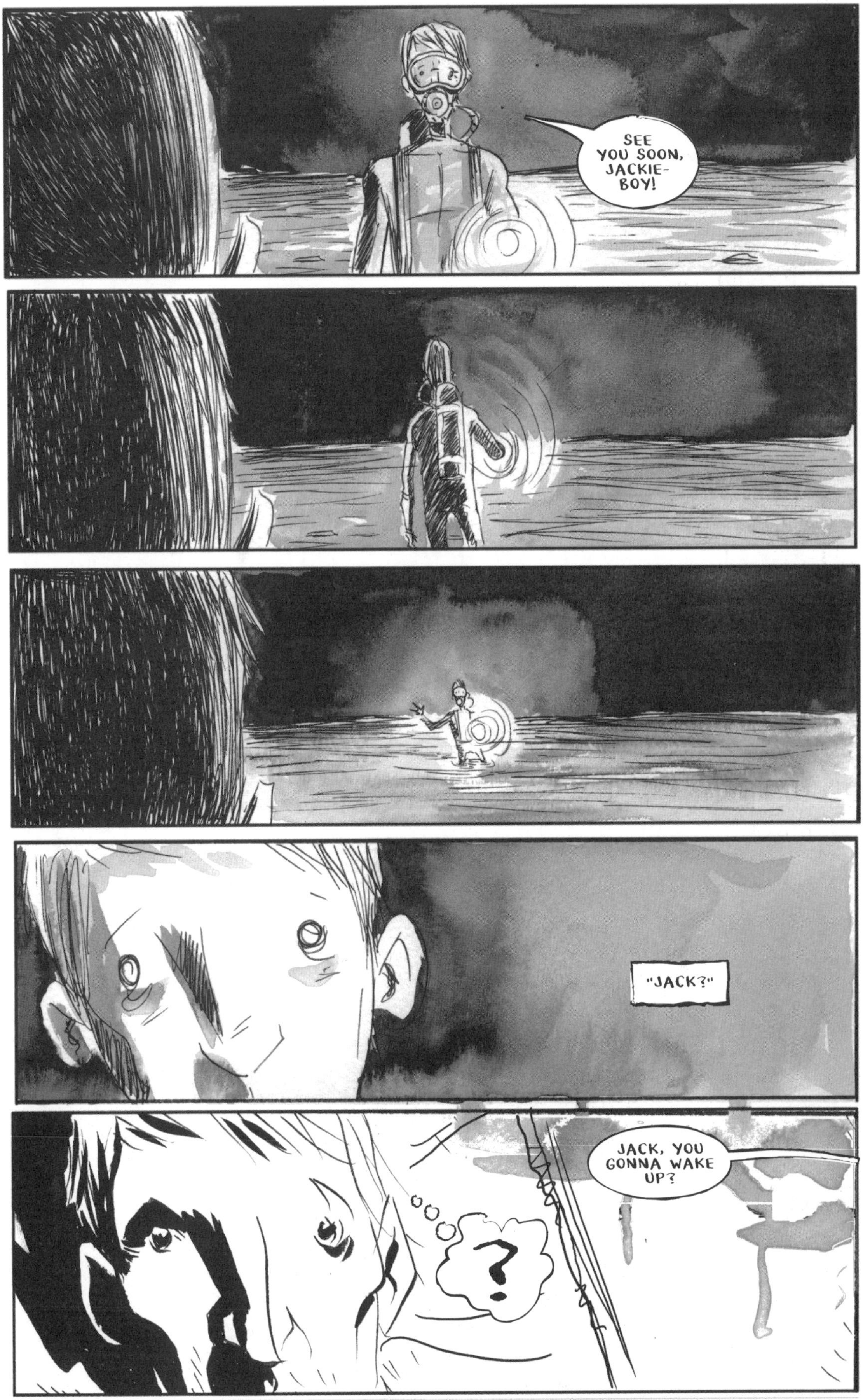
SEE YOU SOON, JACKIE-BOY!
"JACK?"
JACK, YOU GONNA WAKE UP?
?

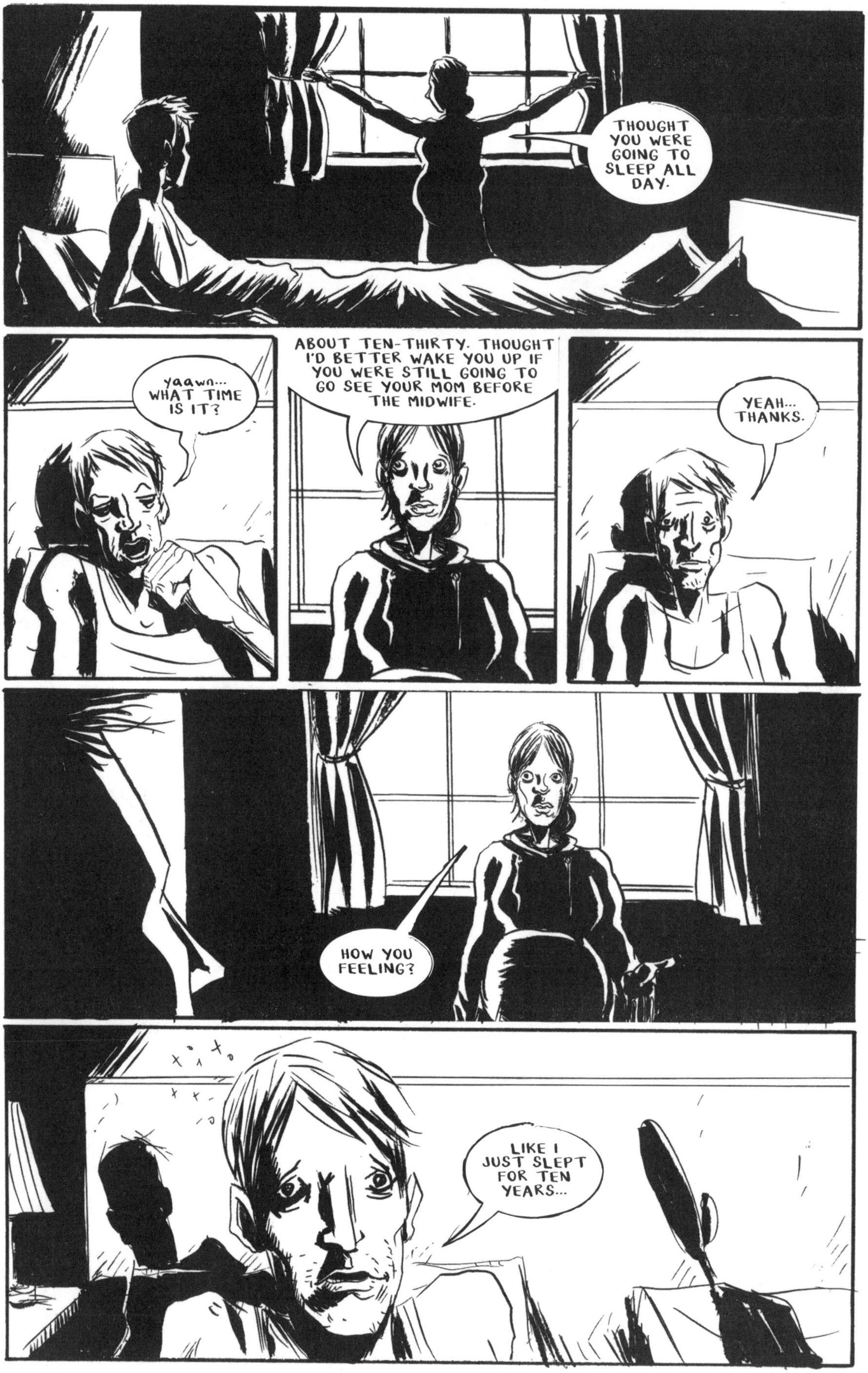
THOUGHT YOU WERE GOING TO SLEEP ALL DAY.
yaawn... WHAT TIME IS IT?
ABOUT TEN-THIRTY. THOUGHT I'D BETTER WAKE YOU UP IF YOU WERE STILL GOING TO GO SEE YOUR MOM BEFORE THE MIDWIFE.
YEAH... THANKS.
HOW YOU FEELING?
LIKE I JUST SLEPT FOR TEN YEARS...

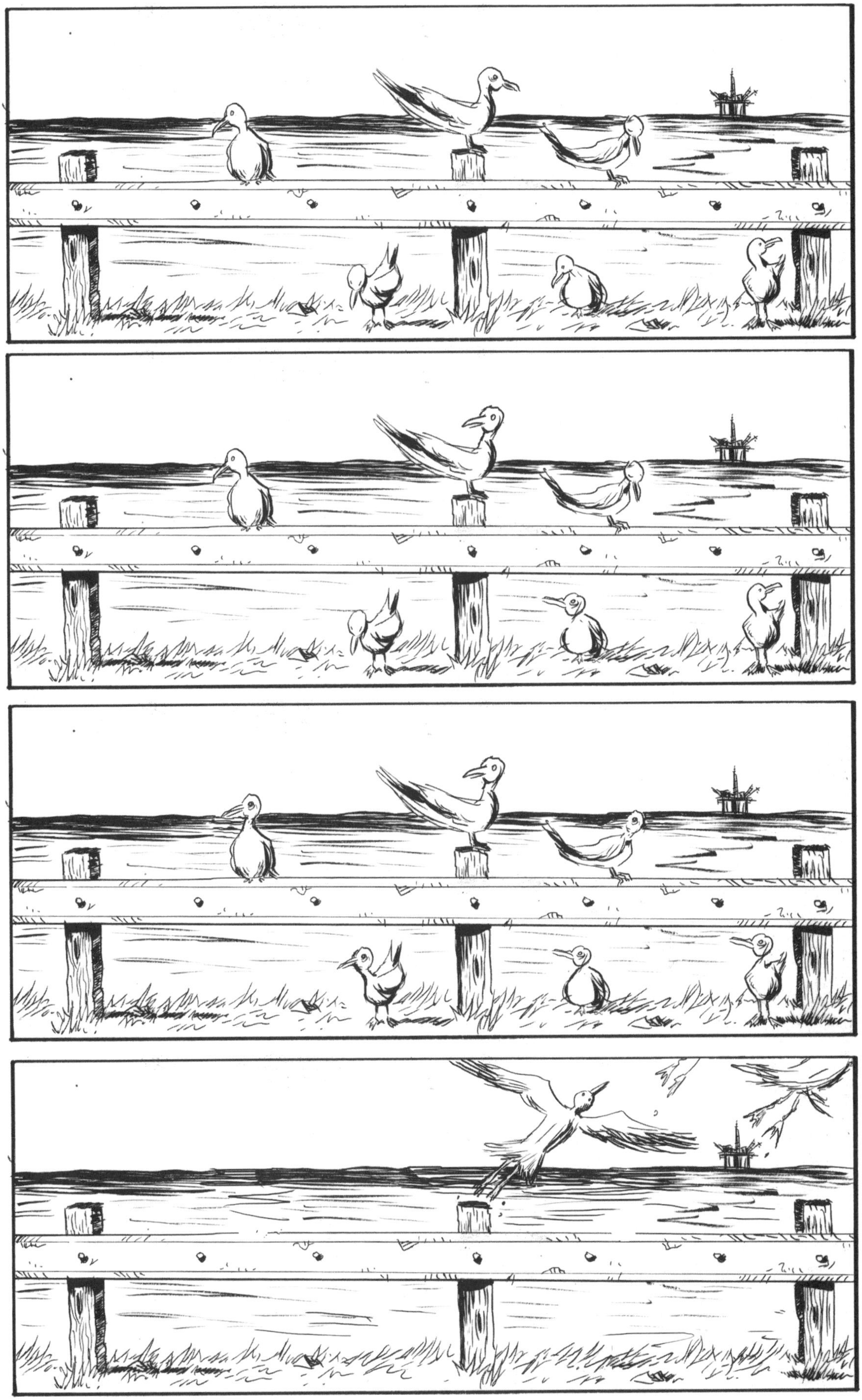

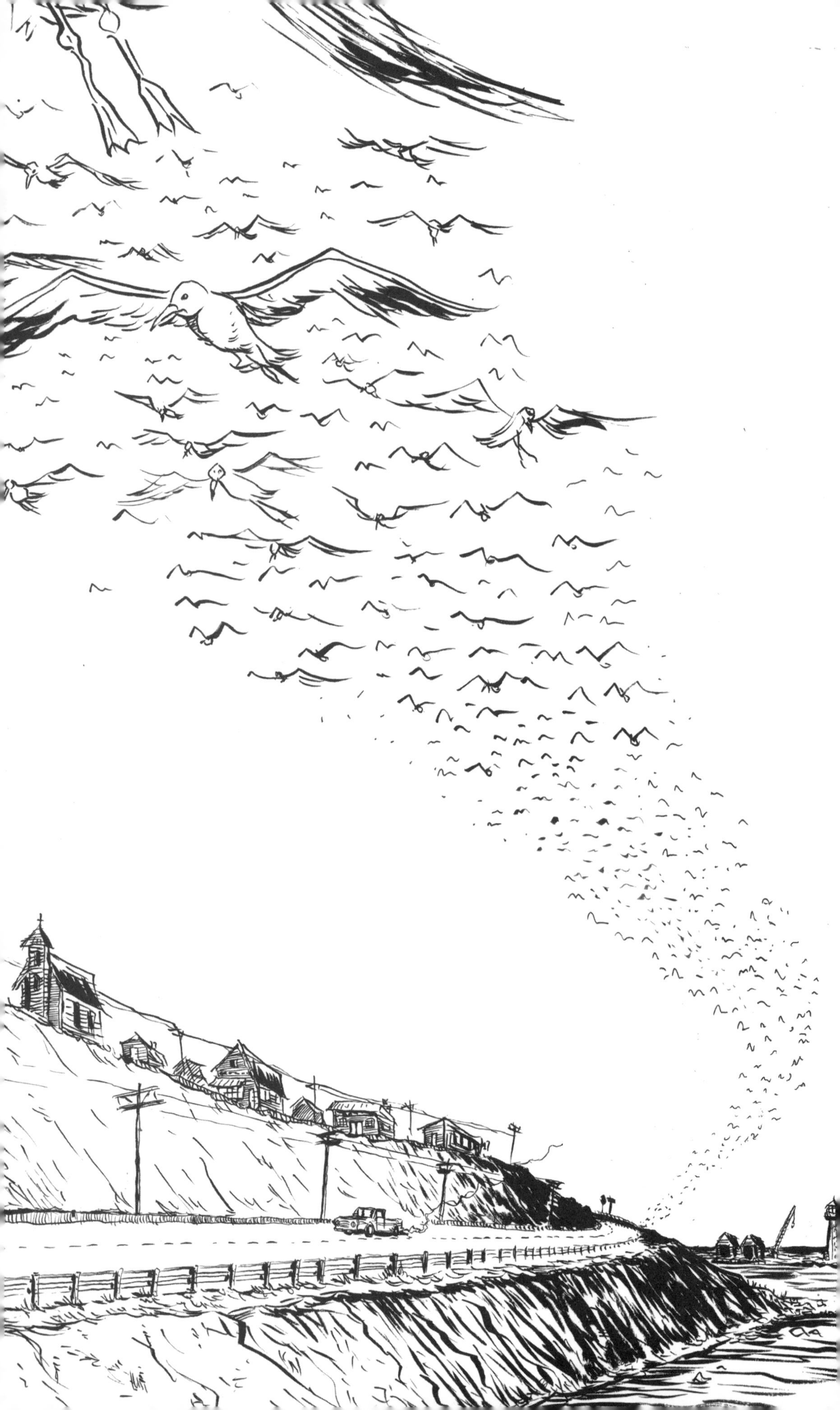

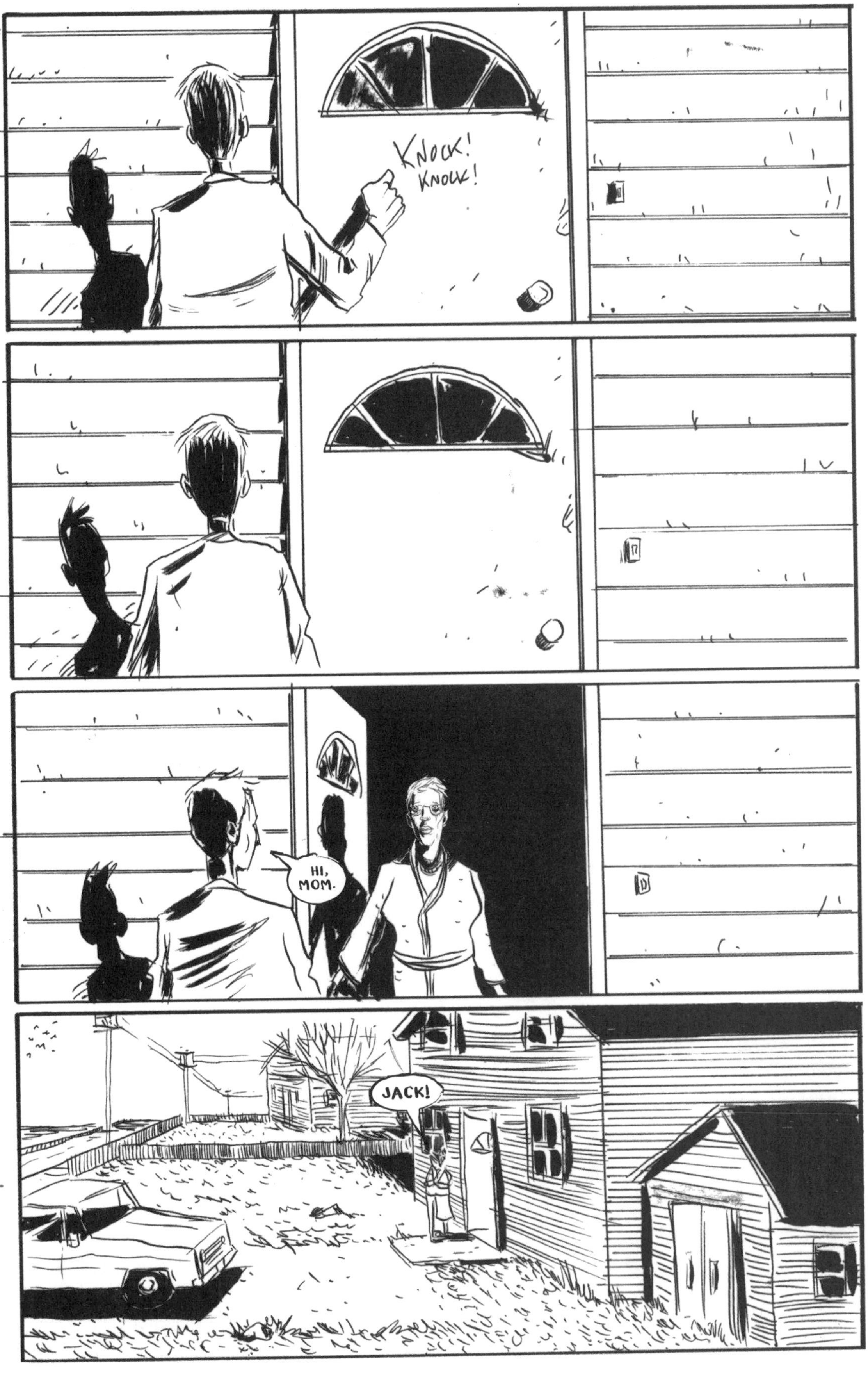
KNOCK! KNOCK!
HI, MOM.
JACK!

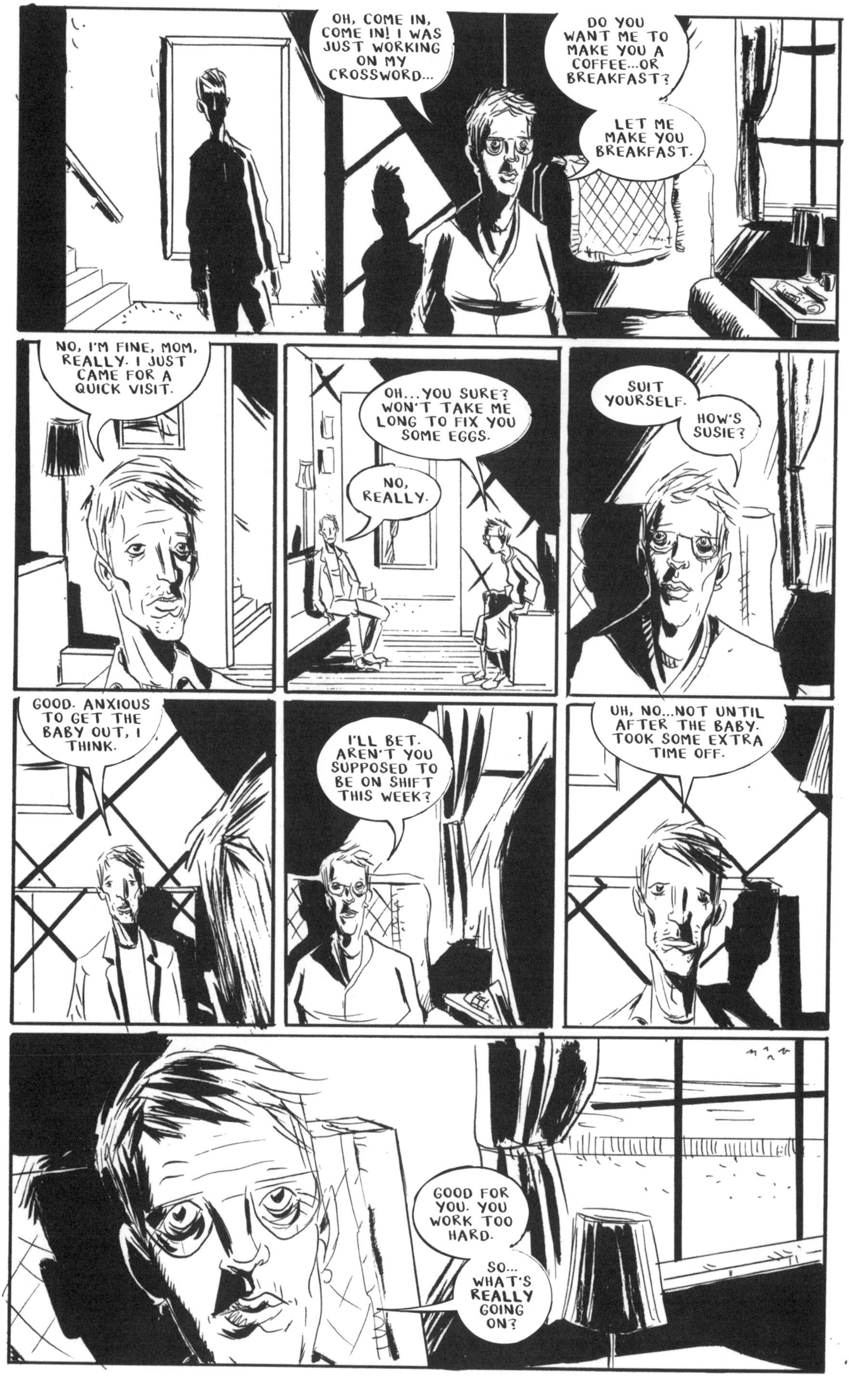
OH, COME IN, COME IN! I WAS JUST WORKING ON MY CROSSWORD...
DO YOU WANT ME TO MAKE YOU A COFFEE...OR BREAKFAST?
LET ME MAKE YOU BREAKFAST.
NO, I'M FINE, MOM, REALLY. I JUST CAME FOR A QUICK VISIT.
OH... YOU SURE? WON'T TAKE ME LONG TO FIX YOU SOME EGGS.
NO, REALLY.
SUIT YOURSELF.
HOW'S SUSIE?
GOOD. ANXIOUS TO GET THE BABY OUT, I THINK.
I'LL BET. AREN'T YOU SUPPOSED TO BE ON SHIFT THIS WEEK?
UH, NO...NOT UNTIL AFTER THE BABY. TOOK SOME EXTRA TIME OFF.
GOOD FOR YOU. YOU WORK TOO HARD.
SO... WHAT'S REALLY GOING ON?

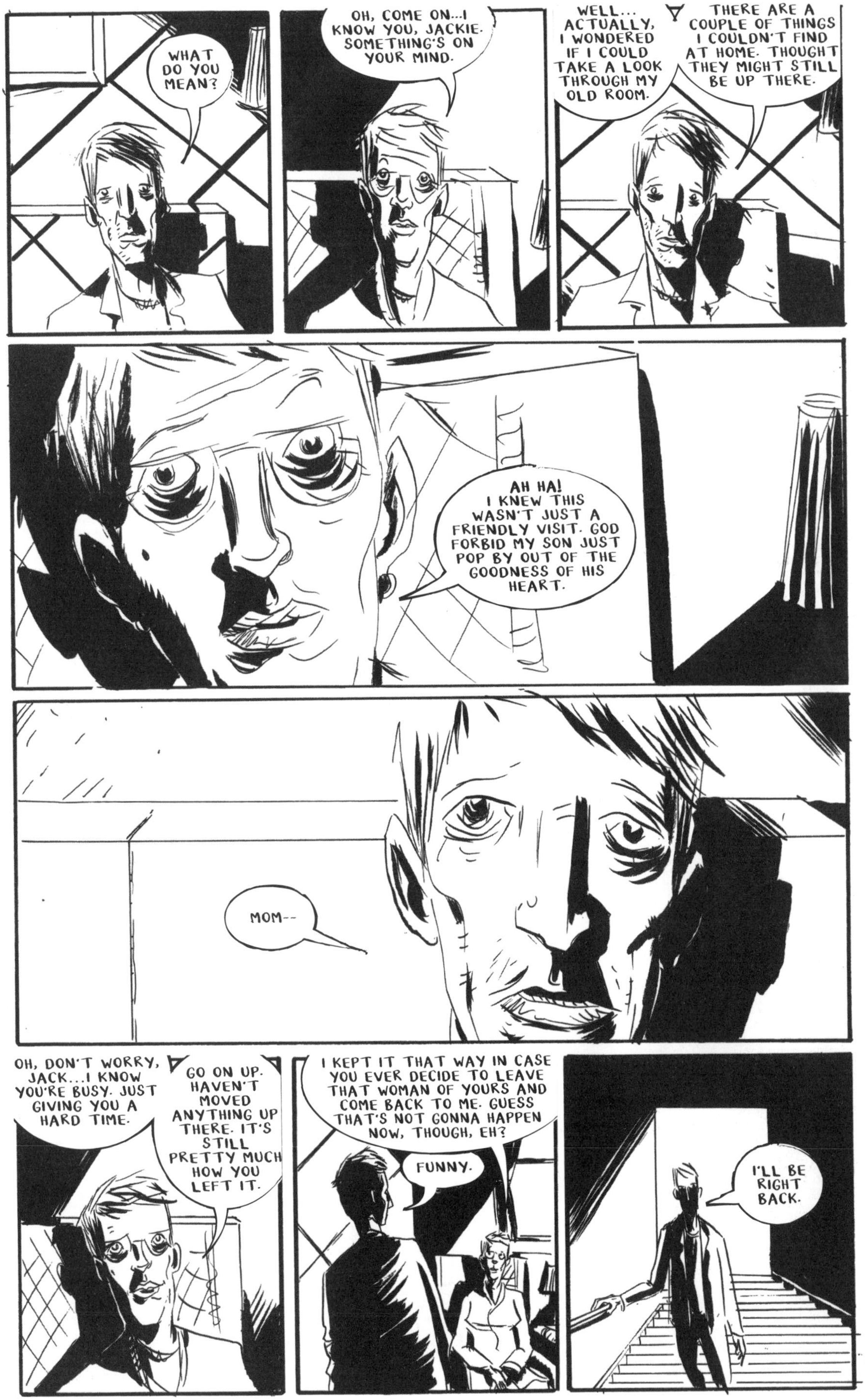
WHAT DO YOU MEAN?
OH, COME ON...I KNOW YOU, JACKIE. SOMETHING'S ON YOUR MIND.
WELL... ACTUALLY, I WONDERED IF I COULD TAKE A LOOK THROUGH MY OLD ROOM.
THERE ARE A COUPLE OF THINGS I COULDN'T FIND AT HOME. THOUGHT THEY MIGHT STILL BE UP THERE.
AH HA! I KNEW THIS WASN'T JUST A FRIENDLY VISIT. GOD FORBID MY SON JUST POP BY OUT OF THE GOODNESS OF HIS HEART.
MOM--
OH, DON'T WORRY, JACK...I KNOW YOU'RE BUSY. JUST GIVING YOU A HARD TIME.
GO ON UP. HAVEN'T MOVED ANYTHING UP THERE. IT'S STILL PRETTY MUCH HOW YOU LEFT IT.
I KEPT IT THAT WAY IN CASE YOU EVER DECIDE TO LEAVE THAT WOMAN OF YOURS AND COME BACK TO ME. GUESS THAT'S NOT GONNA HAPPEN NOW, THOUGH, EH?
FUNNY.
I'LL BE RIGHT BACK.

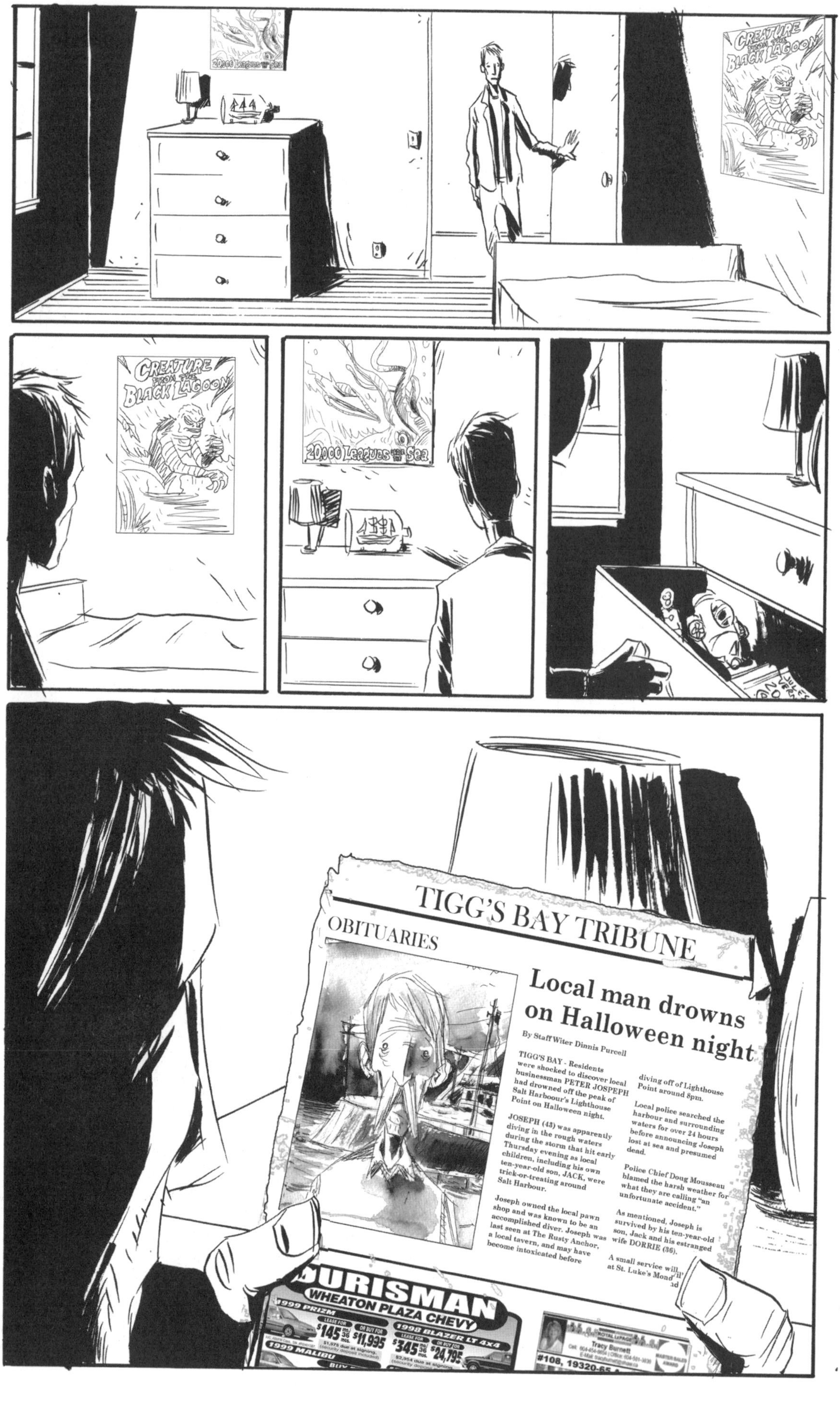

20,000 Leagues under the Sea
CREATURE FROM THE BLACK LAGOON
CREATURE FROM THE BLACK LAGOON
20,000 Leagues under the Sea
TIGG'S BAY TRIBUNE
OBITUARIES
Local man drowns on Halloween night
By Staff Witer Dinnis Purcell
TIGG'S BAY - Residents were shocked to discover local businessman PETER JOSPEPH had drowned off the peak of Salt Harboour's Lighthouse Point on Halloween night.
JOSEPH (43) was apparently diving in the rough waters during the storm that hit early Thursday evening as local children, including his own ten-year-old son, JACK, were trick-or-treating around Salt Harbour.
Joseph owned the local pawn shop and was known to be an accomplished diver. Joseph was last seen at The Rusty Anchor, a local tavern, and may have become intoxicated before diving off of Lighthouse Point around 8pm.
Local police searched the harbour and surrounding waters for over 24 hours before announcing Joseph lost at sea and presumed dead.
Police Chief Doug Mousseau blamed the harsh weather for what they are calling "an unfortunate accident."
As mentioned, Joseph is survived by his ten-year-old son, Jack and his estranged wife DORRIE (36).
A small service will at St. Luke's Mond
URISMAN
WHEATON PLAZA CHEVY
1998 BLAZER LT 4x4
LEASE FOR $145
OR BUY FOR $11,995
LEASE FOR $345
Tracy Burnett

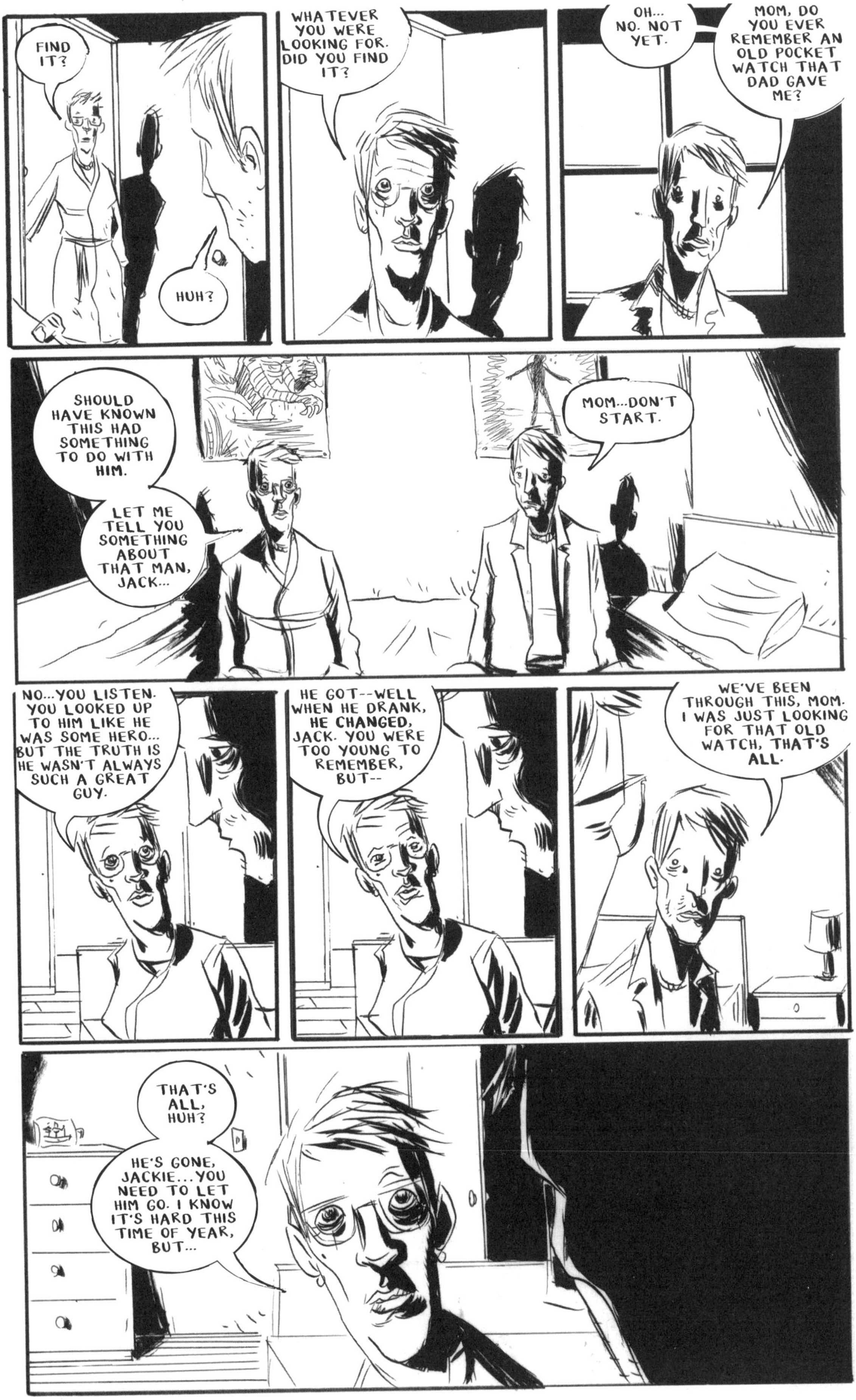
FIND IT?
HUH?
WHATEVER YOU WERE LOOKING FOR. DID YOU FIND IT?
OH... NO. NOT YET.
MOM, DO YOU EVER REMEMBER AN OLD POCKET WATCH THAT DAD GAVE ME?
SHOULD HAVE KNOWN THIS HAD SOMETHING TO DO WITH HIM.
LET ME TELL YOU SOMETHING ABOUT THAT MAN, JACK...
MOM...DON'T START.
NO...YOU LISTEN. YOU LOOKED UP TO HIM LIKE HE WAS SOME HERO... BUT THE TRUTH IS HE WASN'T ALWAYS SUCH A GREAT GUY.
HE GOT--WELL WHEN HE DRANK, HE CHANGED, JACK. YOU WERE TOO YOUNG TO REMEMBER, BUT--
WE'VE BEEN THROUGH THIS, MOM. I WAS JUST LOOKING FOR THAT OLD WATCH, THAT'S ALL.
THAT'S ALL, HUH?
HE'S GONE, JACKIE... YOU NEED TO LET HIM GO. I KNOW IT'S HARD THIS TIME OF YEAR, BUT...

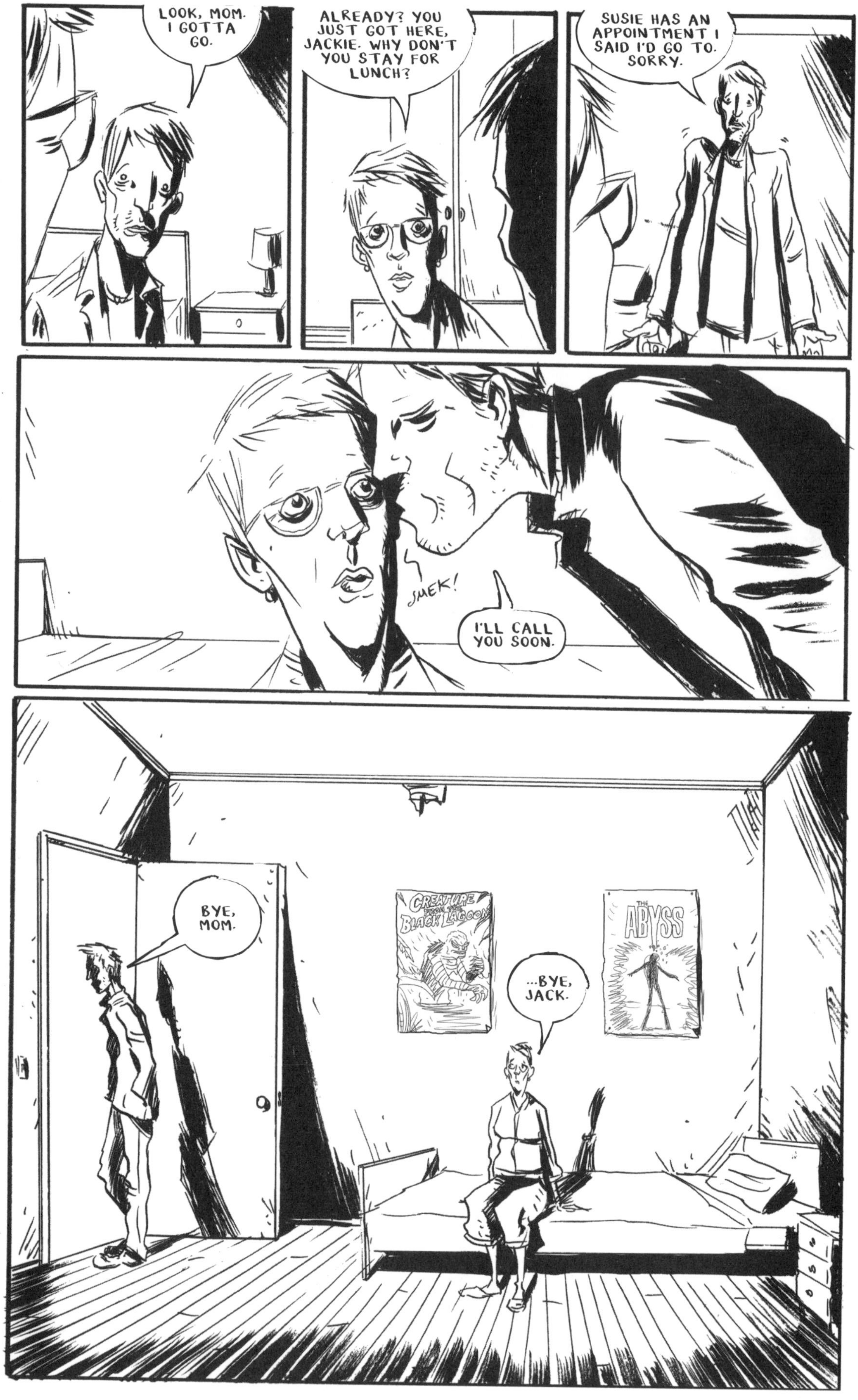
LOOK, MOM. I GOTTA GO.
ALREADY? YOU JUST GOT HERE, JACKIE. WHY DON'T YOU STAY FOR LUNCH?
SUSIE HAS AN APPOINTMENT I SAID I'D GO TO. SORRY.
SMEK!
I'LL CALL YOU SOON.
BYE, MOM.
...BYE, JACK.
CREATURE FROM THE BLACK LAGOON
THE ABYSS

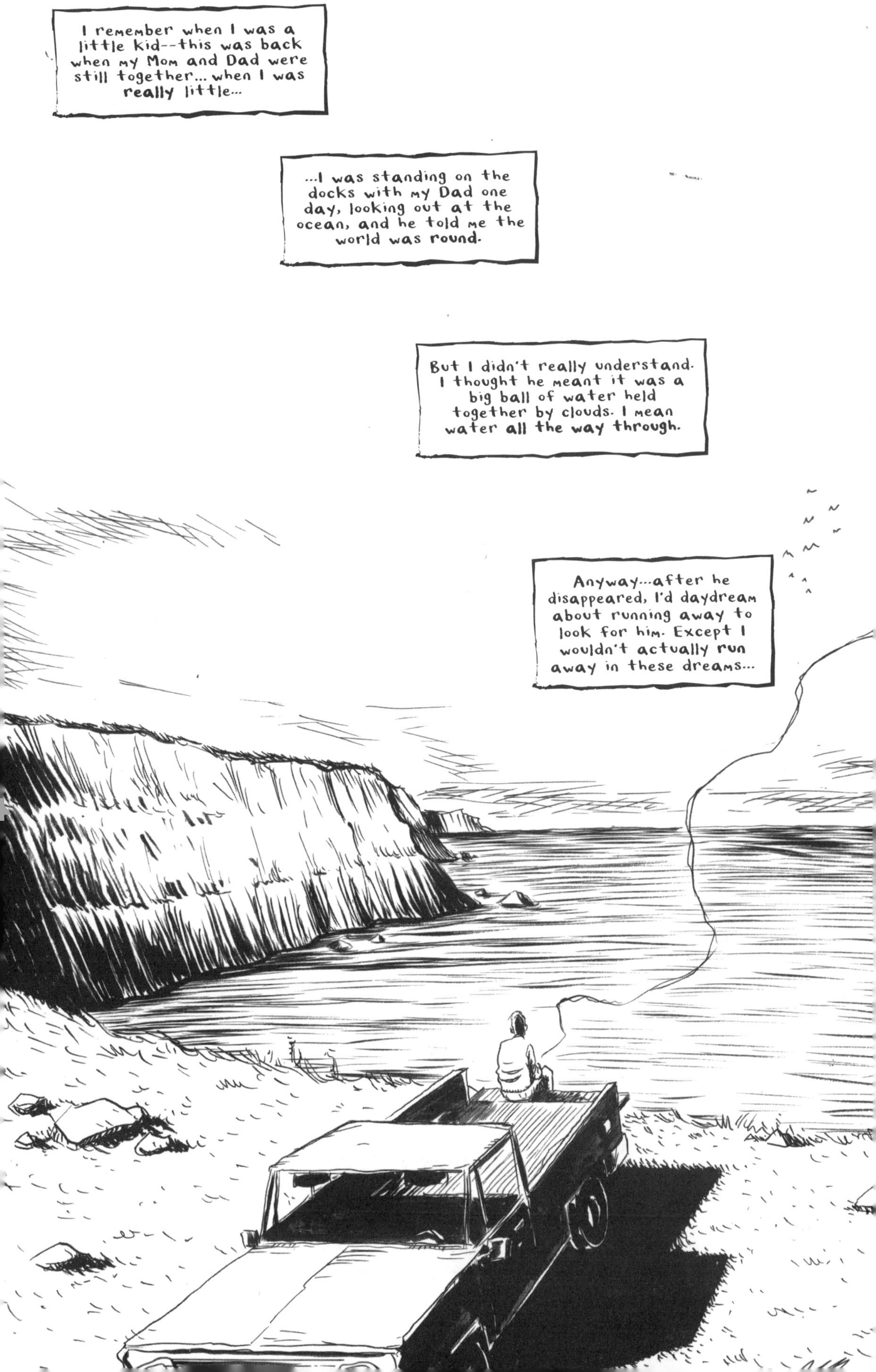
I remember when I was a little kid--this was back when my Mom and Dad were still together... when I was really little...
...I was standing on the docks with my Dad one day, looking out at the ocean, and he told me the world was round.
But I didn't really understand. I thought he meant it was a big ball of water held together by clouds. I mean water all the way through.
Anyway...after he disappeared, I'd daydream about running away to look for him. Except I wouldn't actually run away in these dreams...

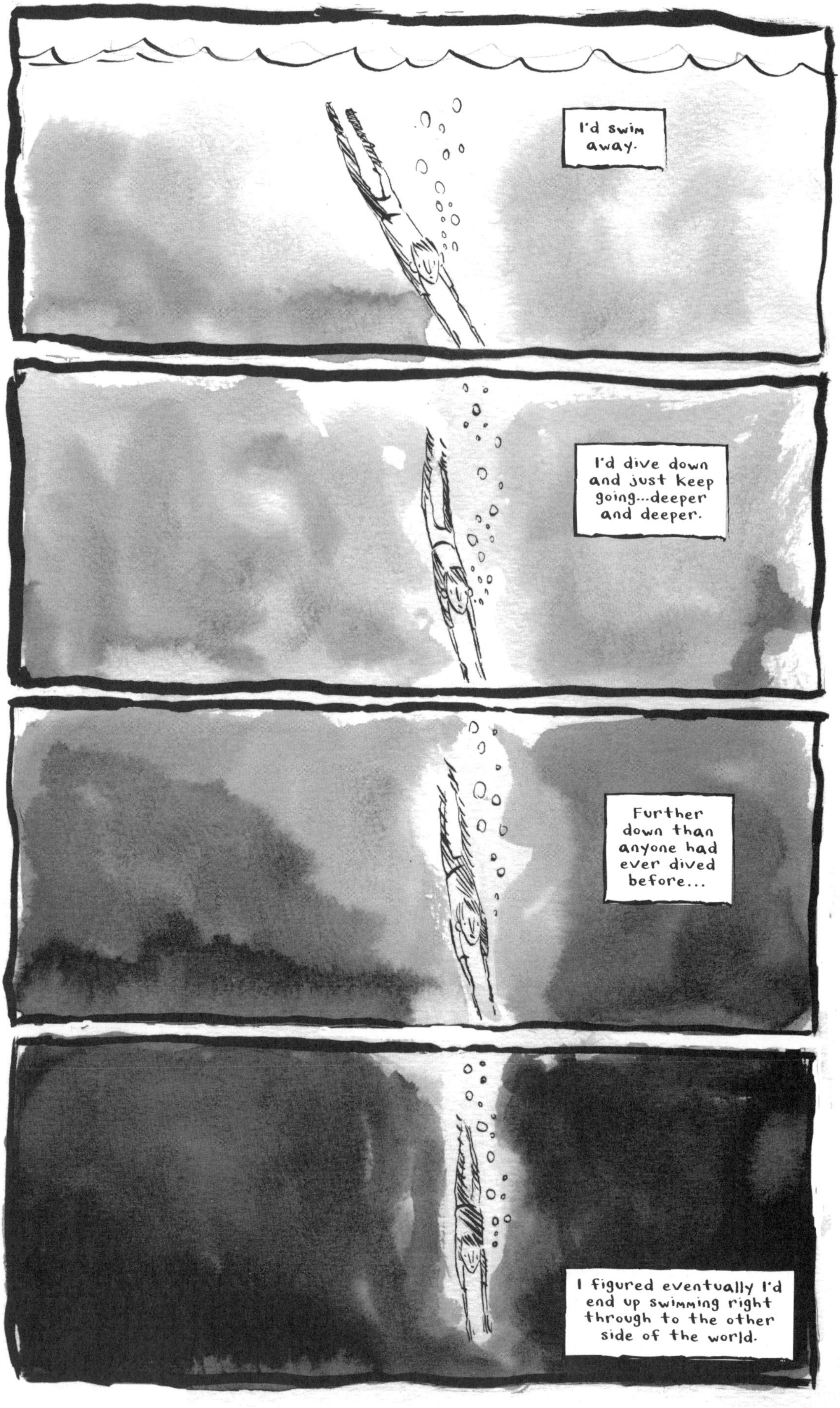
I'd swim away.
I'd dive down and just keep going...deeper and deeper.
Further down than anyone had ever dived before...
I figured eventually I'd end up swimming right through to the other side of the world.

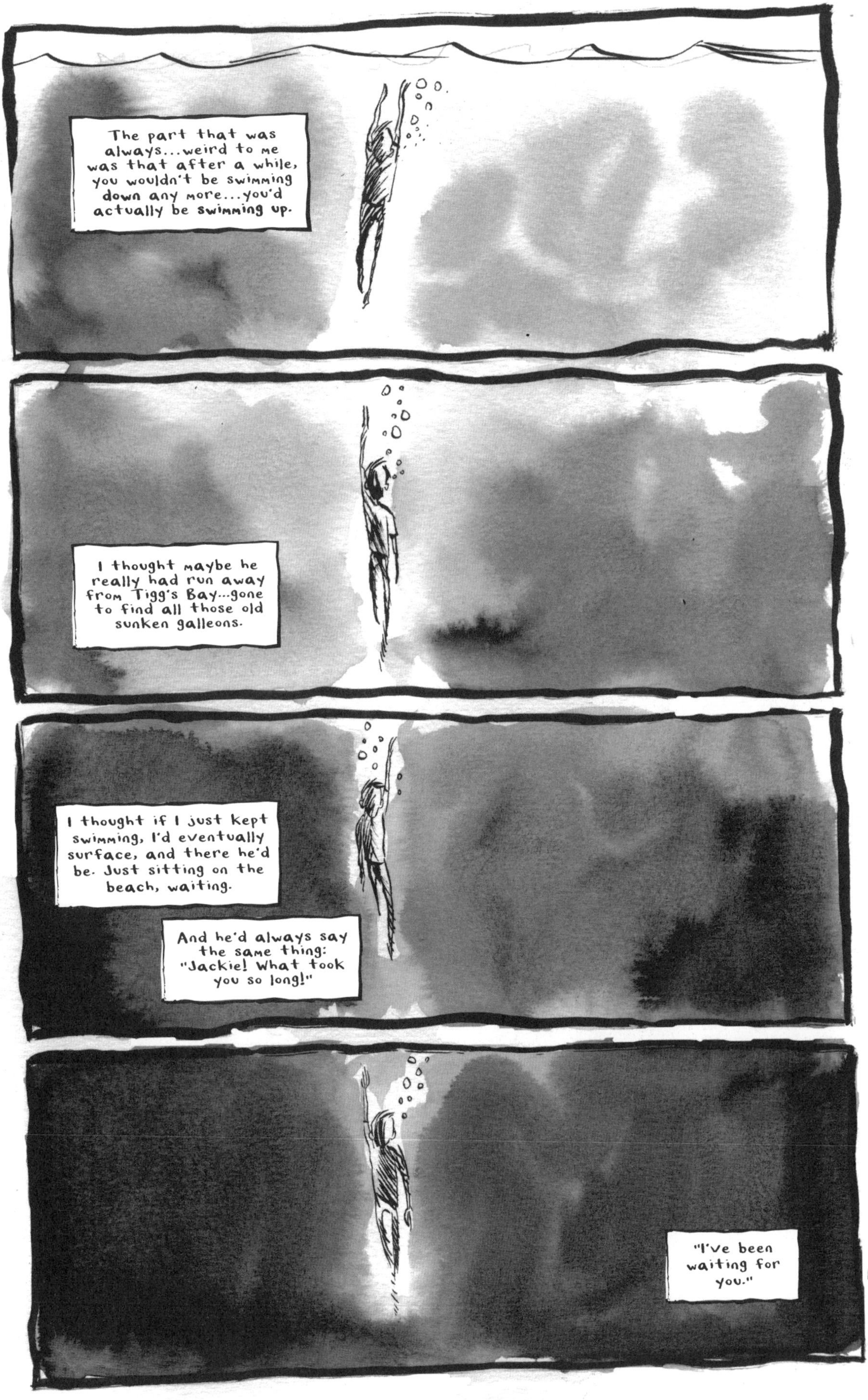
The part that was always...weird to me was that after a while, you wouldn't be swimming down any more...you'd actually be swimming up.
I thought maybe he really had run away from Tigg's Bay...gone to find all those old sunken galleons.
I thought if I just kept swimming, I'd eventually surface, and there he'd be. Just sitting on the beach, waiting.
And he'd always say the same thing: "Jackie! What took you so long!"
"I've been waiting for you."

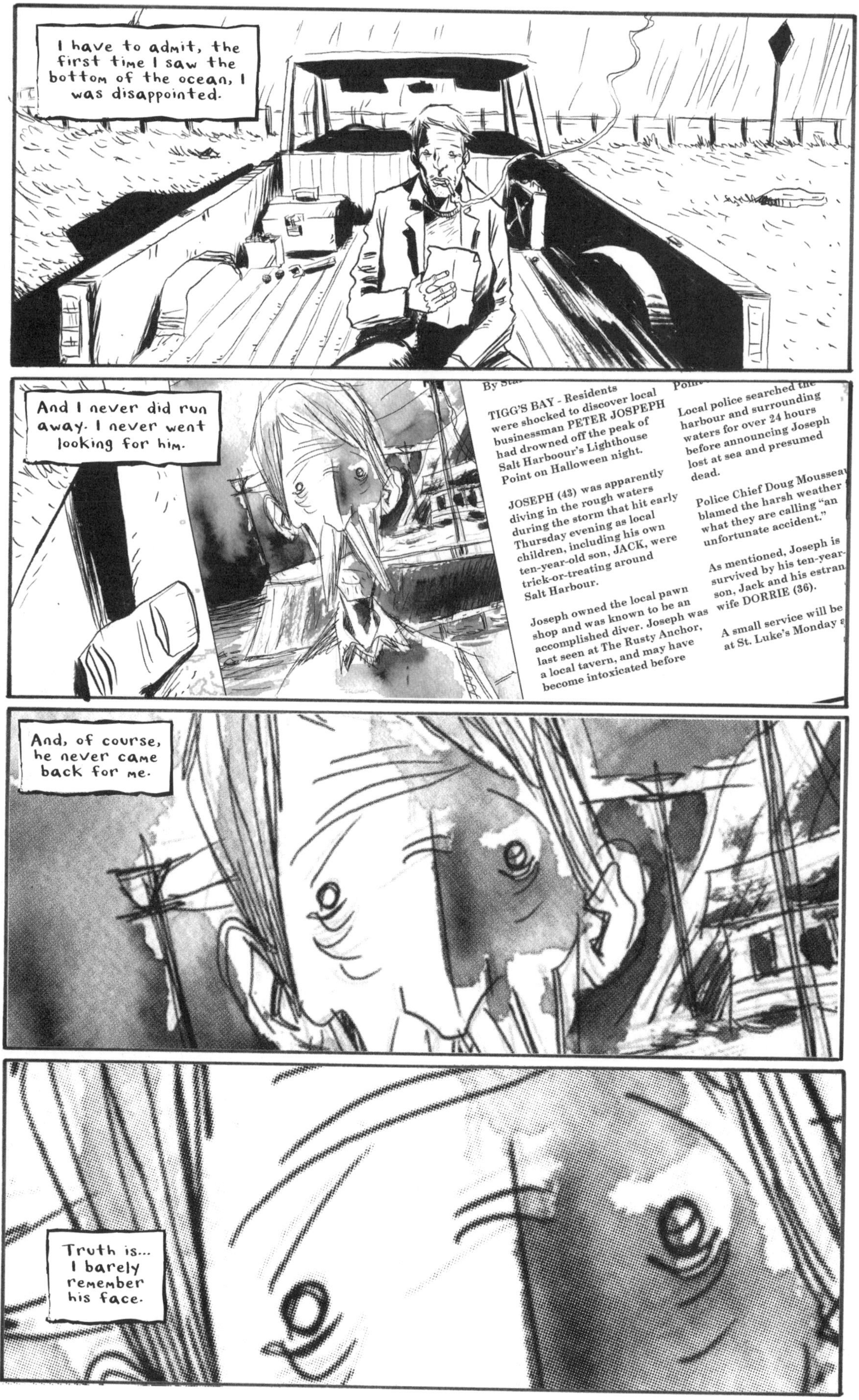
I have to admit, the first time I saw the bottom of the ocean, I was disappointed.
And I never did run away. I never went looking for him.
TIGG'S BAY - Residents were shocked to discover local businessman PETER JOSPEPH had drowned off the peak of Salt Harboour's Lighthouse Point on Halloween night.
JOSEPH (43) was apparently diving in the rough waters during the storm that hit early Thursday evening as local children, including his own ten-year-old son, JACK, were trick-or-treating around Salt Harbour.
Joseph owned the local pawn shop and was known to be an accomplished diver. Joseph was last seen at The Rusty Anchor, a local tavern, and may have become intoxicated before
Local police searched the harbour and surrounding waters for over 24 hours before announcing Joseph lost at sea and presumed dead.
Police Chief Doug Mousseau blamed the harsh weather what they are calling "an unfortunate accident."
As mentioned, Joseph is survived by his ten-year- son, Jack and his estran wife DORRIE (36).
A small service will be at St. Luke's Monday
And, of course, he never came back for me.
Truth is... I barely remember his face.

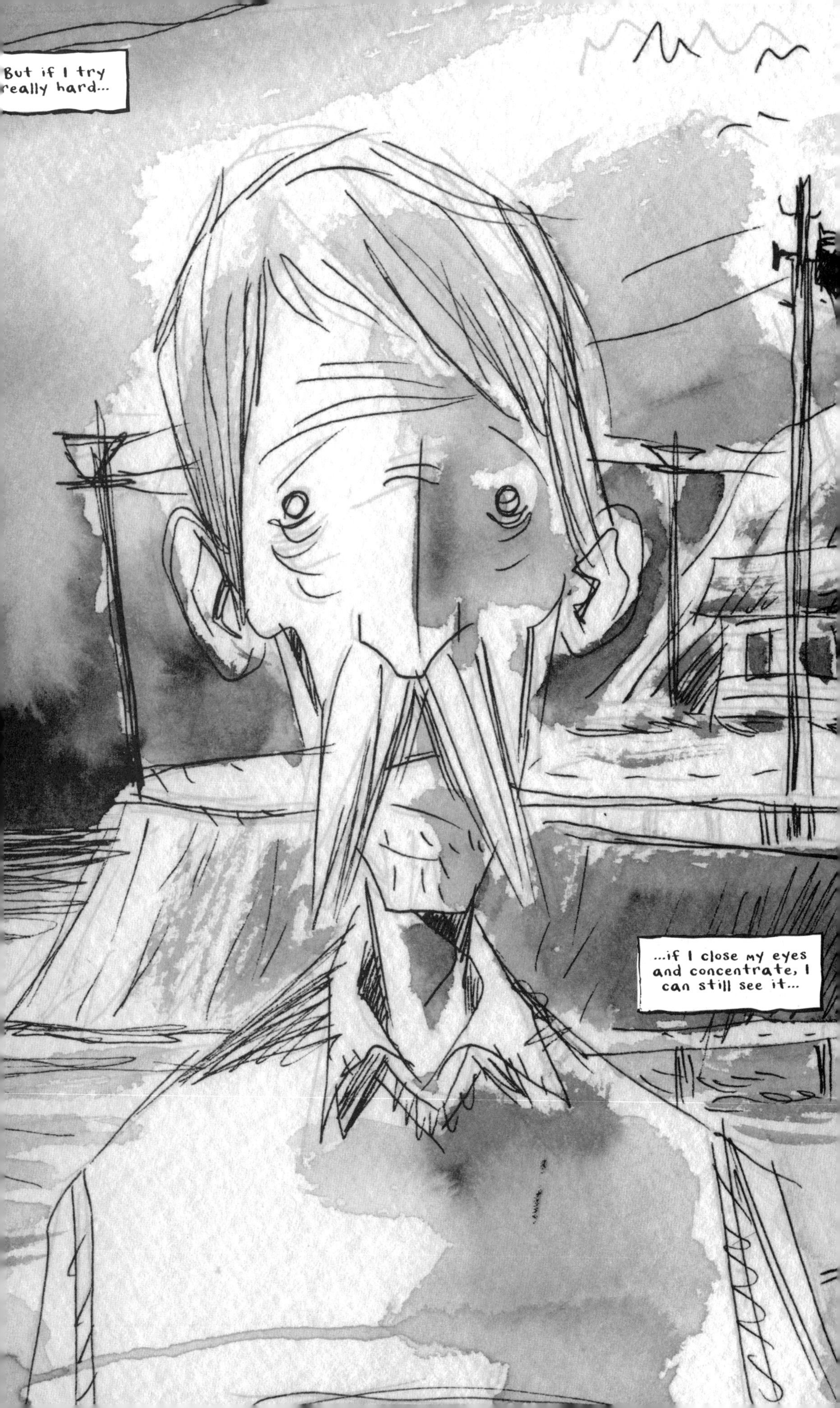
But if I try really hard...
...if I close my eyes and concentrate, I can still see it...

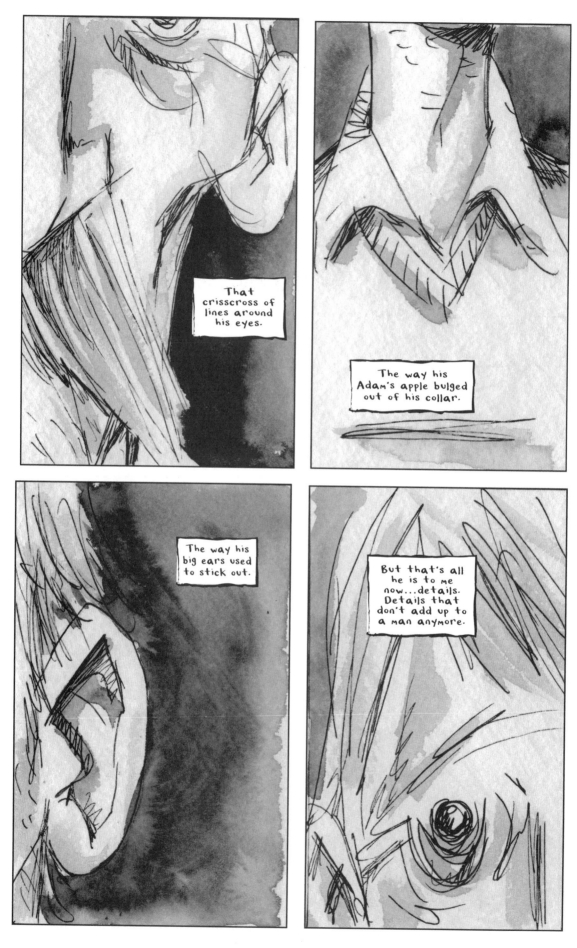

That crisscross of lines around his eyes.

The way his Adam's apple bulged out of his collar.

The way his big ears used to stick out.

But that's all he is to me now...details. Details that don't add up to a man anymore.

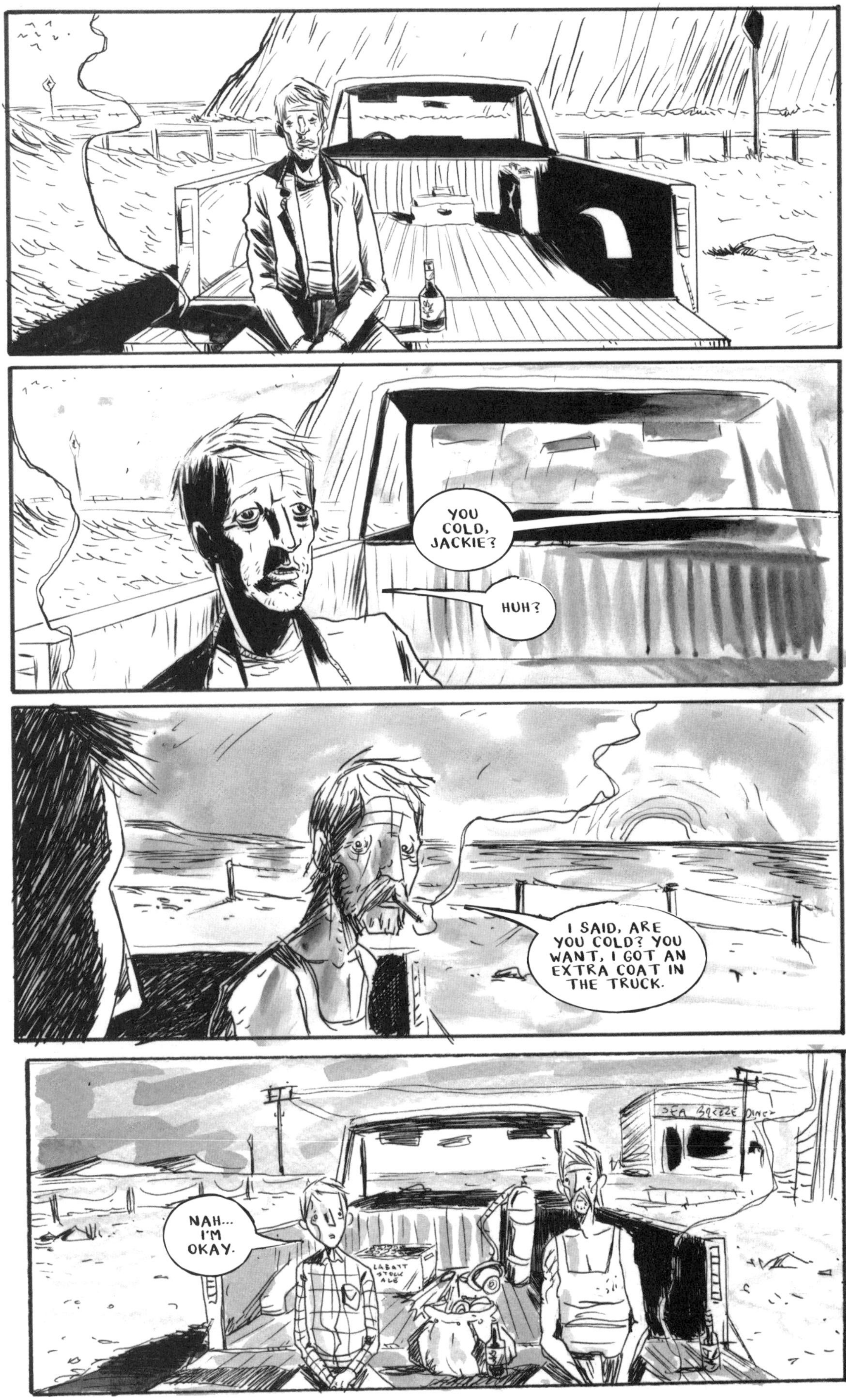
YOU COLD, JACKIE?
HUH?
I SAID, ARE YOU COLD? YOU WANT, I GOT AN EXTRA COAT IN THE TRUCK.
NAH... I'M OKAY.

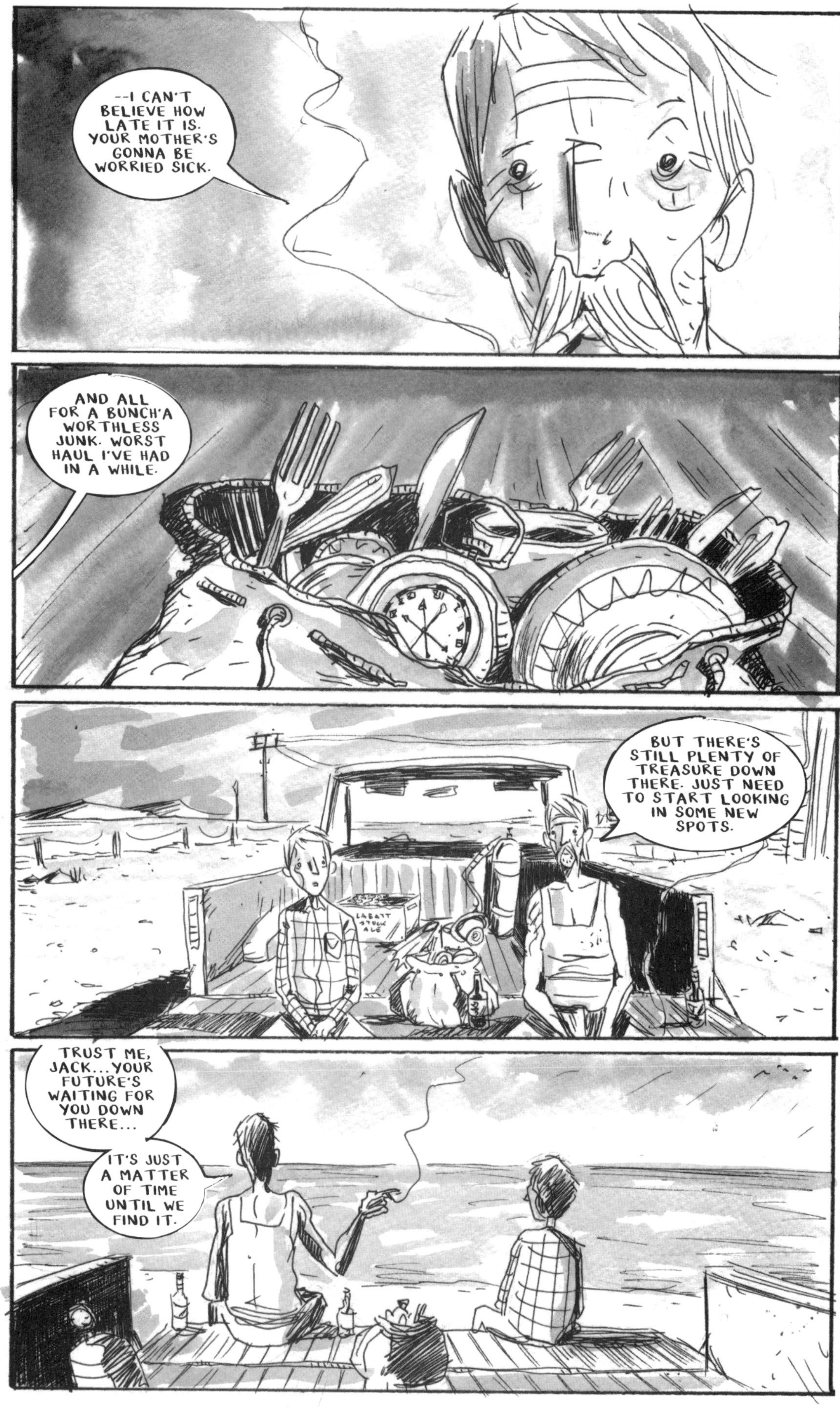

--I CAN'T BELIEVE HOW LATE IT IS. YOUR MOTHER'S GONNA BE WORRIED SICK.
AND ALL FOR A BUNCH'A WORTHLESS JUNK. WORST HAUL I'VE HAD IN A WHILE.
BUT THERE'S STILL PLENTY OF TREASURE DOWN THERE. JUST NEED TO START LOOKING IN SOME NEW SPOTS.
LABATT STOCK ALE
TRUST ME, JACK... YOUR FUTURE'S WAITING FOR YOU DOWN THERE...
IT'S JUST A MATTER OF TIME UNTIL WE FIND IT.

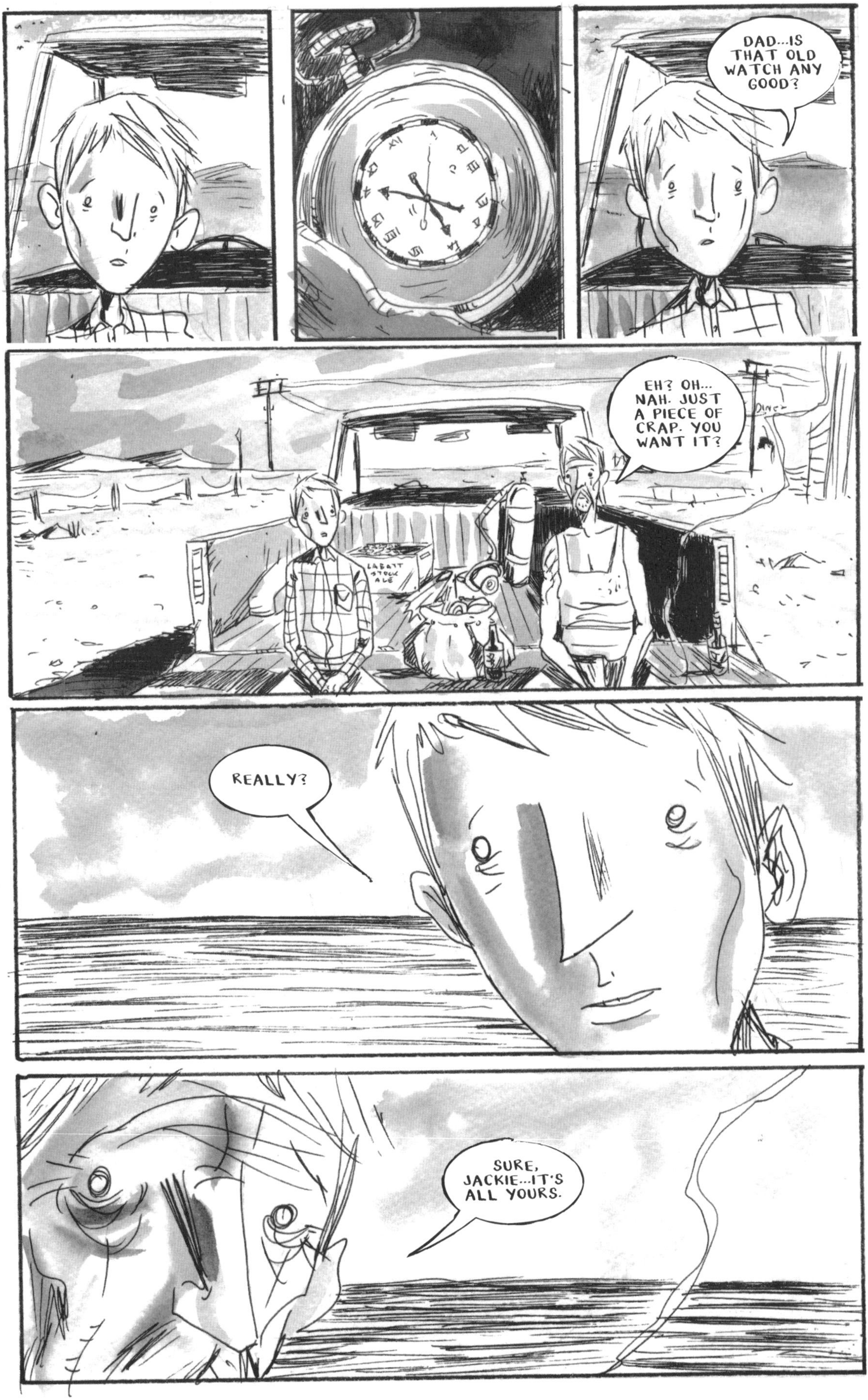
DAD...IS THAT OLD WATCH ANY GOOD?
EH? OH... NAH. JUST A PIECE OF CRAP. YOU WANT IT?
LABATT STOCK ALE
REALLY?
SURE, JACKIE...IT'S ALL YOURS.

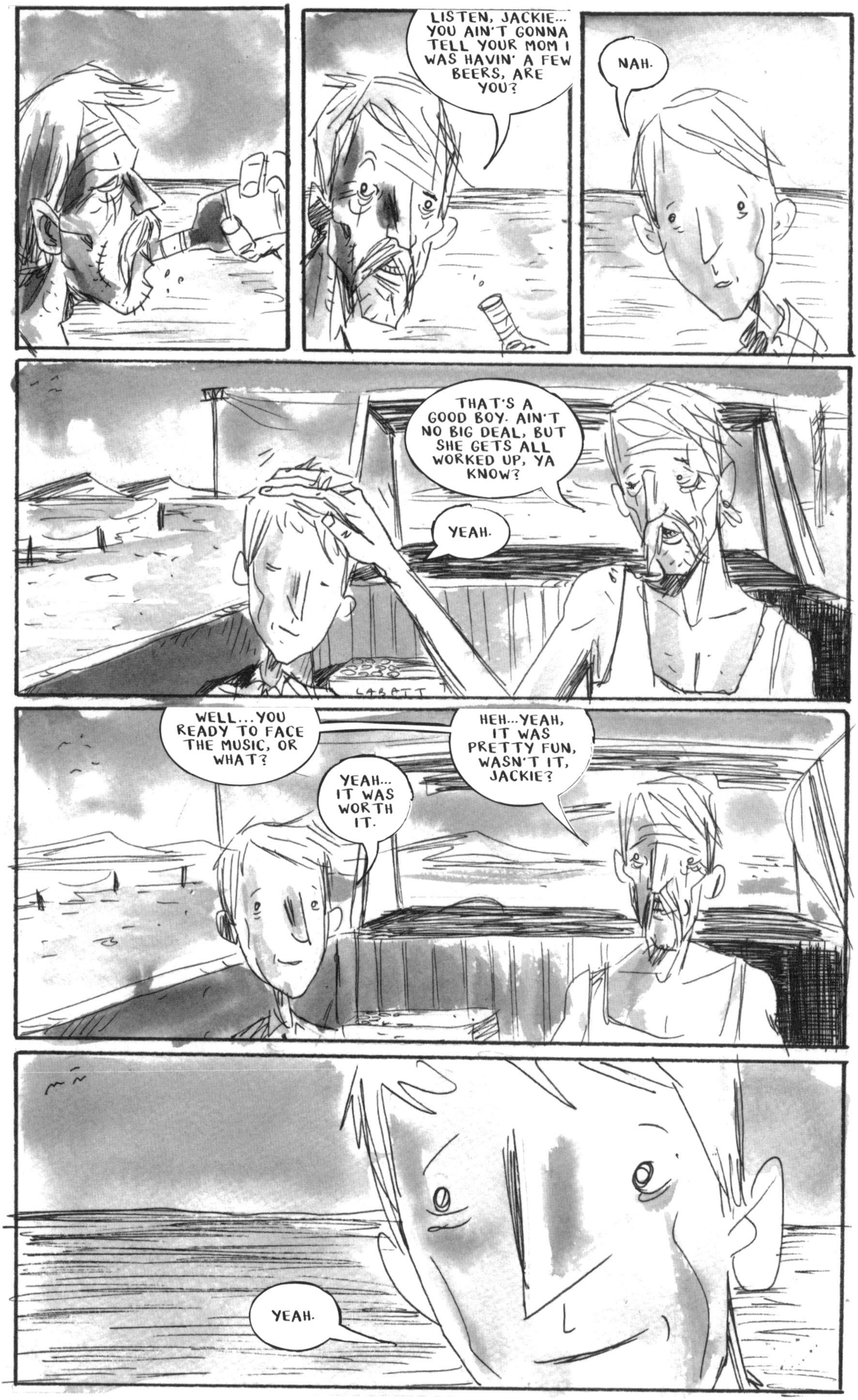
LISTEN, JACKIE... YOU AIN'T GONNA TELL YOUR MOM I WAS HAVIN' A FEW BEERS, ARE YOU?
NAH.
THAT'S A GOOD BOY. AIN'T NO BIG DEAL, BUT SHE GETS ALL WORKED UP, YA KNOW?
YEAH.
LABATT
WELL... YOU READY TO FACE THE MUSIC, OR WHAT?
HEH... YEAH, IT WAS PRETTY FUN, WASN'T IT, JACKIE?
YEAH... IT WAS WORTH IT.
YEAH.

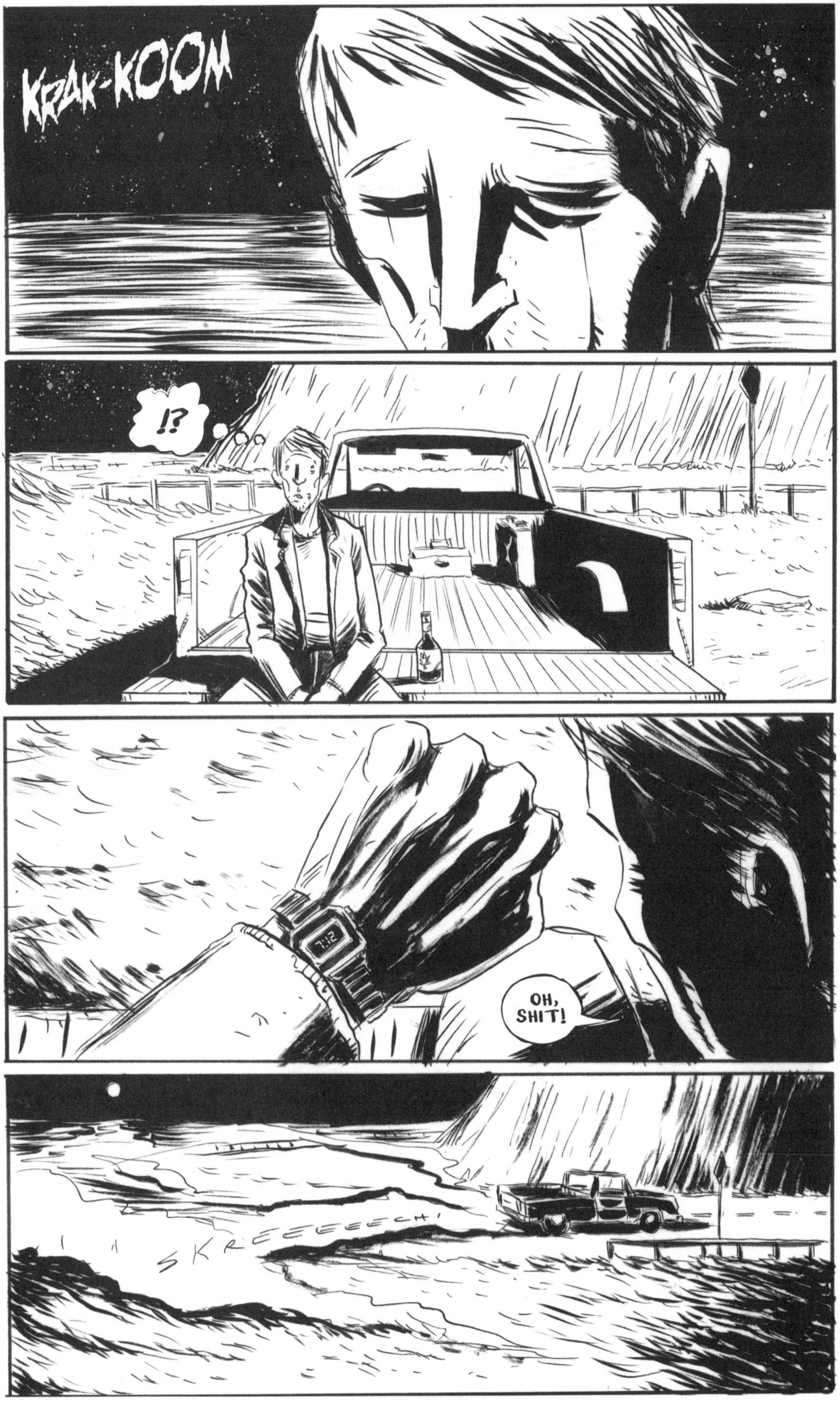
KRAK-KOOM
!?
OH, SHIT!
SKREEEEEEEECH!

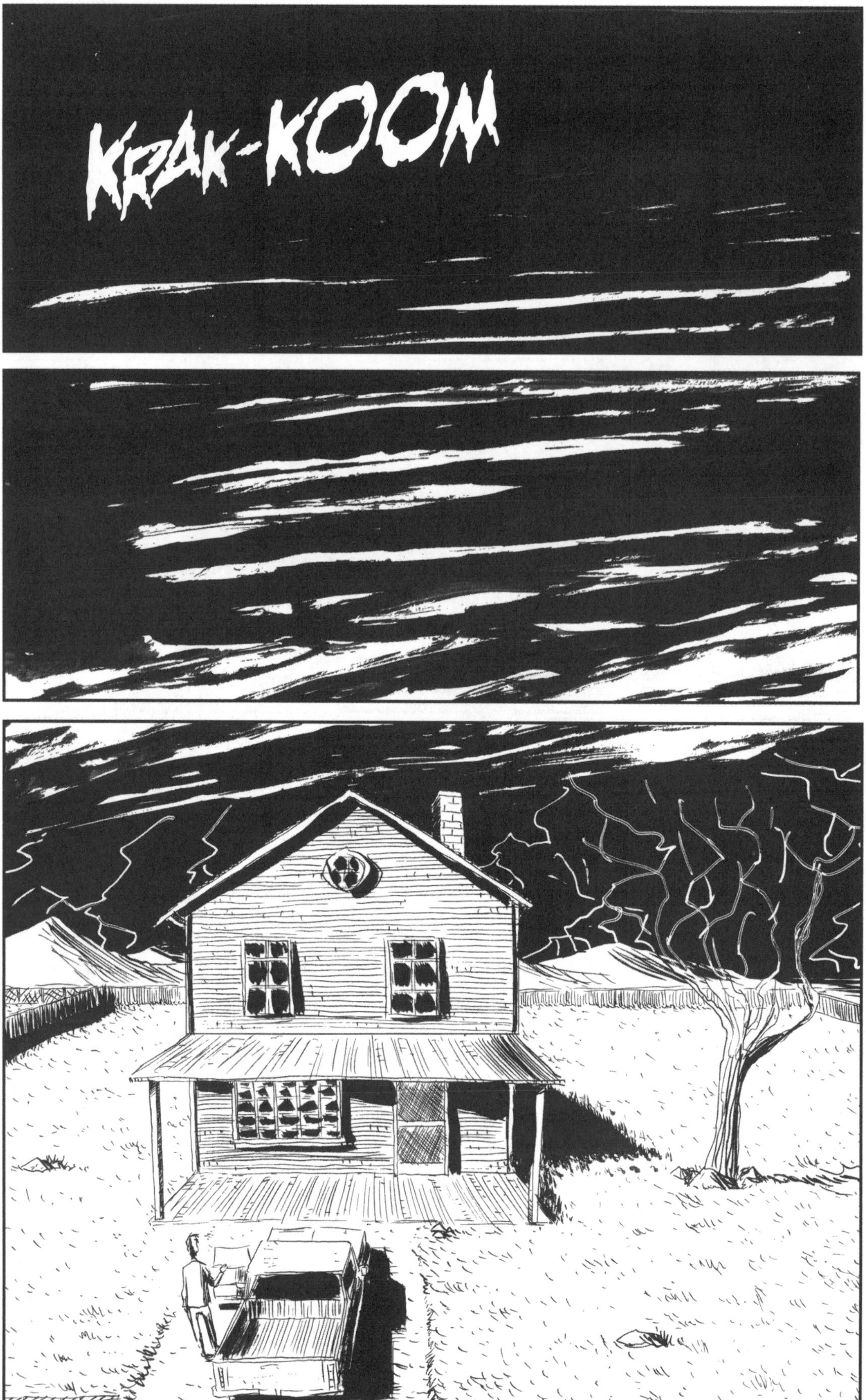
KRAK-KOOM

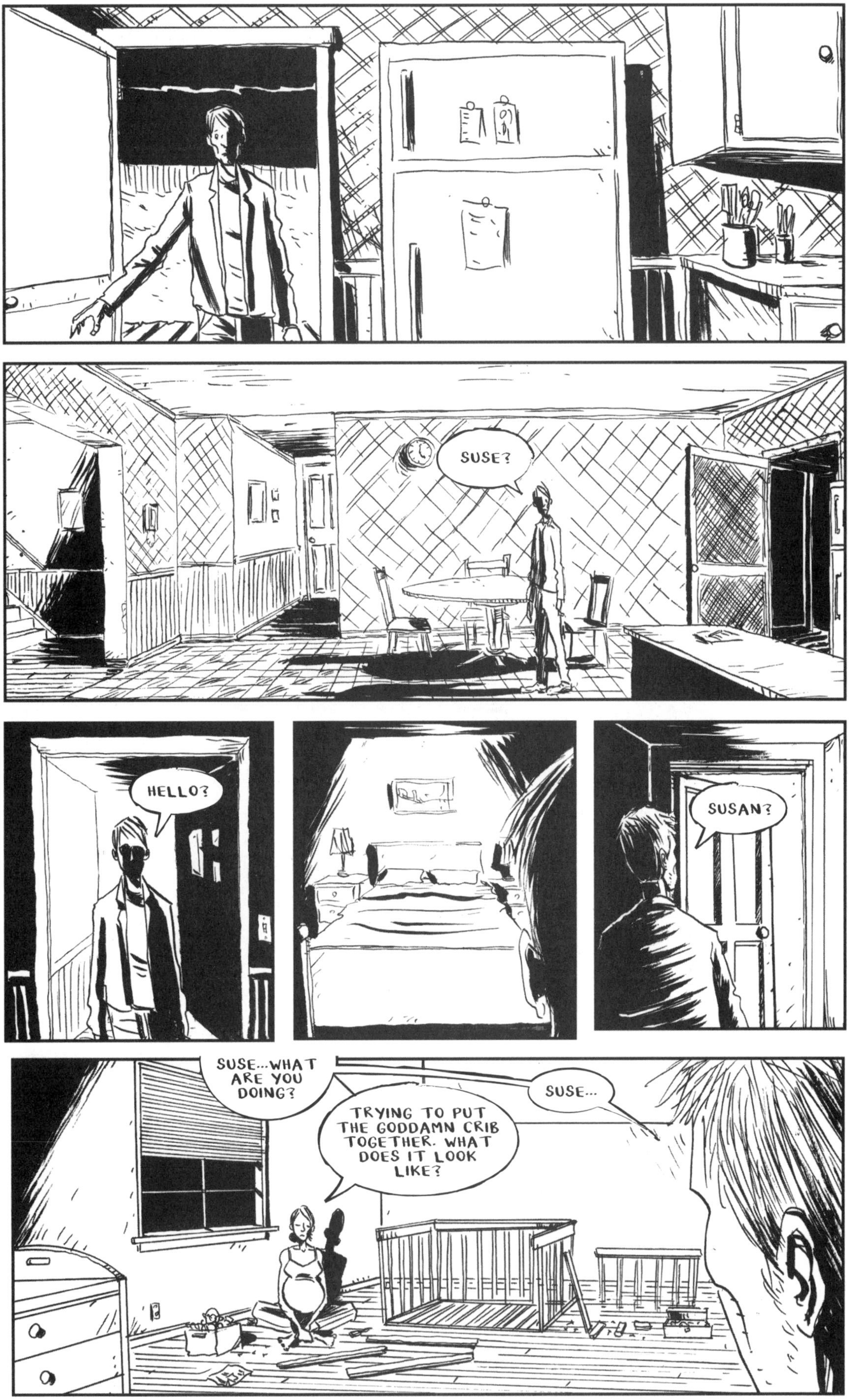
SUSE?
HELLO?
SUSAN?
SUSE...WHAT ARE YOU DOING?
TRYING TO PUT THE GODDAMN CRIB TOGETHER. WHAT DOES IT LOOK LIKE?
SUSE...

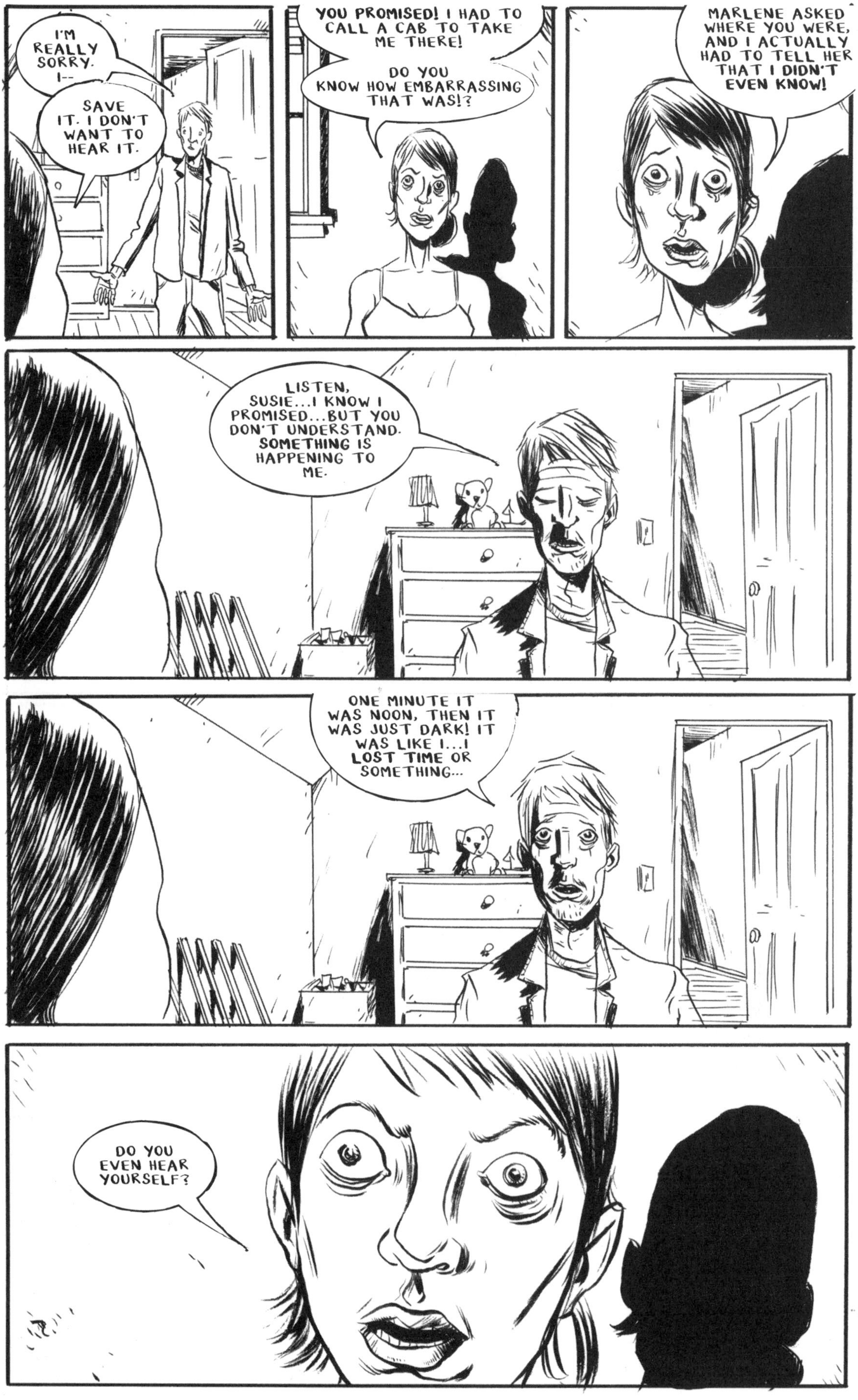
I'M REALLY SORRY. I--
SAVE IT. I DON'T WANT TO HEAR IT.
YOU PROMISED! I HAD TO CALL A CAB TO TAKE ME THERE!
DO YOU KNOW HOW EMBARRASSING THAT WAS!?
MARLENE ASKED WHERE YOU WERE, AND I ACTUALLY HAD TO TELL HER THAT I DIDN'T EVEN KNOW!
LISTEN, SUSIE...I KNOW I PROMISED...BUT YOU DON'T UNDERSTAND. SOMETHING IS HAPPENING TO ME.
ONE MINUTE IT WAS NOON, THEN IT WAS JUST DARK! IT WAS LIKE I...I LOST TIME OR SOMETHING...
DO YOU EVEN HEAR YOURSELF?

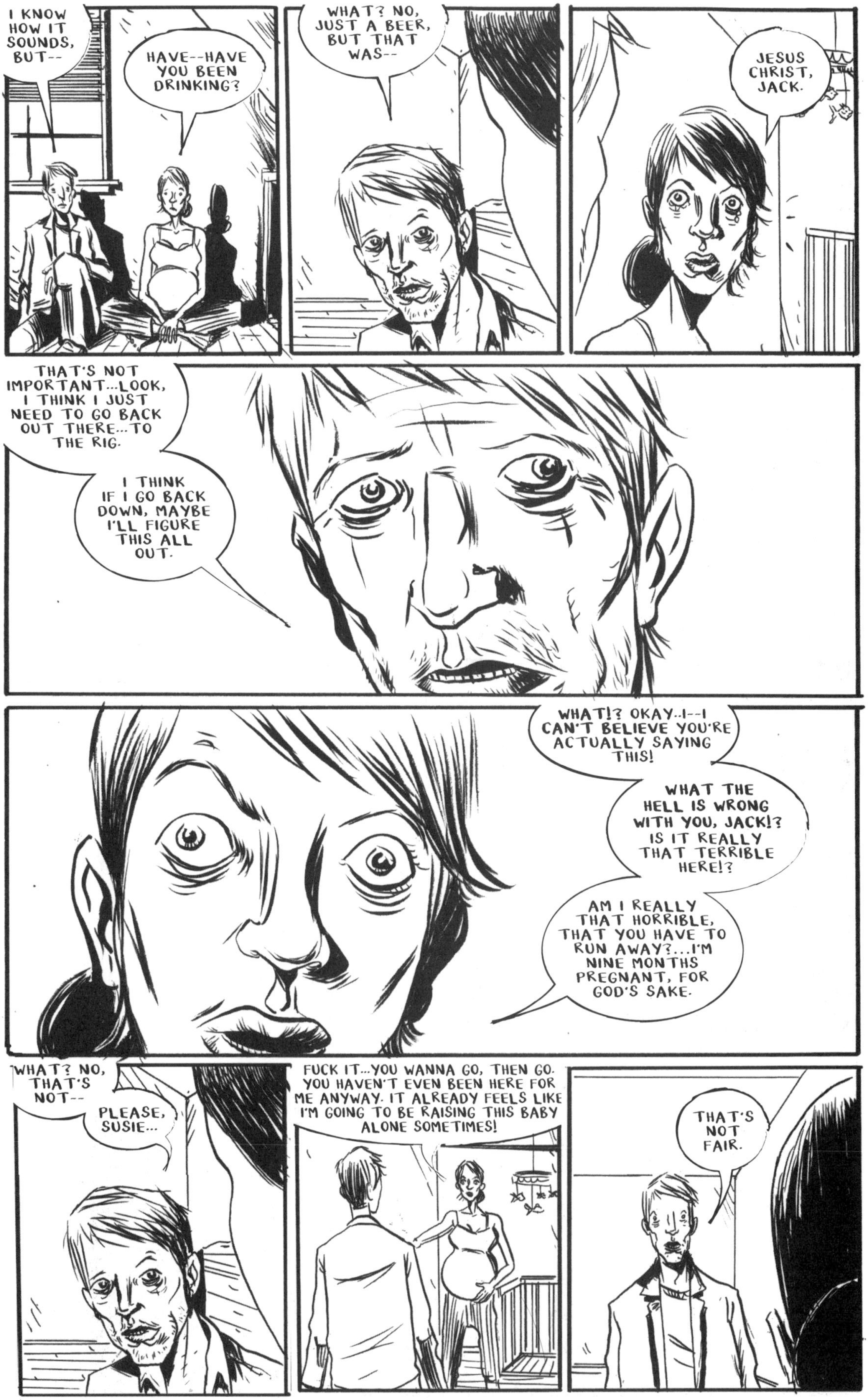
I KNOW HOW IT SOUNDS, BUT--
HAVE--HAVE YOU BEEN DRINKING?
WHAT? NO, JUST A BEER, BUT THAT WAS--
JESUS CHRIST, JACK.
THAT'S NOT IMPORTANT...LOOK, I THINK I JUST NEED TO GO BACK OUT THERE...TO THE RIG.
I THINK IF I GO BACK DOWN, MAYBE I'LL FIGURE THIS ALL OUT.
WHAT!? OKAY..I--I CAN'T BELIEVE YOU'RE ACTUALLY SAYING THIS!
WHAT THE HELL IS WRONG WITH YOU, JACK!? IS IT REALLY THAT TERRIBLE HERE!?
AM I REALLY THAT HORRIBLE, THAT YOU HAVE TO RUN AWAY?...I'M NINE MONTHS PREGNANT, FOR GOD'S SAKE.
WHAT? NO, THAT'S NOT--
PLEASE, SUSIE...
FUCK IT...YOU WANNA GO, THEN GO. YOU HAVEN'T EVEN BEEN HERE FOR ME ANYWAY. IT ALREADY FEELS LIKE I'M GOING TO BE RAISING THIS BABY ALONE SOMETIMES!
THAT'S NOT FAIR.

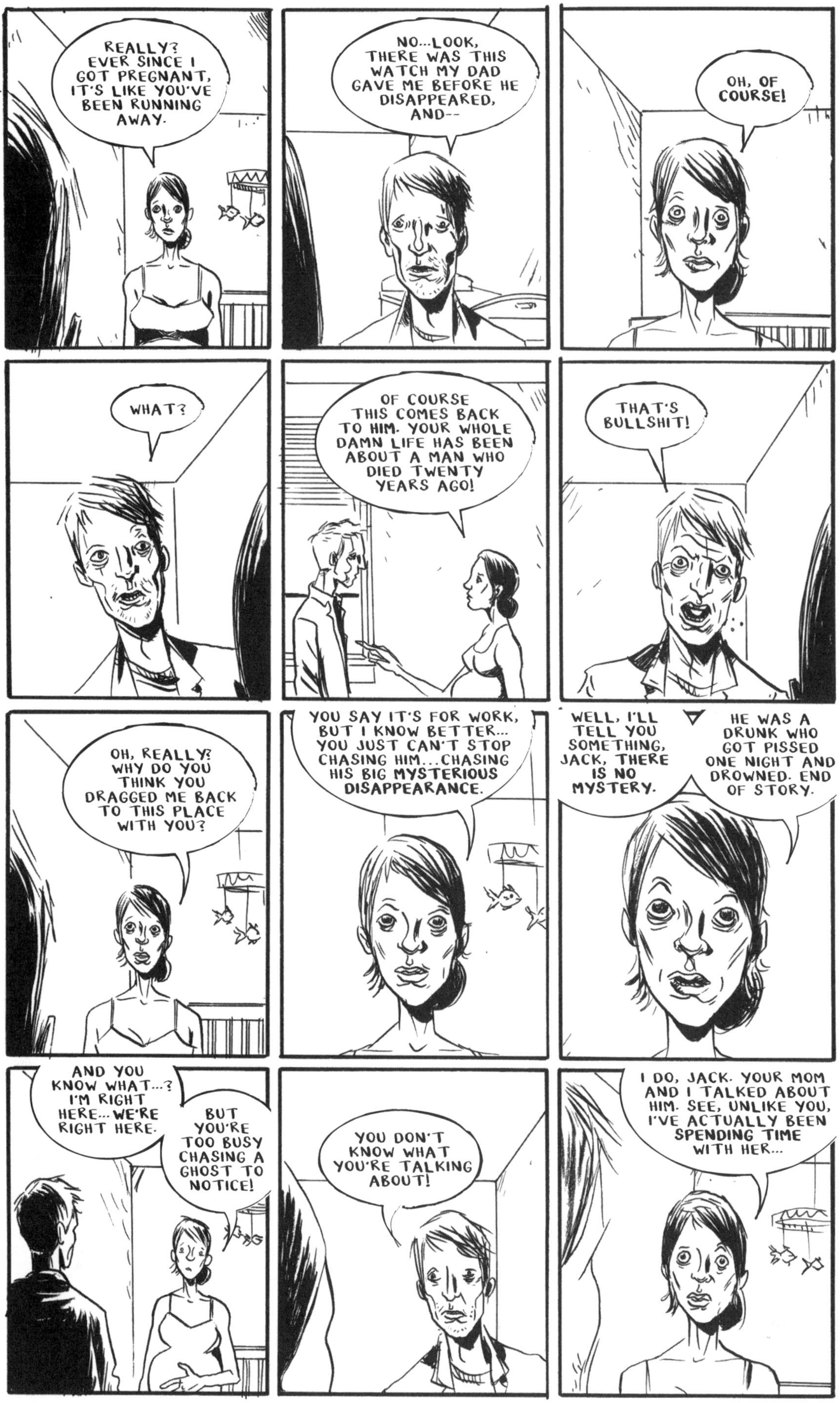
REALLY? EVER SINCE I GOT PREGNANT, IT'S LIKE YOU'VE BEEN RUNNING AWAY.
NO...LOOK, THERE WAS THIS WATCH MY DAD GAVE ME BEFORE HE DISAPPEARED, AND--
OH, OF COURSE!
WHAT?
OF COURSE THIS COMES BACK TO HIM. YOUR WHOLE DAMN LIFE HAS BEEN ABOUT A MAN WHO DIED TWENTY YEARS AGO!
THAT'S BULLSHIT!
OH, REALLY? WHY DO YOU THINK YOU DRAGGED ME BACK TO THIS PLACE WITH YOU?
YOU SAY IT'S FOR WORK, BUT I KNOW BETTER... YOU JUST CAN'T STOP CHASING HIM...CHASING HIS BIG MYSTERIOUS DISAPPEARANCE.
WELL, I'LL TELL YOU SOMETHING, JACK, THERE IS NO MYSTERY.
HE WAS A DRUNK WHO GOT PISSED ONE NIGHT AND DROWNED. END OF STORY.
AND YOU KNOW WHAT...? I'M RIGHT HERE... WE'RE RIGHT HERE.
BUT YOU'RE TOO BUSY CHASING A GHOST TO NOTICE!
YOU DON'T KNOW WHAT YOU'RE TALKING ABOUT!
I DO, JACK. YOUR MOM AND I TALKED ABOUT HIM. SEE, UNLIKE YOU, I'VE ACTUALLY BEEN SPENDING TIME WITH HER...

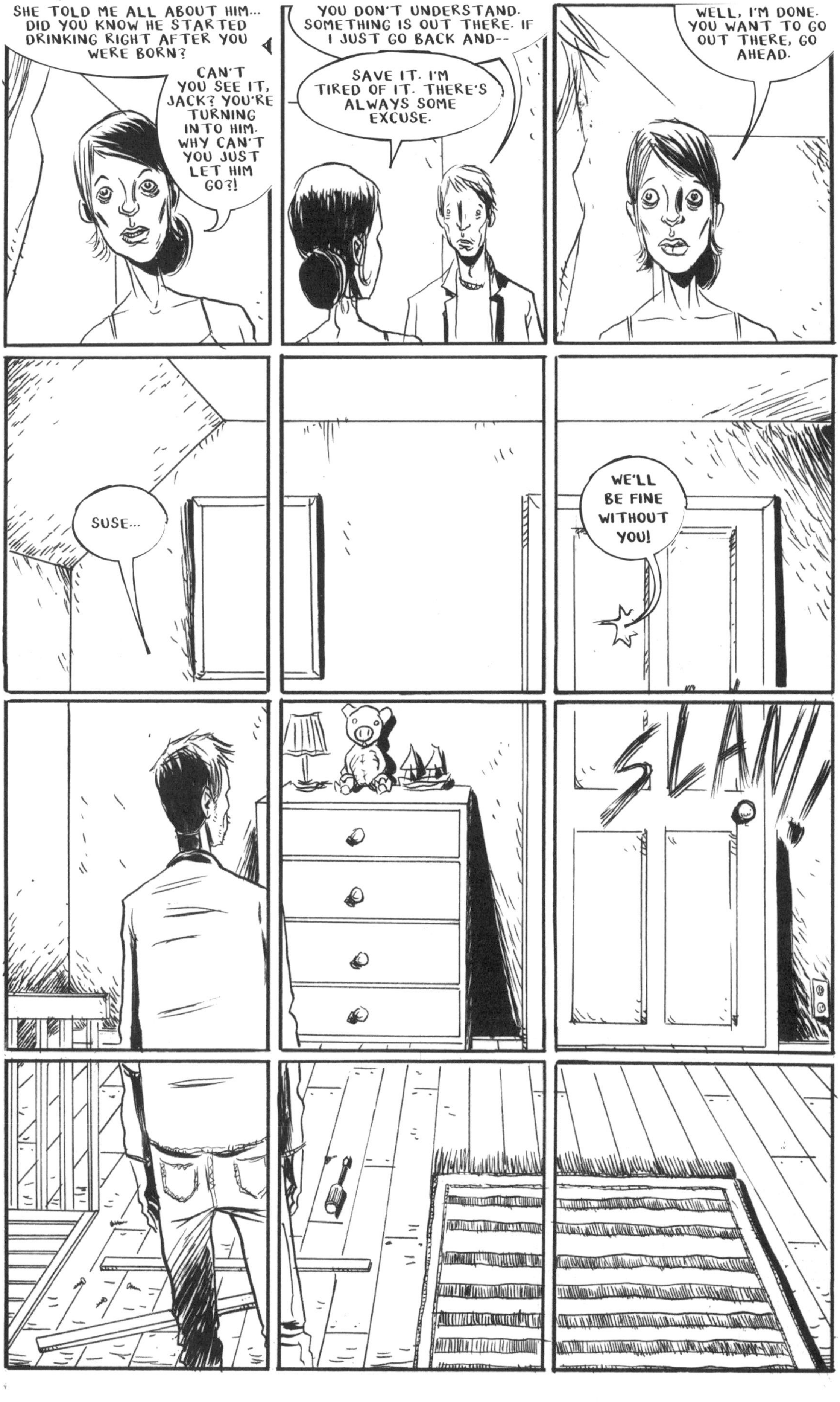
SHE TOLD ME ALL ABOUT HIM... DID YOU KNOW HE STARTED DRINKING RIGHT AFTER YOU WERE BORN?
CAN'T YOU SEE IT, JACK? YOU'RE TURNING INTO HIM. WHY CAN'T YOU JUST LET HIM GO?!
YOU DON'T UNDERSTAND. SOMETHING IS OUT THERE. IF I JUST GO BACK AND--
SAVE IT. I'M TIRED OF IT. THERE'S ALWAYS SOME EXCUSE.
WELL, I'M DONE. YOU WANT TO GO OUT THERE, GO AHEAD.
SUSE...
WE'LL BE FINE WITHOUT YOU!
SLAM!

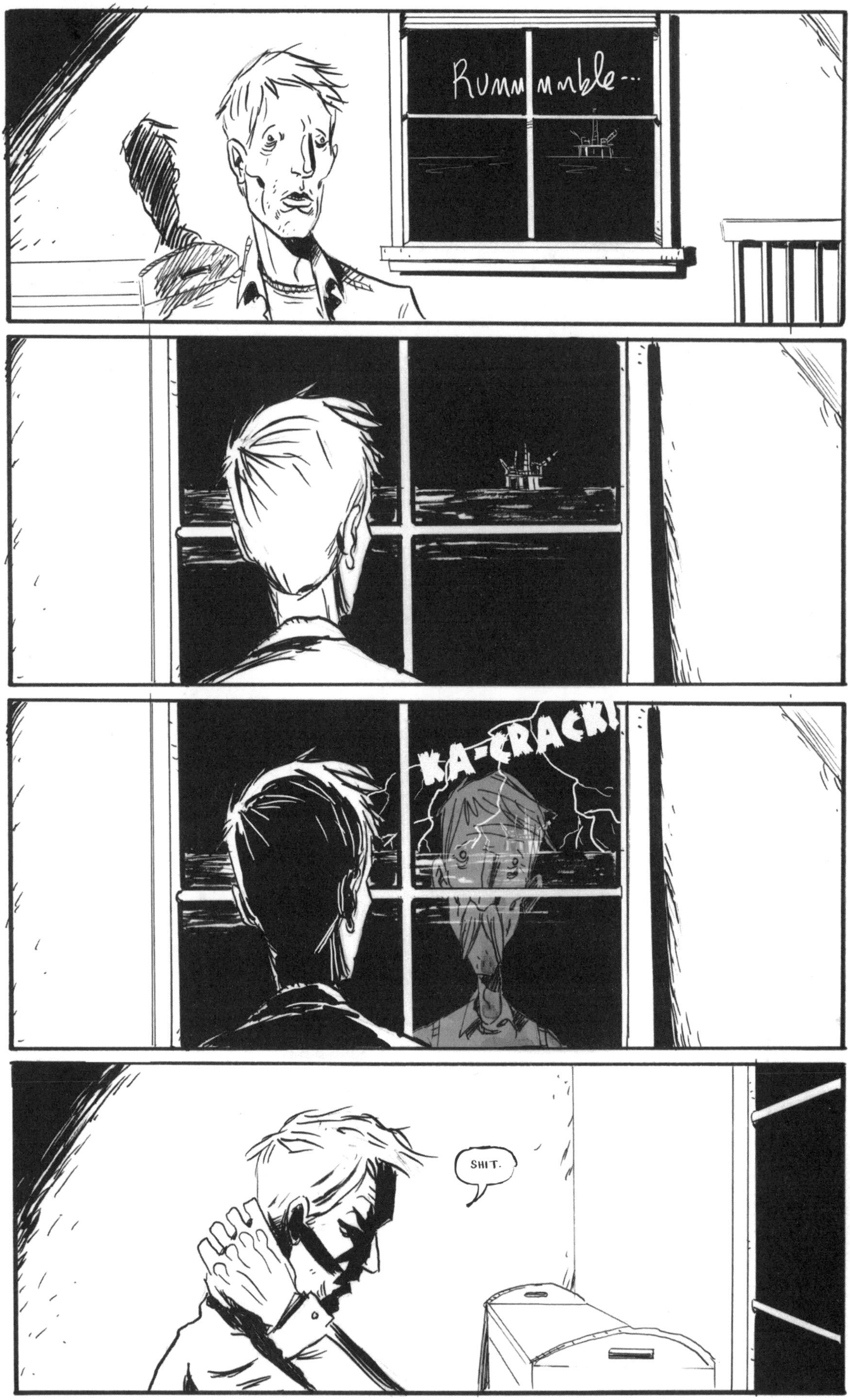
Rummmmble...
KA-CRACK!
SHIT.

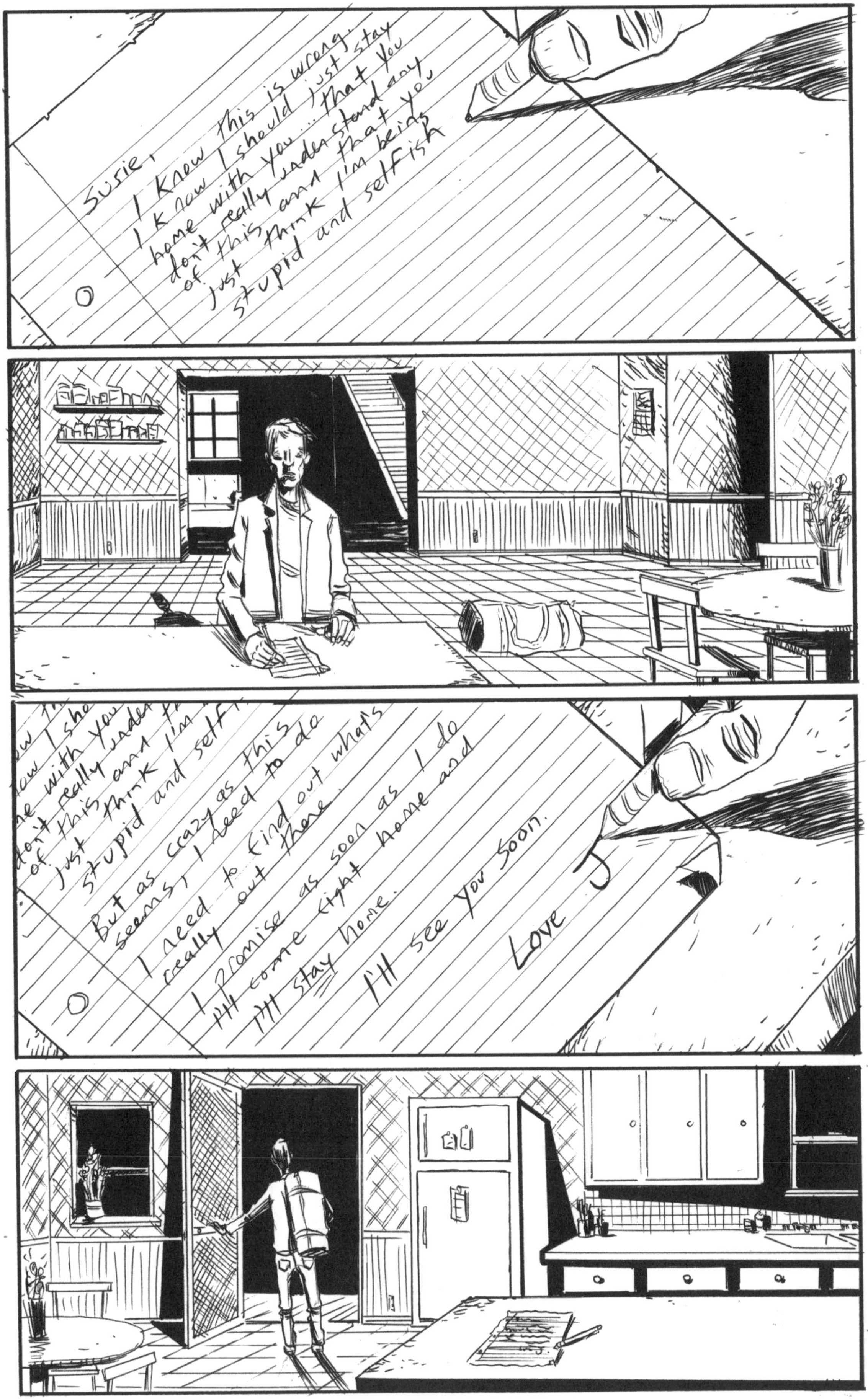
Susie,
I know this is wrong.
I know I should just stay
home with you... that you
don't really understand any
of this, and that you
just think I'm being
stupid and selfish
But as crazy as this
seems, I need to do
I need to find out what's
really out there.
I promise as soon as I do
I'll come right home and
I'll stay home.
I'll see you soon.
Love J

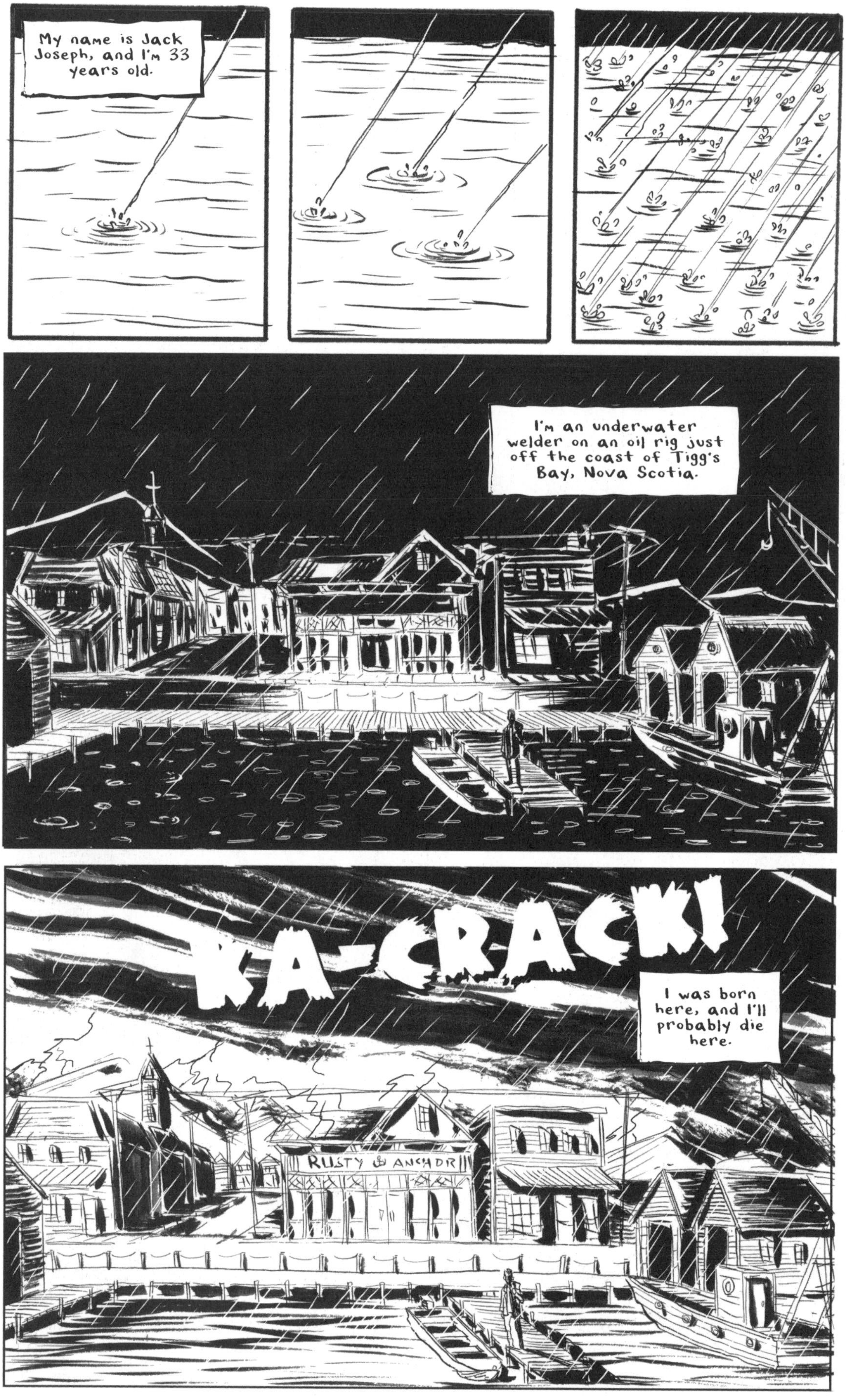
My name is Jack Joseph, and I'm 33 years old.
I'm an underwater welder on an oil rig just off the coast of Tigg's Bay, Nova Scotia.
KA-CRACK!
I was born here, and I'll probably die here.
RUSTY ANCHOR

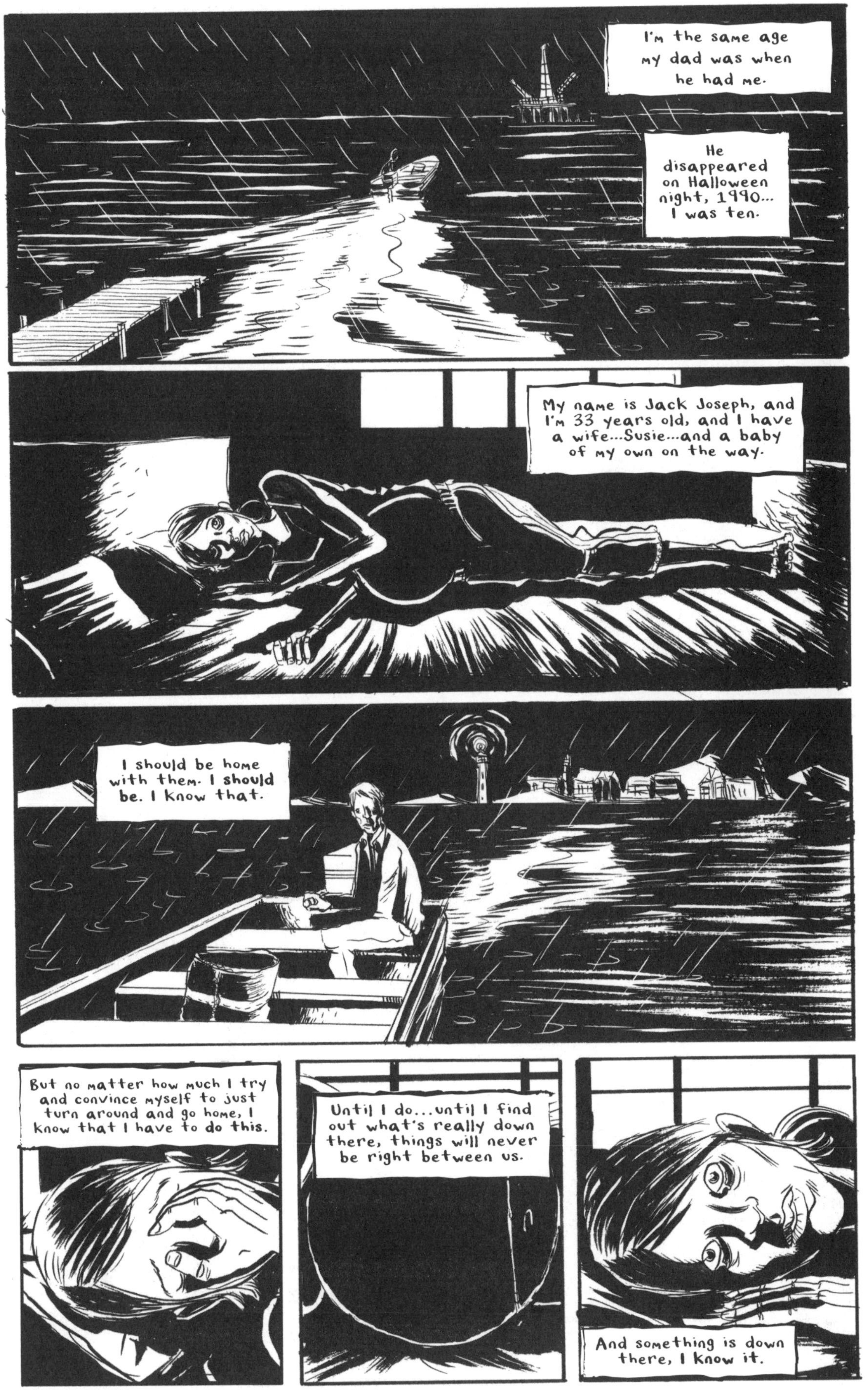
I'm the same age my dad was when he had me.
He disappeared on Halloween night, 1990... I was ten.
My name is Jack Joseph, and I'm 33 years old, and I have a wife...Susie...and a baby of my own on the way.
I should be home with them. I should be. I know that.
But no matter how much I try and convince myself to just turn around and go home, I know that I have to do this.
Until I do...until I find out what's really down there, things will never be right between us.
And something is down there, I know it.

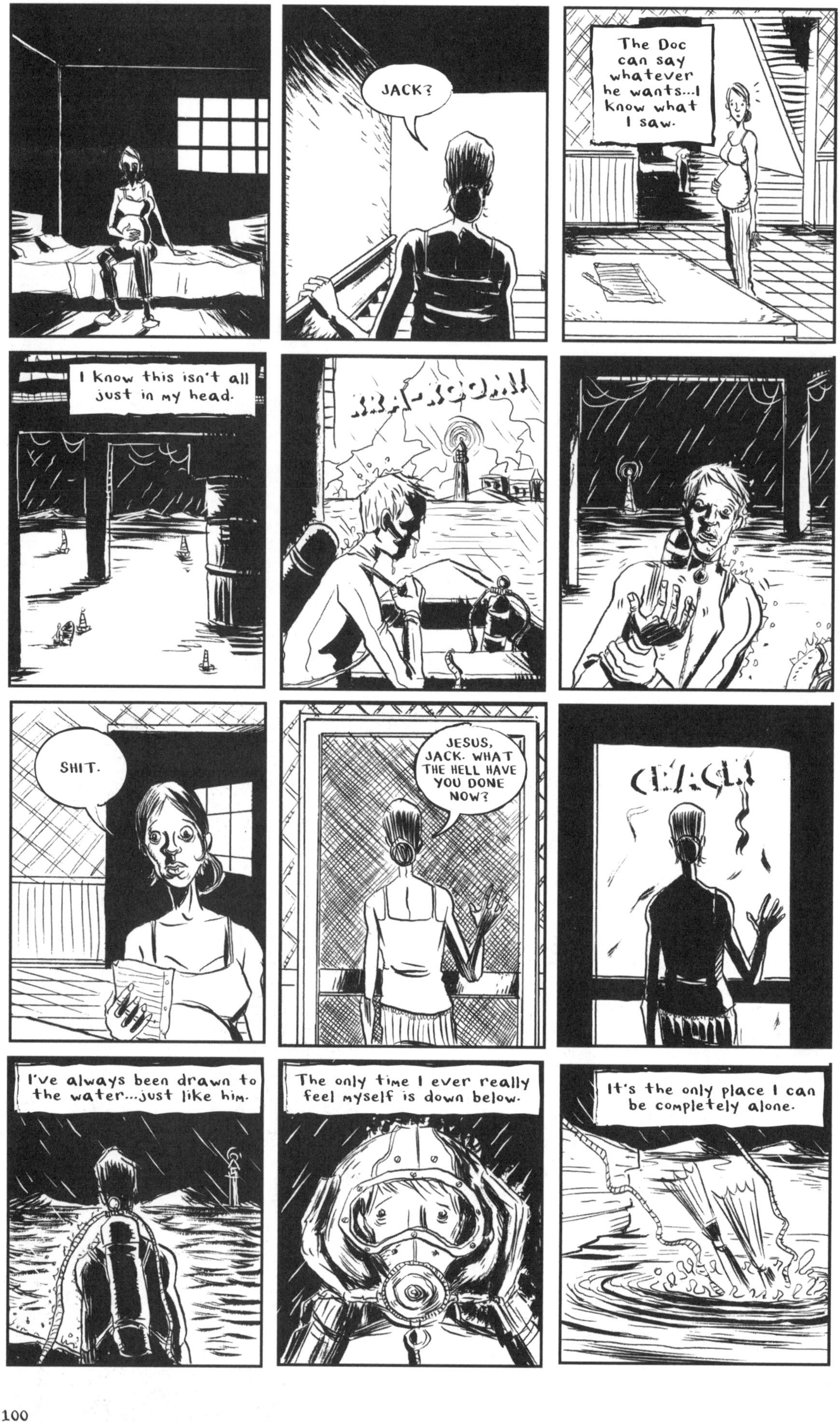
JACK?
The Doc can say whatever he wants...I know what I saw.
I know this isn't all just in my head.
KA-BOOM!!
SHIT.
JESUS, JACK. WHAT THE HELL HAVE YOU DONE NOW?
CRACK!
I've always been drawn to the water...just like him.
The only time I ever really feel myself is down below.
It's the only place I can be completely alone.

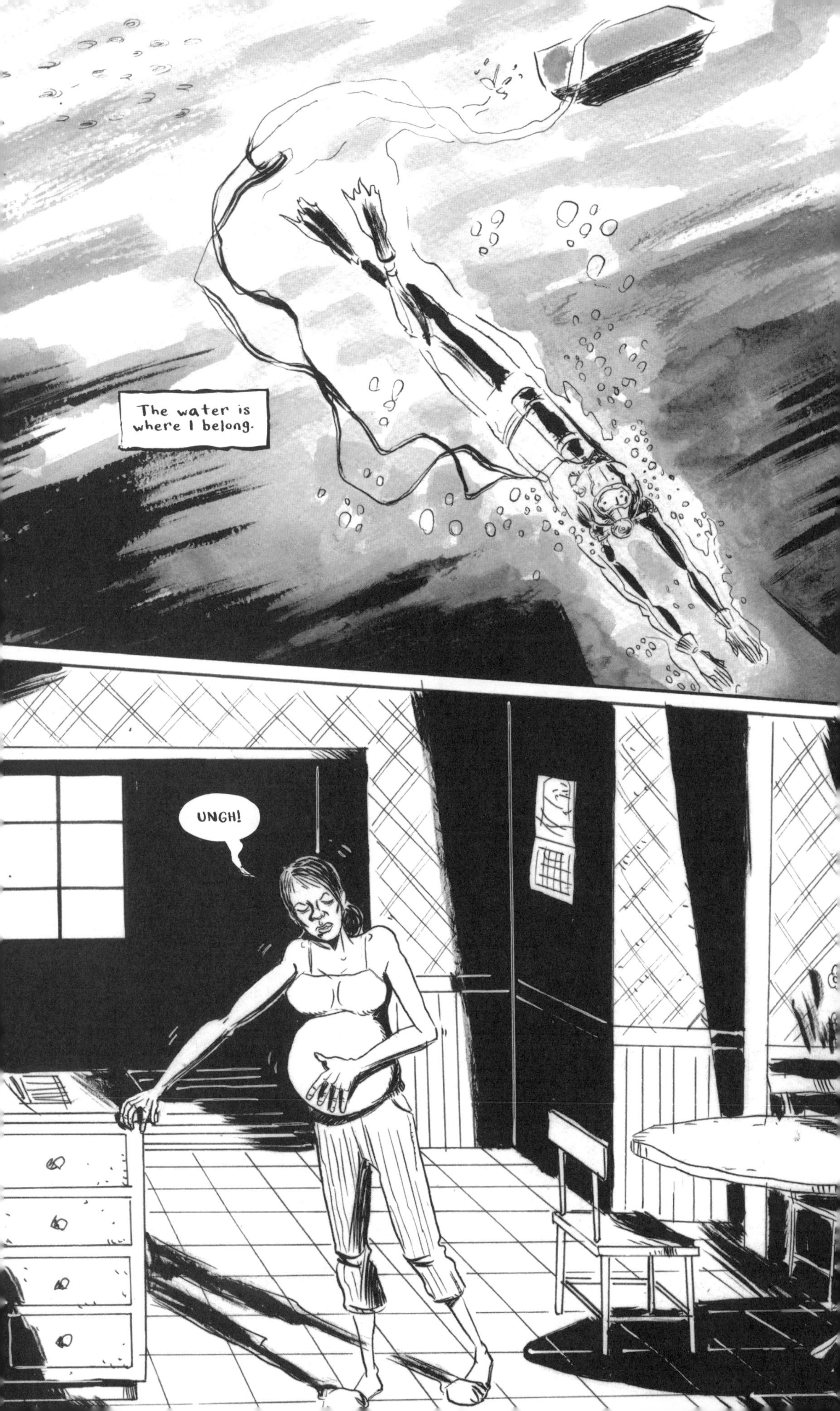
The water is where I belong.
UNGH!

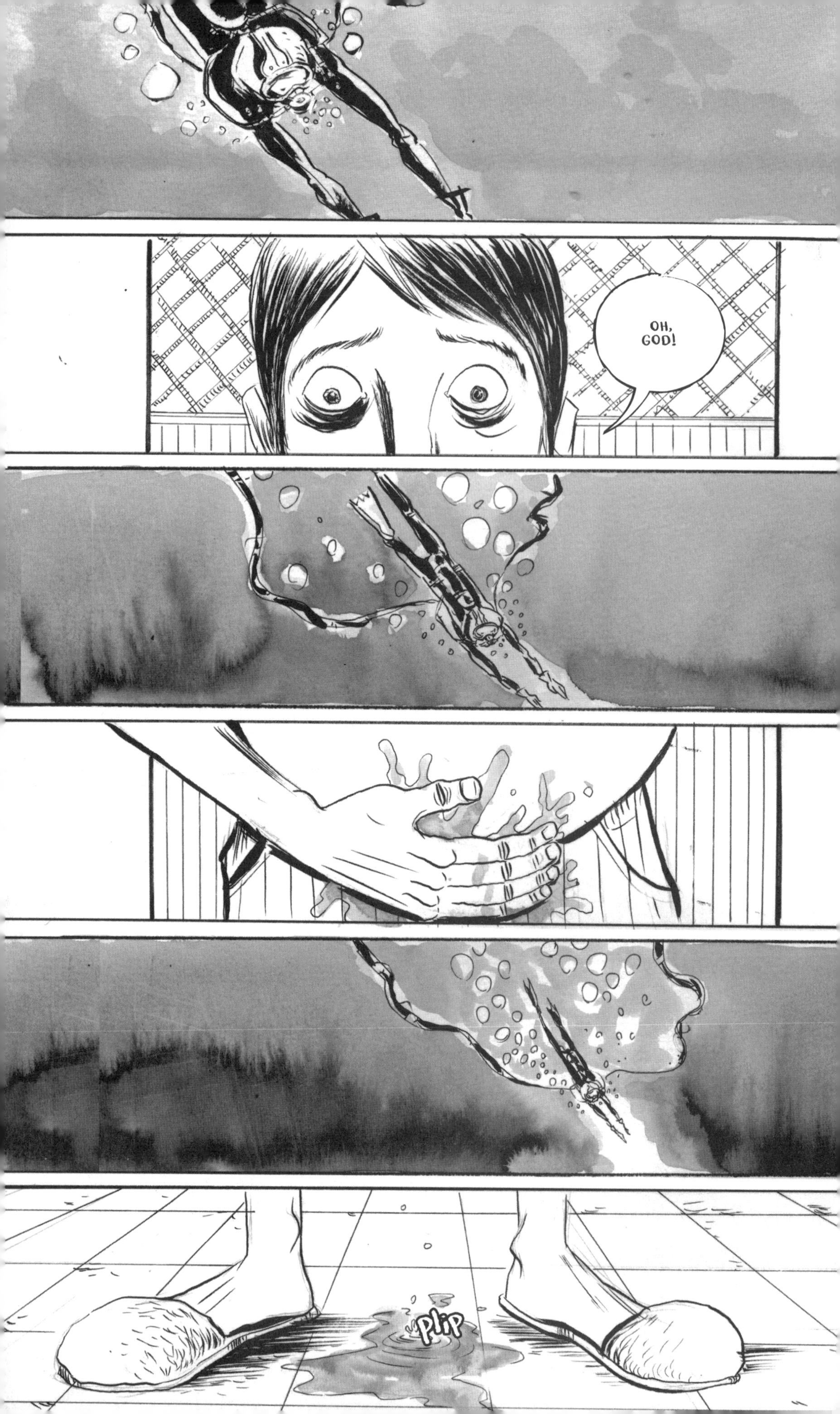
OH, GOD!
PLIP

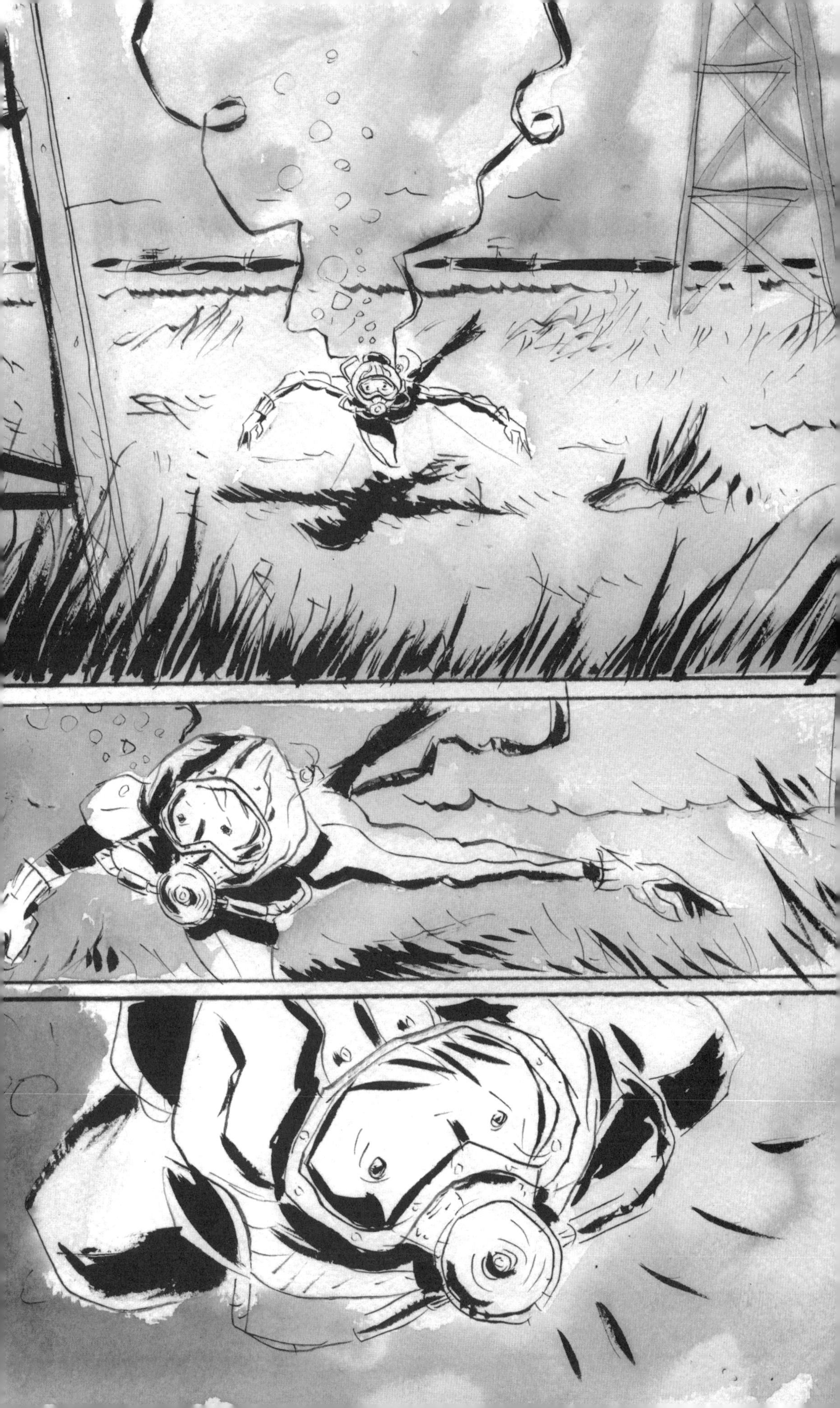

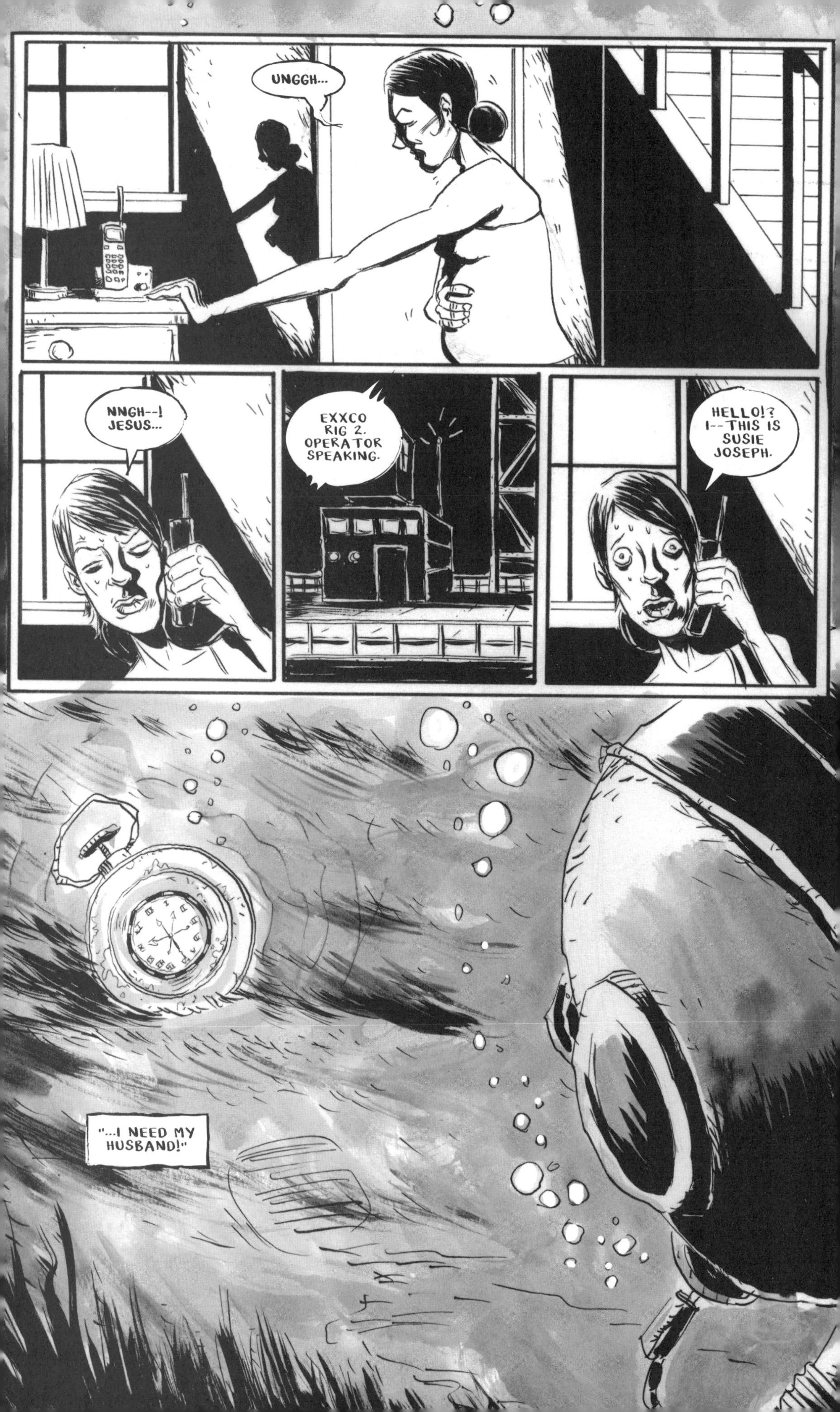
UNGGH...
NNGH--! JESUS...
EXXCO RIG 2. OPERATOR SPEAKING.
HELLO!? I--THIS IS SUSIE JOSEPH.
"...I NEED MY HUSBAND!"

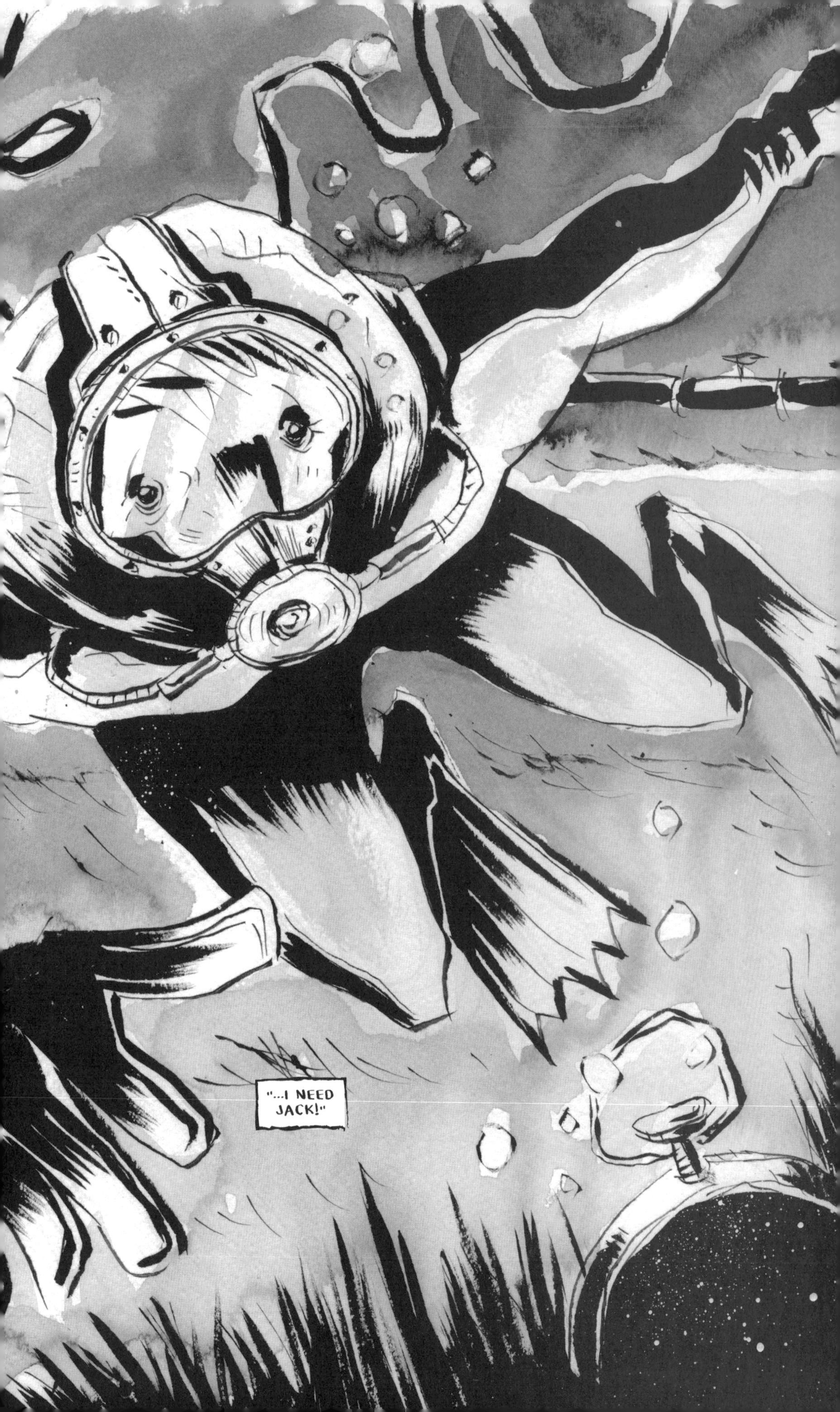
"...I NEED JACK!"

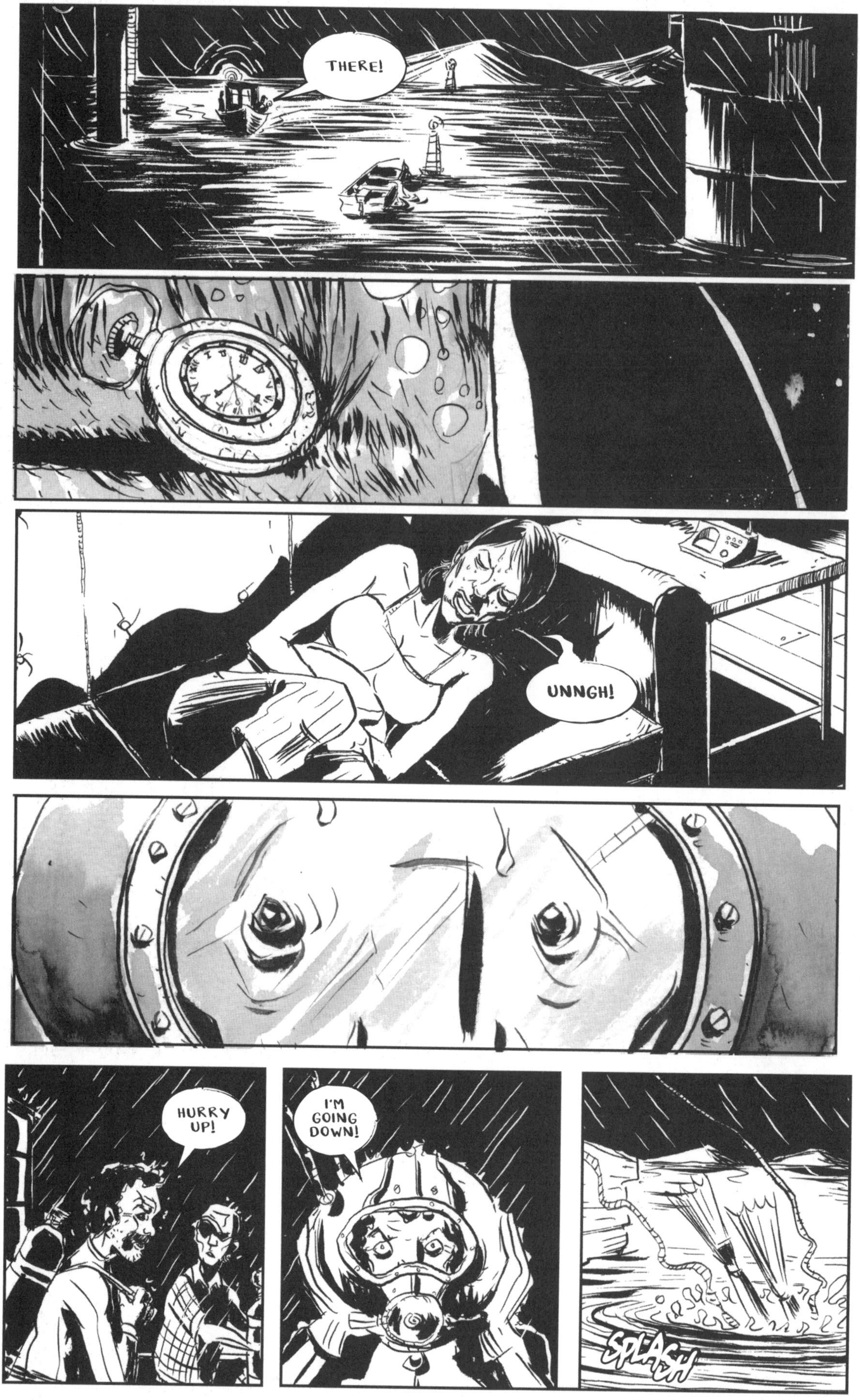
THERE!
UNNGH!
HURRY UP!
I'M GOING DOWN!
SPLASH

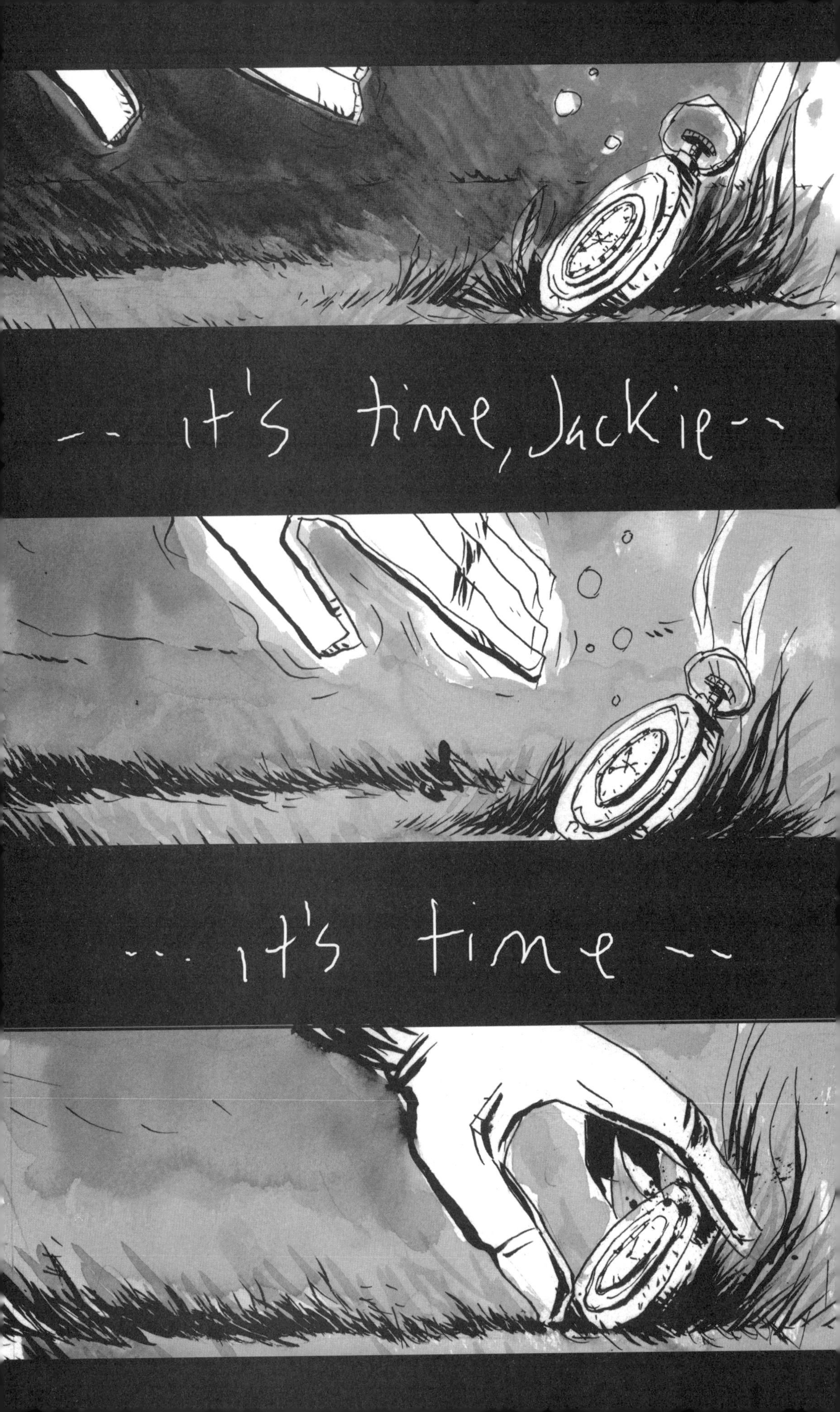
--- it's time, Jackie---
... it's time ---

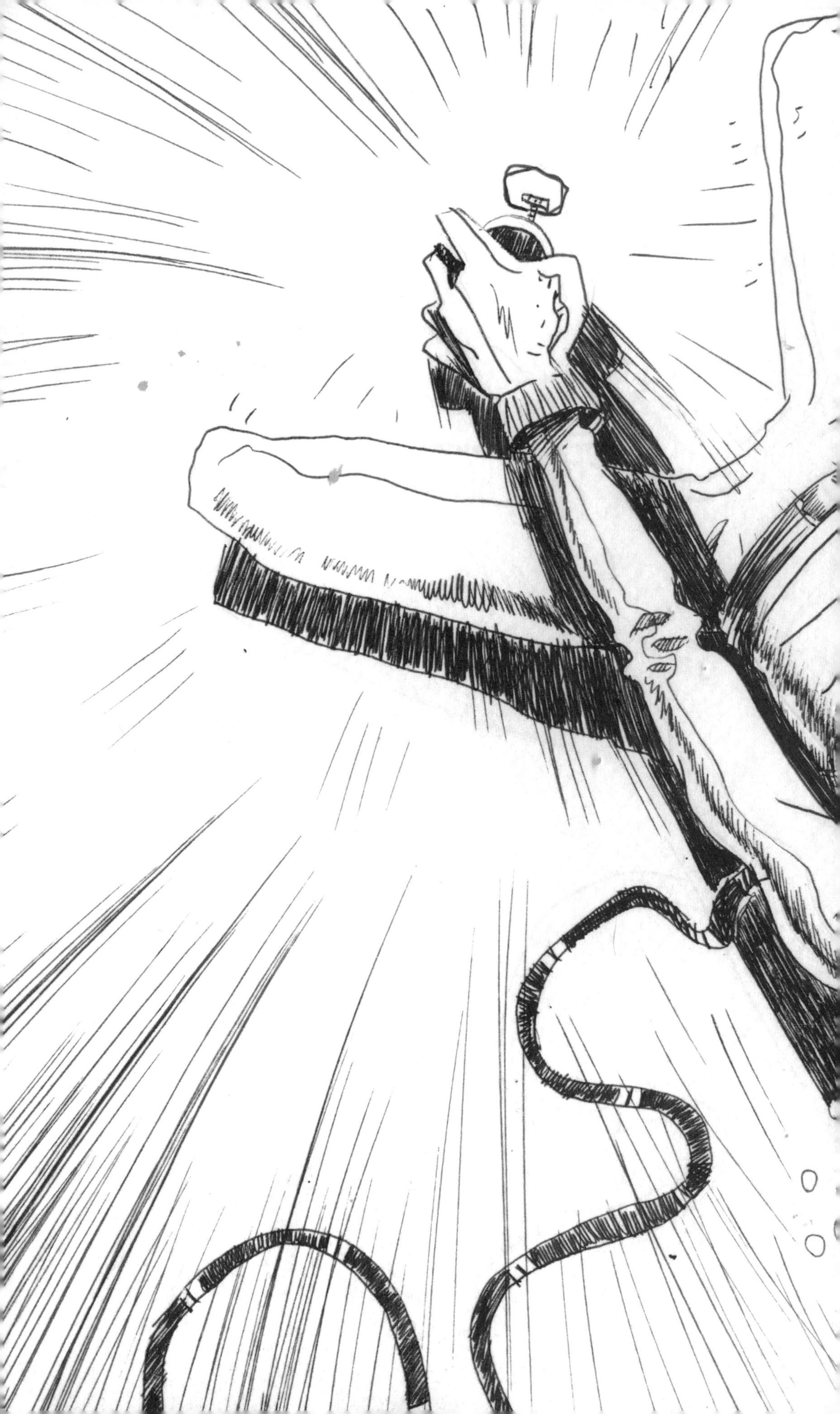

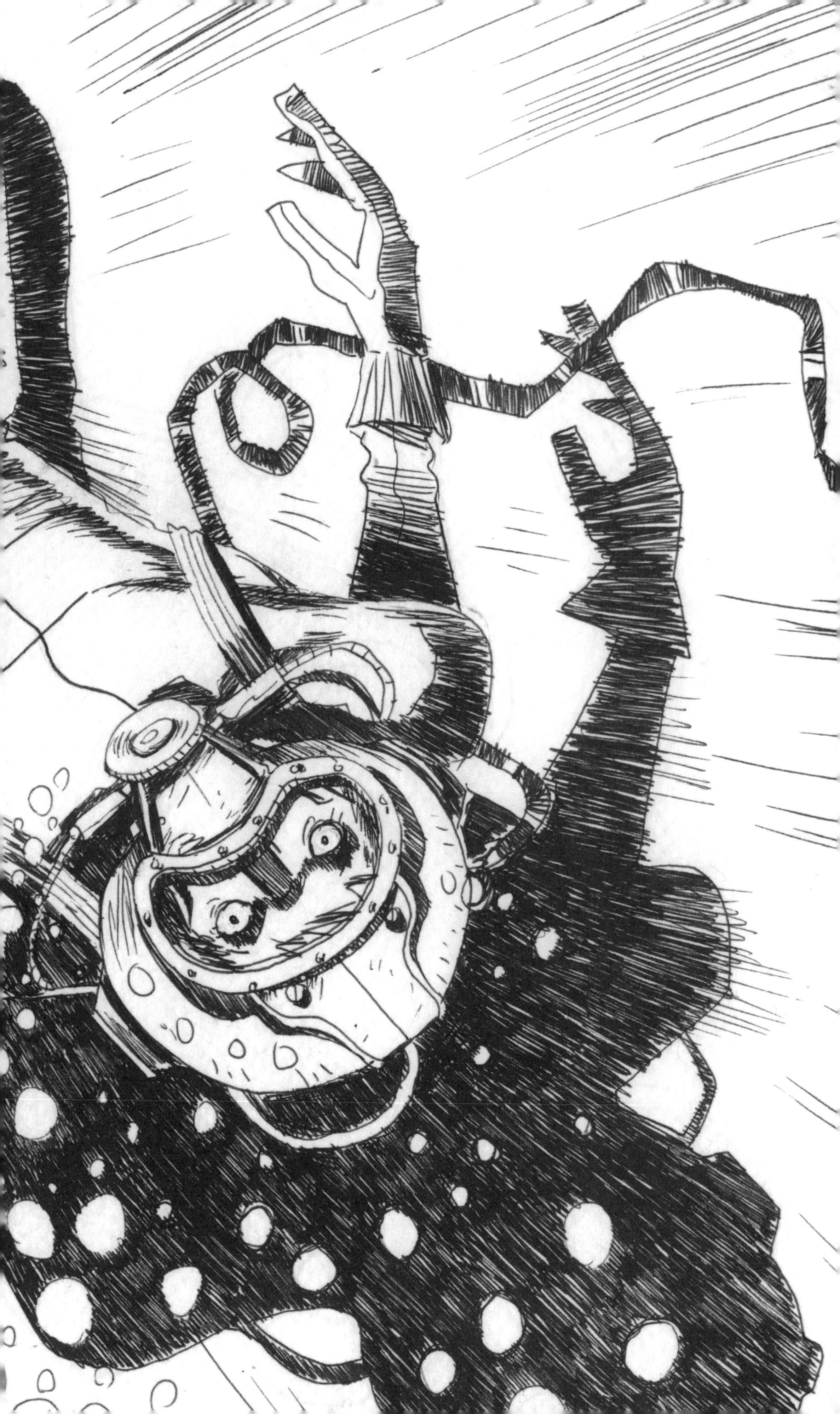

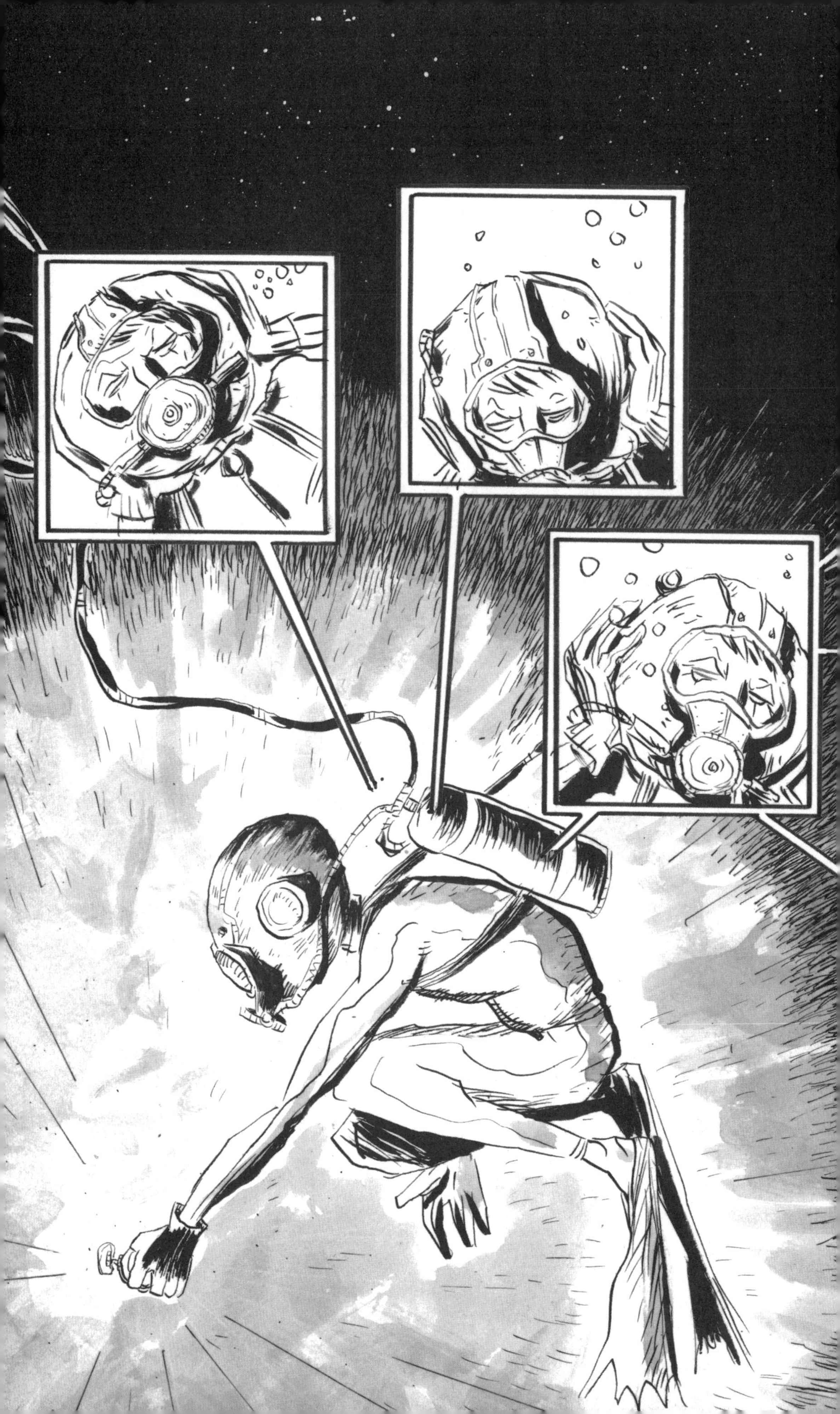

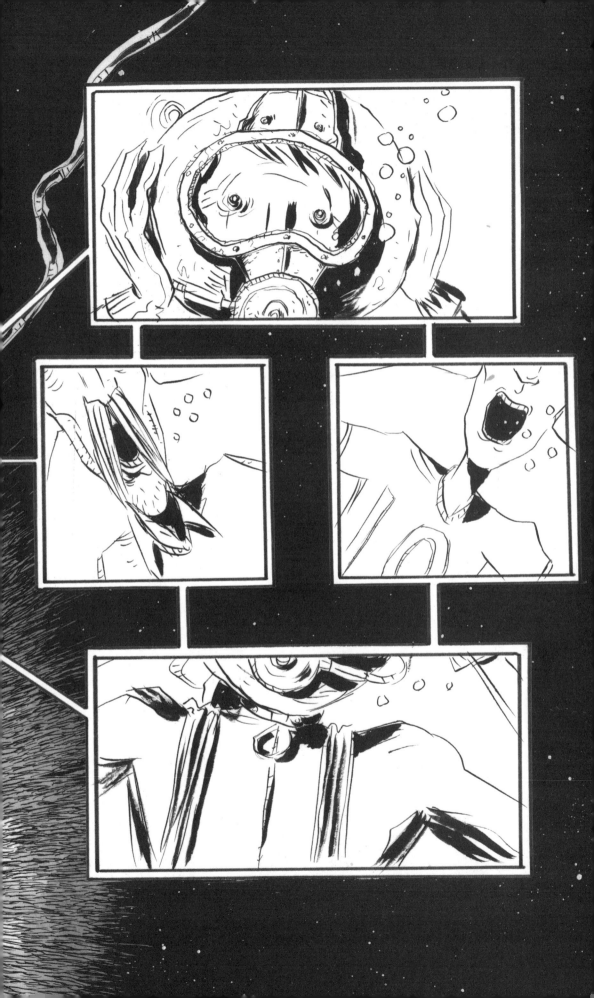

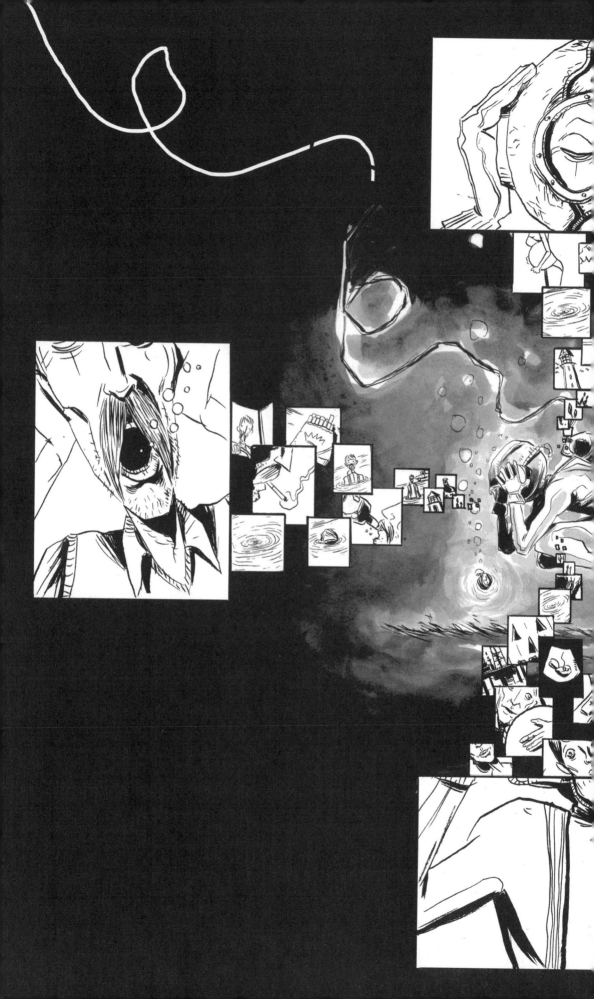

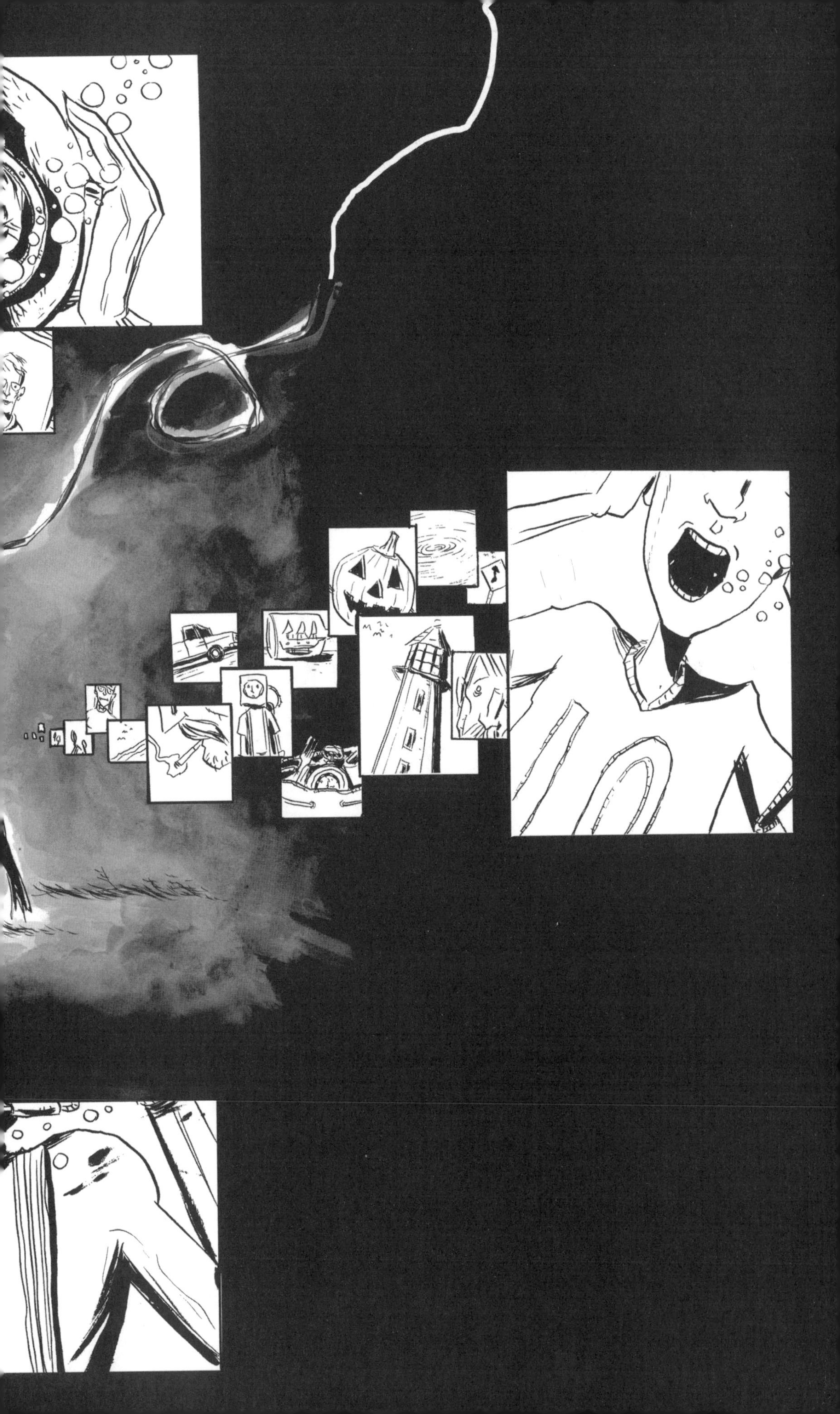

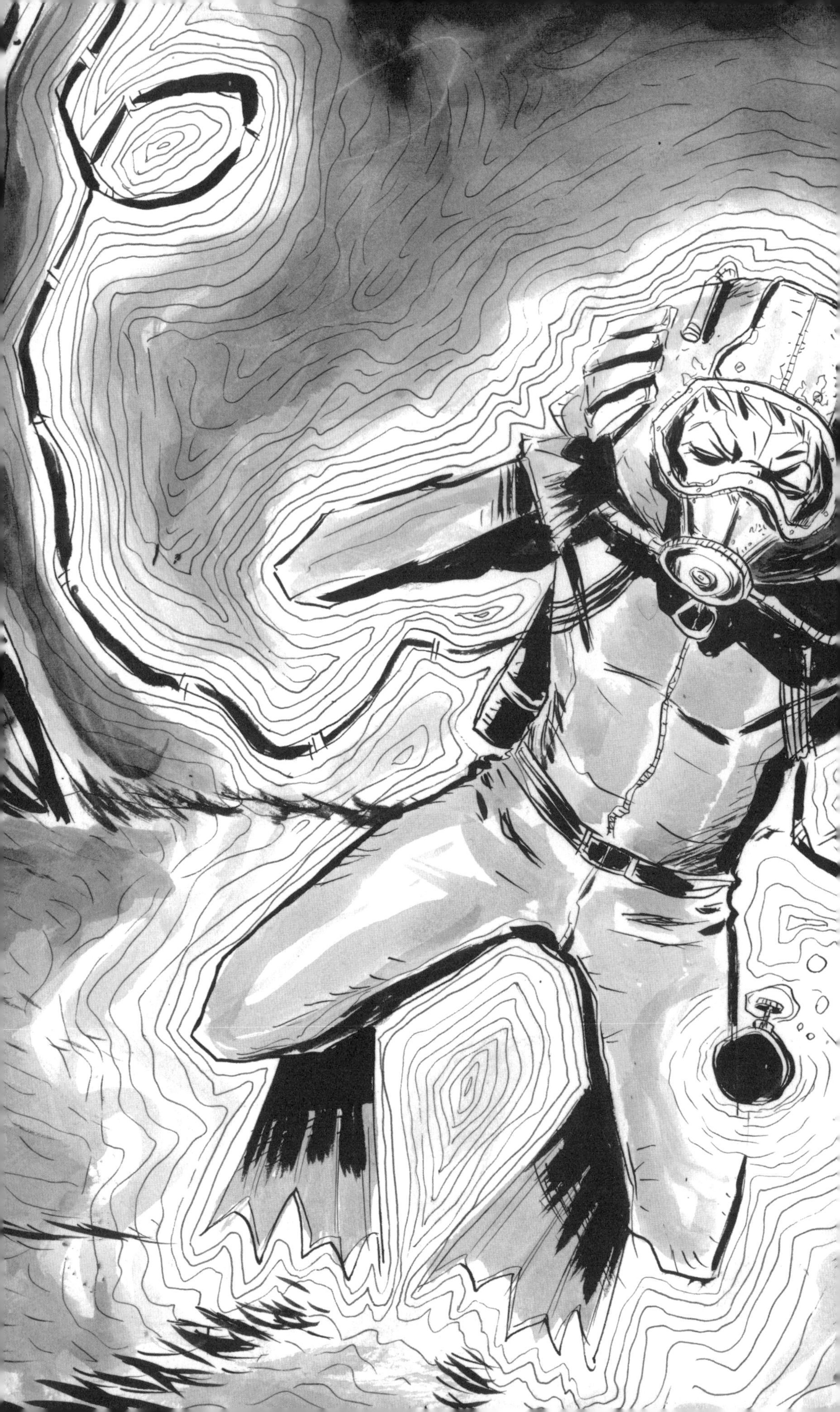

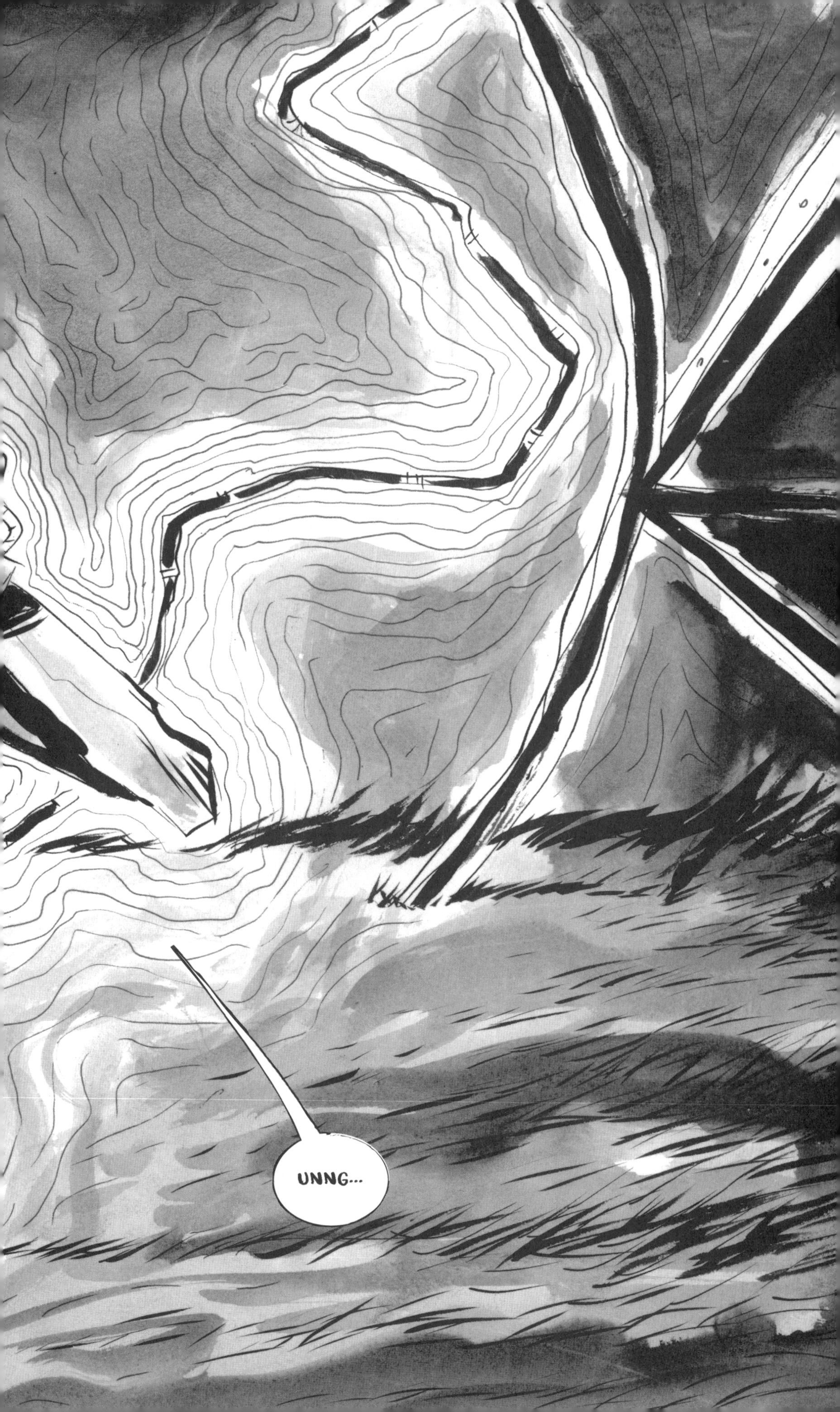
UNNG...

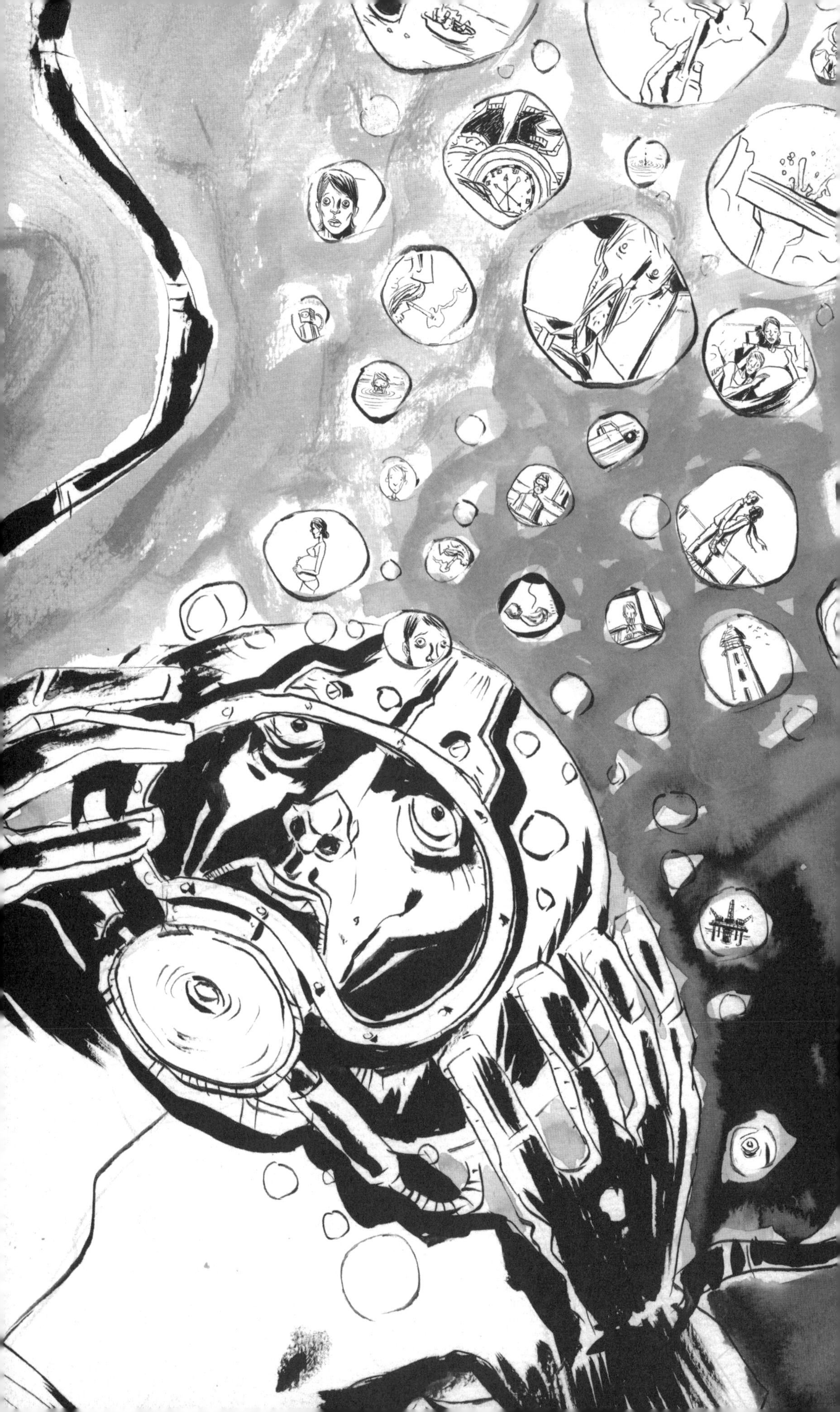

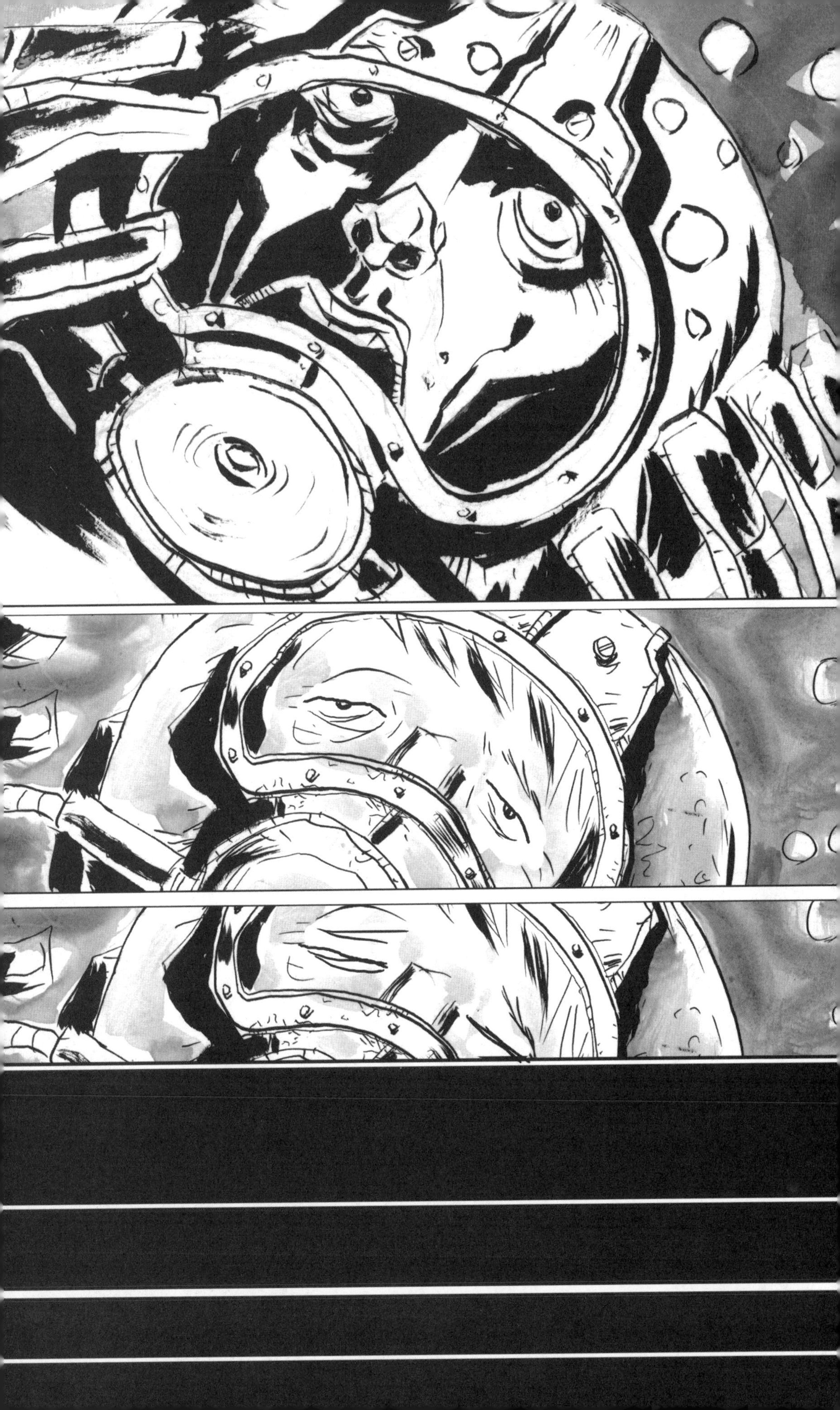

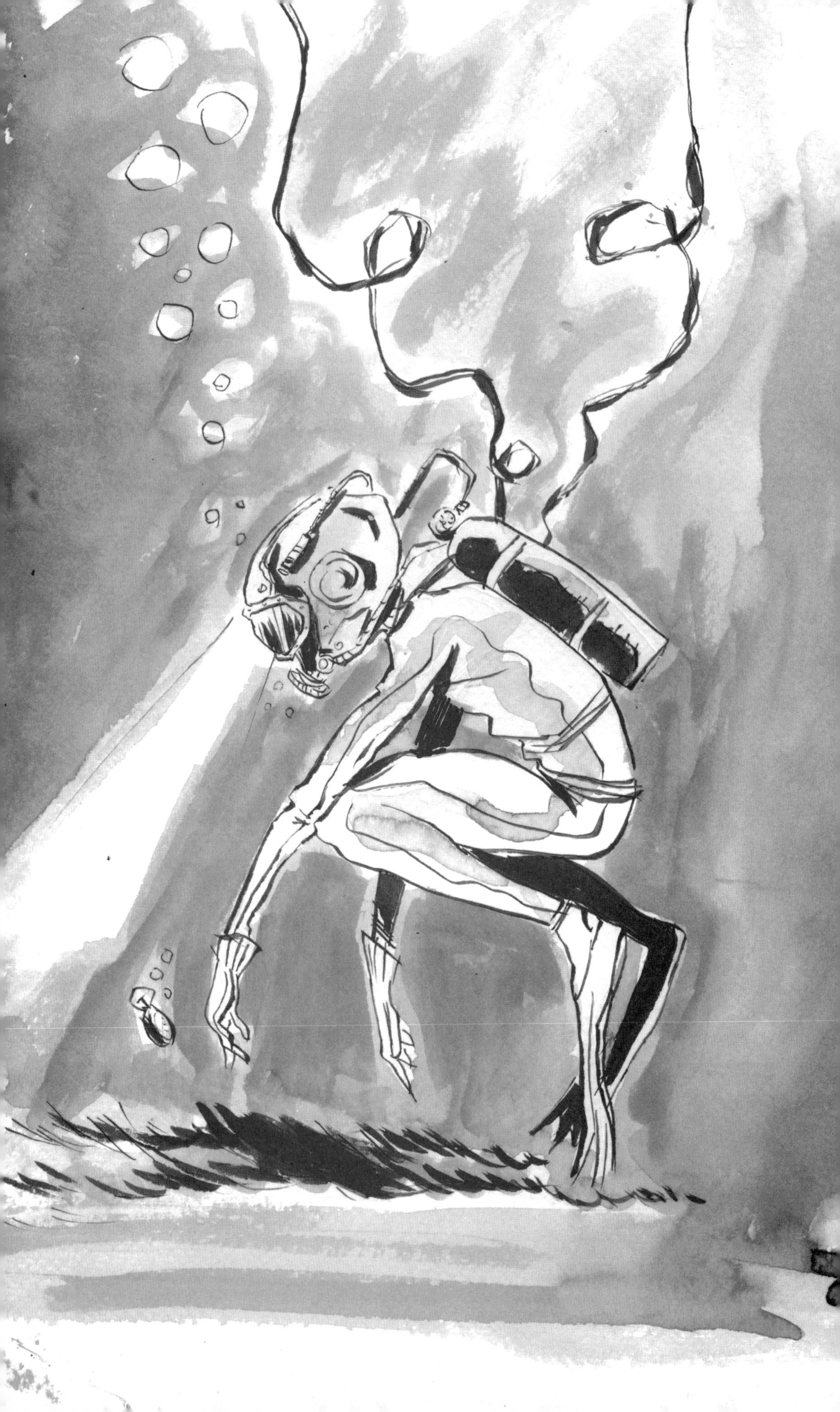

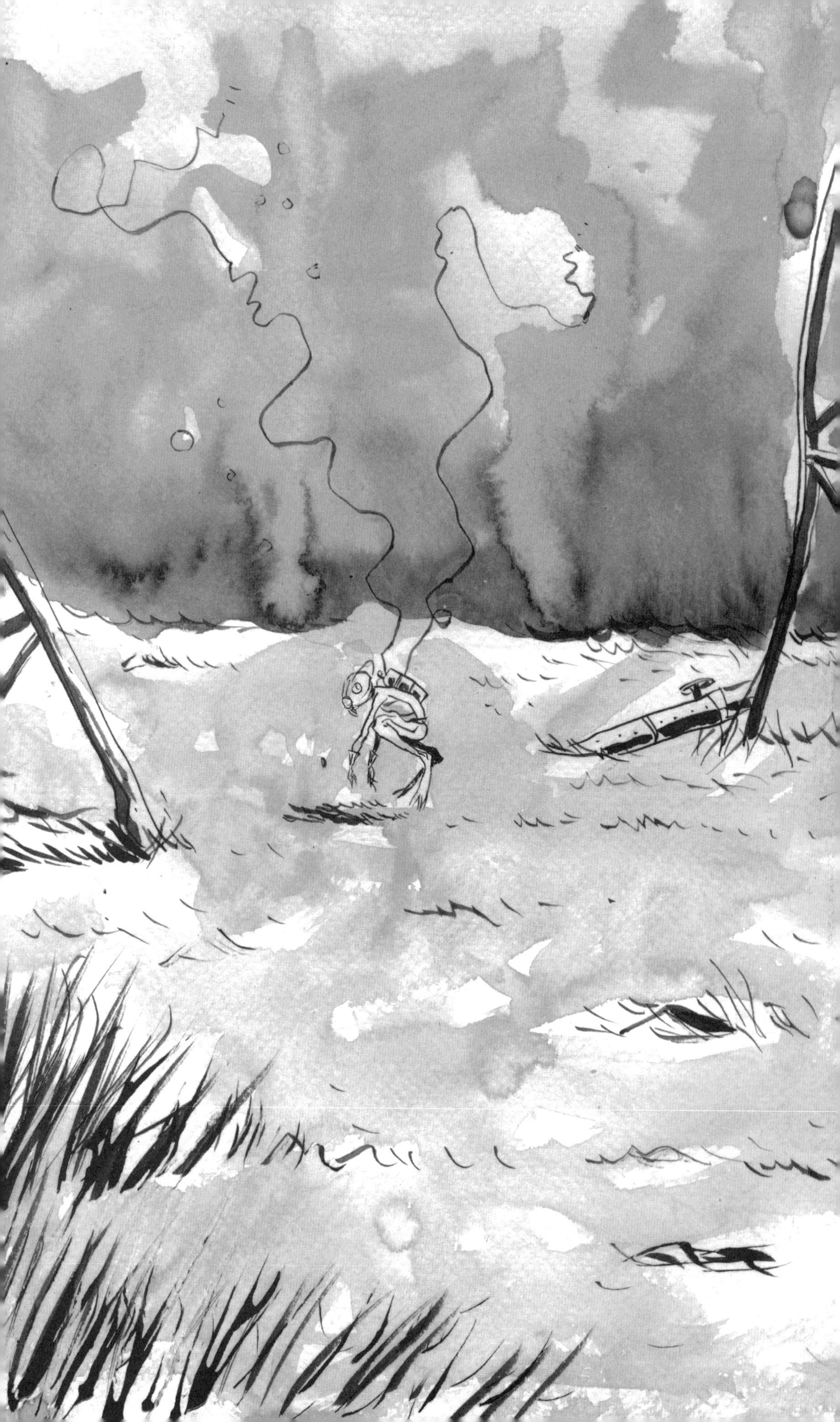

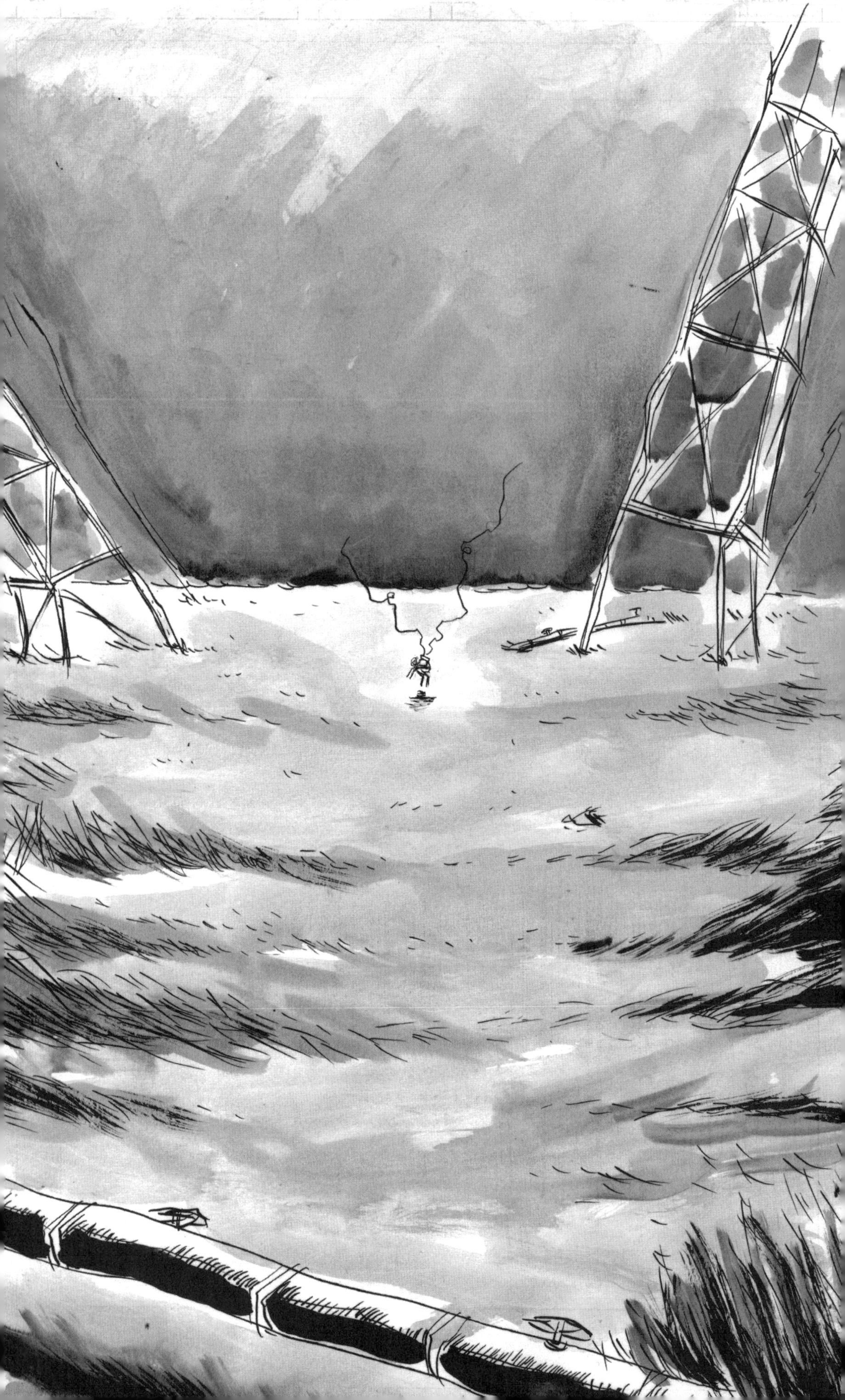

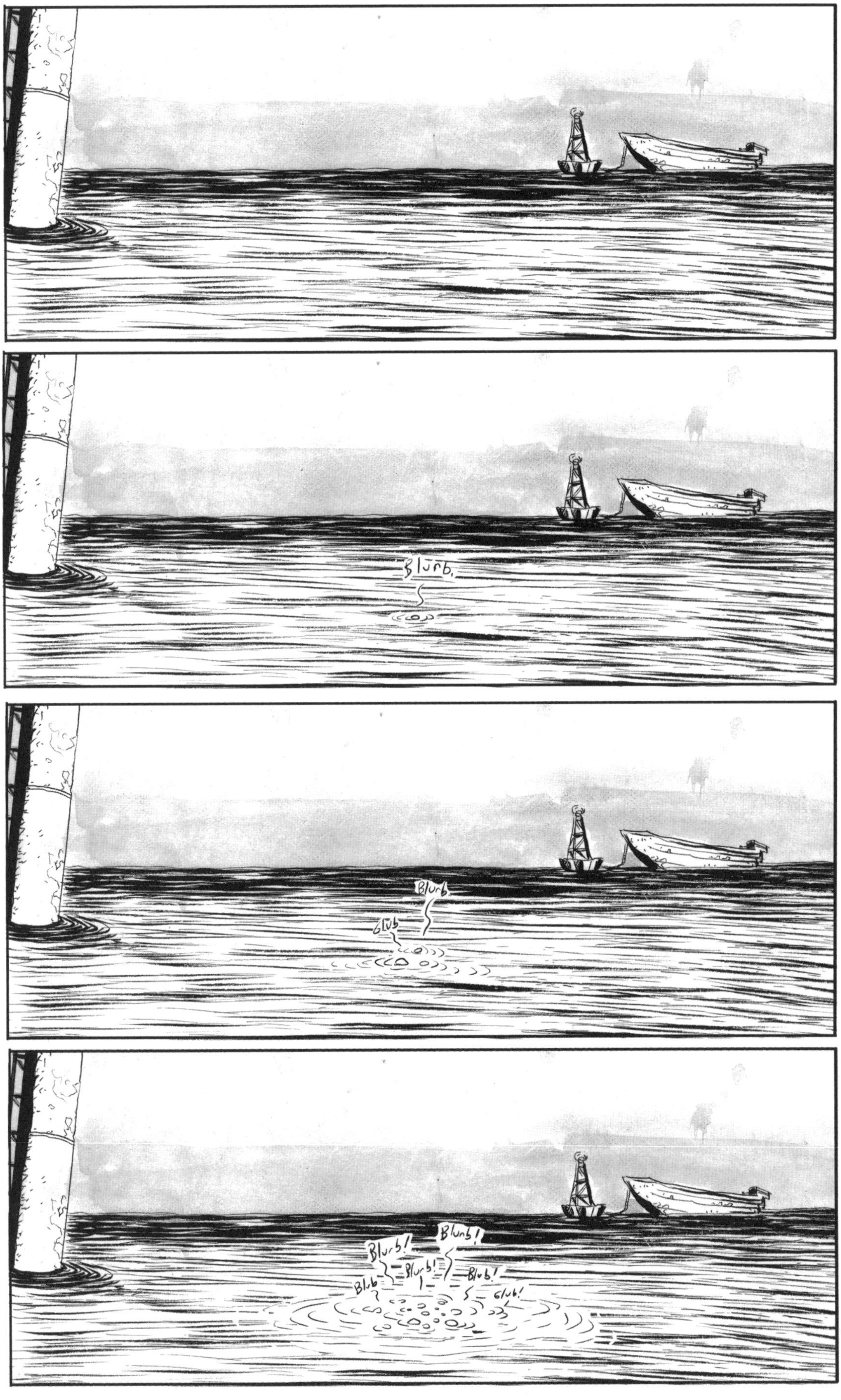
Blurb.
Blurb
Glub
Blurb!
Blunb!
Blurb!
Blub
Blub!
Glub!

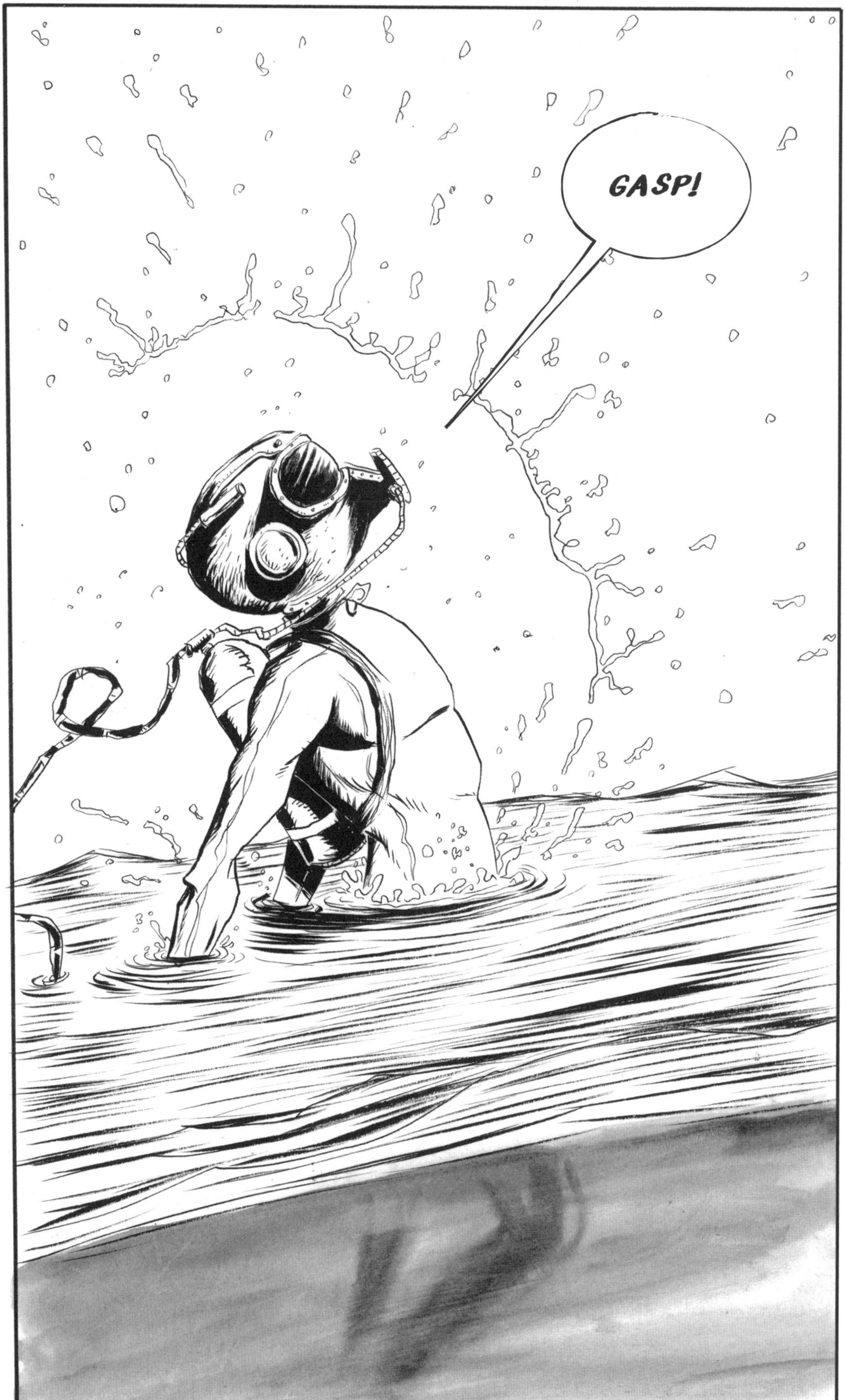
GASP!

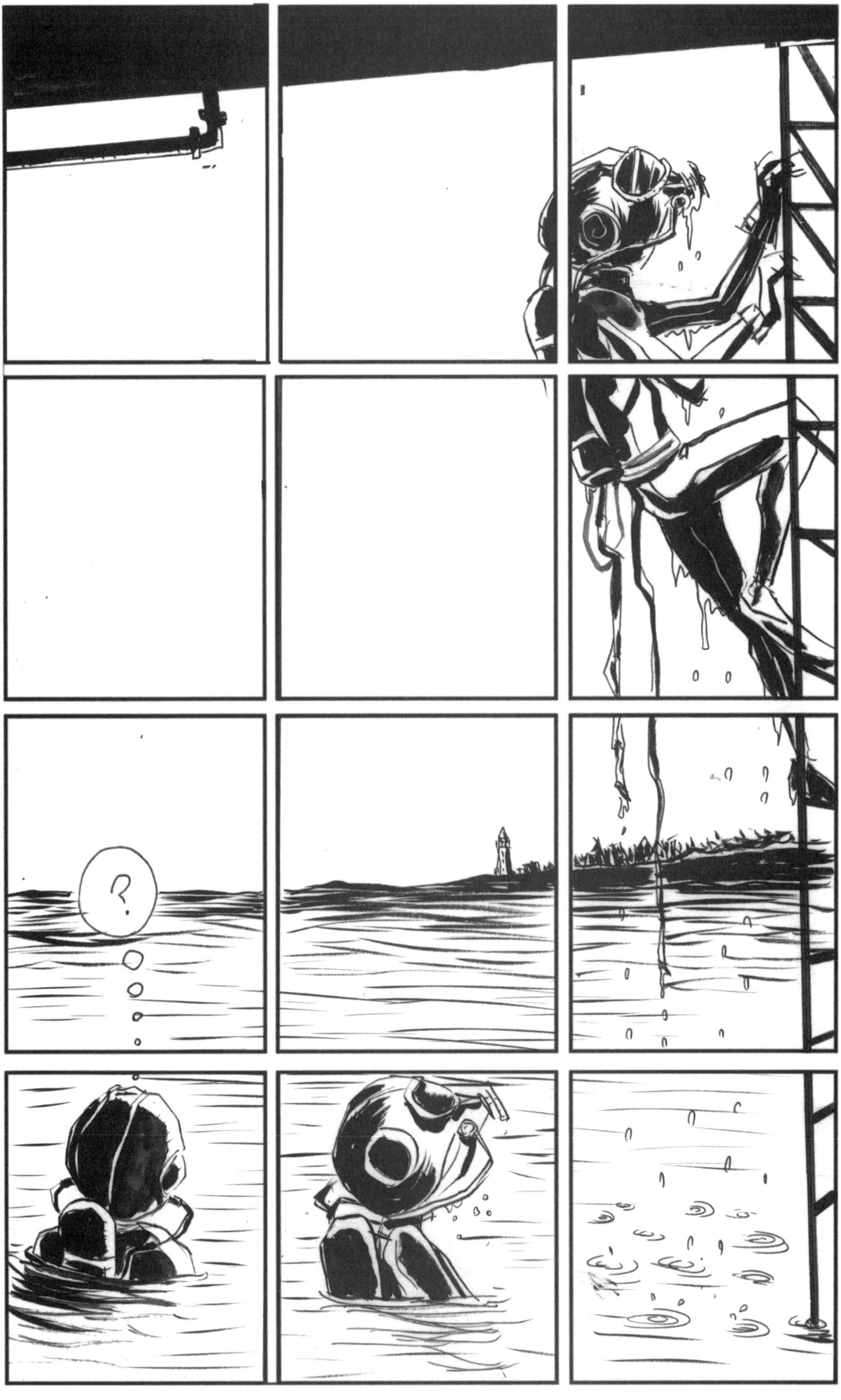
?

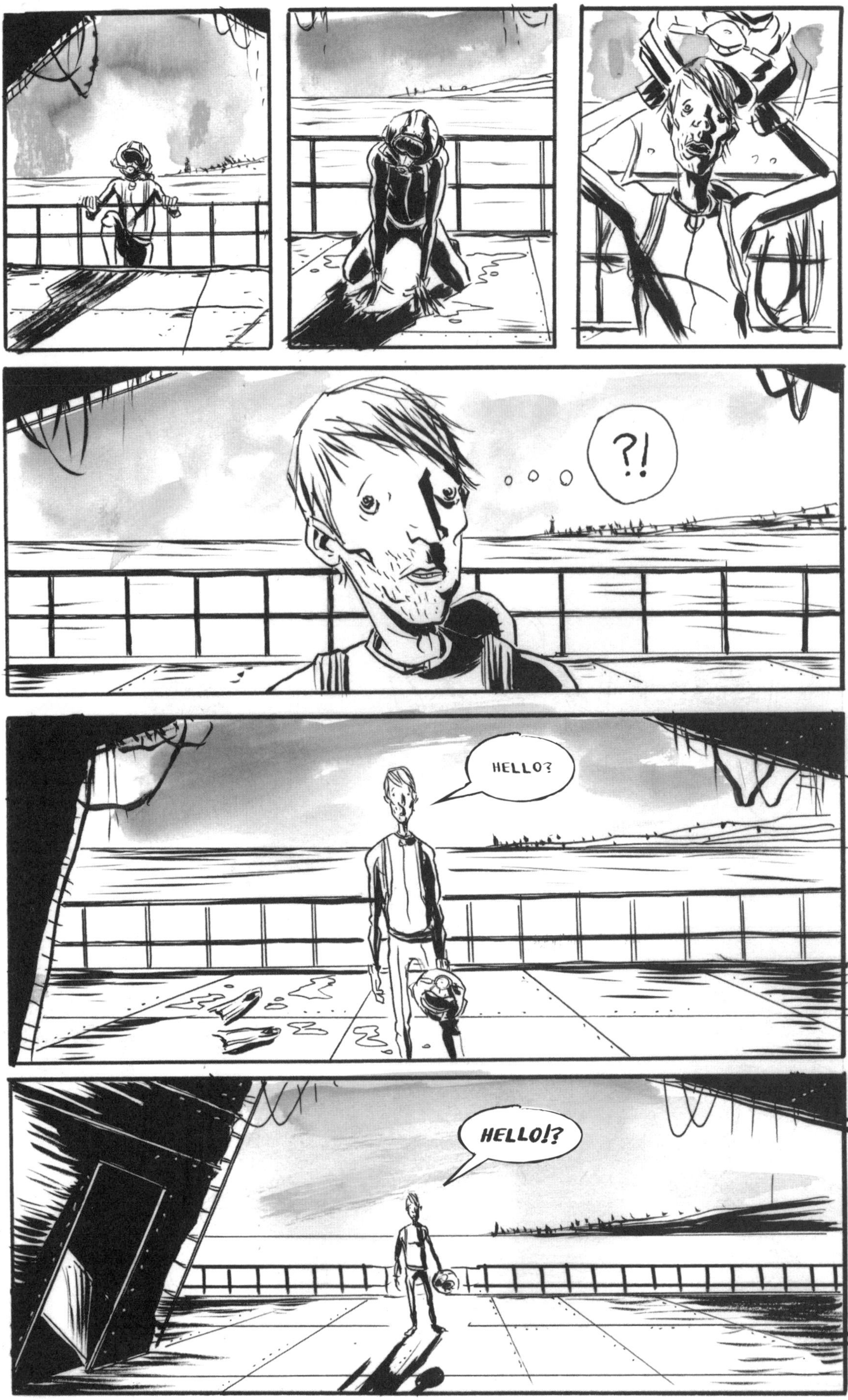
?!
HELLO?
HELLO!?

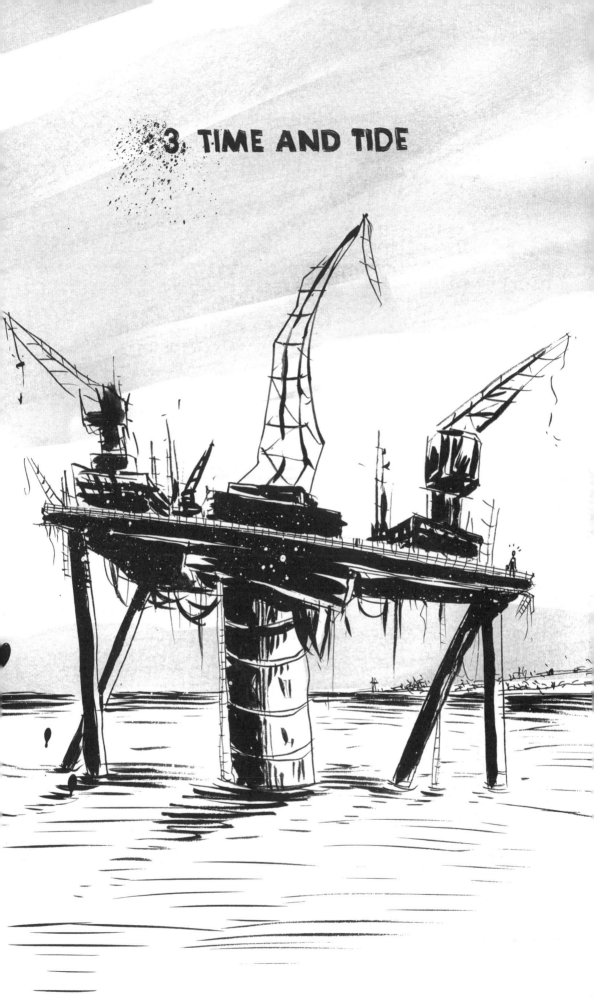

3. TIME AND TIDE

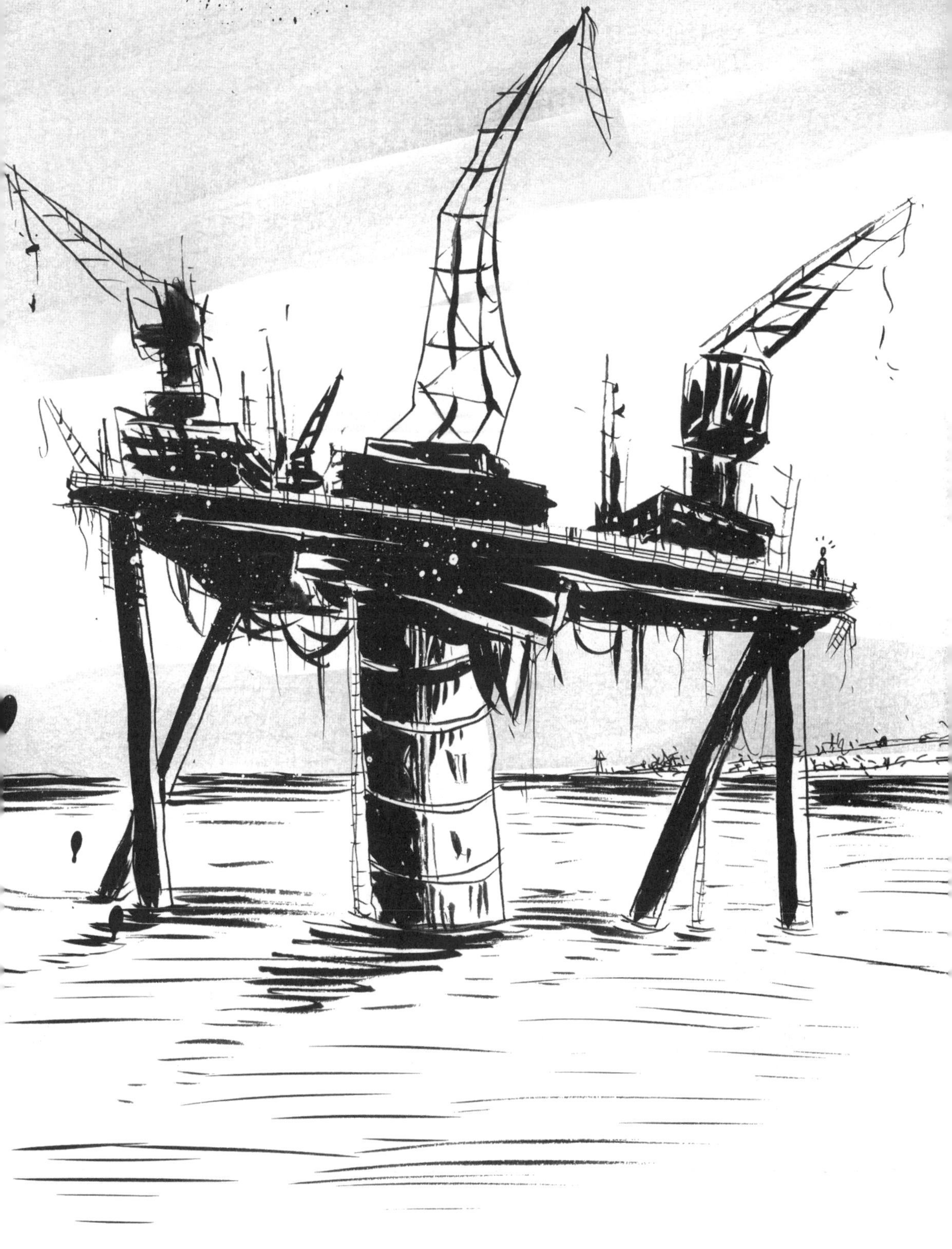

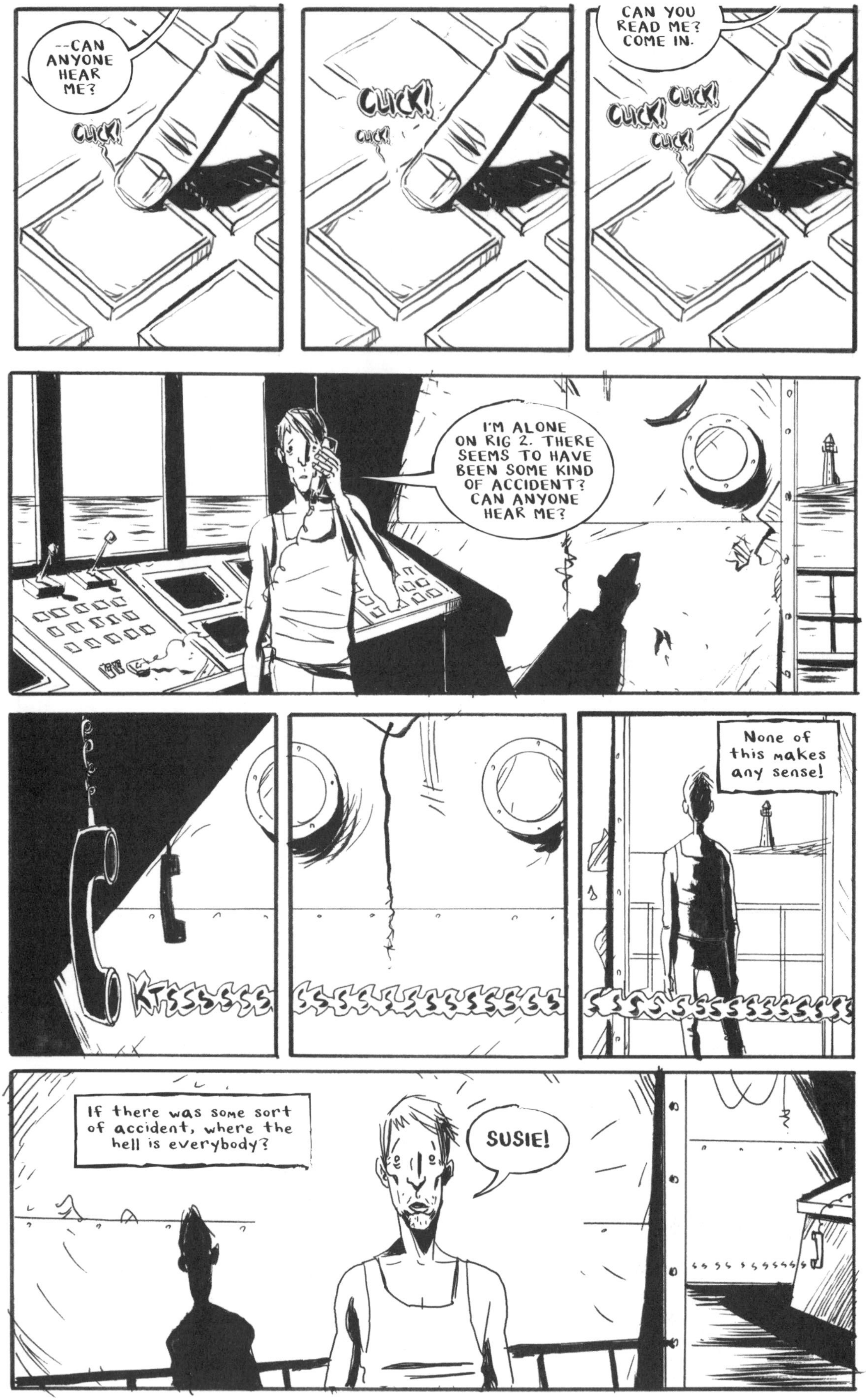
--CAN ANYONE HEAR ME?
CLICK!
CLICK!
CLICK!
CAN YOU READ ME? COME IN.
CLICK!
CLICK!
CLICK!
I'M ALONE ON RIG 2. THERE SEEMS TO HAVE BEEN SOME KIND OF ACCIDENT? CAN ANYONE HEAR ME?
KTSSSSSS
None of this makes any sense!
If there was some sort of accident, where the hell is everybody?
SUSIE!

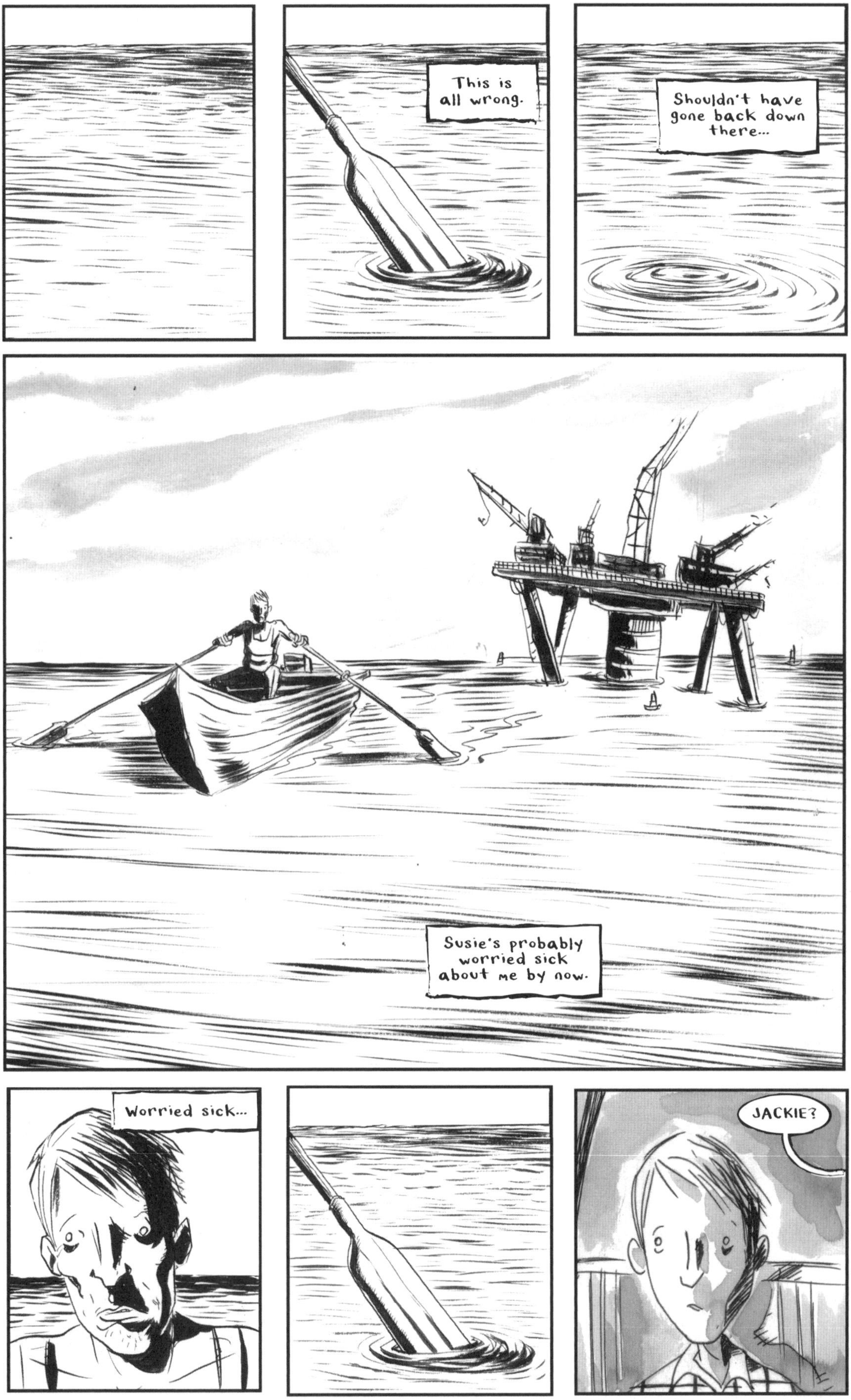
This is all wrong.
Shouldn't have gone back down there...
Susie's probably worried sick about me by now.
Worried sick...
JACKIE?

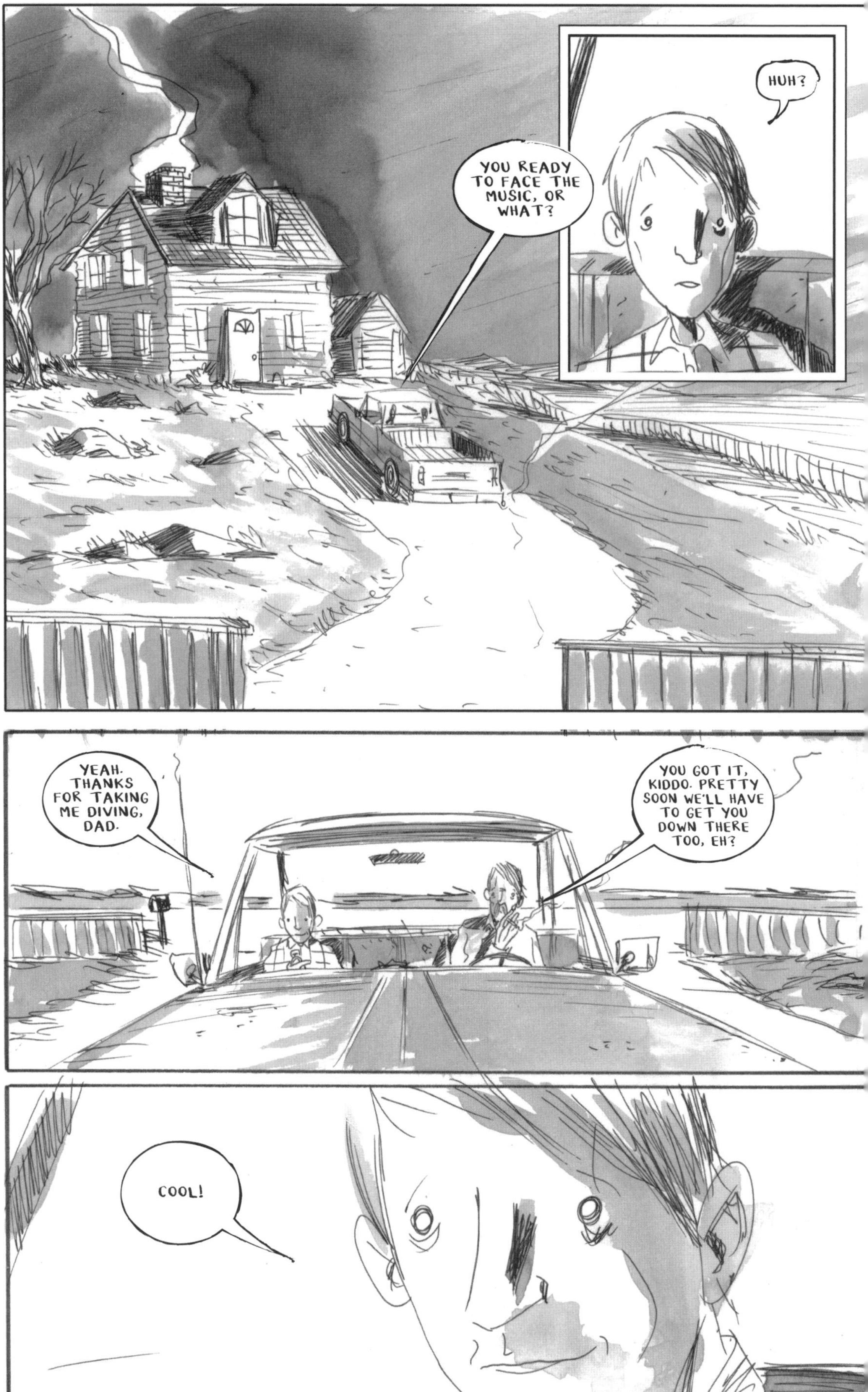
YOU READY TO FACE THE MUSIC, OR WHAT?
HUH?
YEAH. THANKS FOR TAKING ME DIVING, DAD.
YOU GOT IT, KIDDO. PRETTY SOON WE'LL HAVE TO GET YOU DOWN THERE TOO, EH?
COOL!

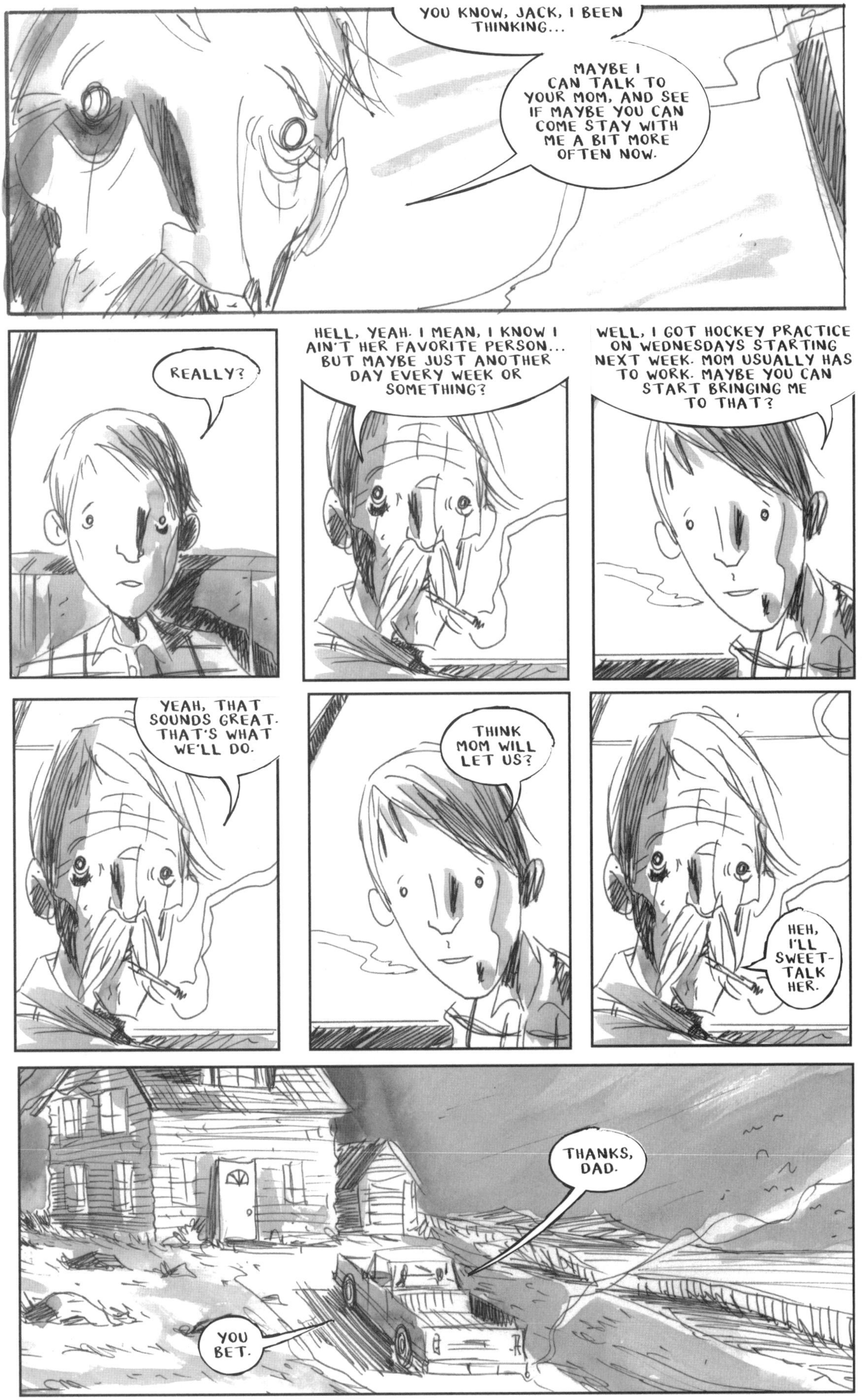
YOU KNOW, JACK, I BEEN THINKING...
MAYBE I CAN TALK TO YOUR MOM, AND SEE IF MAYBE YOU CAN COME STAY WITH ME A BIT MORE OFTEN NOW.
REALLY?
HELL, YEAH. I MEAN, I KNOW I AIN'T HER FAVORITE PERSON... BUT MAYBE JUST ANOTHER DAY EVERY WEEK OR SOMETHING?
WELL, I GOT HOCKEY PRACTICE ON WEDNESDAYS STARTING NEXT WEEK. MOM USUALLY HAS TO WORK. MAYBE YOU CAN START BRINGING ME TO THAT?
YEAH, THAT SOUNDS GREAT. THAT'S WHAT WE'LL DO.
THINK MOM WILL LET US?
HEH, I'LL SWEET-TALK HER.
THANKS, DAD.
YOU BET.

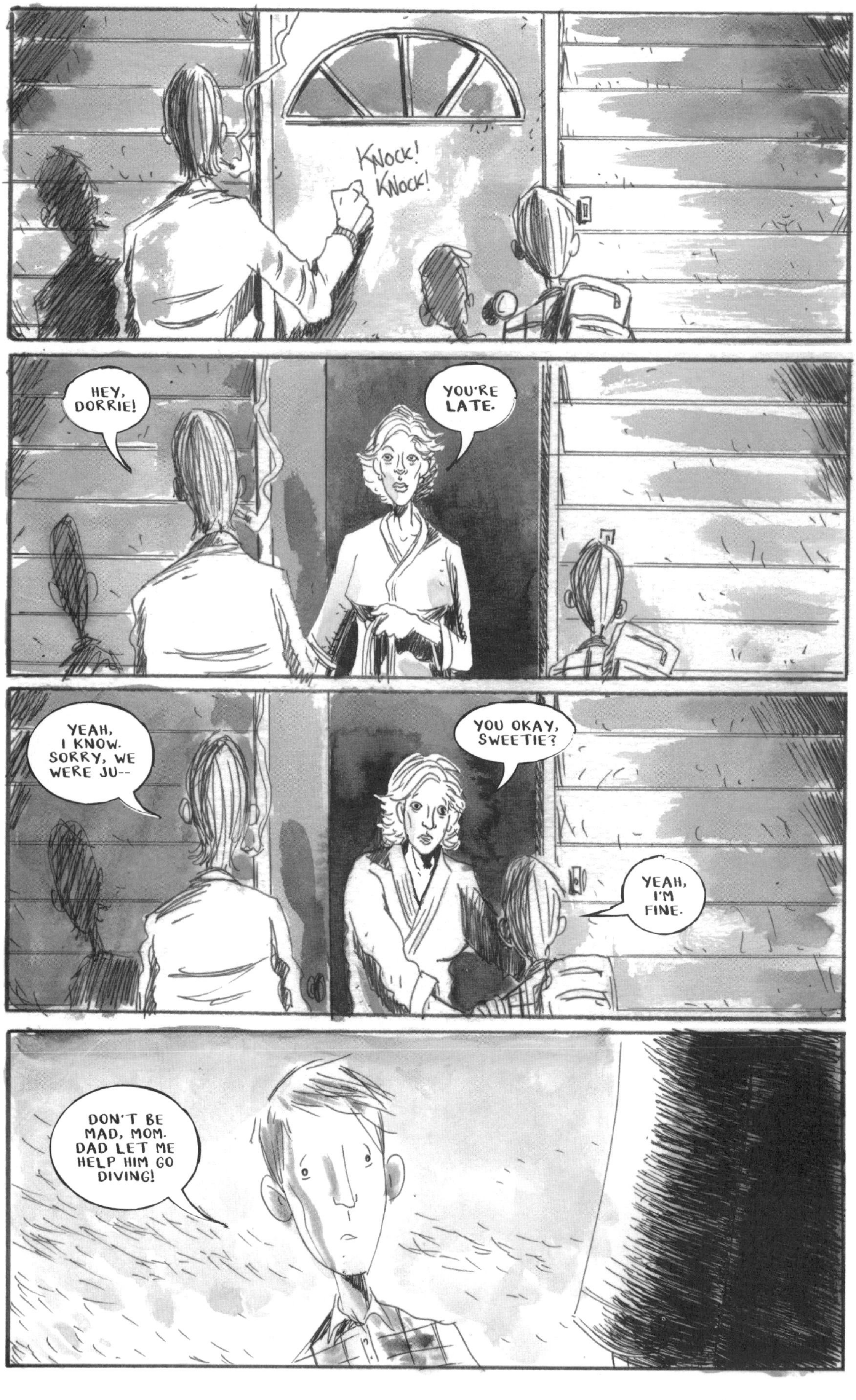
KNOCK! KNOCK!
HEY, DORRIE!
YOU'RE LATE.
YEAH, I KNOW. SORRY, WE WERE JU--
YOU OKAY, SWEETIE?
YEAH, I'M FINE.
DON'T BE MAD, MOM. DAD LET ME HELP HIM GO DIVING!

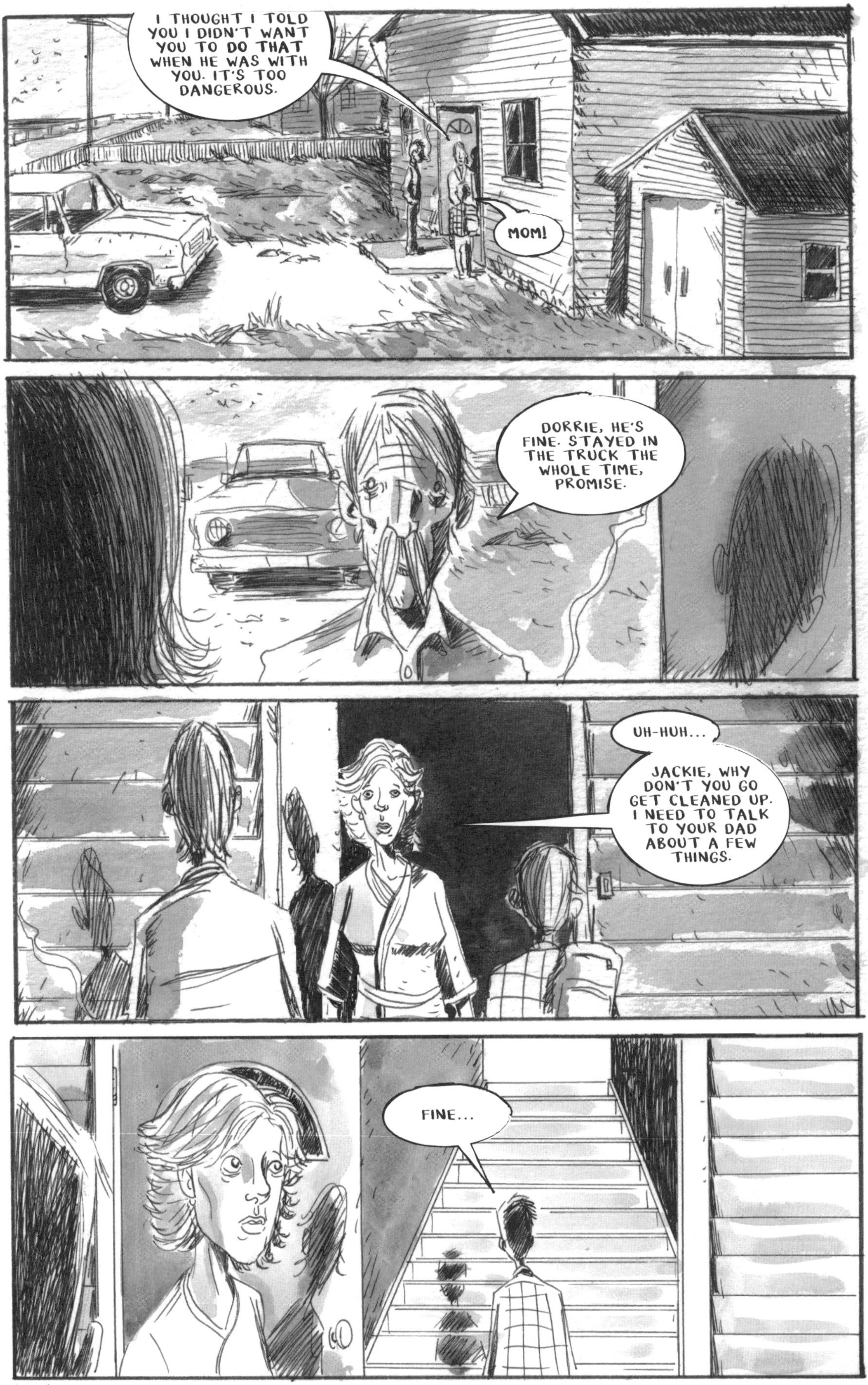
I THOUGHT I TOLD YOU I DIDN'T WANT YOU TO DO THAT WHEN HE WAS WITH YOU. IT'S TOO DANGEROUS.
MOM!
DORRIE, HE'S FINE. STAYED IN THE TRUCK THE WHOLE TIME, PROMISE.
UH-HUH...
JACKIE, WHY DON'T YOU GO GET CLEANED UP. I NEED TO TALK TO YOUR DAD ABOUT A FEW THINGS.
FINE...

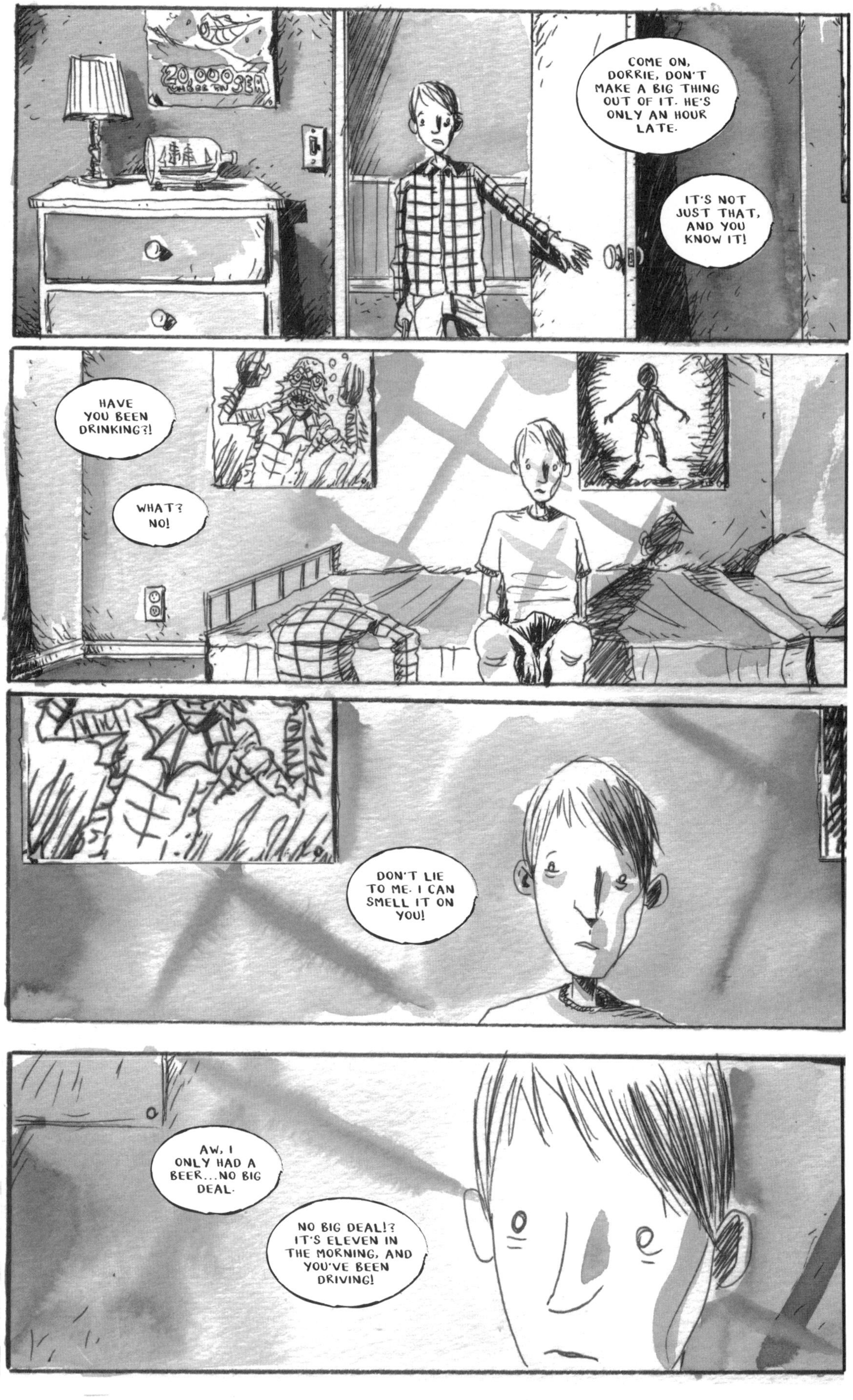
COME ON, DORRIE, DON'T MAKE A BIG THING OUT OF IT. HE'S ONLY AN HOUR LATE.
IT'S NOT JUST THAT, AND YOU KNOW IT!
HAVE YOU BEEN DRINKING?!
WHAT? NO!
DON'T LIE TO ME. I CAN SMELL IT ON YOU!
AW, I ONLY HAD A BEER... NO BIG DEAL.
NO BIG DEAL!? IT'S ELEVEN IN THE MORNING, AND YOU'VE BEEN DRIVING!

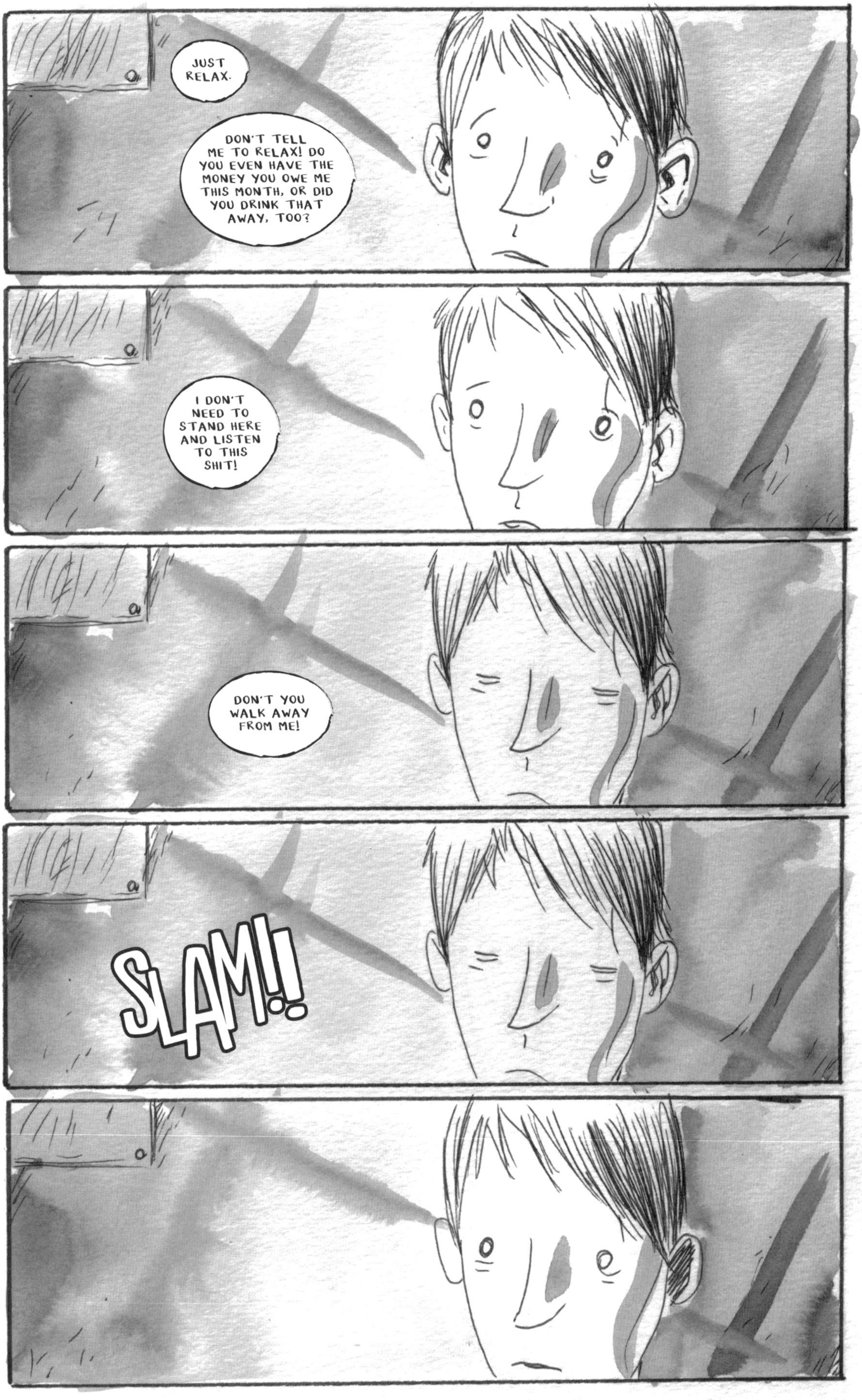
JUST RELAX.
DON'T TELL ME TO RELAX! DO YOU EVEN HAVE THE MONEY YOU OWE ME THIS MONTH, OR DID YOU DRINK THAT AWAY, TOO?
I DON'T NEED TO STAND HERE AND LISTEN TO THIS SHIT!
DON'T YOU WALK AWAY FROM ME!
SLAM!!

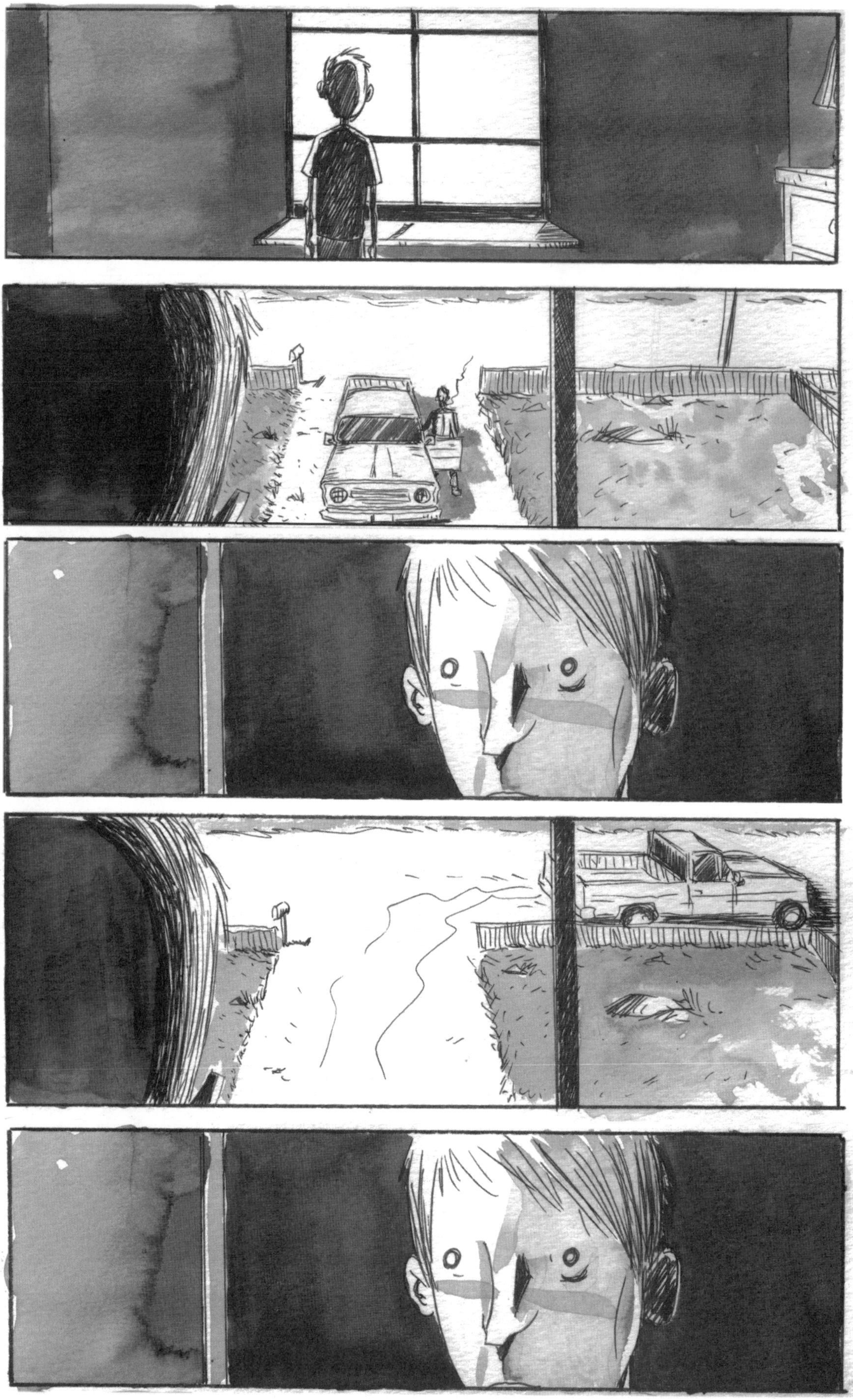

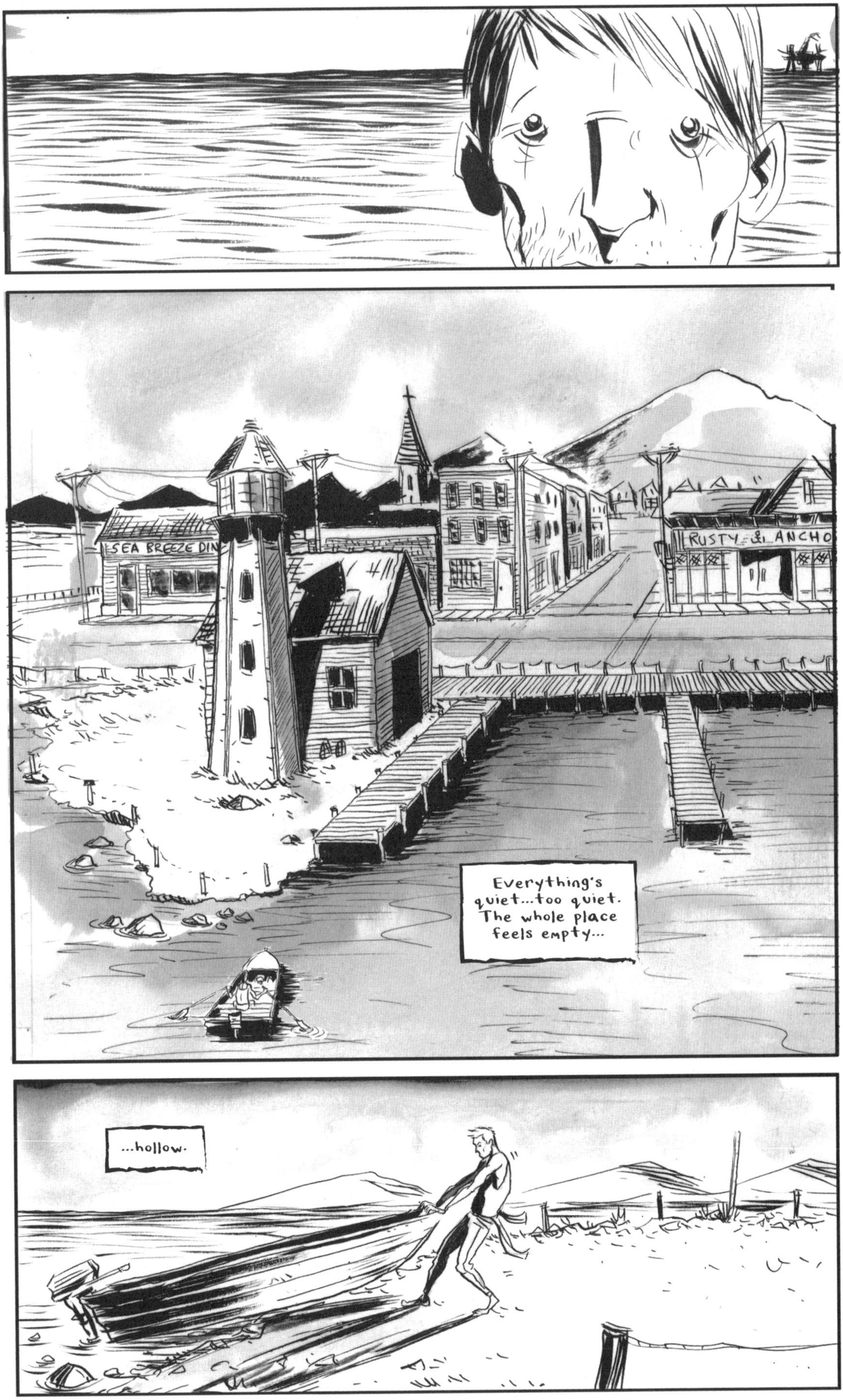
SEA BREEZE DIN
RUSTY & ANCHO
Everything's quiet...too quiet. The whole place feels empty...
...hollow.

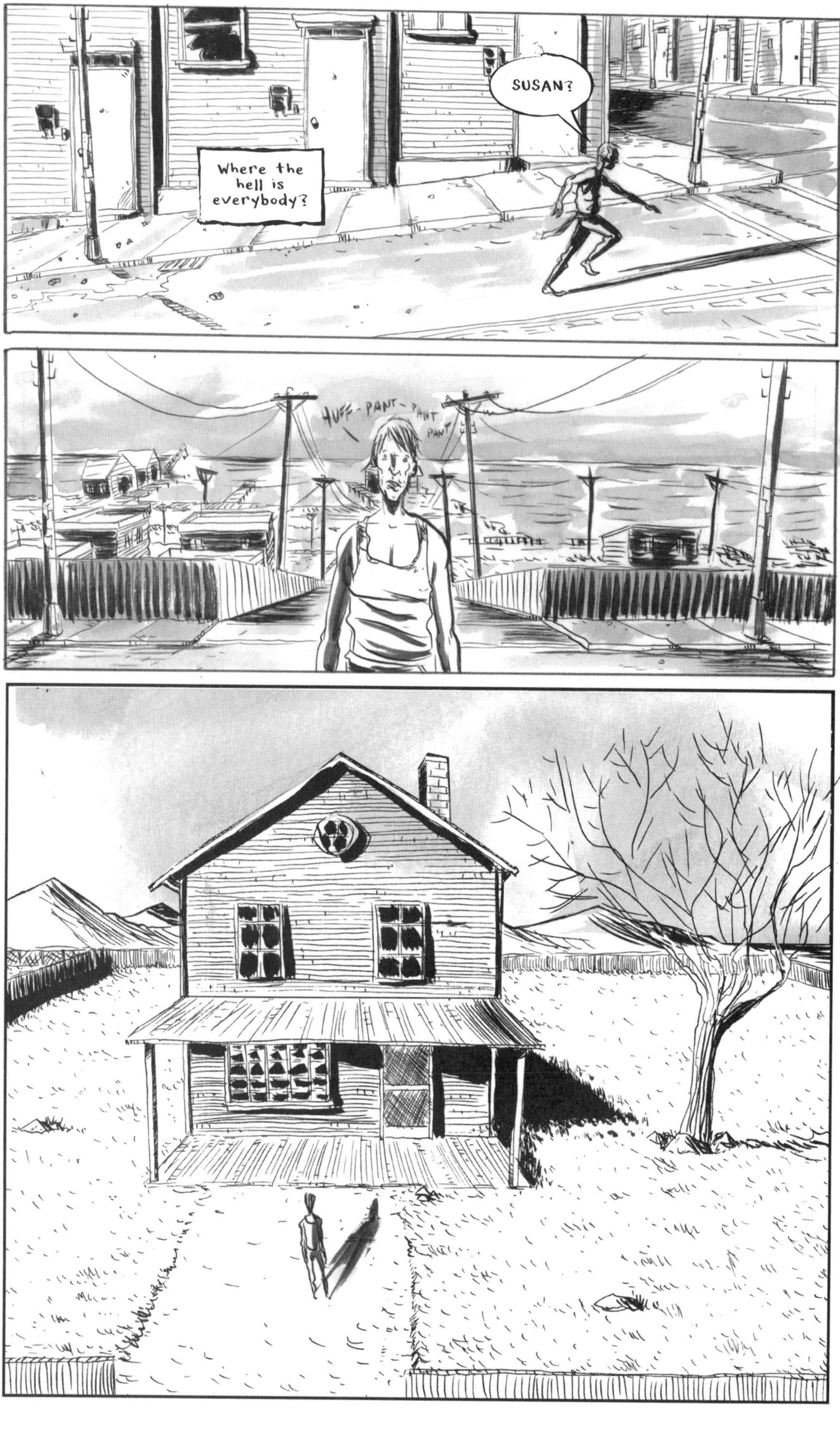
Where the hell is everybody?
SUSAN?
HUFF-PANT-PANT
PANT

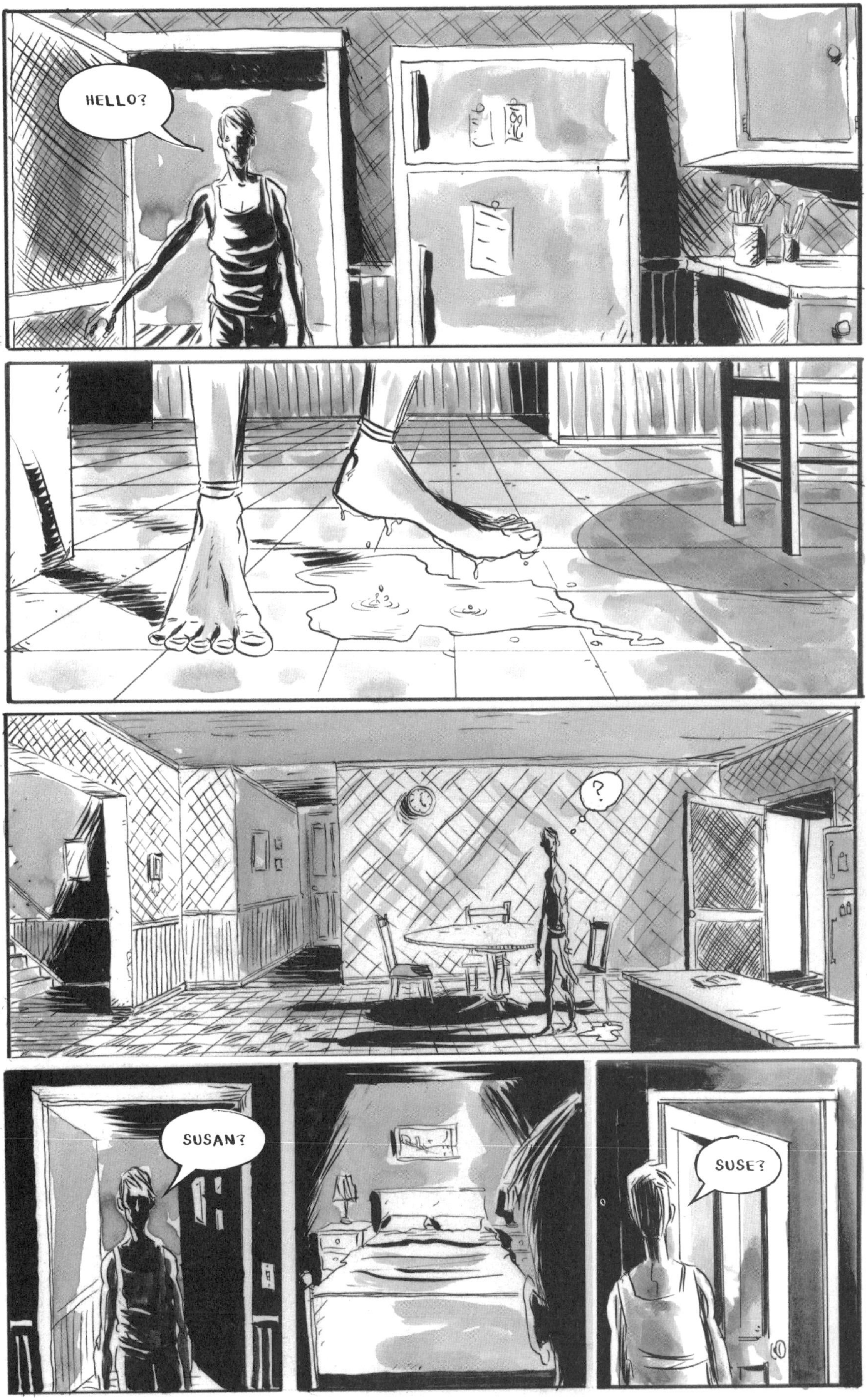
HELLO?
?
SUSAN?
SUSE?

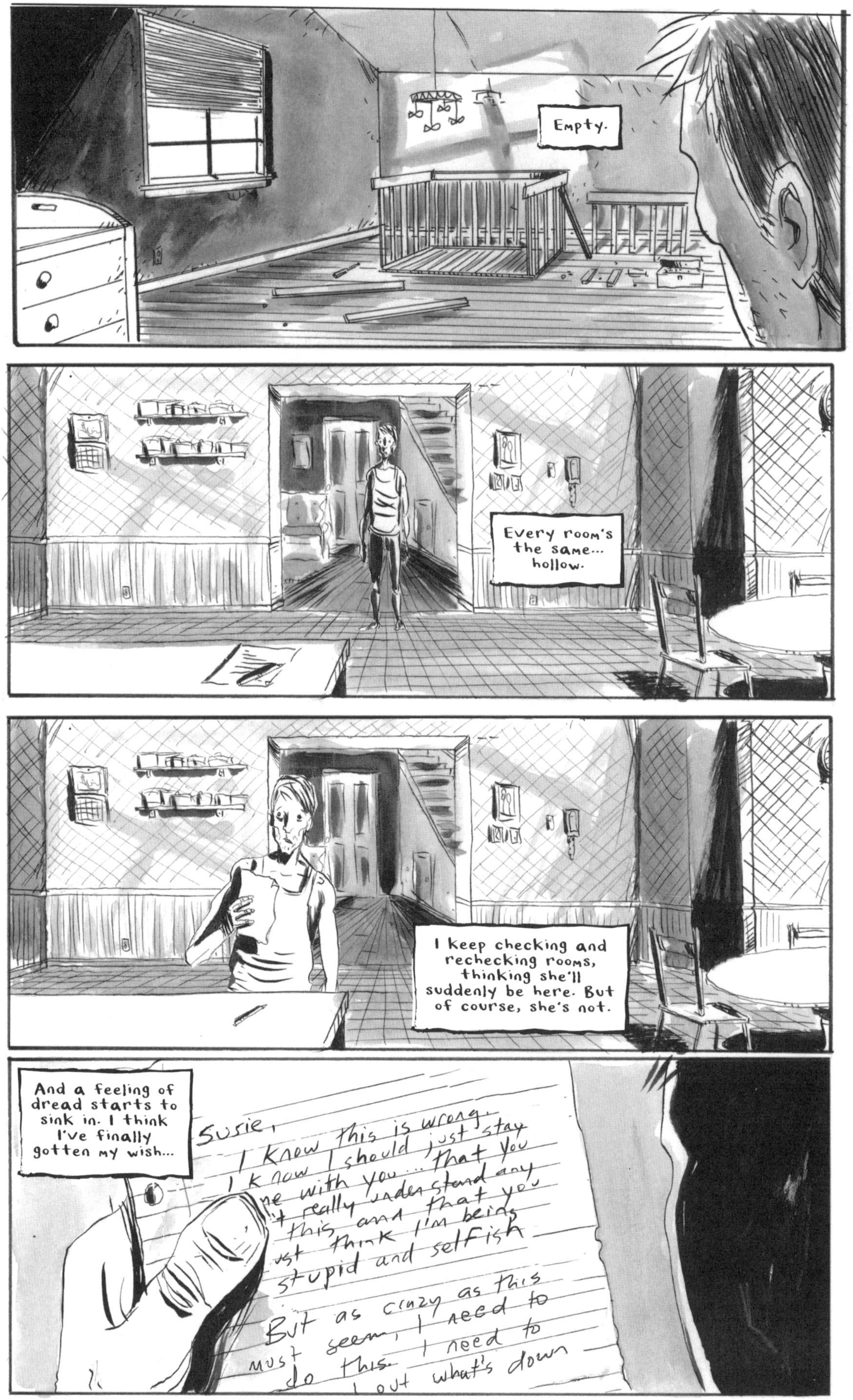
Empty.
Every room's the same... hollow.
I keep checking and rechecking rooms, thinking she'll suddenly be here. But of course, she's not.
And a feeling of dread starts to sink in. I think I've finally gotten my wish...
Susie,
I know this is wrong.
I know I should just stay
with you... that you
really understand any
this and that you
think I'm being
stupid and selfish
But as crazy as this
must seem, I need to
do this. I need to
out what's down

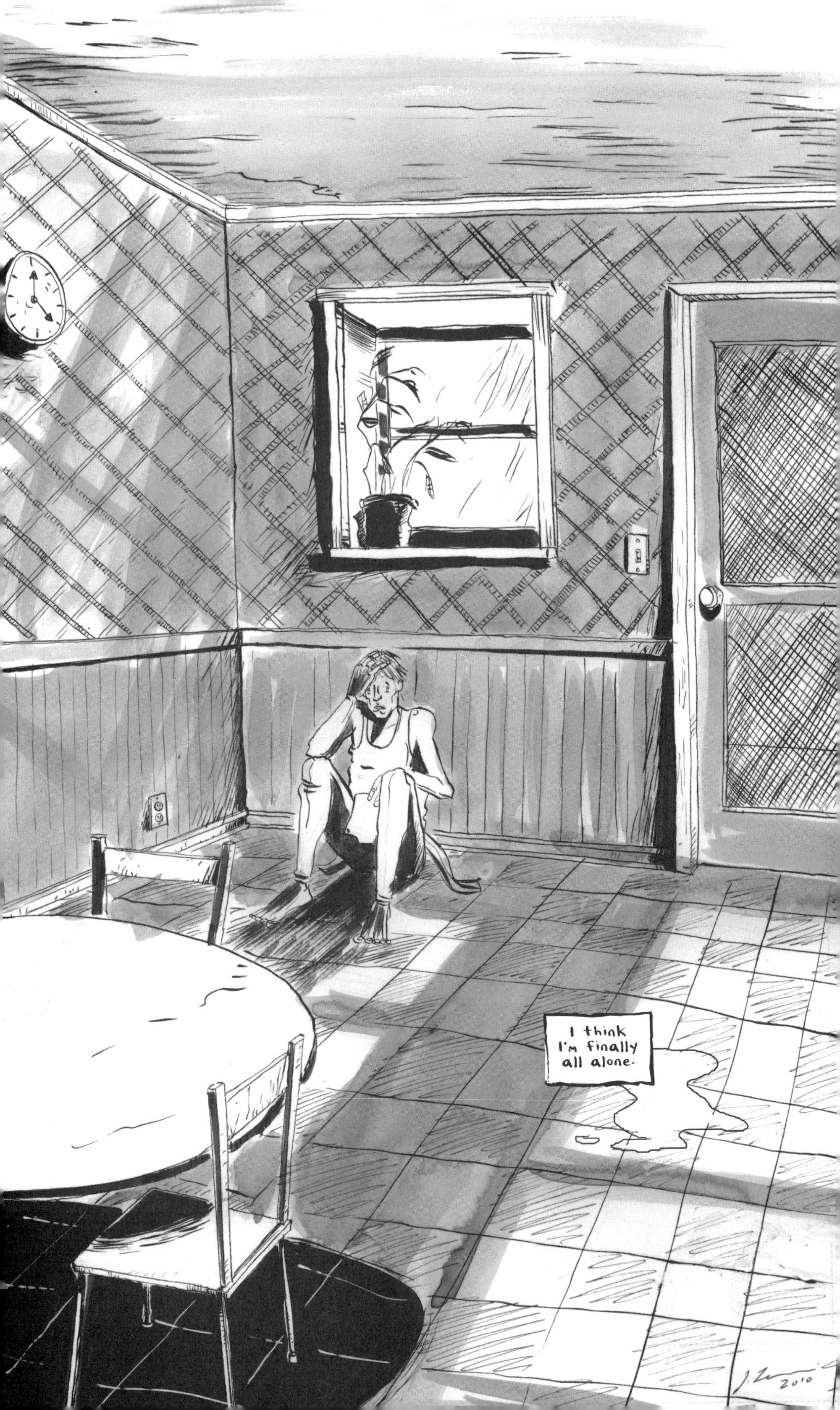
I think
I'm finally
all alone.
J. L.
2010

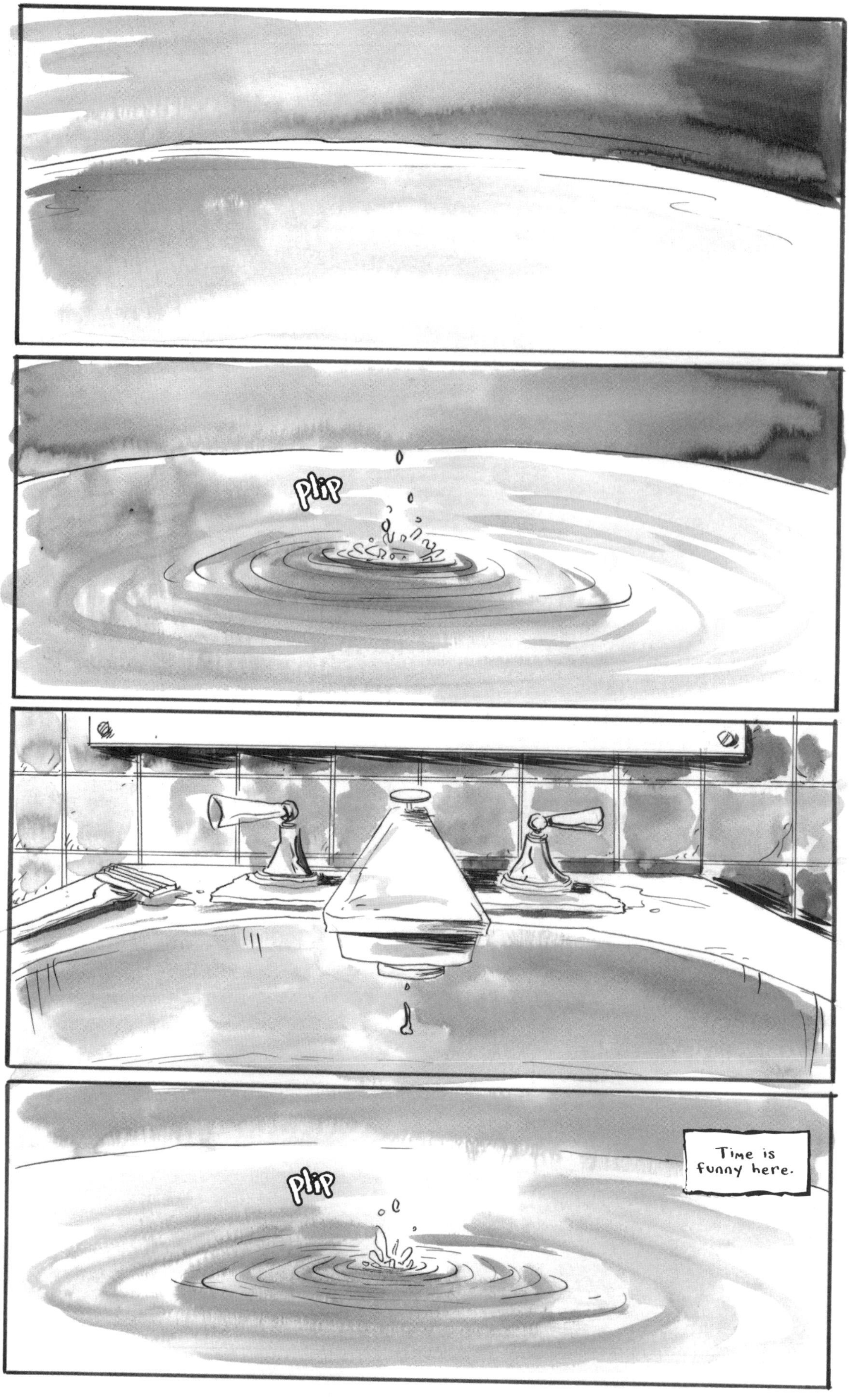
plip
plip
Time is funny here.

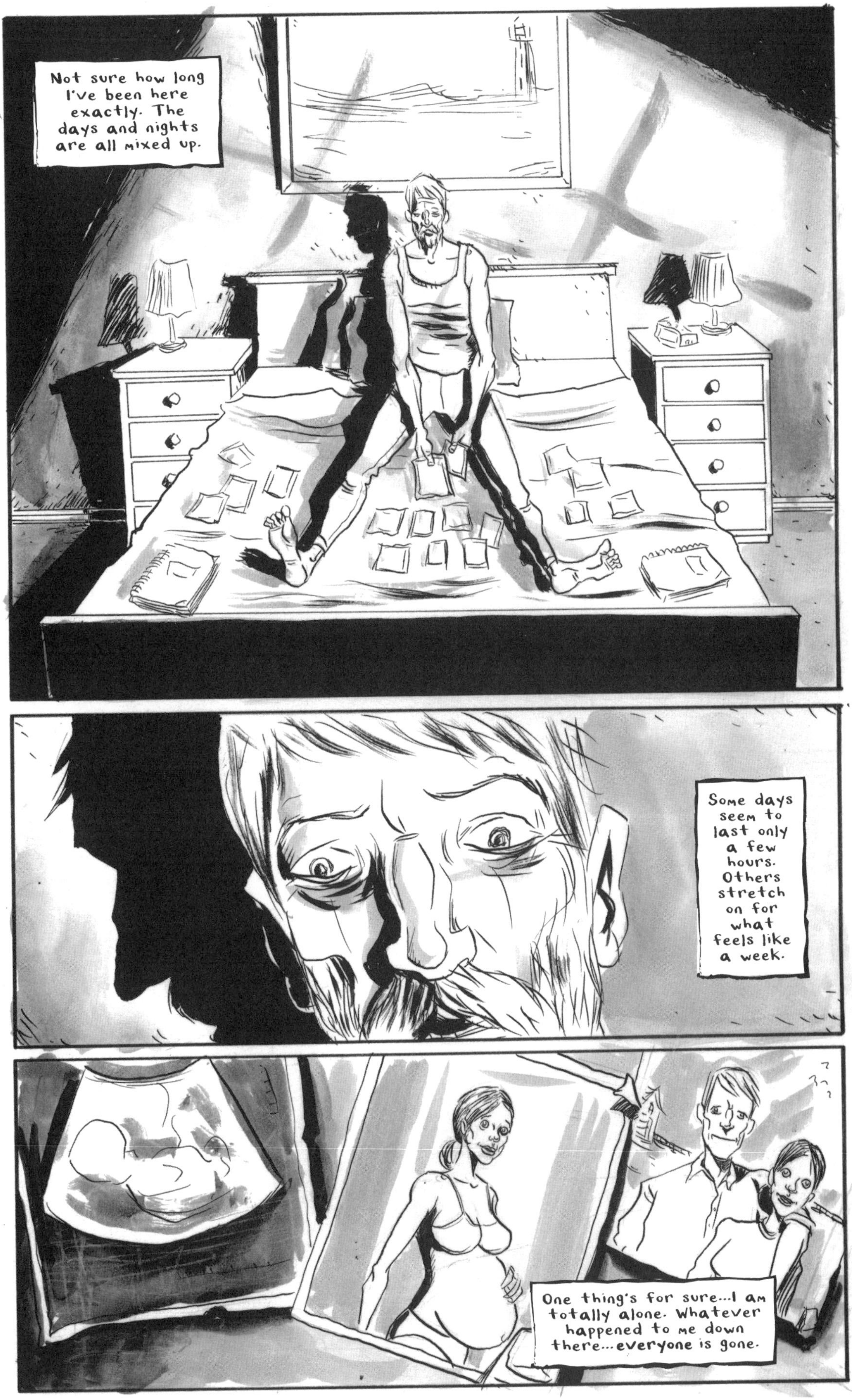
Not sure how long I've been here exactly. The days and nights are all mixed up.
Some days seem to last only a few hours. Others stretch on for what feels like a week.
One thing's for sure...I am totally alone. Whatever happened to me down there...everyone is gone.

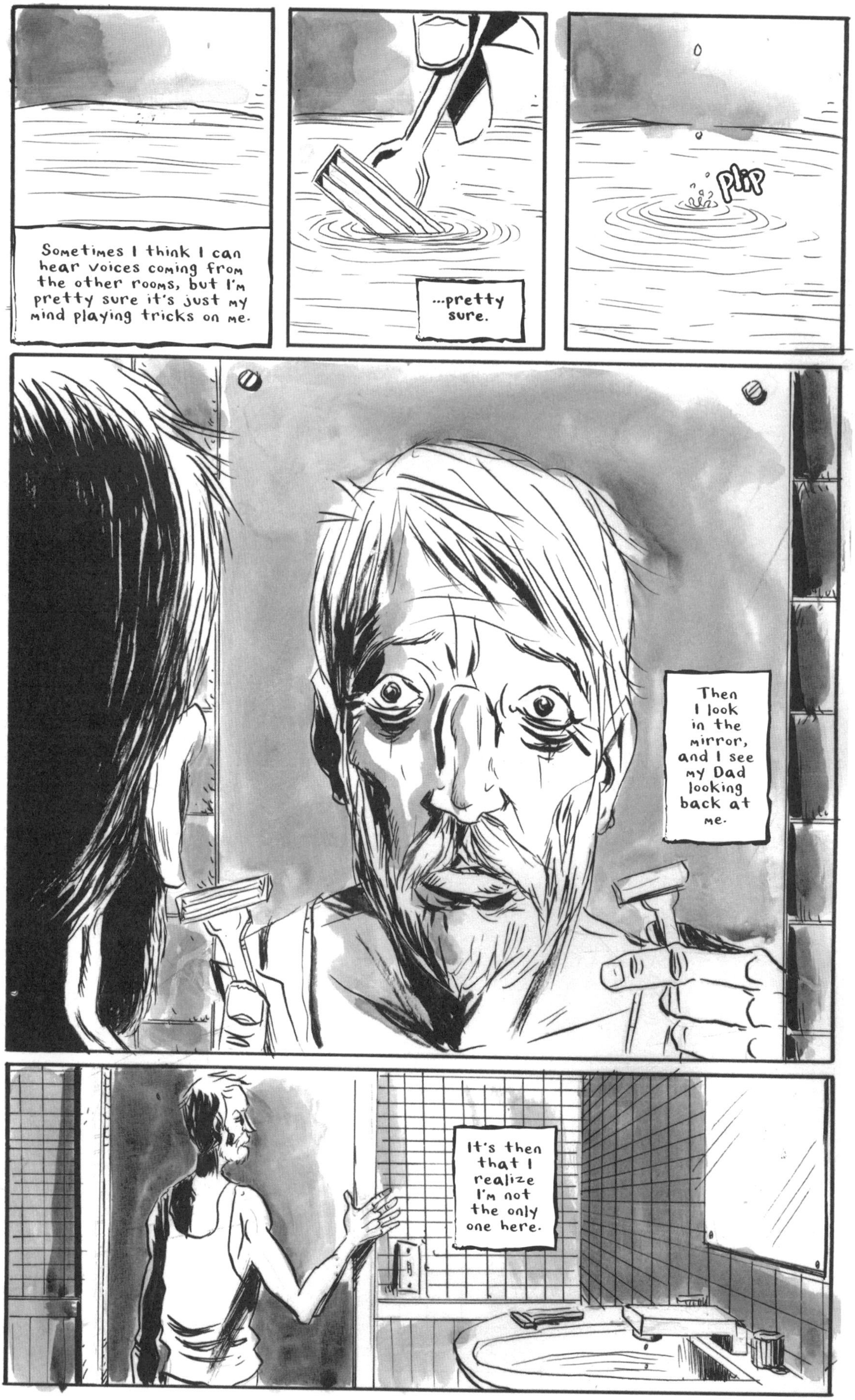
Sometimes I think I can hear voices coming from the other rooms, but I'm pretty sure it's just my mind playing tricks on me.
...pretty sure.
PLIP
Then I look in the mirror, and I see my Dad looking back at me.
It's then that I realize I'm not the only one here.

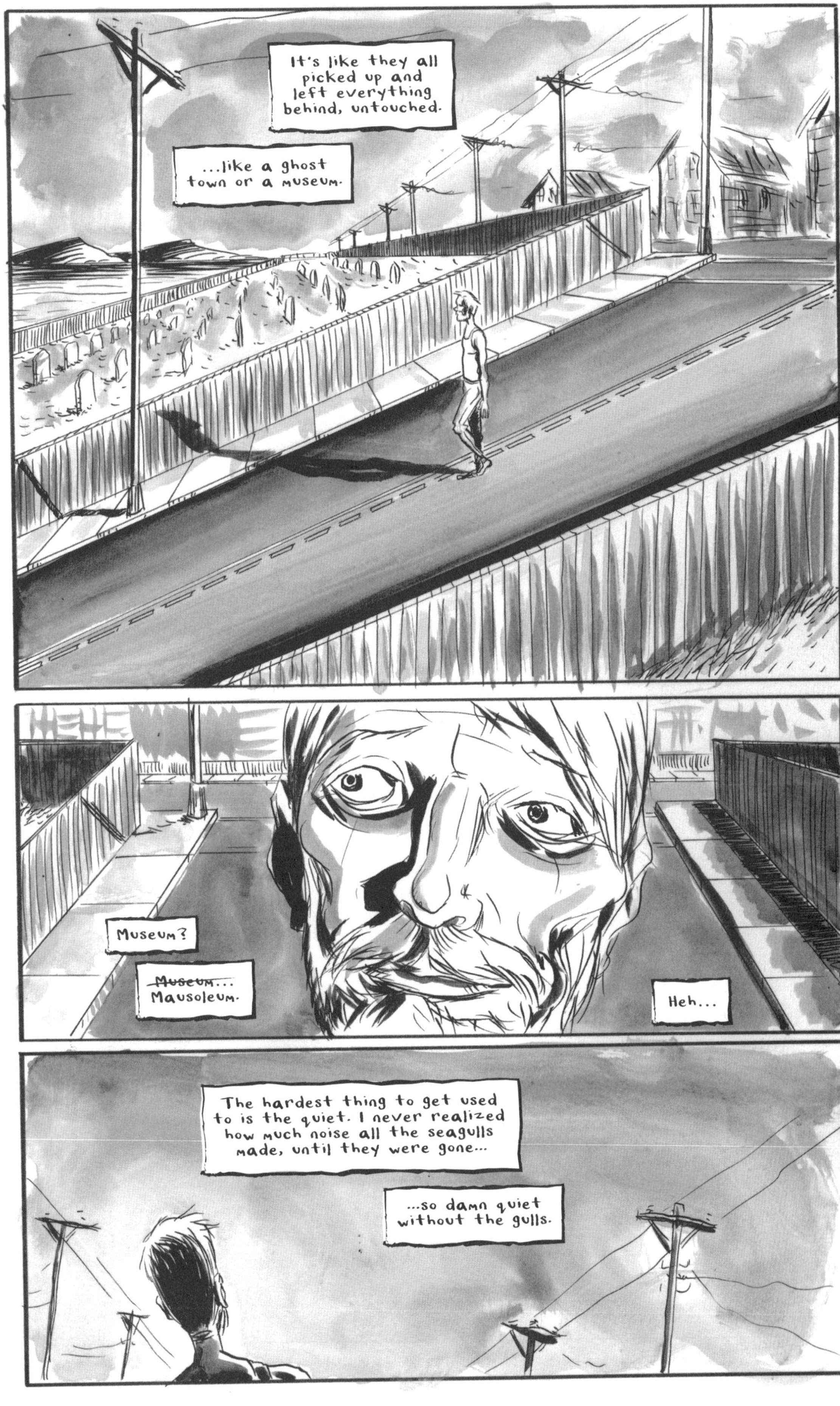
It's like they all picked up and left everything behind, untouched.
...like a ghost town or a museum.
Museum?
~~Museum~~... Mausoleum.
Heh...
The hardest thing to get used to is the quiet. I never realized how much noise all the seagulls made, until they were gone...
...so damn quiet without the gulls.

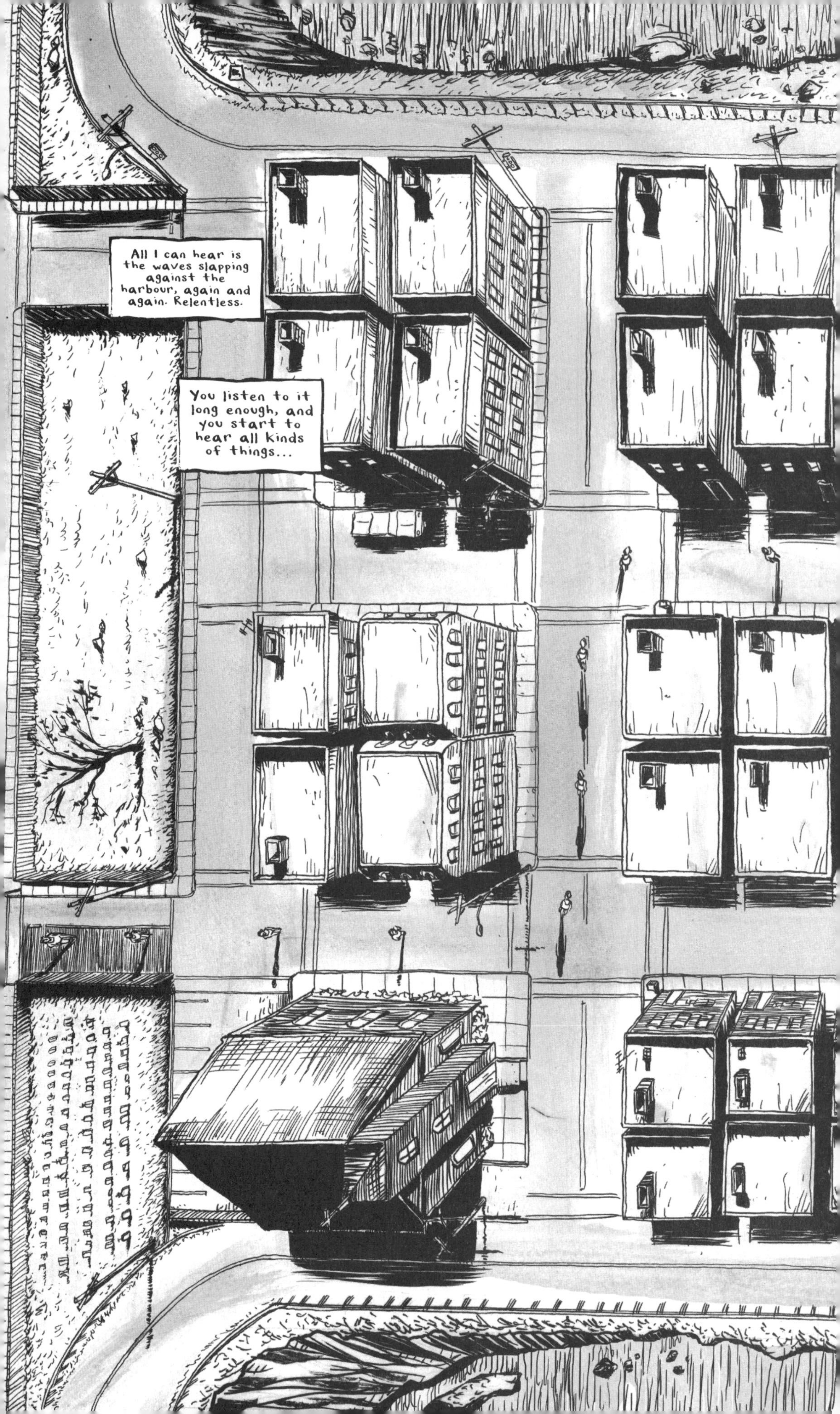
All I can hear is the waves slapping against the harbour, again and again. Relentless.
You listen to it long enough, and you start to hear all kinds of things...

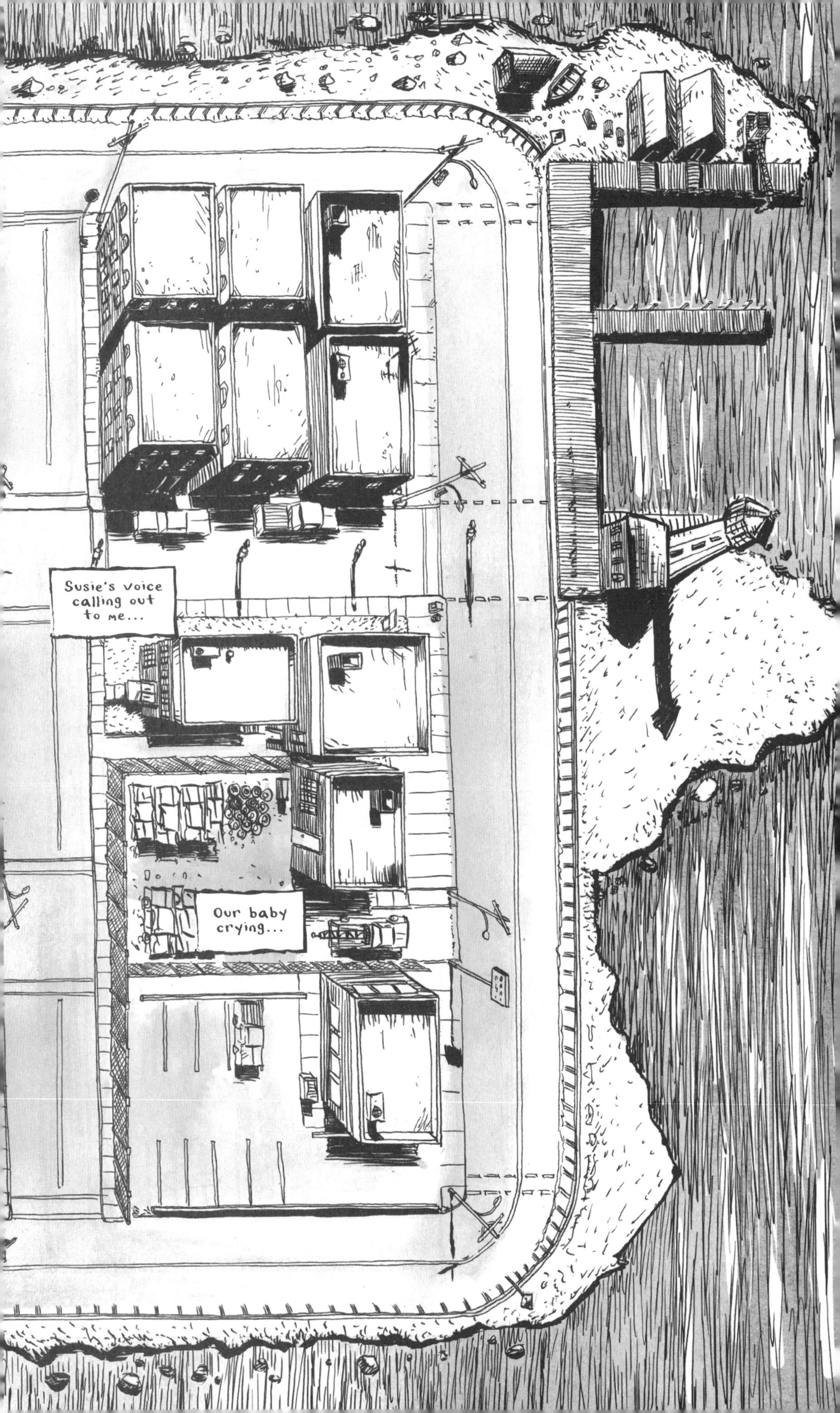
Susie's voice calling out to me...
Our baby crying...

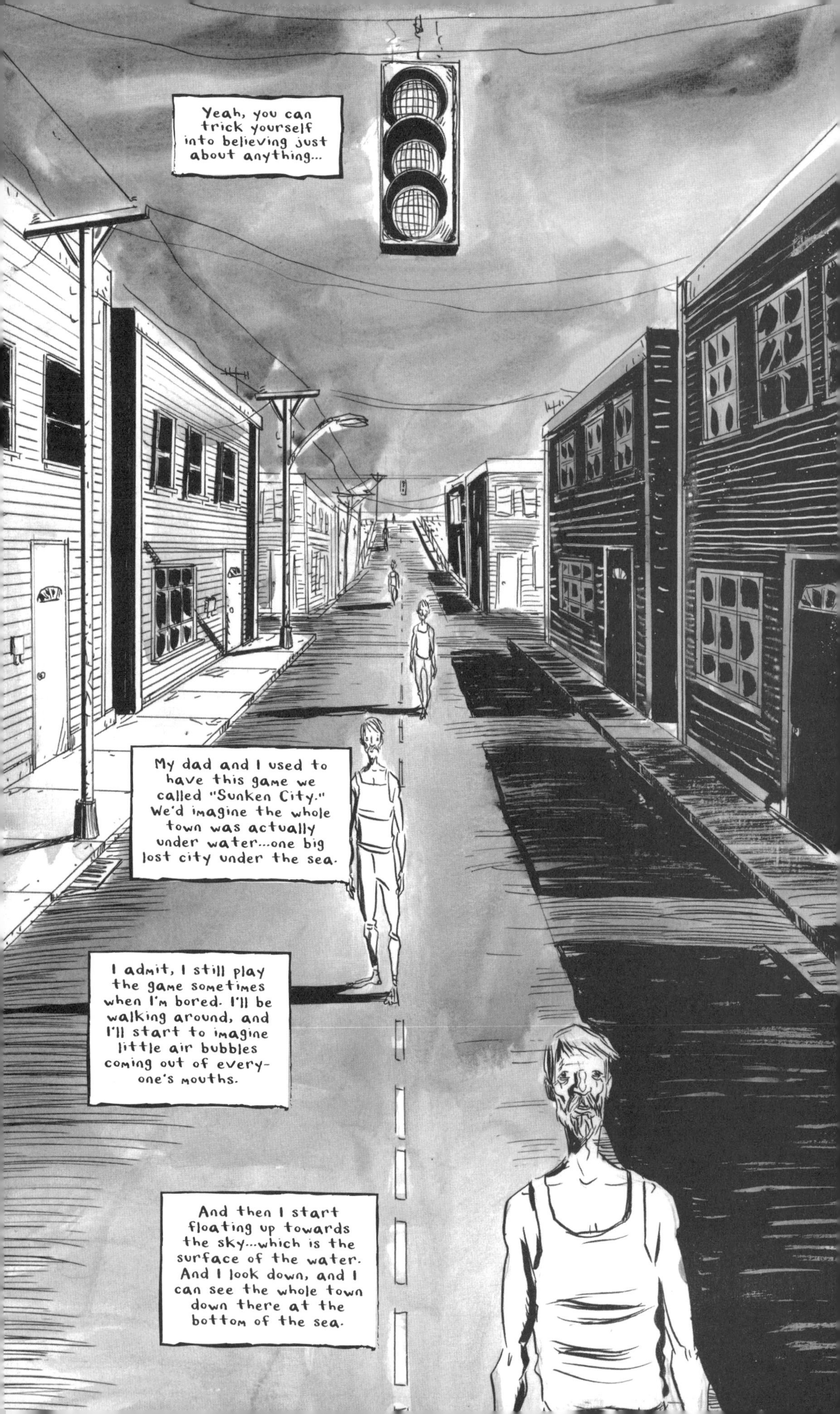
Yeah, you can trick yourself into believing just about anything...
My dad and I used to have this game we called "Sunken City." We'd imagine the whole town was actually under water...one big lost city under the sea.
I admit, I still play the game sometimes when I'm bored. I'll be walking around, and I'll start to imagine little air bubbles coming out of every-one's mouths.
And then I start floating up towards the sky...which is the surface of the water. And I look down, and I can see the whole town down there at the bottom of the sea.

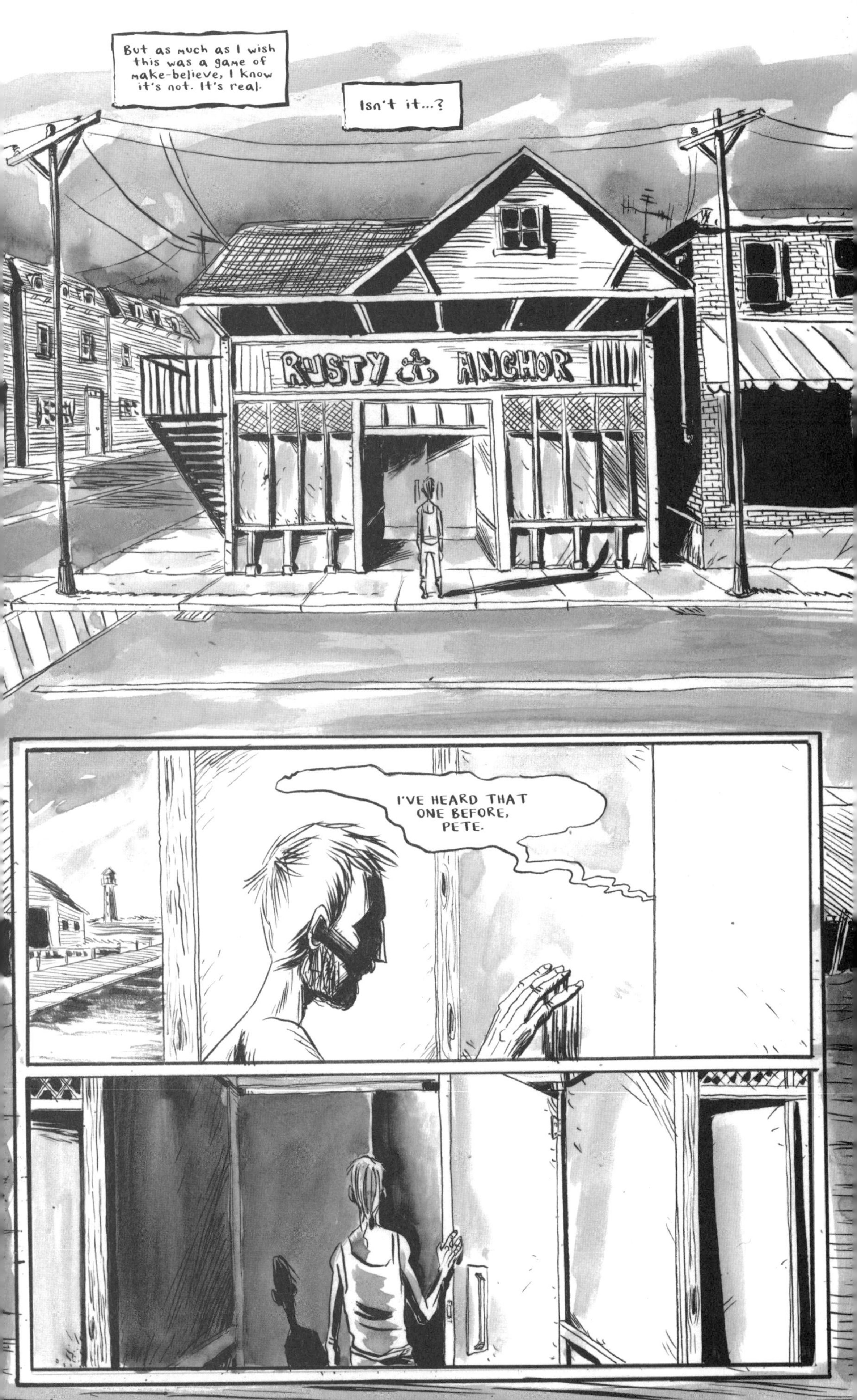
But as much as I wish this was a game of make-believe, I know it's not. It's real.
Isn't it...?
RUSTY ANCHOR
I'VE HEARD THAT ONE BEFORE, PETE.

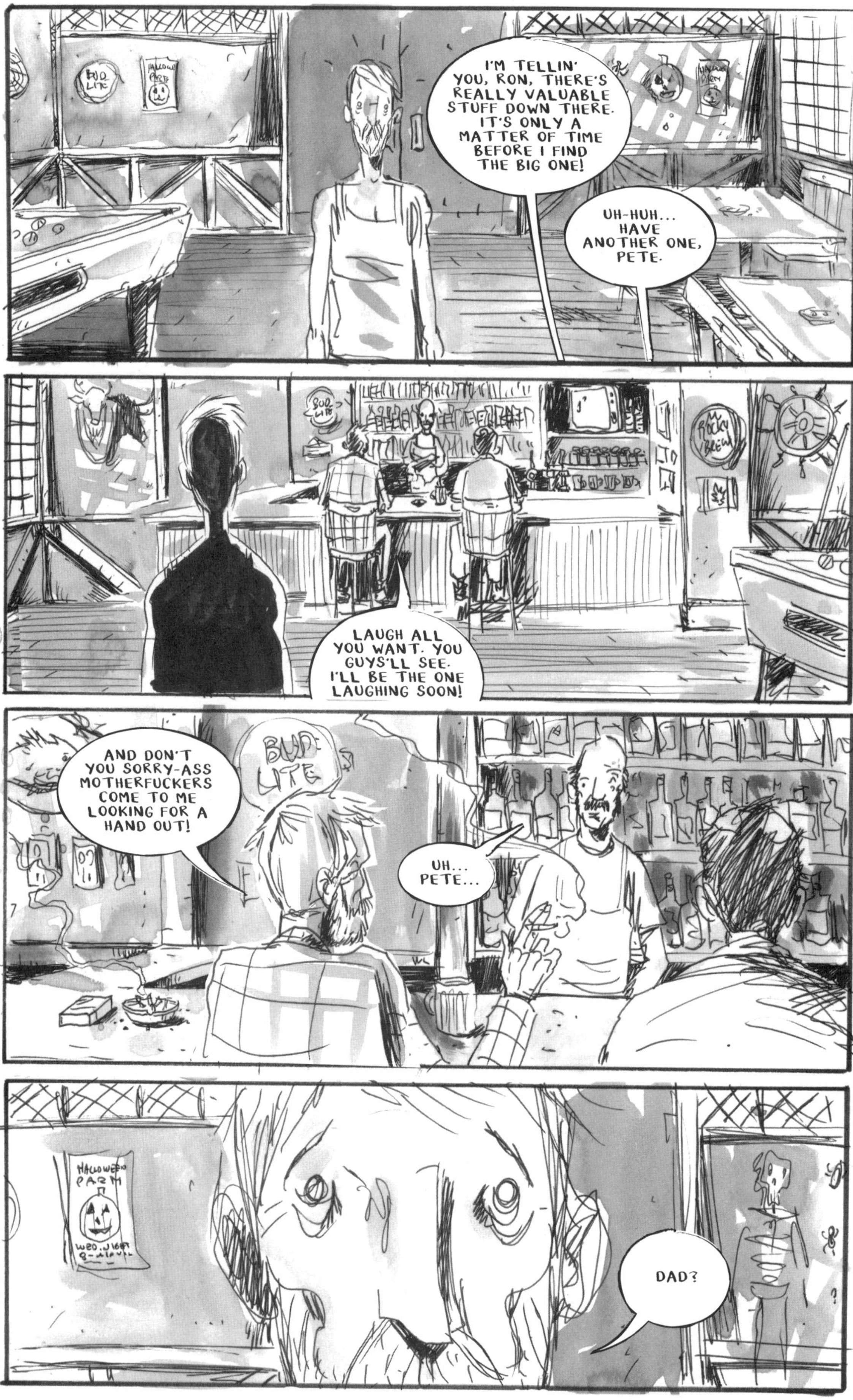
BUD LITE
HALLOWEEN PARTY
I'M TELLIN' YOU, RON, THERE'S REALLY VALUABLE STUFF DOWN THERE. IT'S ONLY A MATTER OF TIME BEFORE I FIND THE BIG ONE!
UH-HUH... HAVE ANOTHER ONE, PETE.
BUD LITE
ROCKY BREW
LAUGH ALL YOU WANT. YOU GUYS'LL SEE. I'LL BE THE ONE LAUGHING SOON!
BUD LITE
AND DON'T YOU SORRY-ASS MOTHERFUCKERS COME TO ME LOOKING FOR A HAND OUT!
UH... PETE...
HALLOWEEN PARTY
DAD?

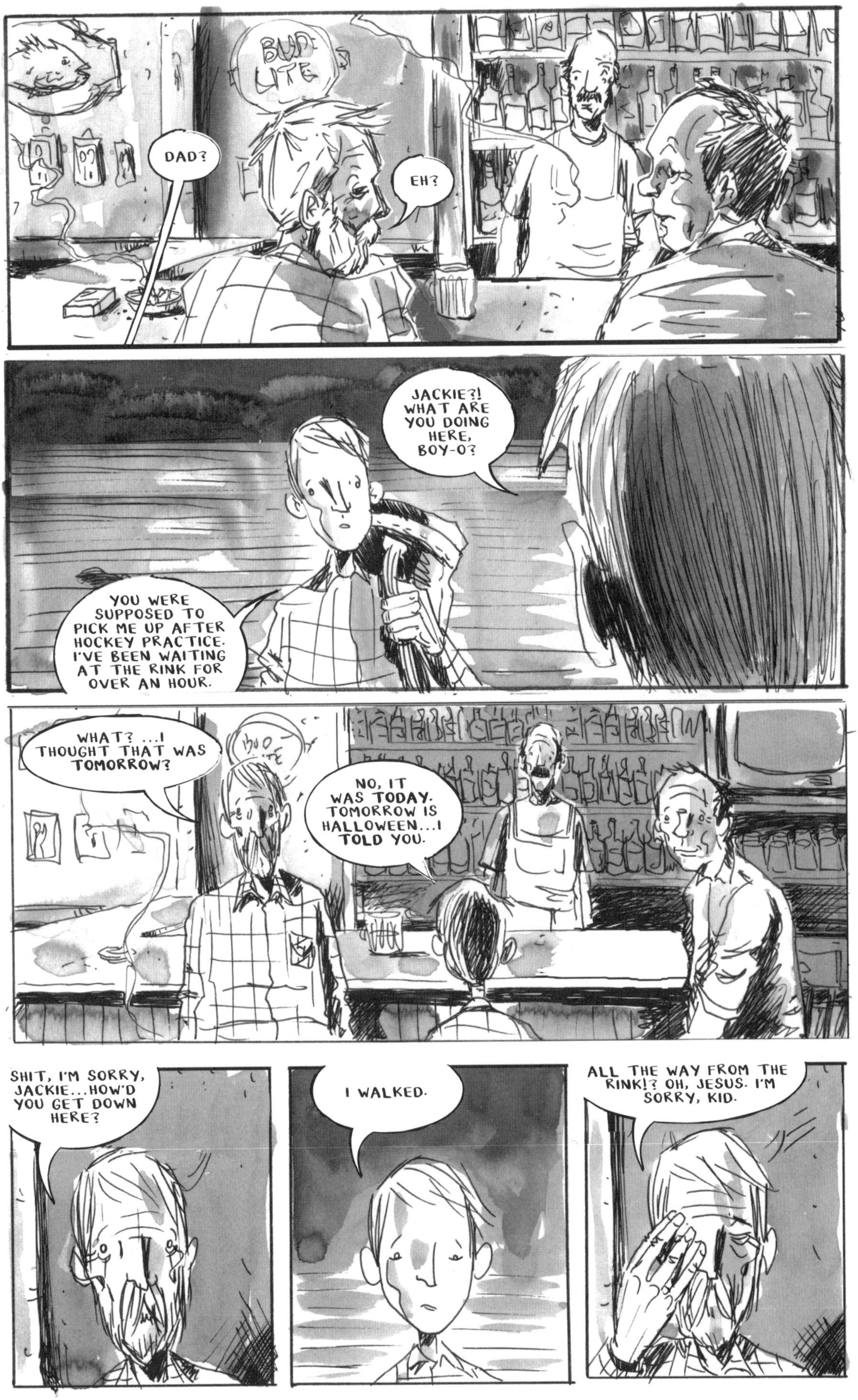
BUD LITE
DAD?
EH?
JACKIE?! WHAT ARE YOU DOING HERE, BOY-O?
YOU WERE SUPPOSED TO PICK ME UP AFTER HOCKEY PRACTICE. I'VE BEEN WAITING AT THE RINK FOR OVER AN HOUR.
WHAT? ...I THOUGHT THAT WAS TOMORROW?
NO, IT WAS TODAY. TOMORROW IS HALLOWEEN...I TOLD YOU.
SHIT, I'M SORRY, JACKIE...HOW'D YOU GET DOWN HERE?
I WALKED.
ALL THE WAY FROM THE RINK!? OH, JESUS. I'M SORRY, KID.

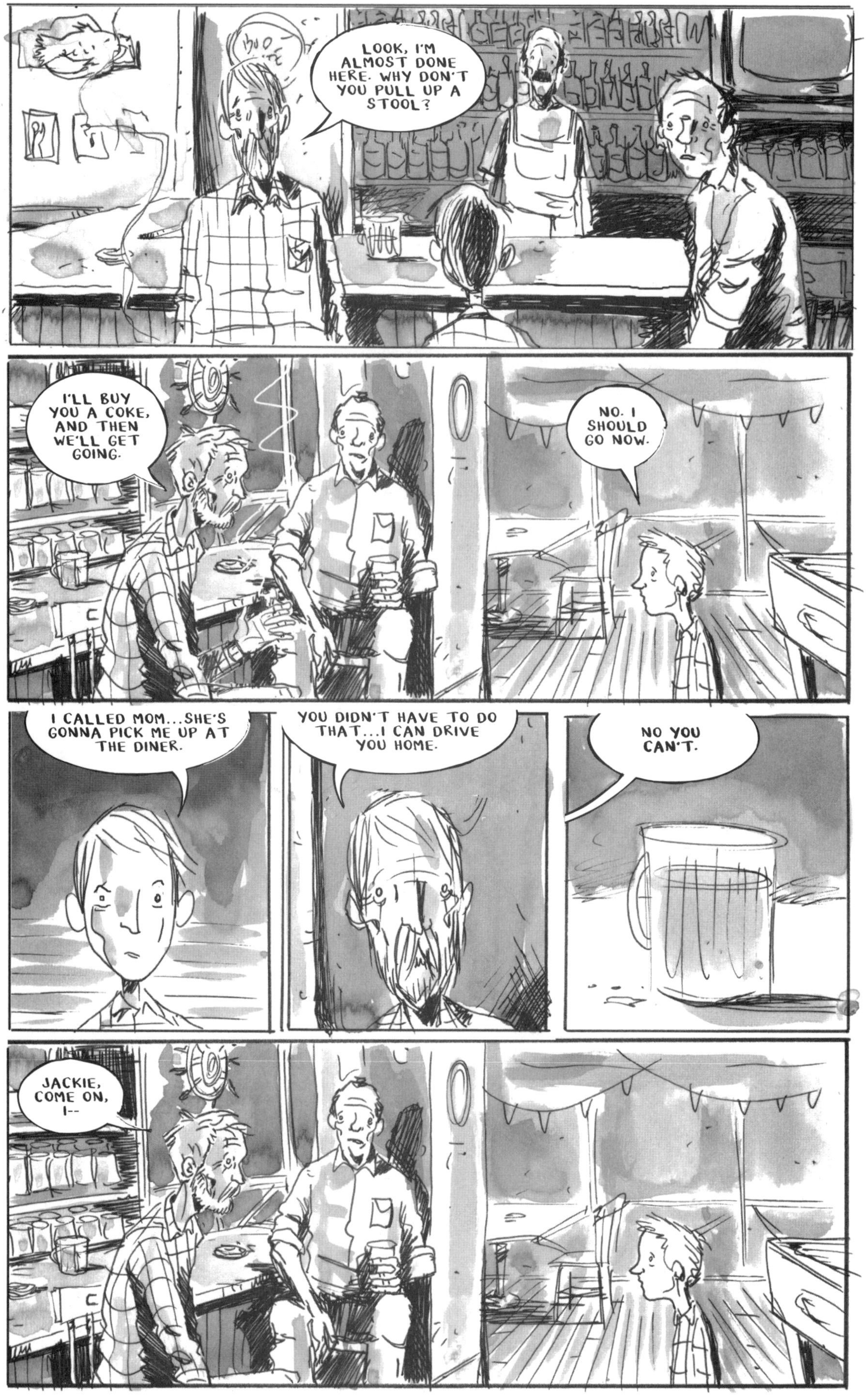
LOOK, I'M ALMOST DONE HERE. WHY DON'T YOU PULL UP A STOOL?
I'LL BUY YOU A COKE, AND THEN WE'LL GET GOING.
NO. I SHOULD GO NOW.
I CALLED MOM...SHE'S GONNA PICK ME UP AT THE DINER.
YOU DIDN'T HAVE TO DO THAT...I CAN DRIVE YOU HOME.
NO YOU CAN'T.
JACKIE, COME ON, I--

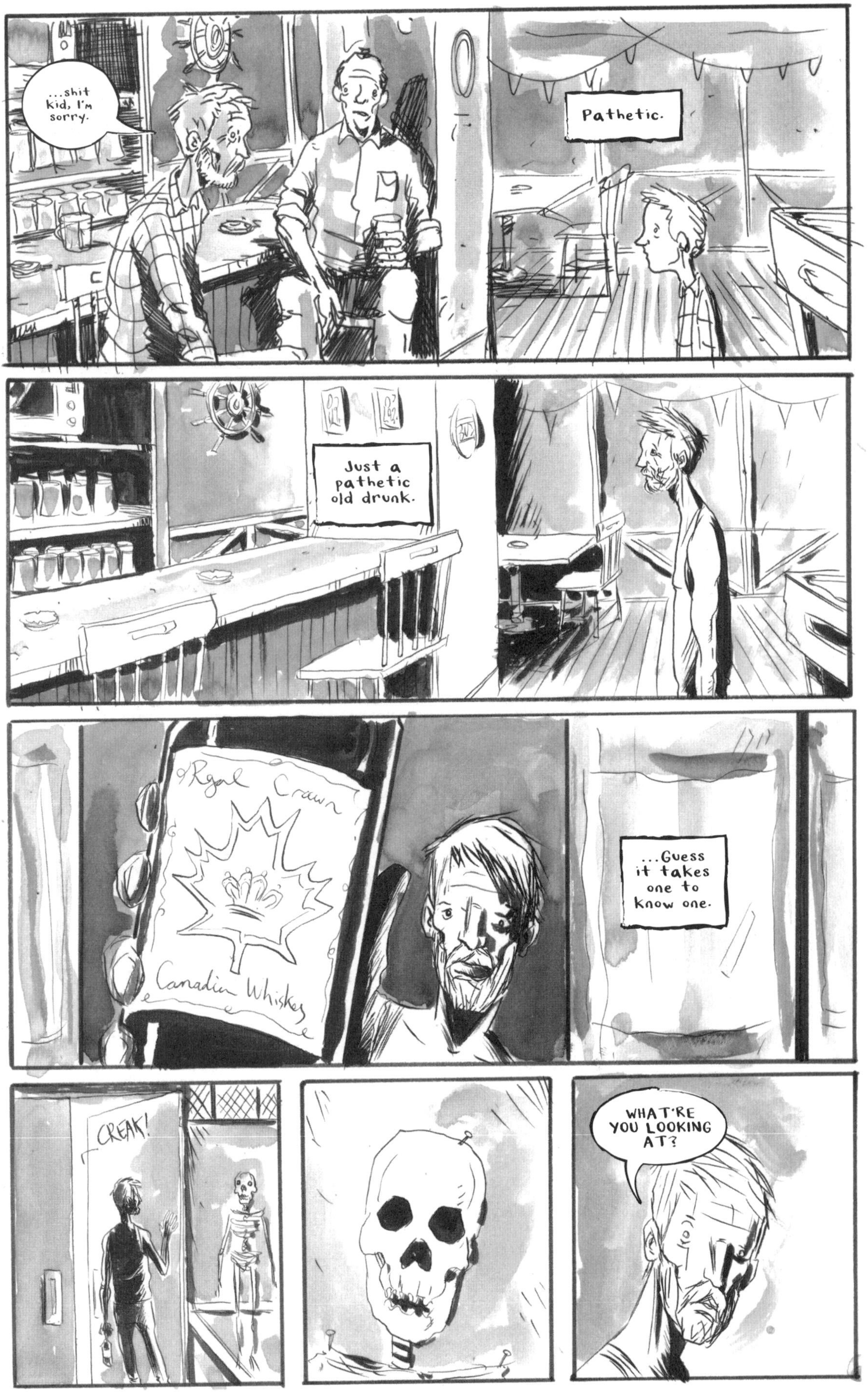
...shit kid, I'm sorry.
Pathetic.
Just a pathetic old drunk.
Regal Crown
Canadian Whiskey
...Guess it takes one to know one.
CREAK!
WHAT'RE YOU LOOKING AT?

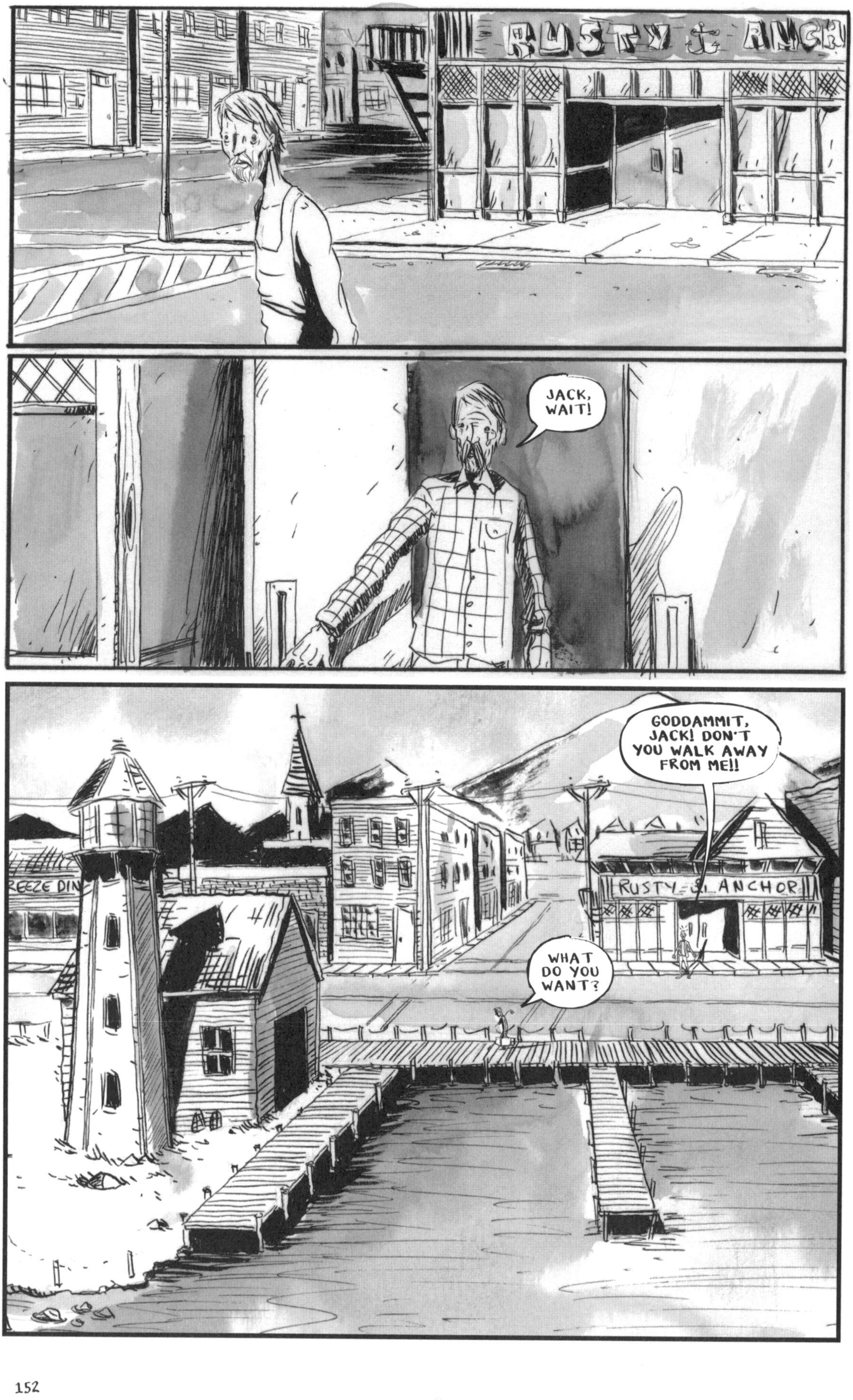
RUSTY ANCH
JACK, WAIT!
GODDAMMIT, JACK! DON'T YOU WALK AWAY FROM ME!!
REEZE DIN
RUSTY ANCHOR
WHAT DO YOU WANT?

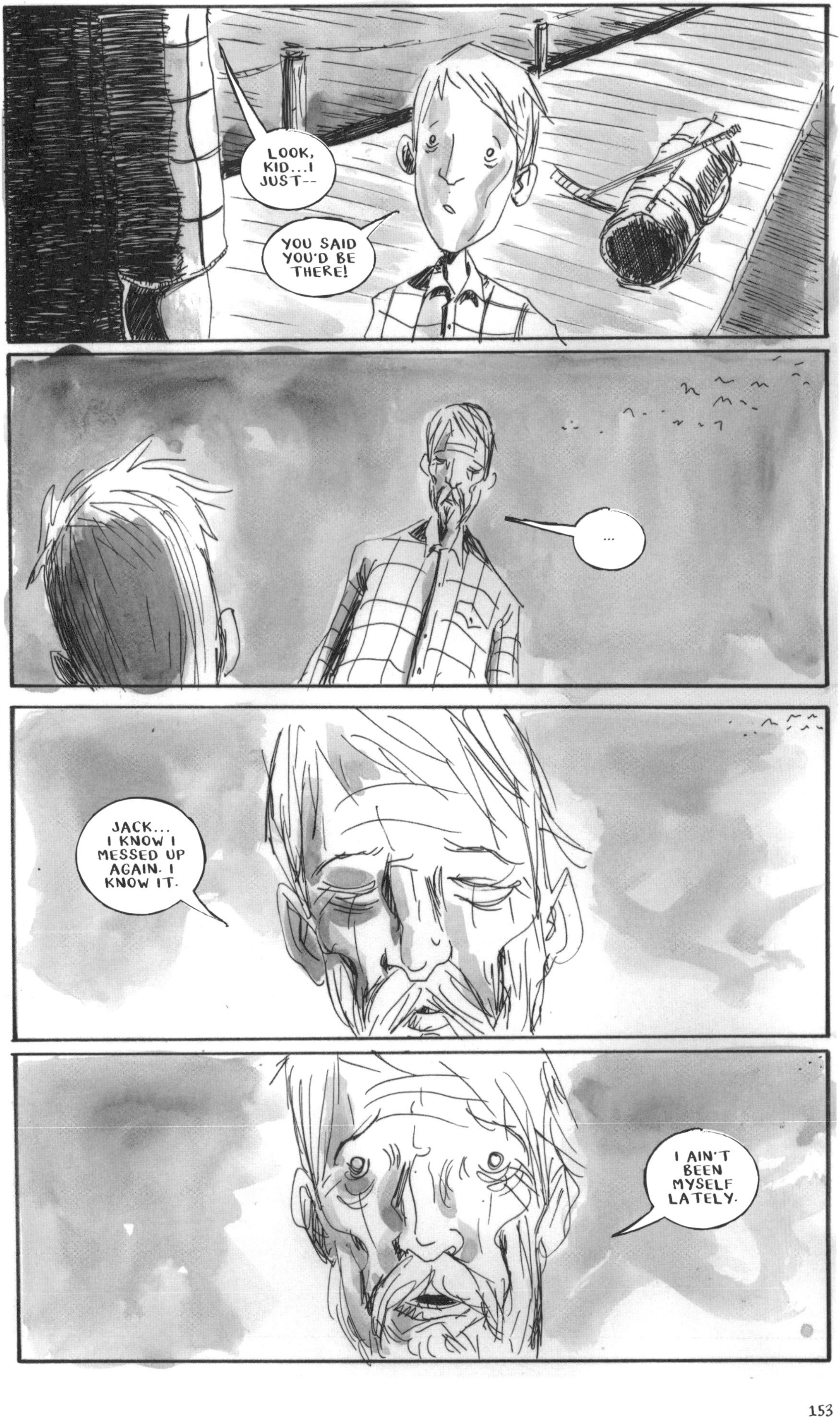
LOOK, KID...I JUST--
YOU SAID YOU'D BE THERE!
...
JACK... I KNOW I MESSED UP AGAIN. I KNOW IT.
I AIN'T BEEN MYSELF LATELY.

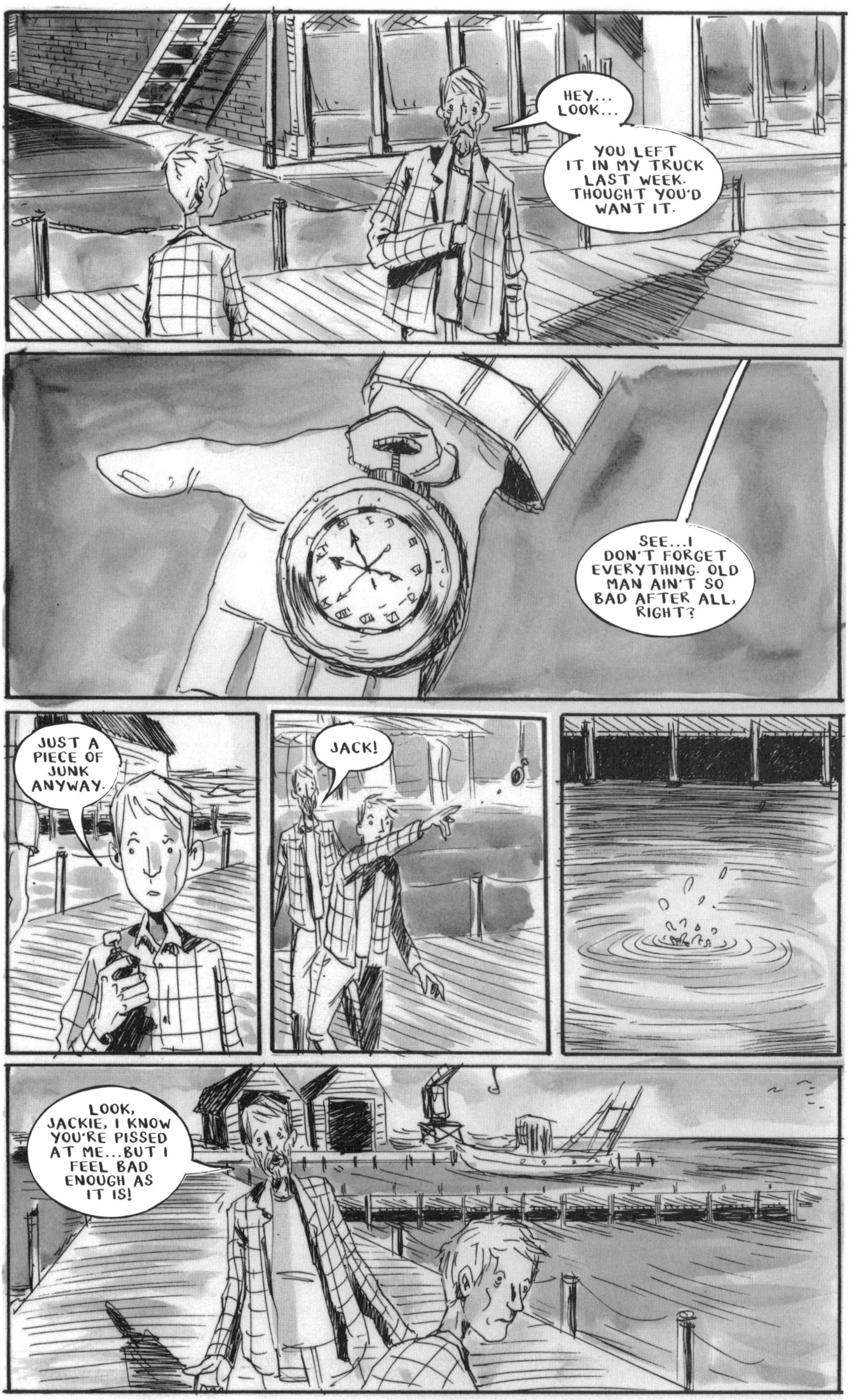
HEY... LOOK...
YOU LEFT IT IN MY TRUCK LAST WEEK. THOUGHT YOU'D WANT IT.
SEE...I DON'T FORGET EVERYTHING. OLD MAN AIN'T SO BAD AFTER ALL, RIGHT?
JUST A PIECE OF JUNK ANYWAY.
JACK!
LOOK, JACKIE, I KNOW YOU'RE PISSED AT ME...BUT I FEEL BAD ENOUGH AS IT IS!

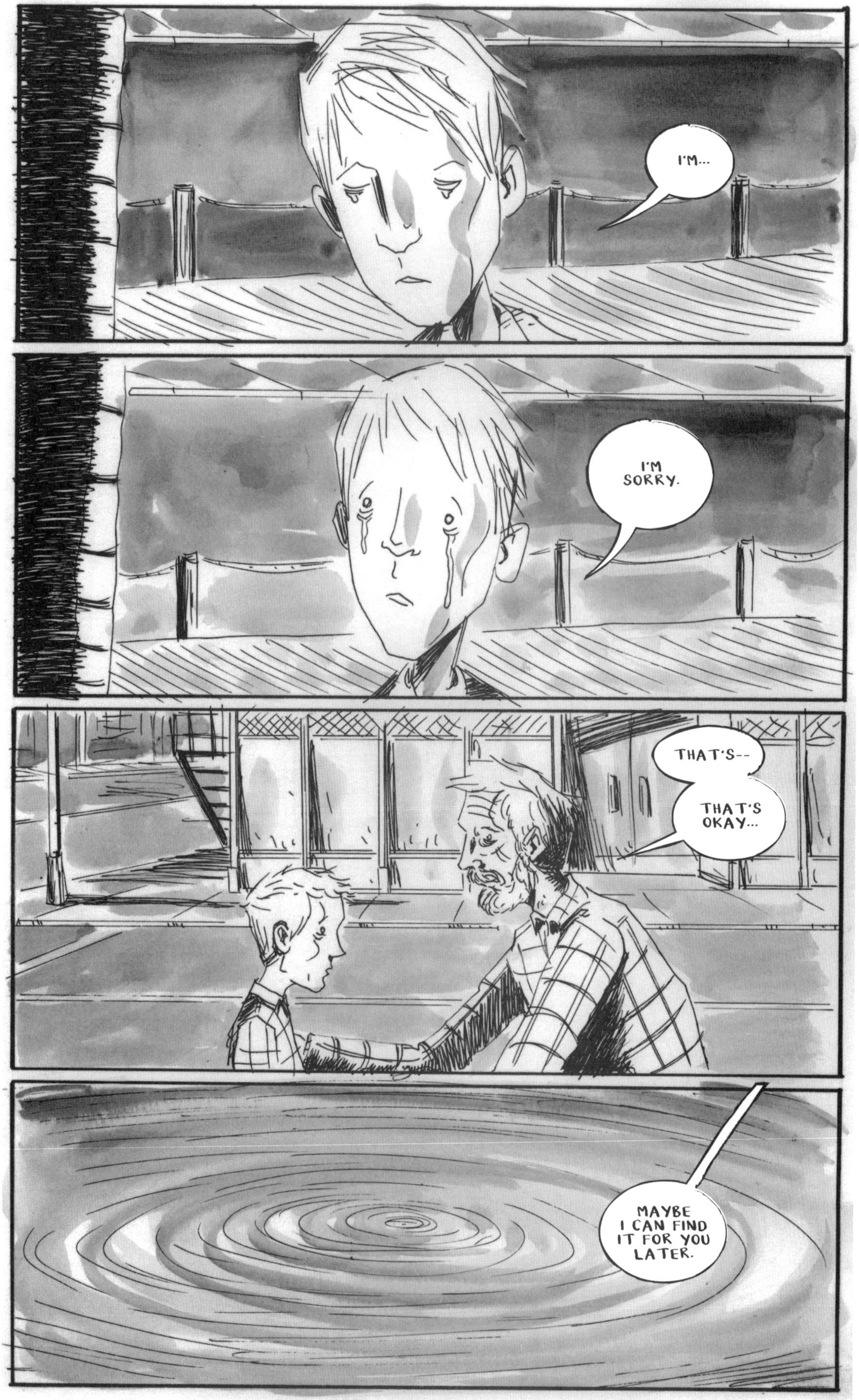
I'M...
I'M SORRY.
THAT'S--
THAT'S OKAY...
MAYBE I CAN FIND IT FOR YOU LATER.

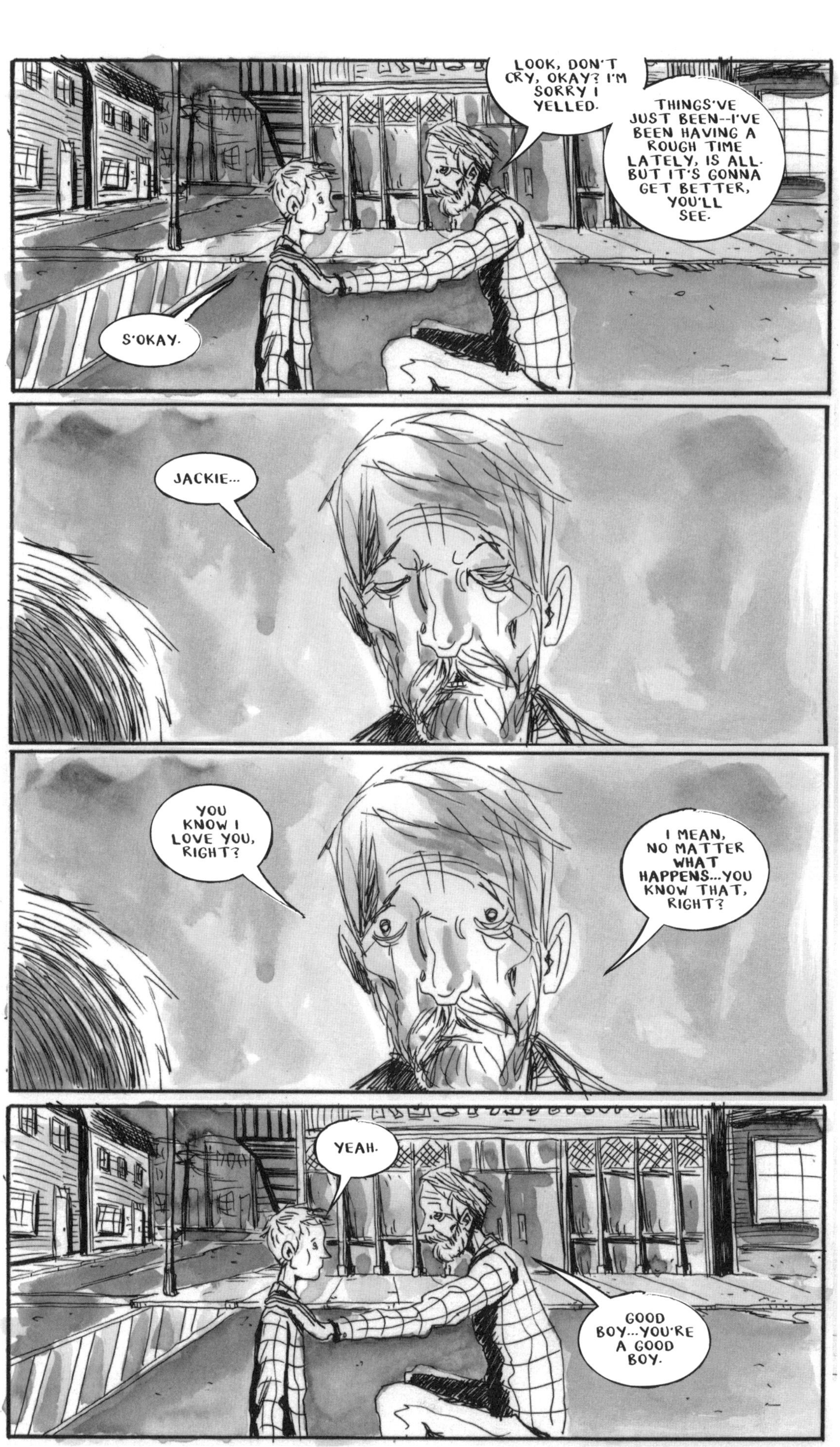
LOOK, DON'T CRY, OKAY? I'M SORRY I YELLED.
THINGS'VE JUST BEEN--I'VE BEEN HAVING A ROUGH TIME LATELY, IS ALL. BUT IT'S GONNA GET BETTER, YOU'LL SEE.
S'OKAY.
JACKIE...
YOU KNOW I LOVE YOU, RIGHT?
I MEAN, NO MATTER WHAT HAPPENS...YOU KNOW THAT, RIGHT?
YEAH.
GOOD BOY...YOU'RE A GOOD BOY.

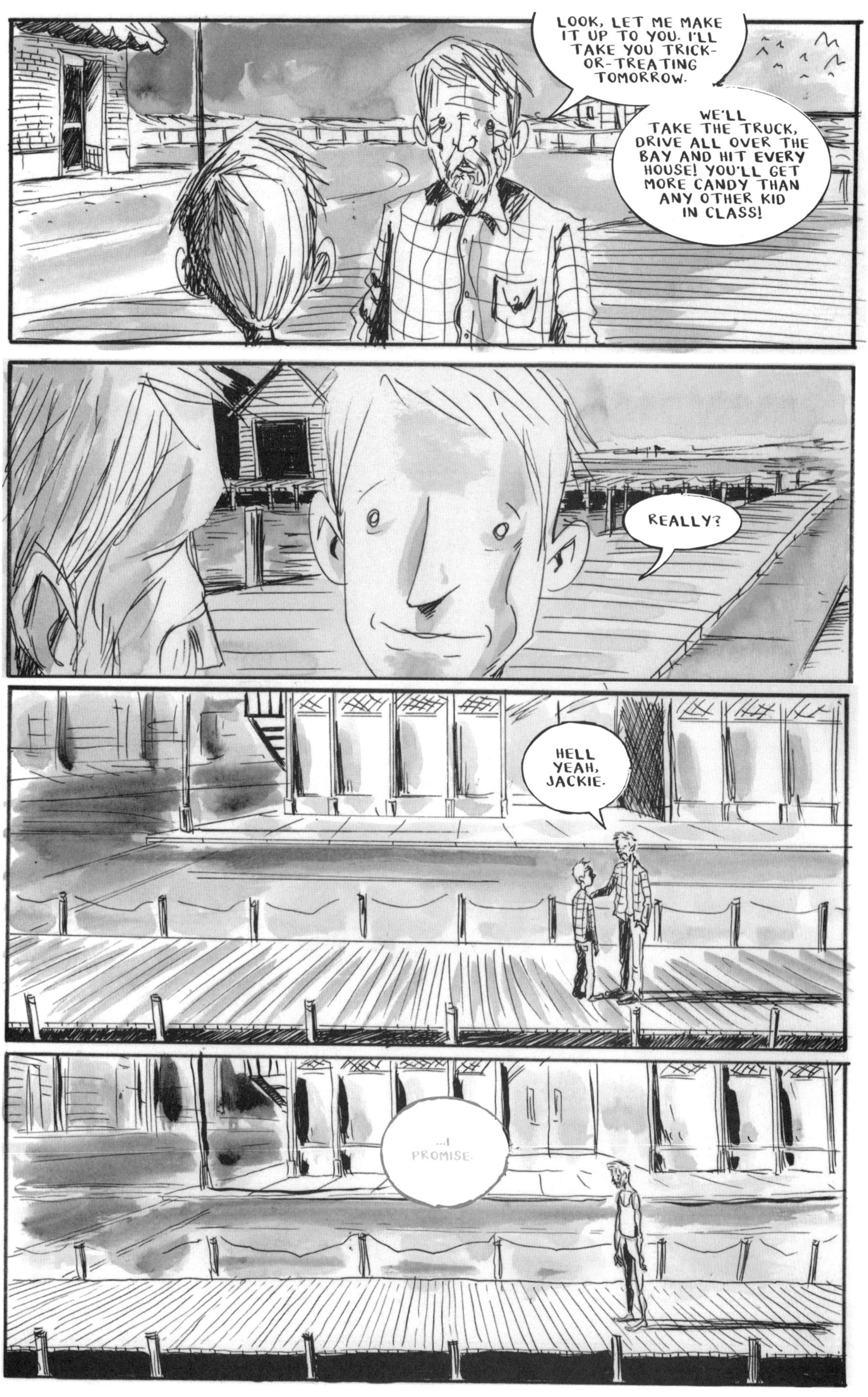
LOOK, LET ME MAKE IT UP TO YOU. I'LL TAKE YOU TRICK-OR-TREATING TOMORROW.
WE'LL TAKE THE TRUCK, DRIVE ALL OVER THE BAY AND HIT EVERY HOUSE! YOU'LL GET MORE CANDY THAN ANY OTHER KID IN CLASS!
REALLY?
HELL YEAH, JACKIE.
...I PROMISE.

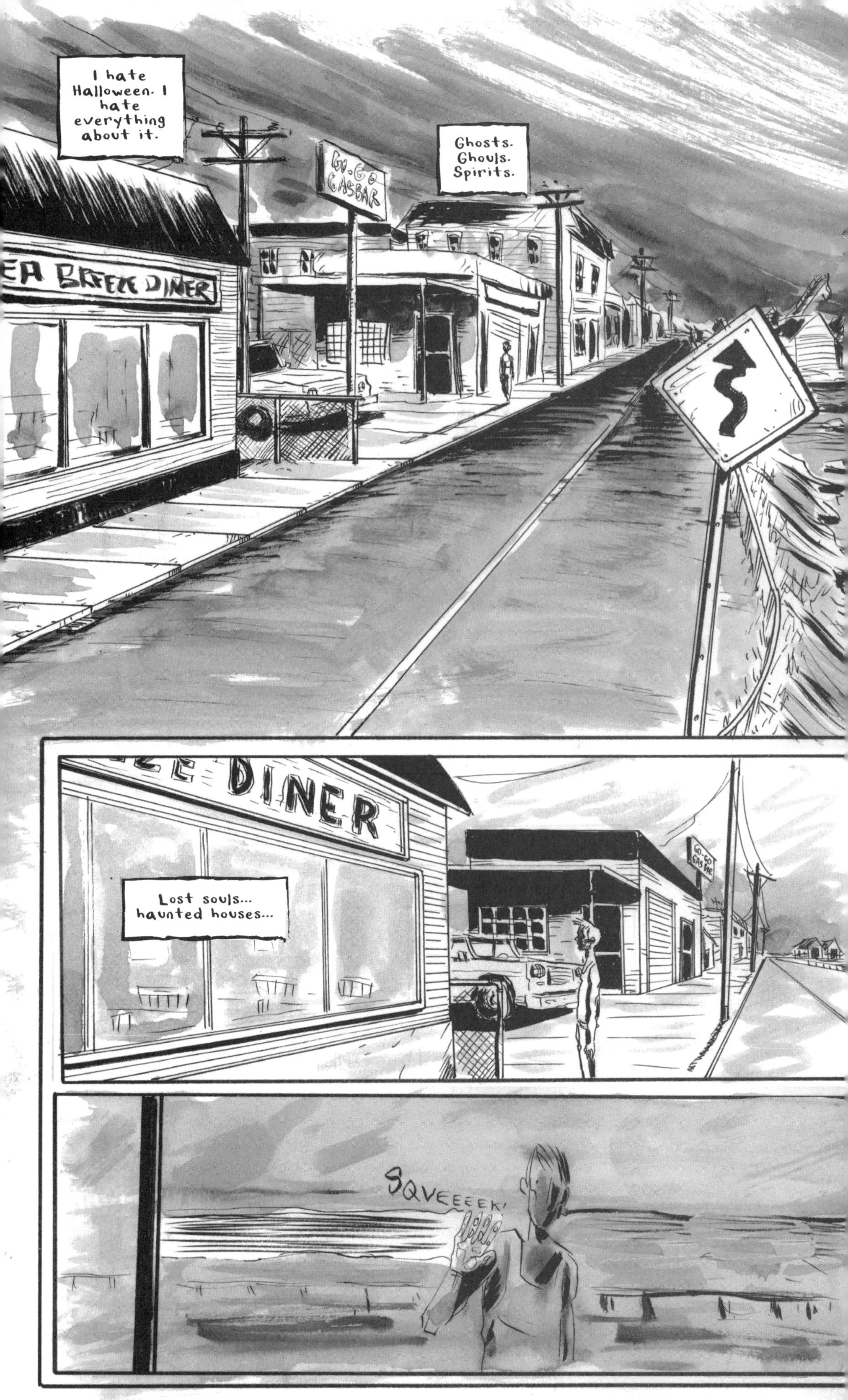
I hate Halloween. I hate everything about it.
GO-GO GASBAR
Ghosts. Ghouls. Spirits.
EA BREEZE DINER
DINER
GO-GO GAS BAR
Lost souls... haunted houses...
SQVEEEEK!

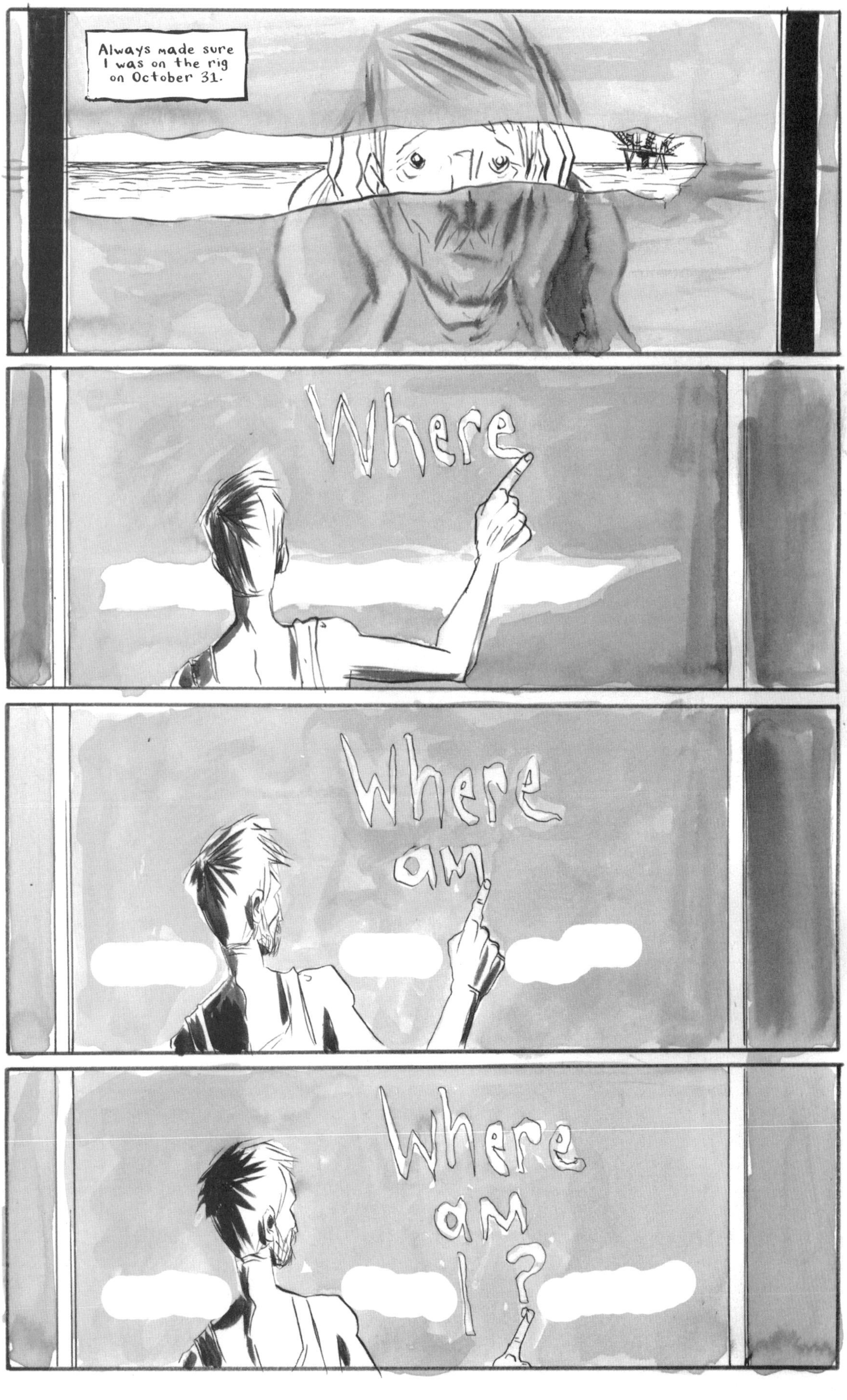
Always made sure I was on the rig on October 31.
Where
Where am
Where am I?

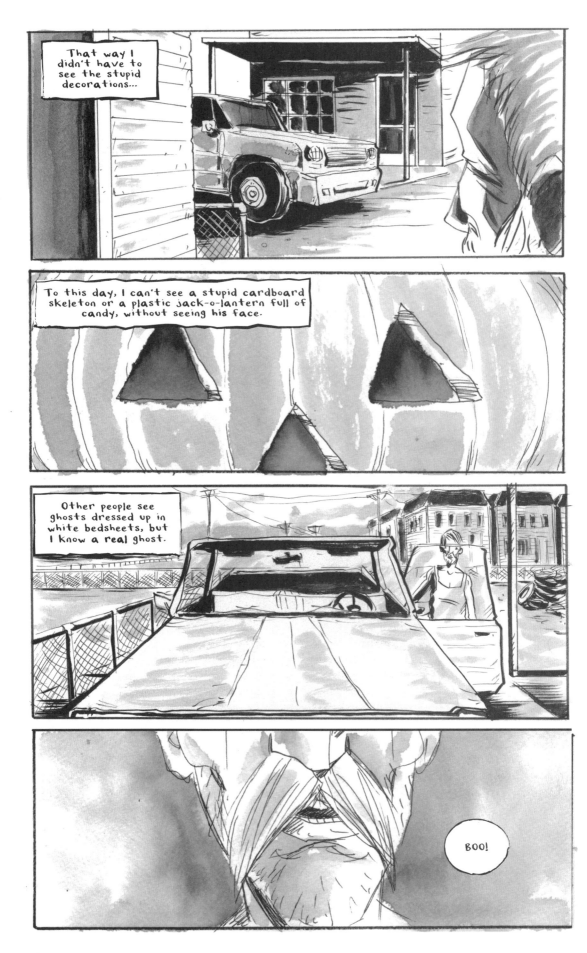

That way I didn't have to see the stupid decorations...

To this day, I can't see a stupid cardboard skeleton or a plastic jack-o-lantern full of candy, without seeing his face.

Other people see ghosts dressed up in white bedsheets, but I know a real ghost.

BOO!

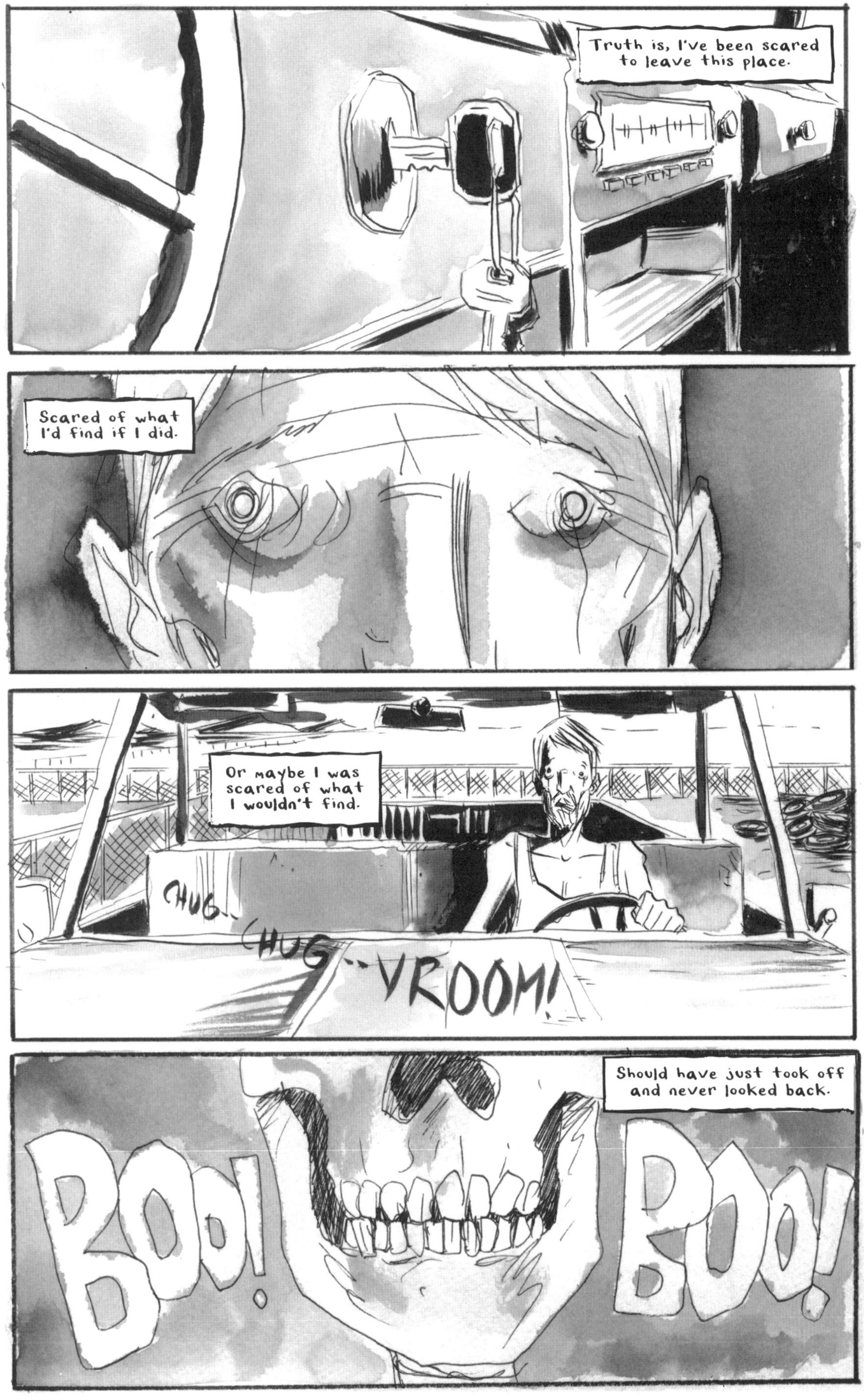
Truth is, I've been scared to leave this place.
Scared of what I'd find if I did.
Or maybe I was scared of what I wouldn't find.
CHUG--
CHUG--VROOM!
Should have just took off and never looked back.
BOOM!
BOOM!

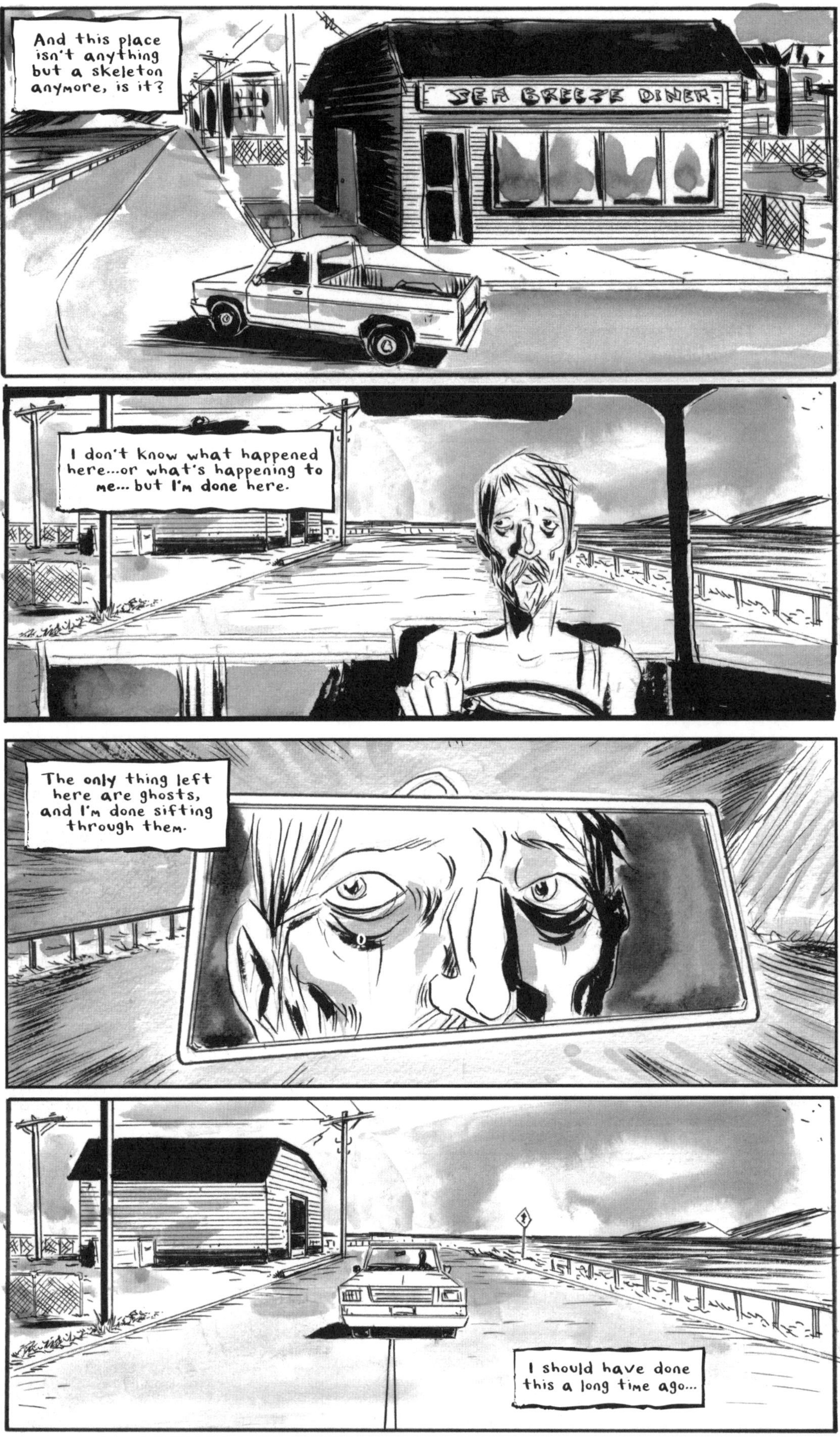
And this place isn't anything but a skeleton anymore, is it?
SEA BREEZE DINER
I don't know what happened here...or what's happening to me... but I'm done here.
The only thing left here are ghosts, and I'm done sifting through them.
I should have done this a long time ago...

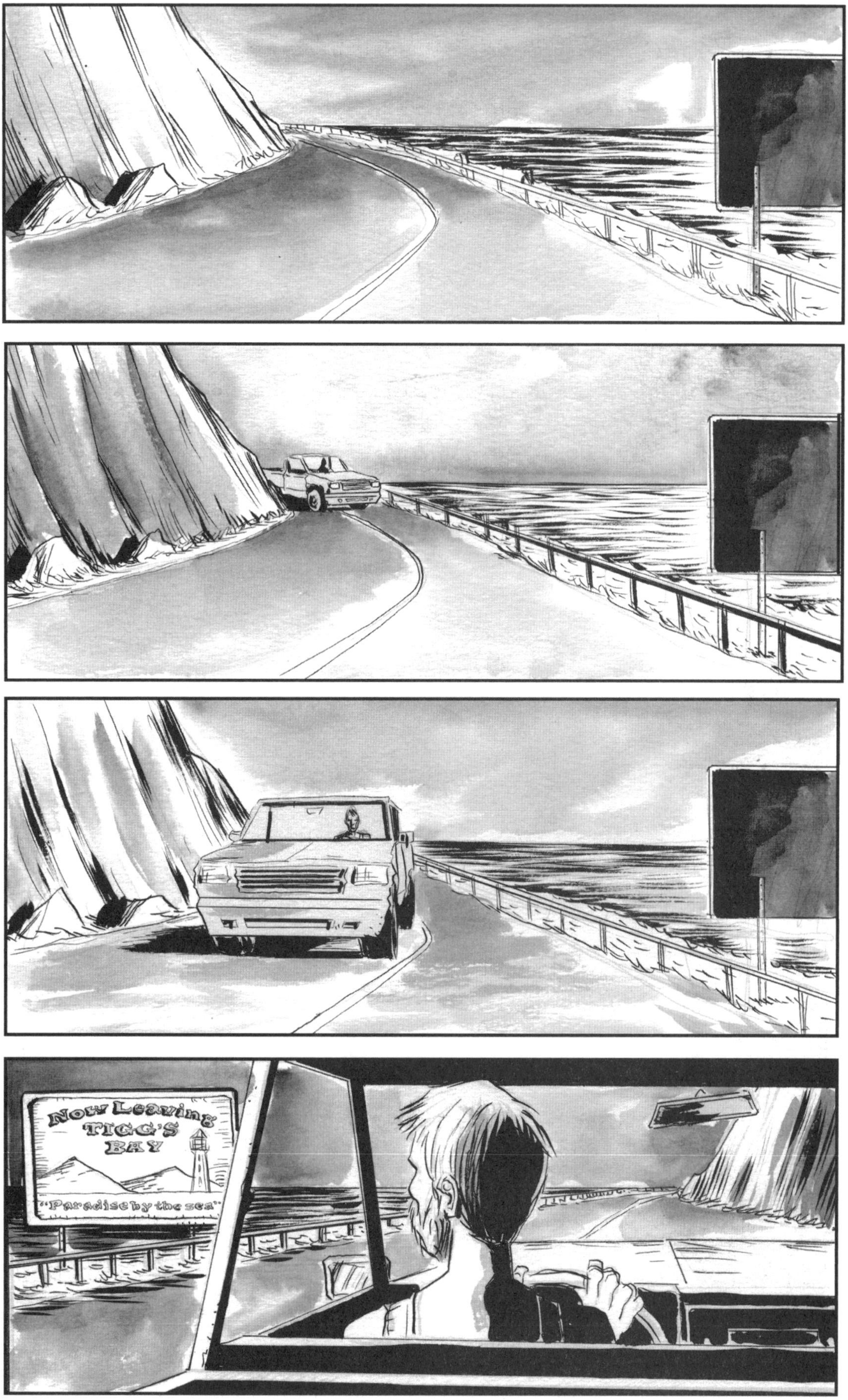
Now Leaving
TIGG'S
BAY
"Paradise by the sea"

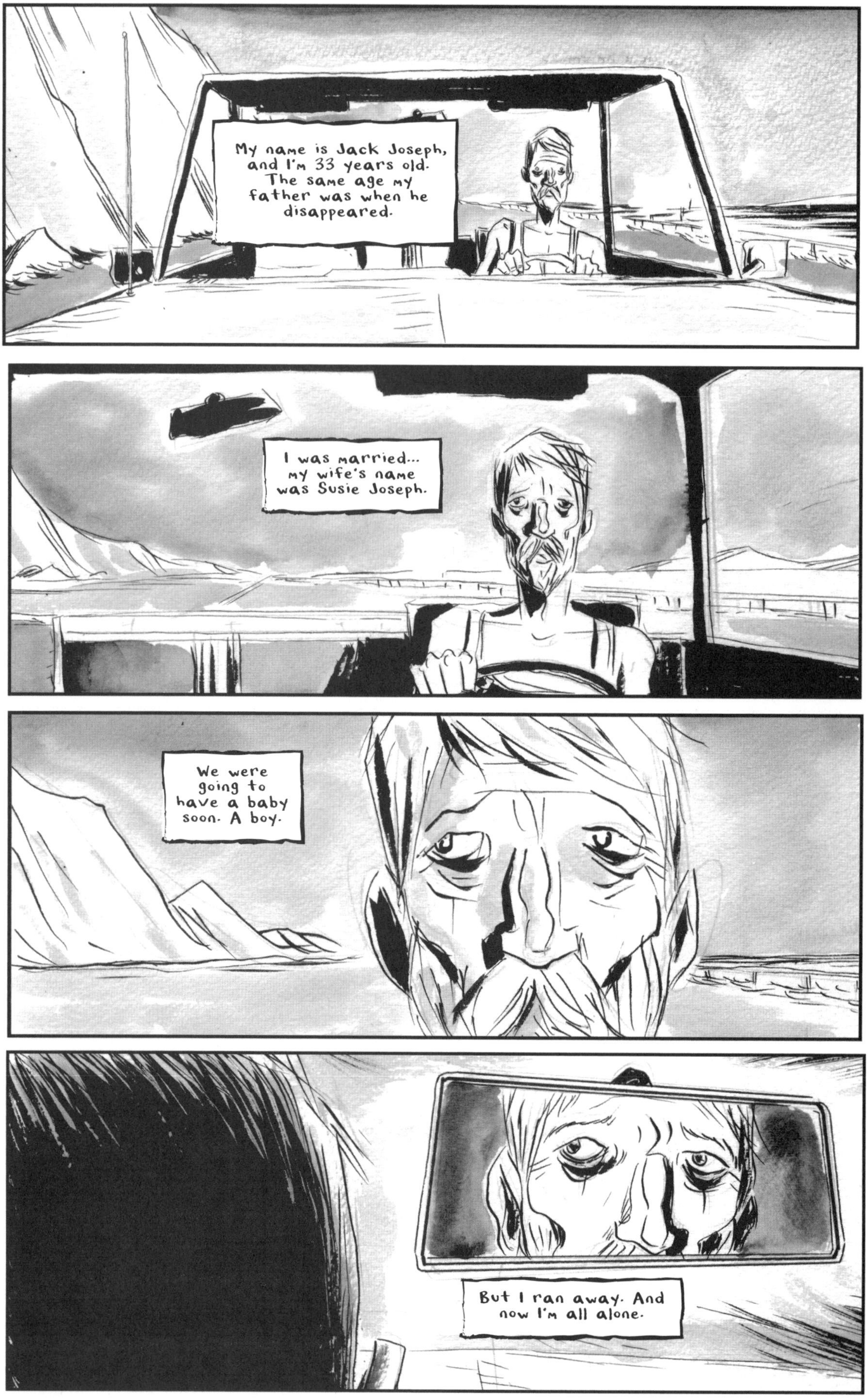
My name is Jack Joseph, and I'm 33 years old. The same age my father was when he disappeared.
I was married... my wife's name was Susie Joseph.
We were going to have a baby soon. A boy.
But I ran away. And now I'm all alone.

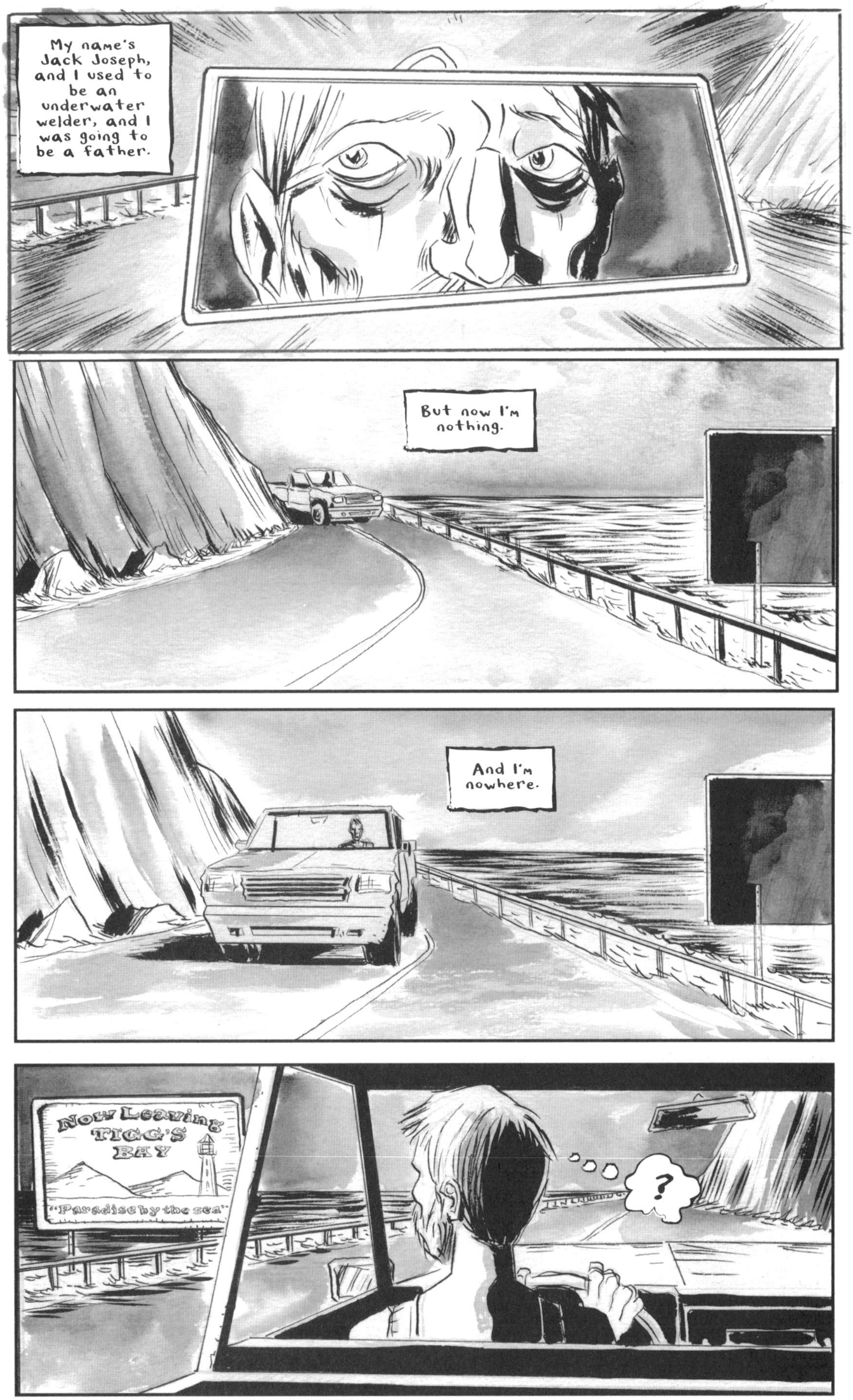
My name's Jack Joseph, and I used to be an underwater welder, and I was going to be a father.
But now I'm nothing.
And I'm nowhere.
Now Leaving TIGG'S BAY
"Paradise by the sea"
?

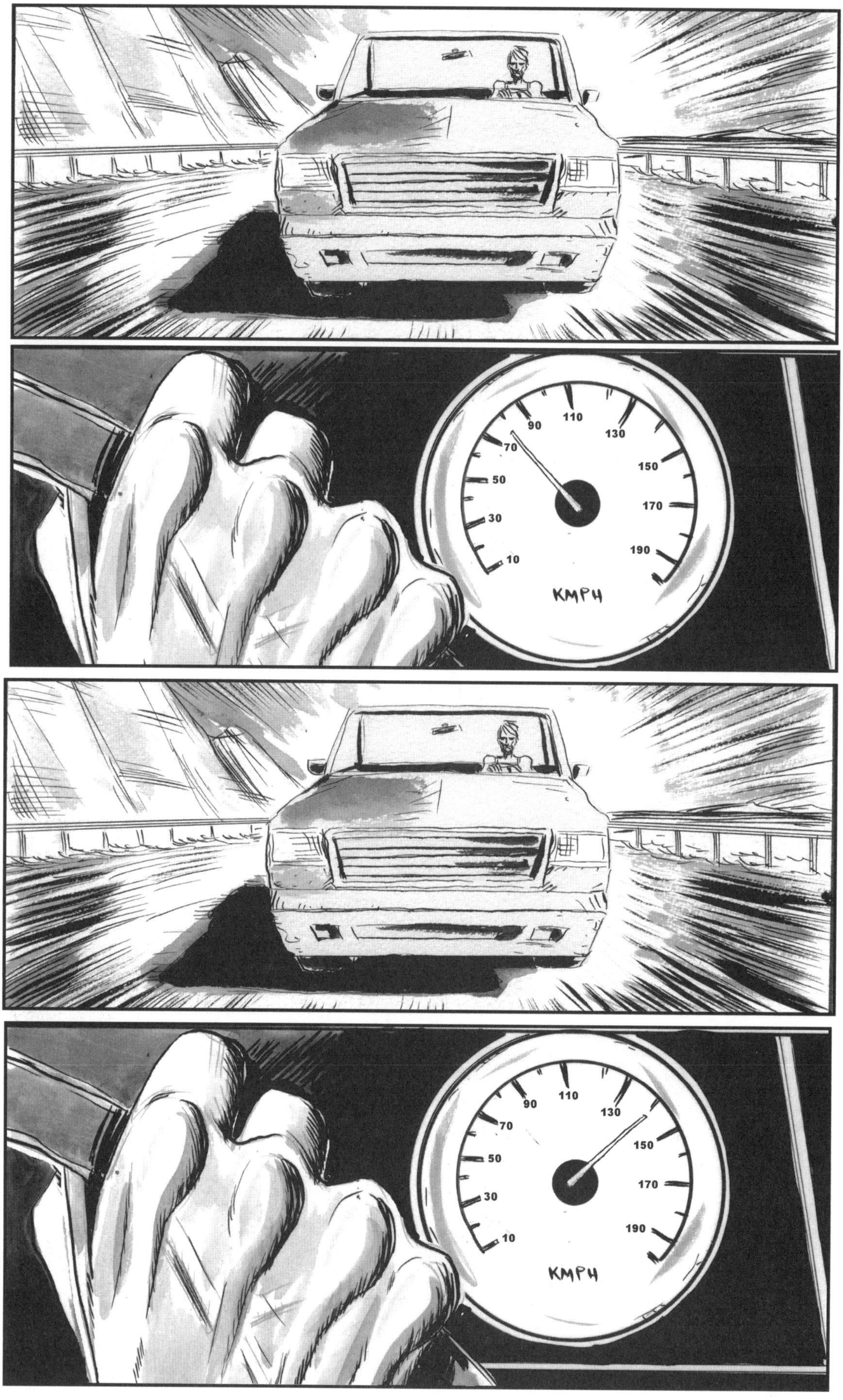
10 30 50 70 90 110 130 150 170 190
KMPH
10 30 50 70 90 110 130 150 170 190
KMPH

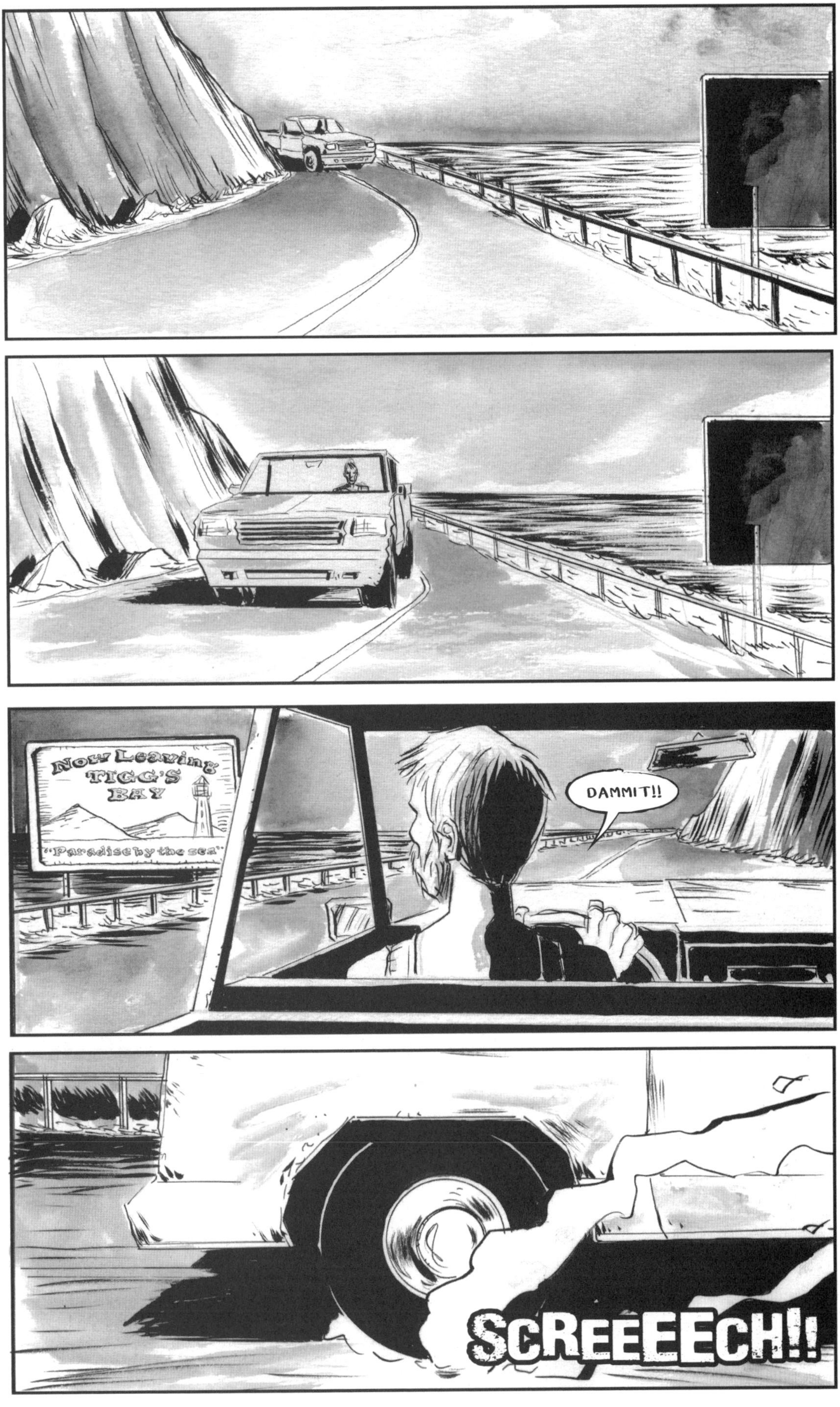
Now Leaving
TIGG'S
BAY
"Paradise by the sea"
DAMMIT!!
SCREEEECH!!

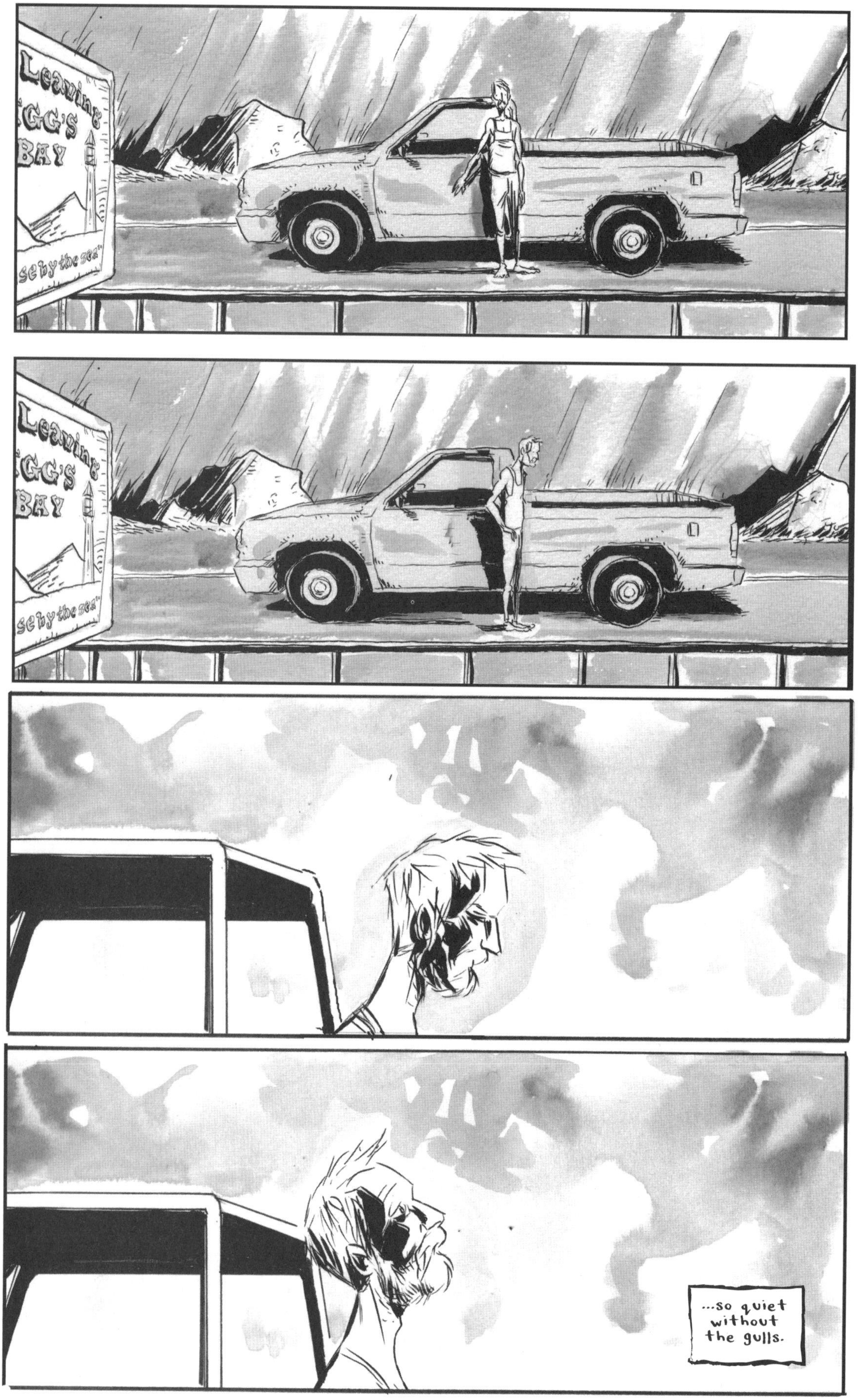
Leaving
GG'S
BAY
se by the sea"
...so quiet without the gulls.

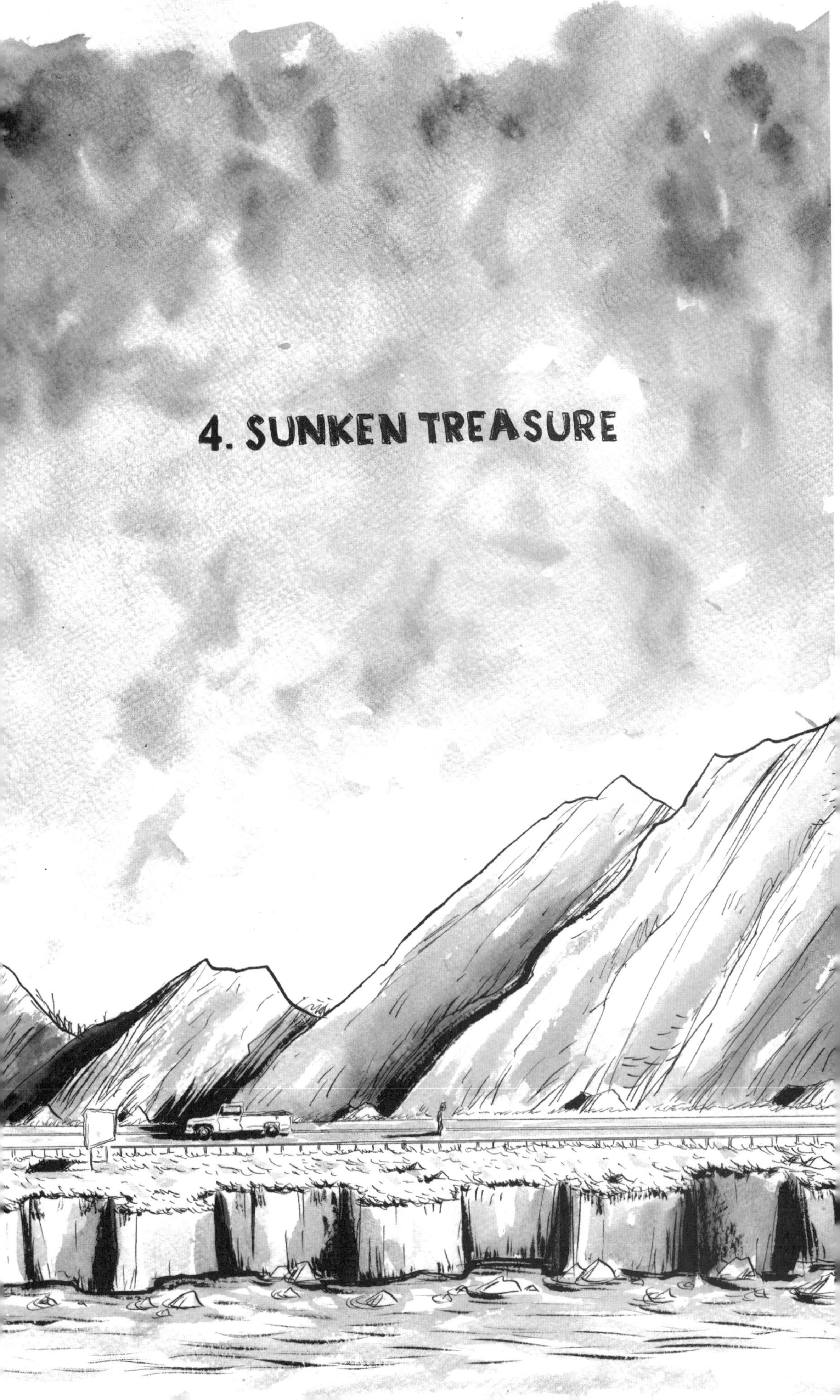
4. SUNKEN TREASURE

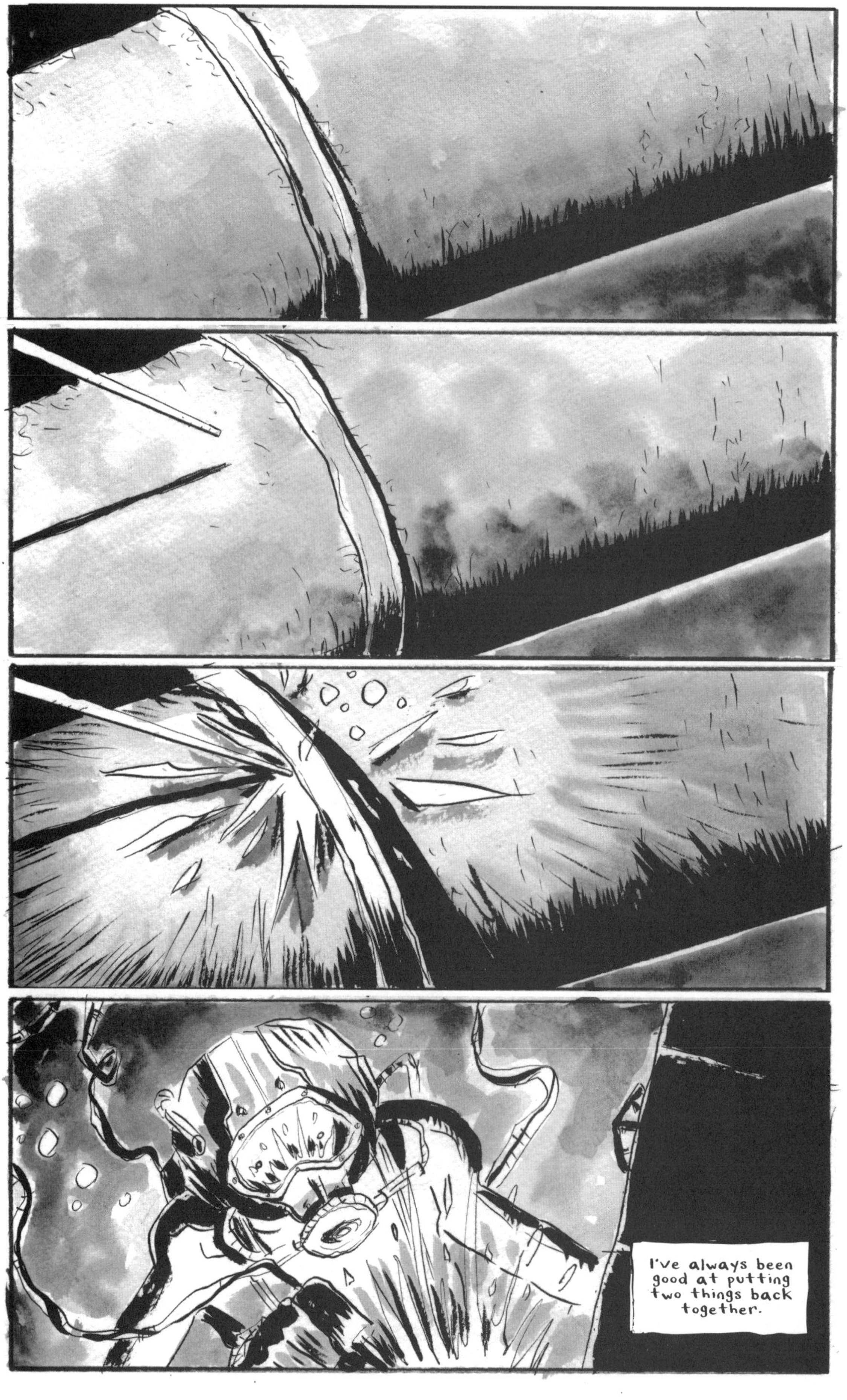
I've always been good at putting two things back together.

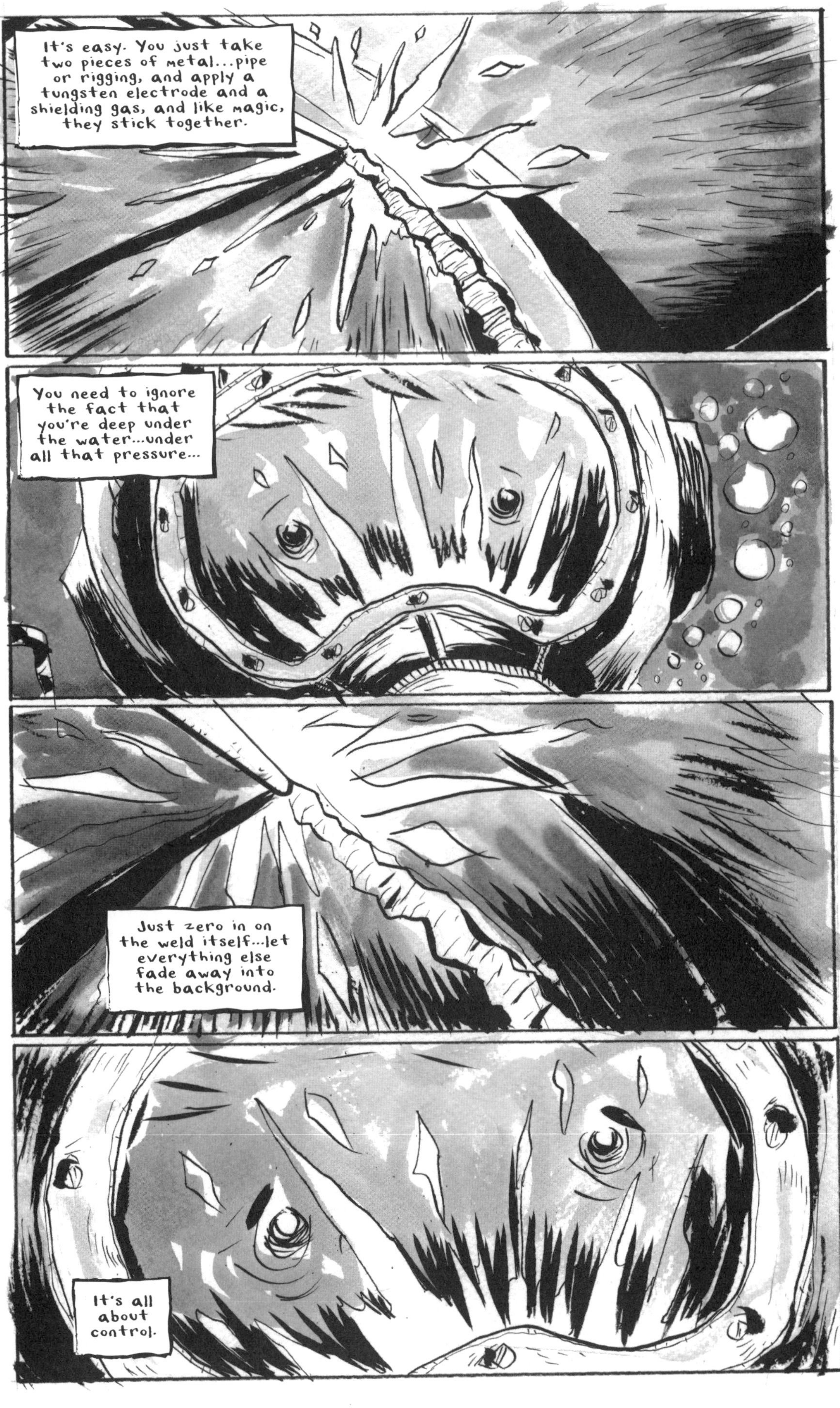
It's easy. You just take two pieces of metal...pipe or rigging, and apply a tungsten electrode and a shielding gas, and like magic, they stick together.
You need to ignore the fact that you're deep under the water...under all that pressure...
Just zero in on the weld itself...let everything else fade away into the background.
It's all about control.

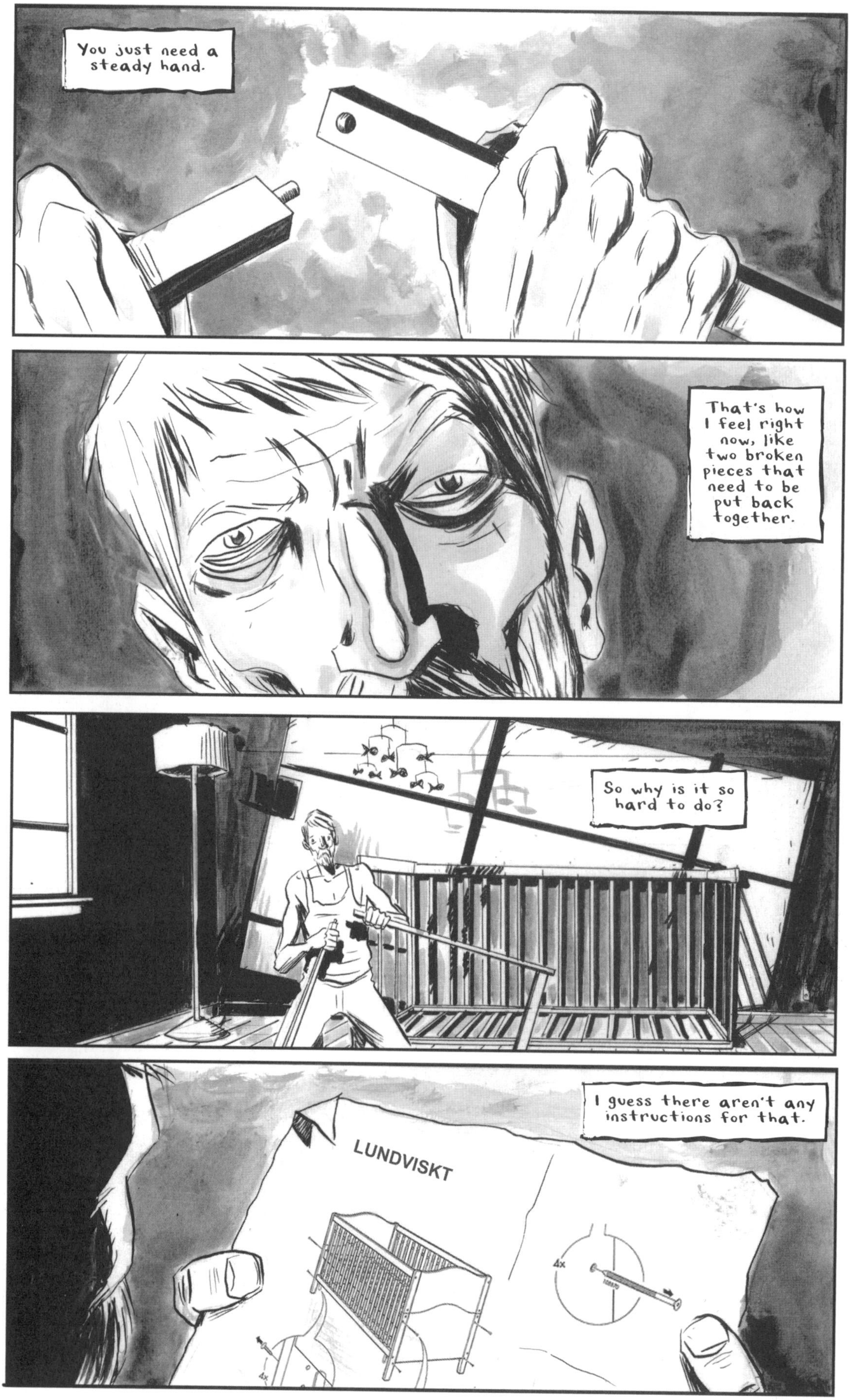
You just need a steady hand.
That's how I feel right now, like two broken pieces that need to be put back together.
So why is it so hard to do?
I guess there aren't any instructions for that.
LUNDVISKT
4x
4x

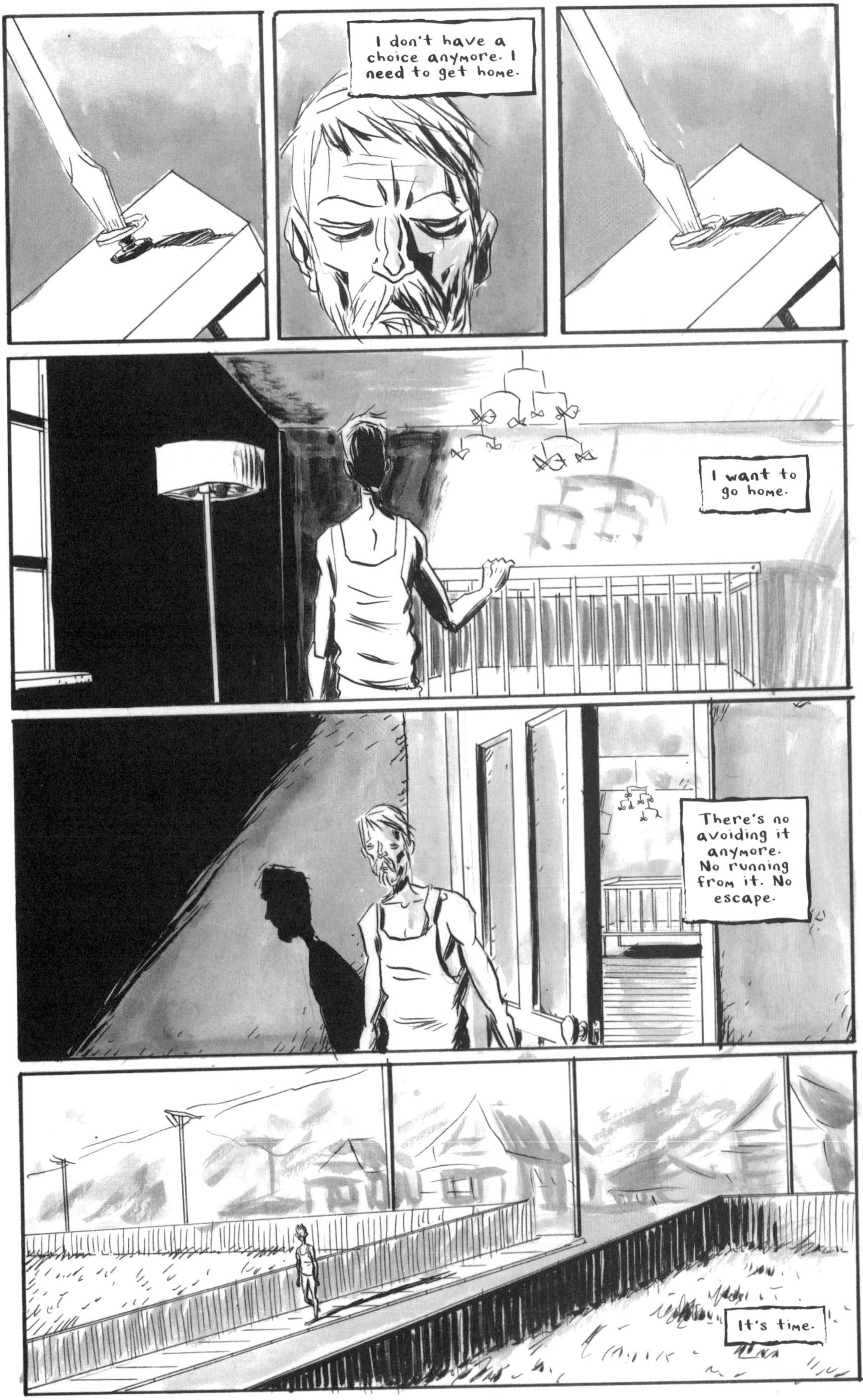
I don't have a choice anymore. I need to get home.
I want to go home.
There's no avoiding it anymore. No running from it. No escape.
It's time.

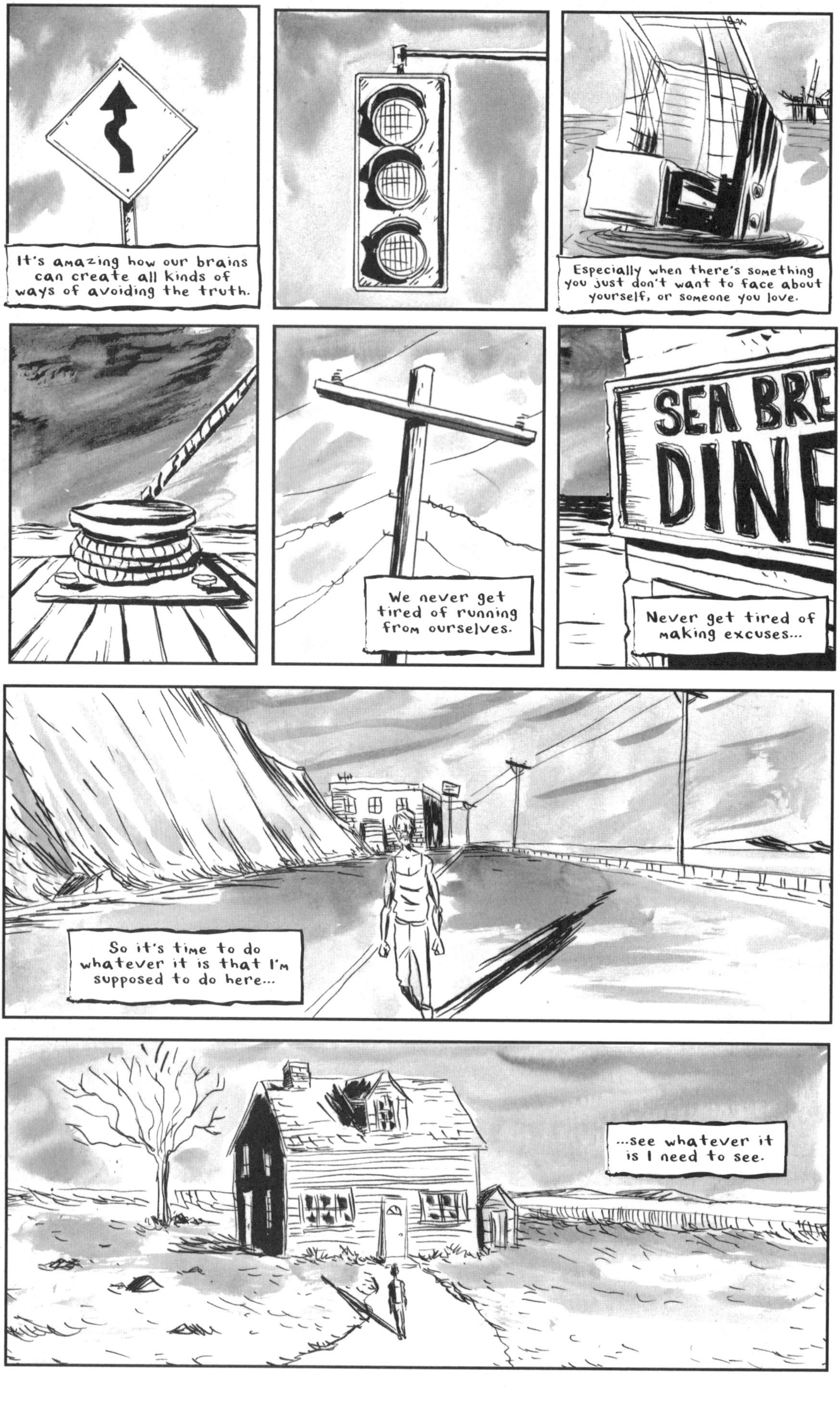
It's amazing how our brains can create all kinds of ways of avoiding the truth.
Especially when there's something you just don't want to face about yourself, or someone you love.
We never get tired of running from ourselves.
SEA BRE
DINE
Never get tired of making excuses...
So it's time to do whatever it is that I'm supposed to do here...
...see whatever it is I need to see.

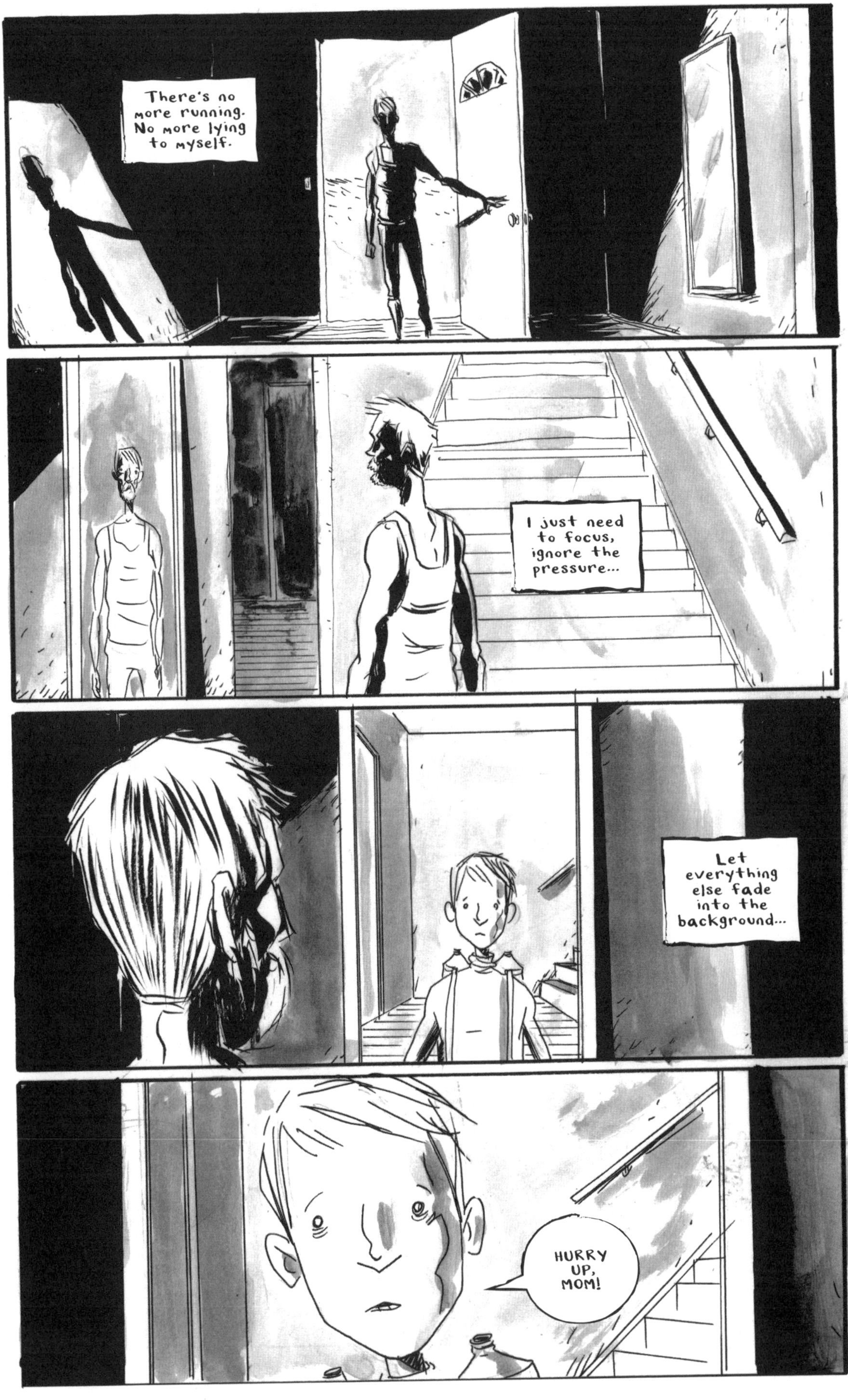
There's no more running. No more lying to myself.
I just need to focus, ignore the pressure...
Let everything else fade into the background...
HURRY UP, MOM!

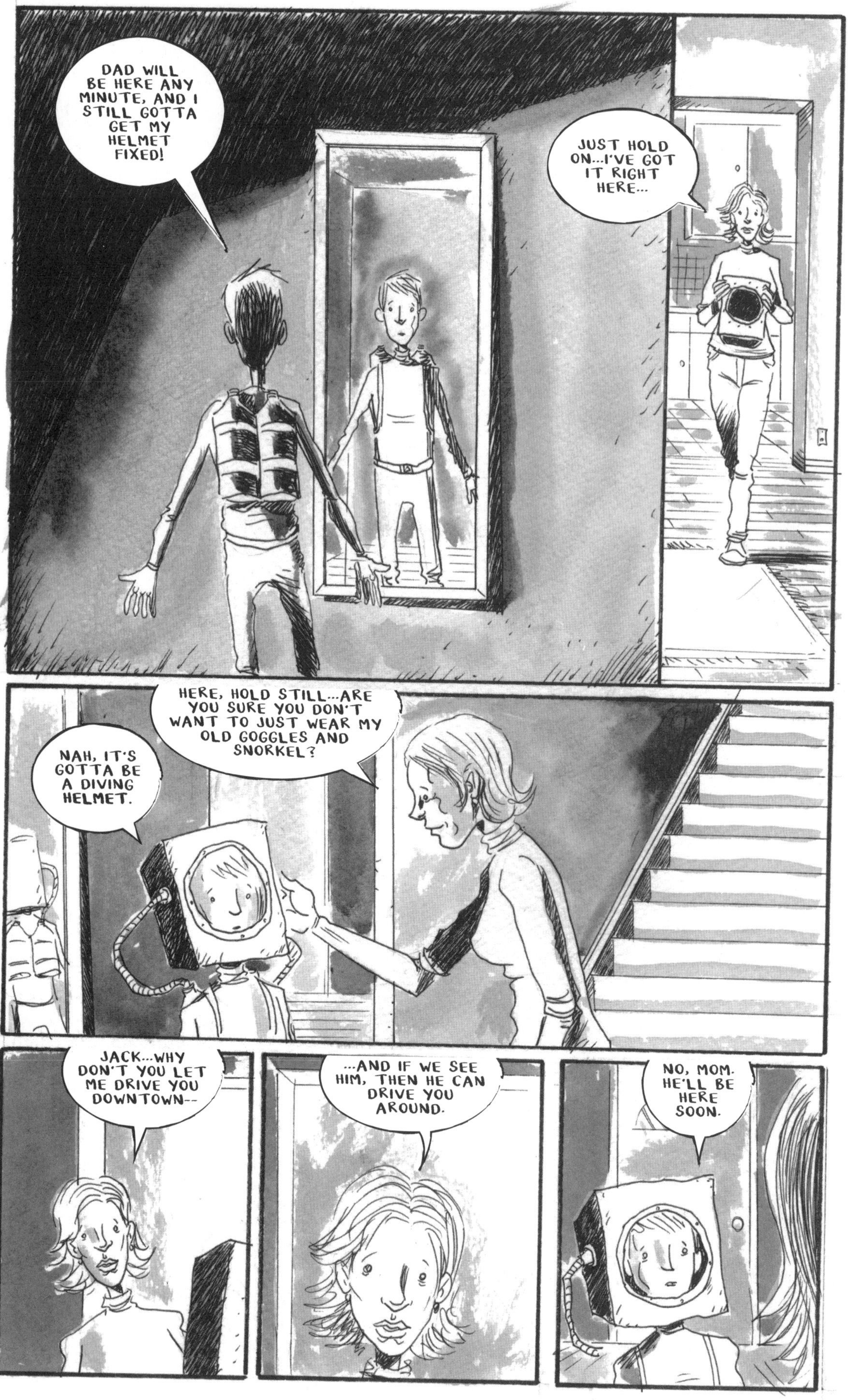
DAD WILL BE HERE ANY MINUTE, AND I STILL GOTTA GET MY HELMET FIXED!
JUST HOLD ON...I'VE GOT IT RIGHT HERE...
HERE, HOLD STILL...ARE YOU SURE YOU DON'T WANT TO JUST WEAR MY OLD GOGGLES AND SNORKEL?
NAH, IT'S GOTTA BE A DIVING HELMET.
JACK...WHY DON'T YOU LET ME DRIVE YOU DOWNTOWN--
...AND IF WE SEE HIM, THEN HE CAN DRIVE YOU AROUND.
NO, MOM. HE'LL BE HERE SOON.

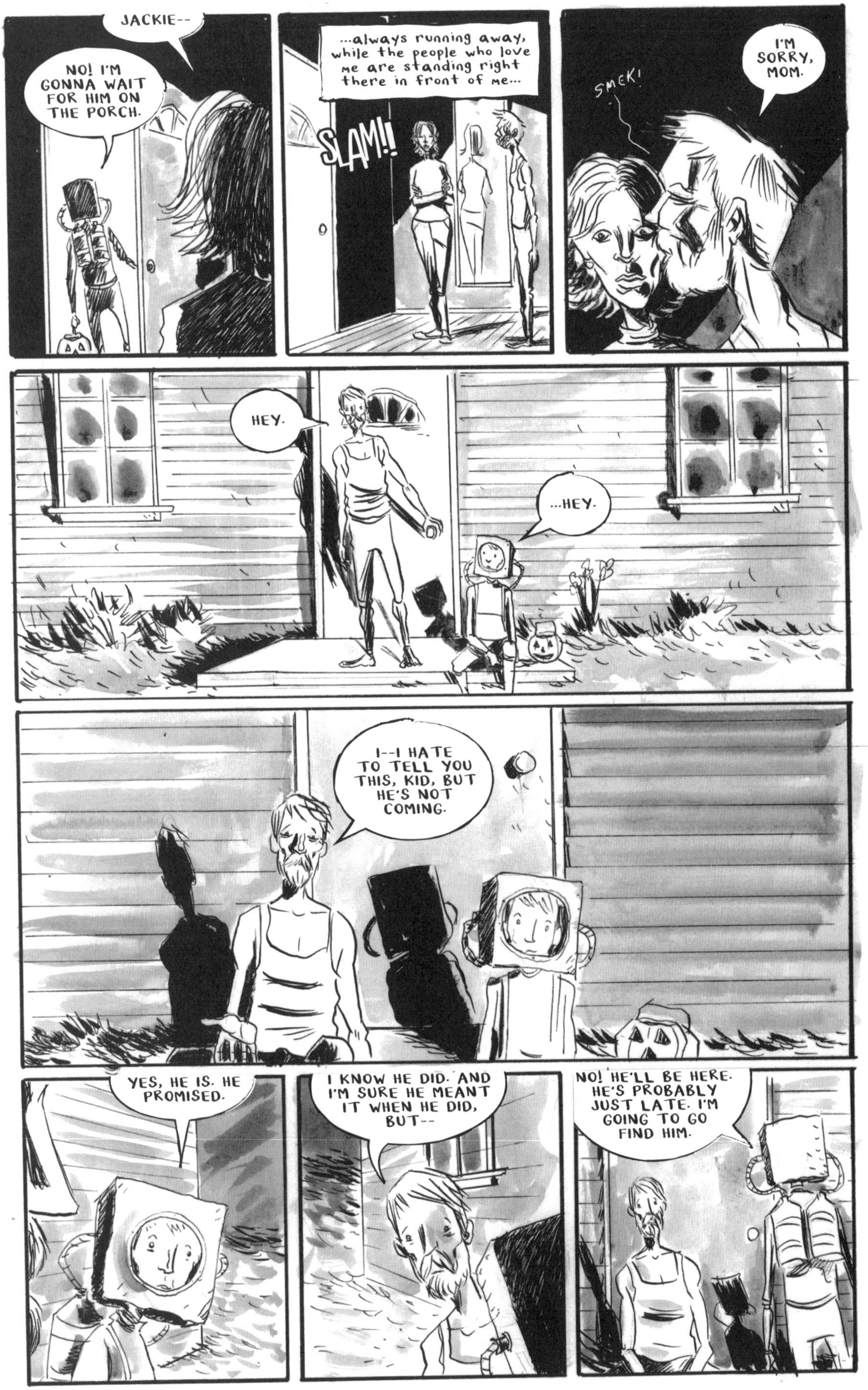
JACKIE--
NO! I'M GONNA WAIT FOR HIM ON THE PORCH.
...always running away, while the people who love me are standing right there in front of me...
SLAM!!
SMEK!
I'M SORRY, MOM.
HEY.
...HEY.
I--I HATE TO TELL YOU THIS, KID, BUT HE'S NOT COMING.
YES, HE IS. HE PROMISED.
I KNOW HE DID. AND I'M SURE HE MEANT IT WHEN HE DID, BUT--
NO! HE'LL BE HERE. HE'S PROBABLY JUST LATE. I'M GOING TO GO FIND HIM.

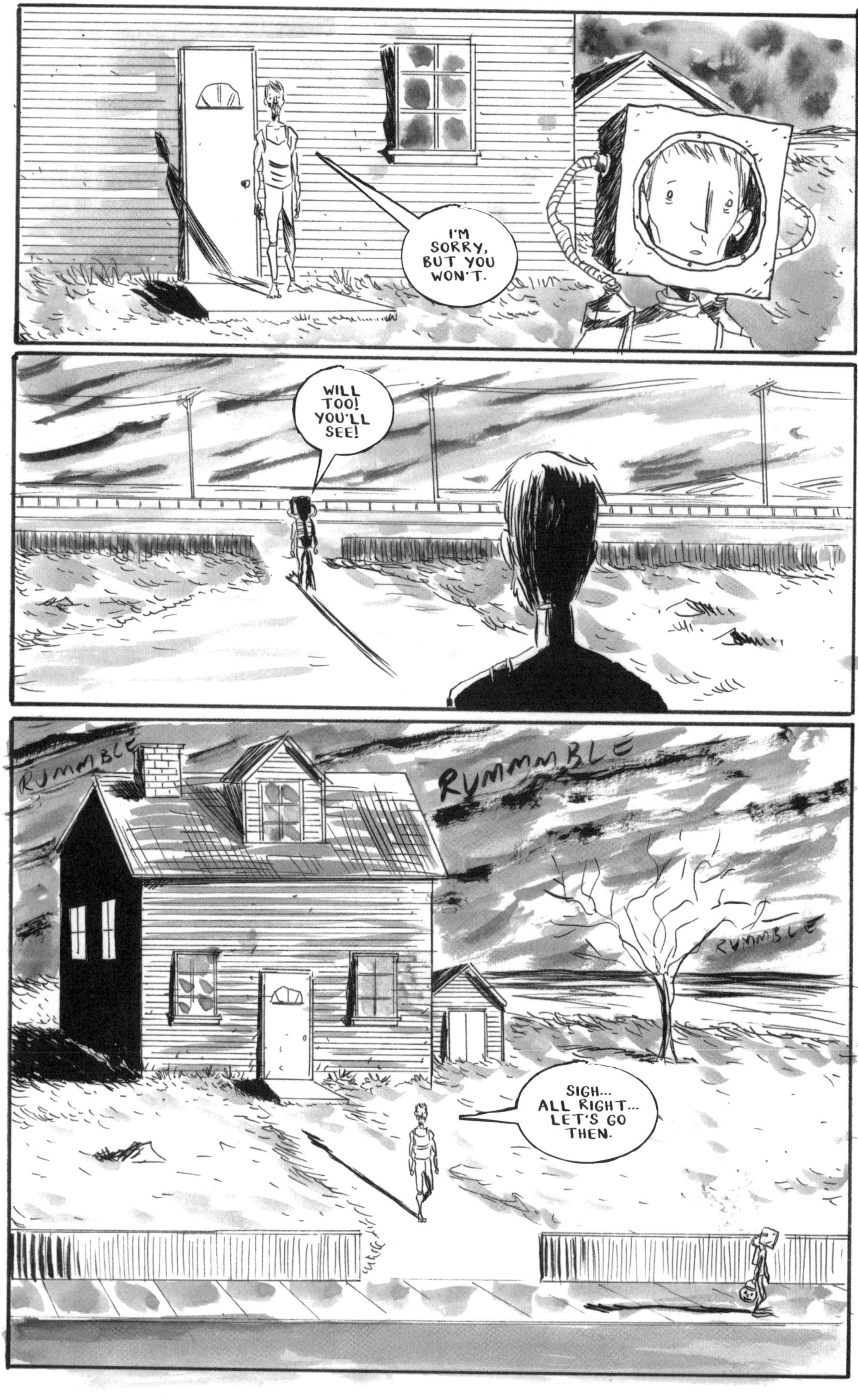
I'M SORRY, BUT YOU WON'T.
WILL TOO! YOU'LL SEE!
RUMMBLE
RUMMMBLE
RUMMBLE
SIGH... ALL RIGHT... LET'S GO THEN.

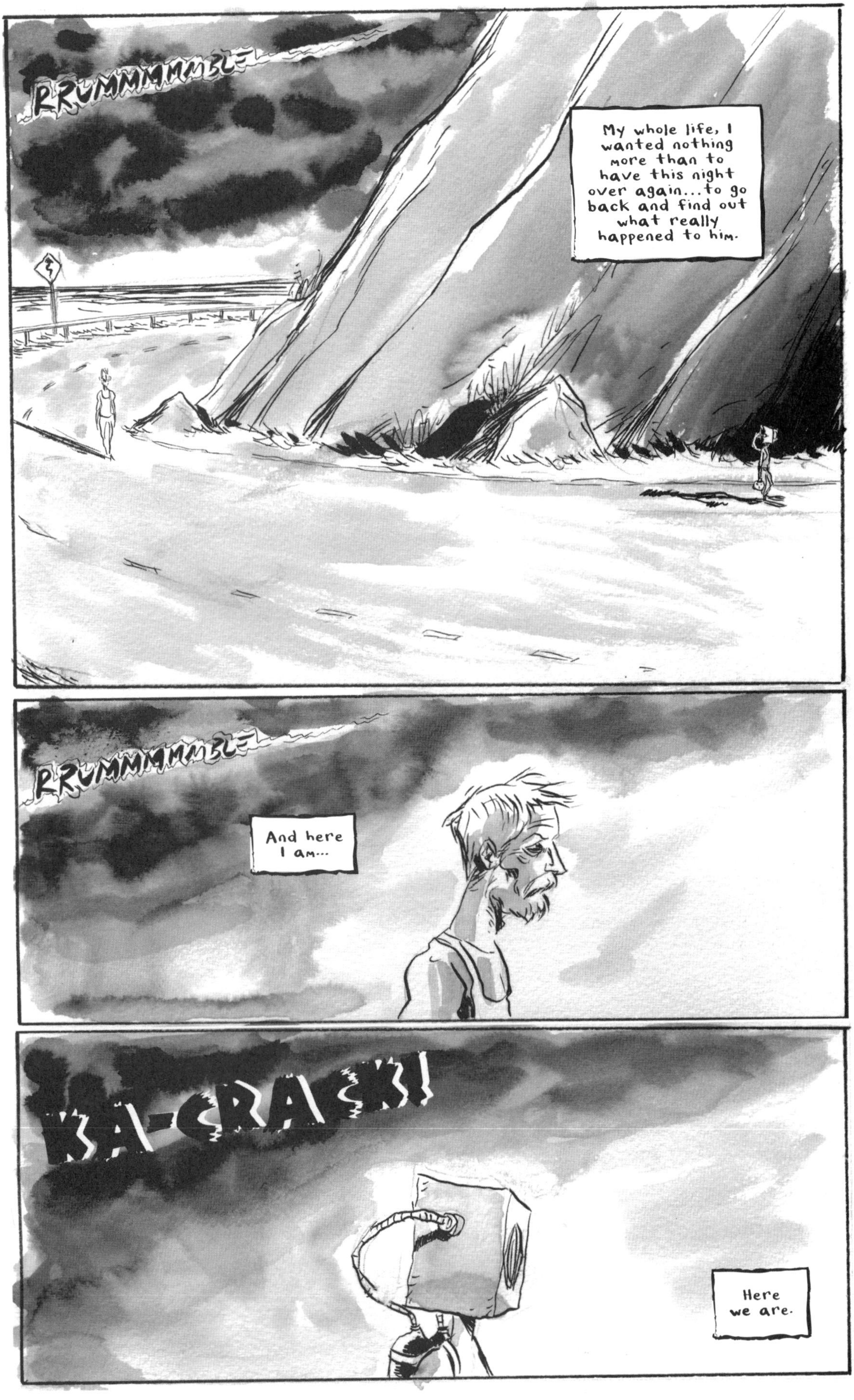
RRUMMMMMBLE
My whole life, I wanted nothing more than to have this night over again... to go back and find out what really happened to him.
RRUMMMMMBLE
And here I am...
KA-CRACK!
Here we are.

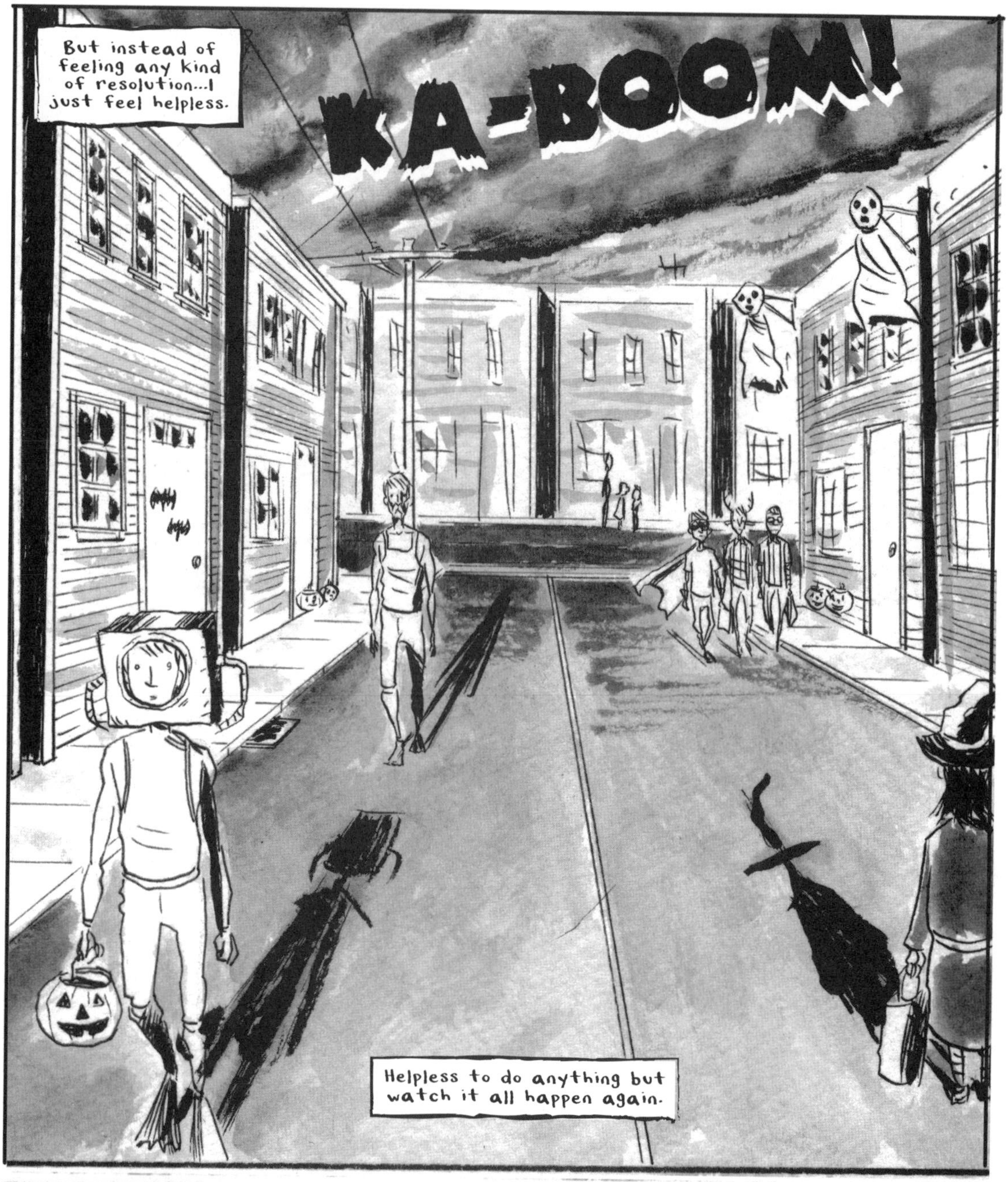
But instead of feeling any kind of resolution...I just feel helpless.
KA-BOOM!
Helpless to do anything but watch it all happen again.

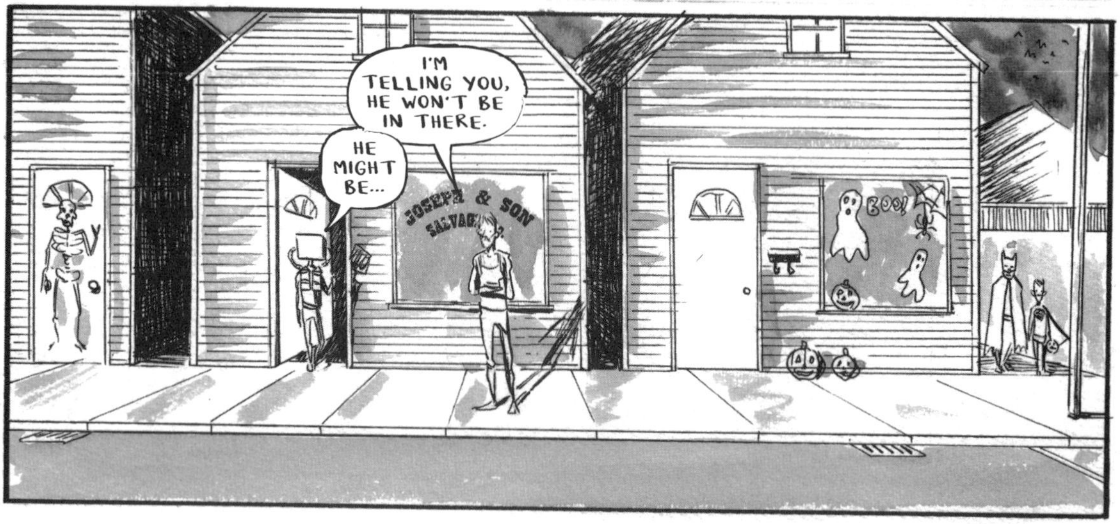
I'M TELLING YOU, HE WON'T BE IN THERE.
HE MIGHT BE...
JOSEPH & SON
BOO!

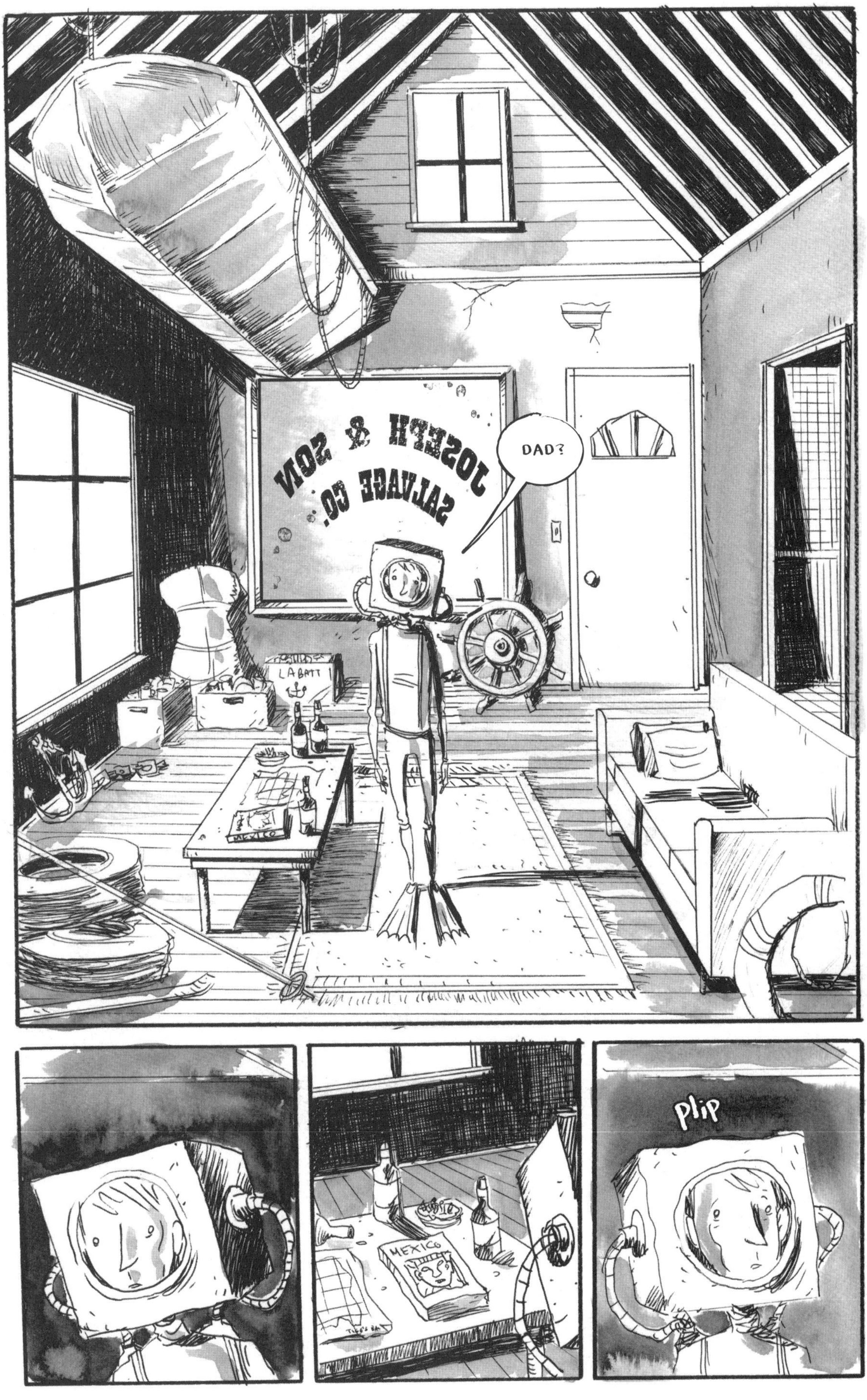
JOSEPH & SON
SALVAGE CO.
LABATT
MEXICO
DAD?
MEXICO
plip

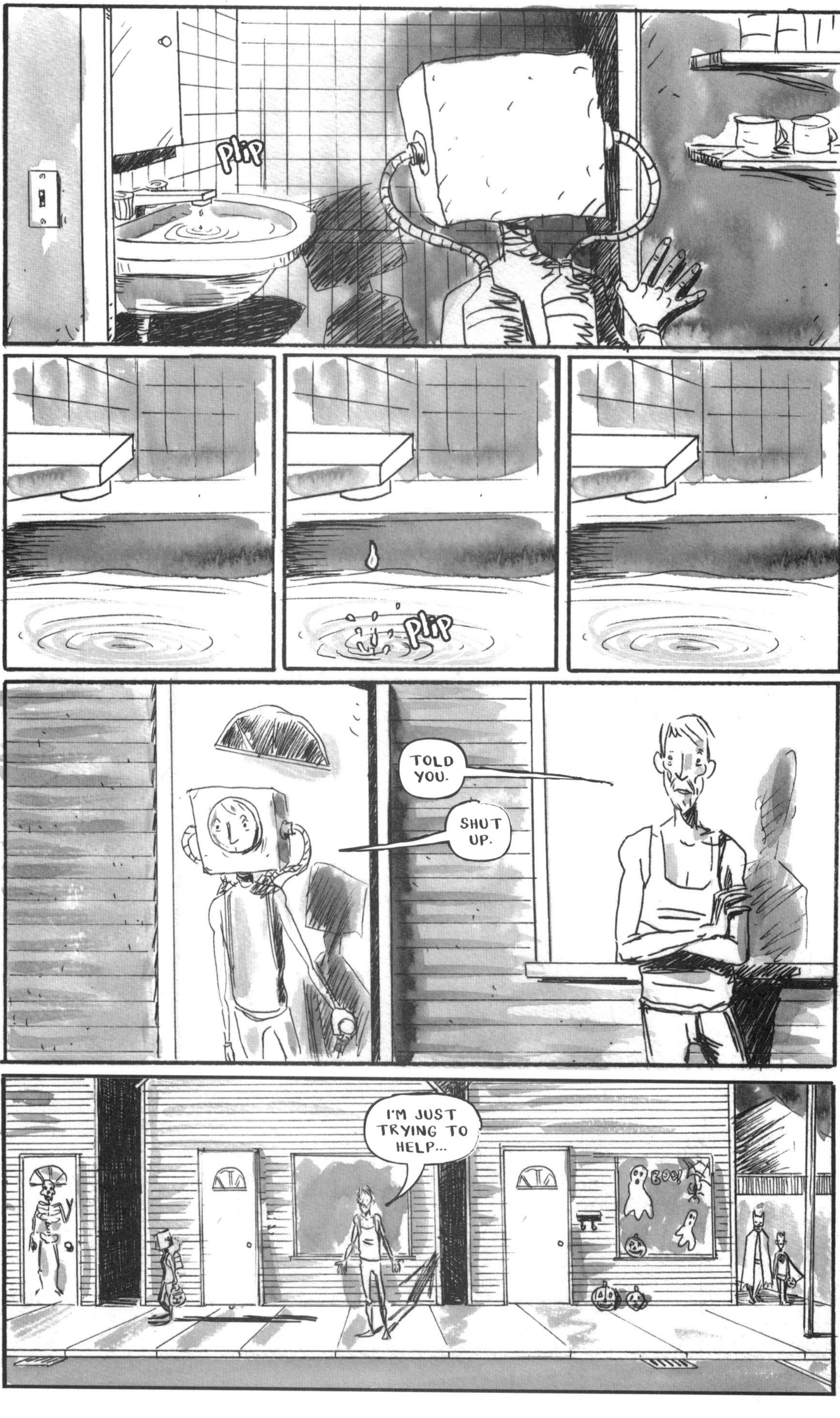

PLIP
PLIP
TOLD YOU.
SHUT UP.
I'M JUST TRYING TO HELP...
BOO!

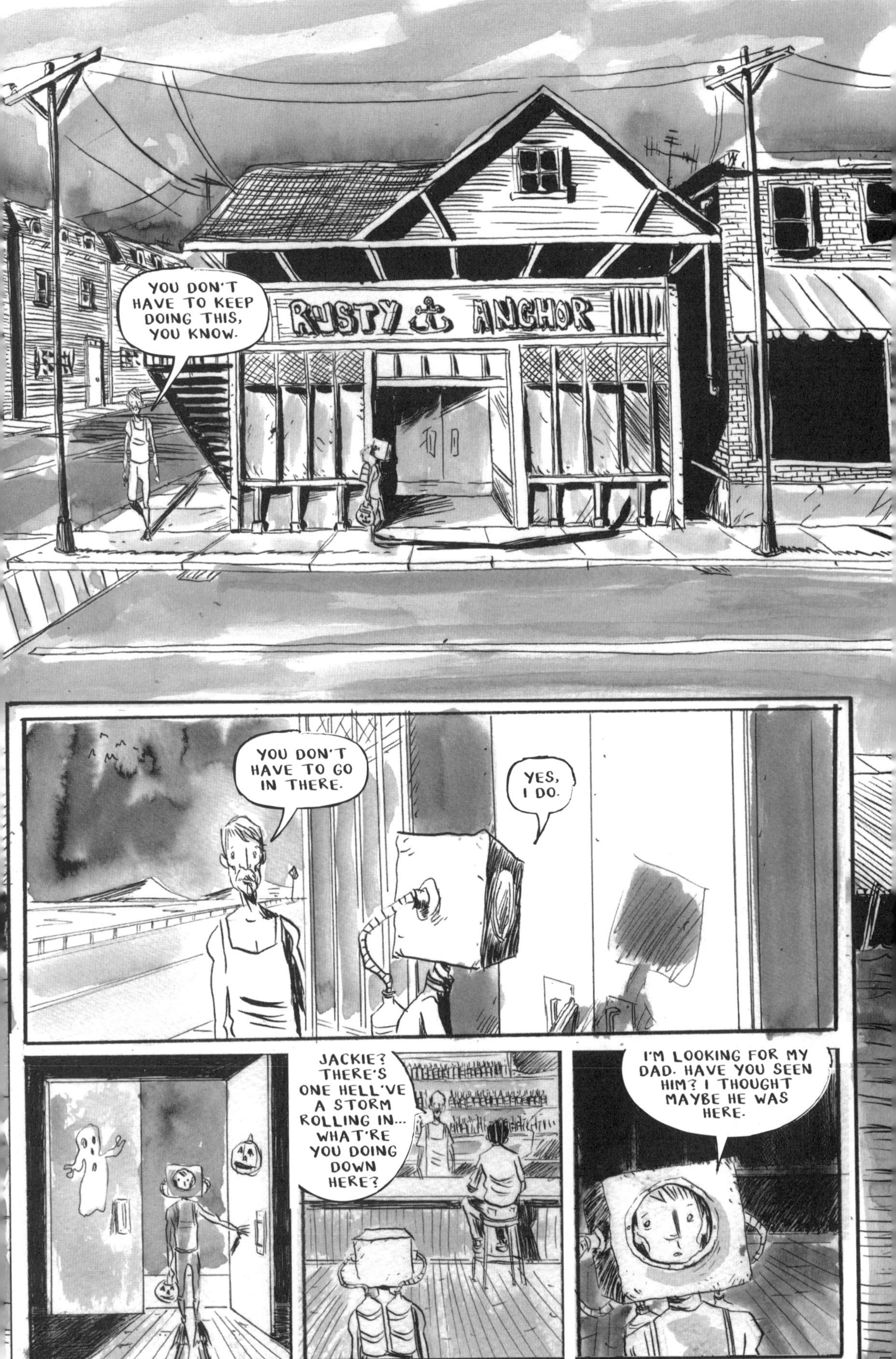

RUSTY ANCHOR
YOU DON'T HAVE TO KEEP DOING THIS, YOU KNOW.
YOU DON'T HAVE TO GO IN THERE.
YES, I DO.
JACKIE? THERE'S ONE HELL'VE A STORM ROLLING IN... WHAT'RE YOU DOING DOWN HERE?
I'M LOOKING FOR MY DAD. HAVE YOU SEEN HIM? I THOUGHT MAYBE HE WAS HERE.

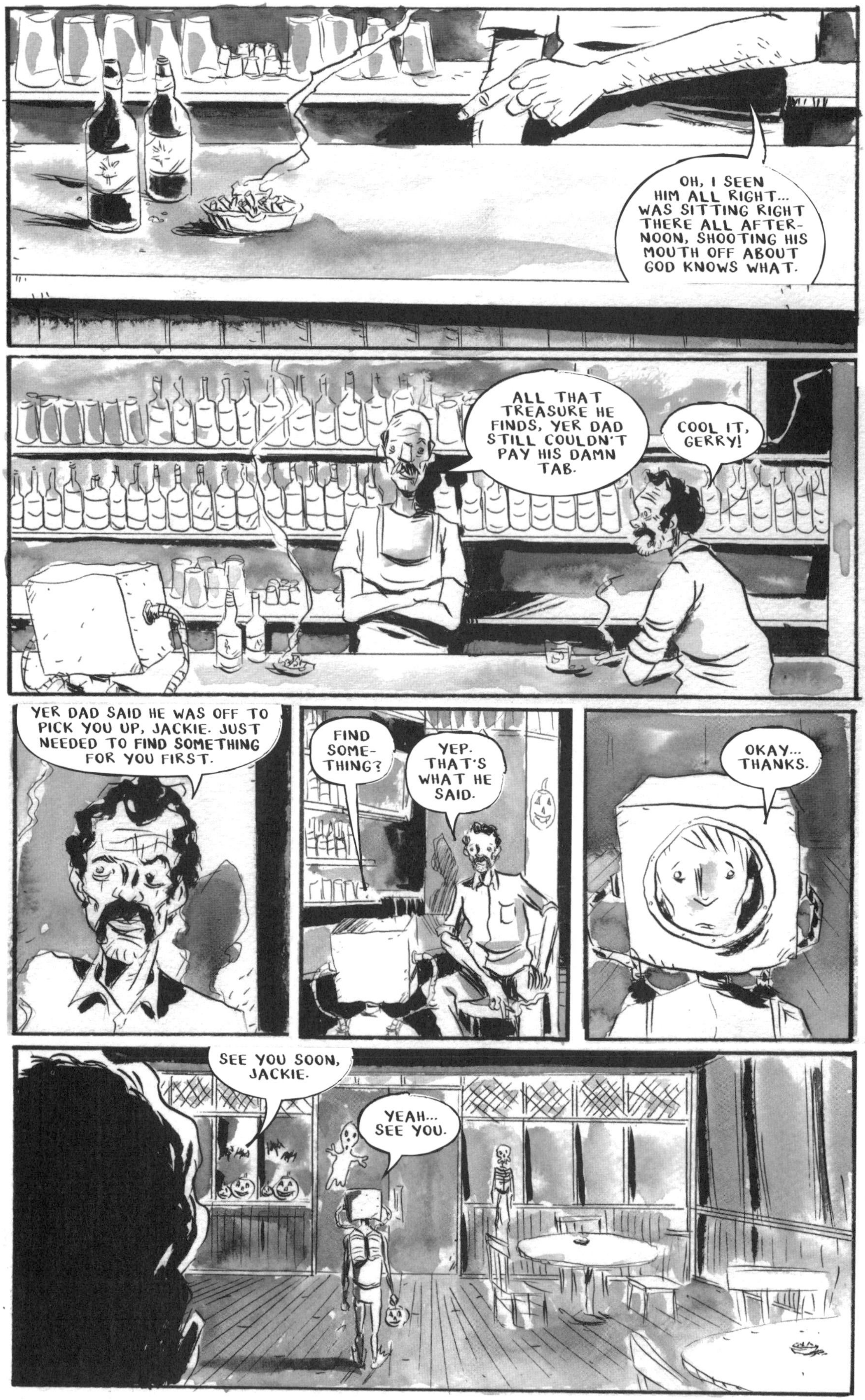

OH, I SEEN HIM ALL RIGHT... WAS SITTING RIGHT THERE ALL AFTER-NOON, SHOOTING HIS MOUTH OFF ABOUT GOD KNOWS WHAT.
ALL THAT TREASURE HE FINDS, YER DAD STILL COULDN'T PAY HIS DAMN TAB.
COOL IT, GERRY!
YER DAD SAID HE WAS OFF TO PICK YOU UP, JACKIE. JUST NEEDED TO FIND SOMETHING FOR YOU FIRST.
FIND SOME-THING?
YEP. THAT'S WHAT HE SAID.
OKAY... THANKS.
SEE YOU SOON, JACKIE.
YEAH... SEE YOU.

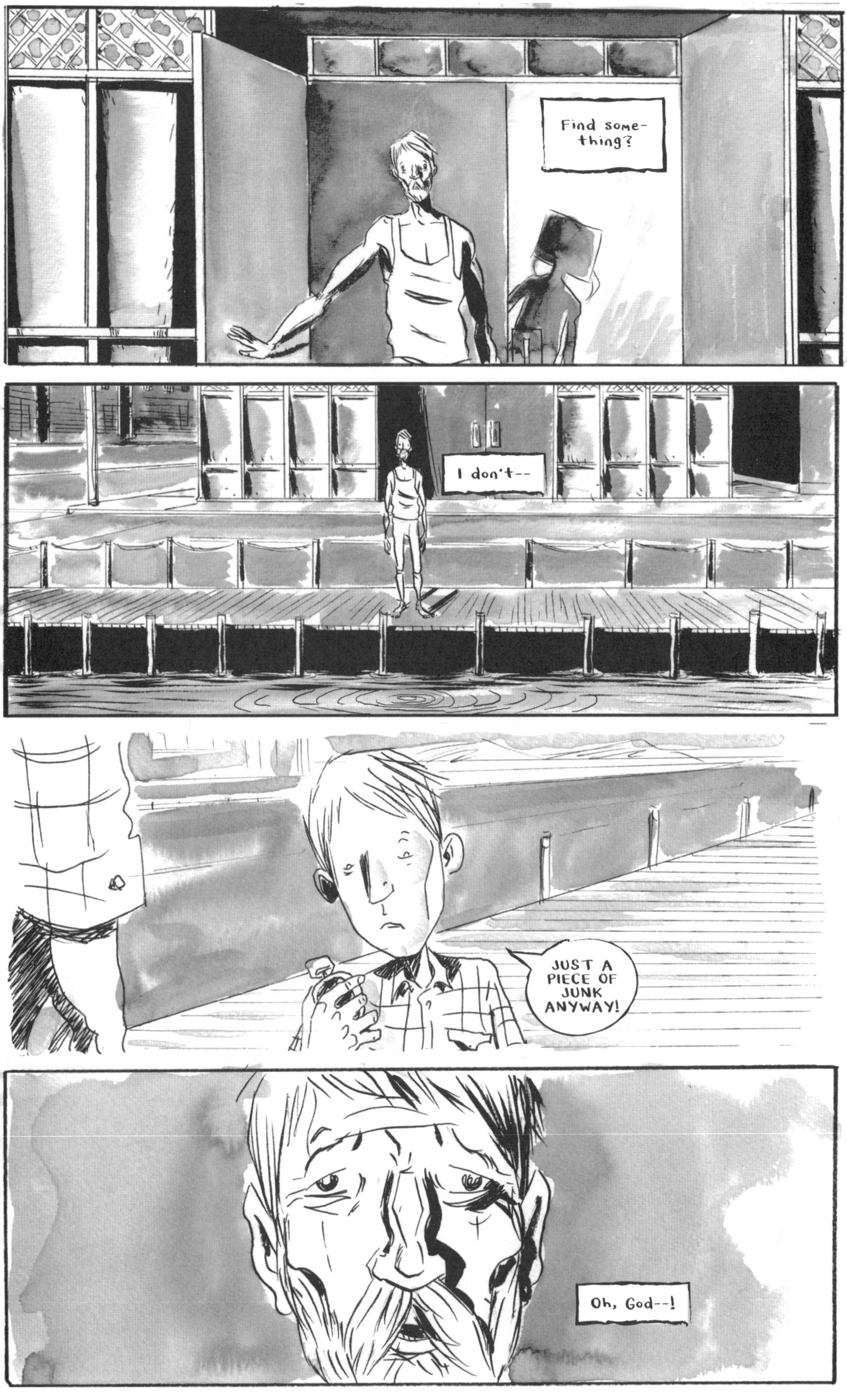
Find something?
I don't--
JUST A PIECE OF JUNK ANYWAY!
Oh, God--!

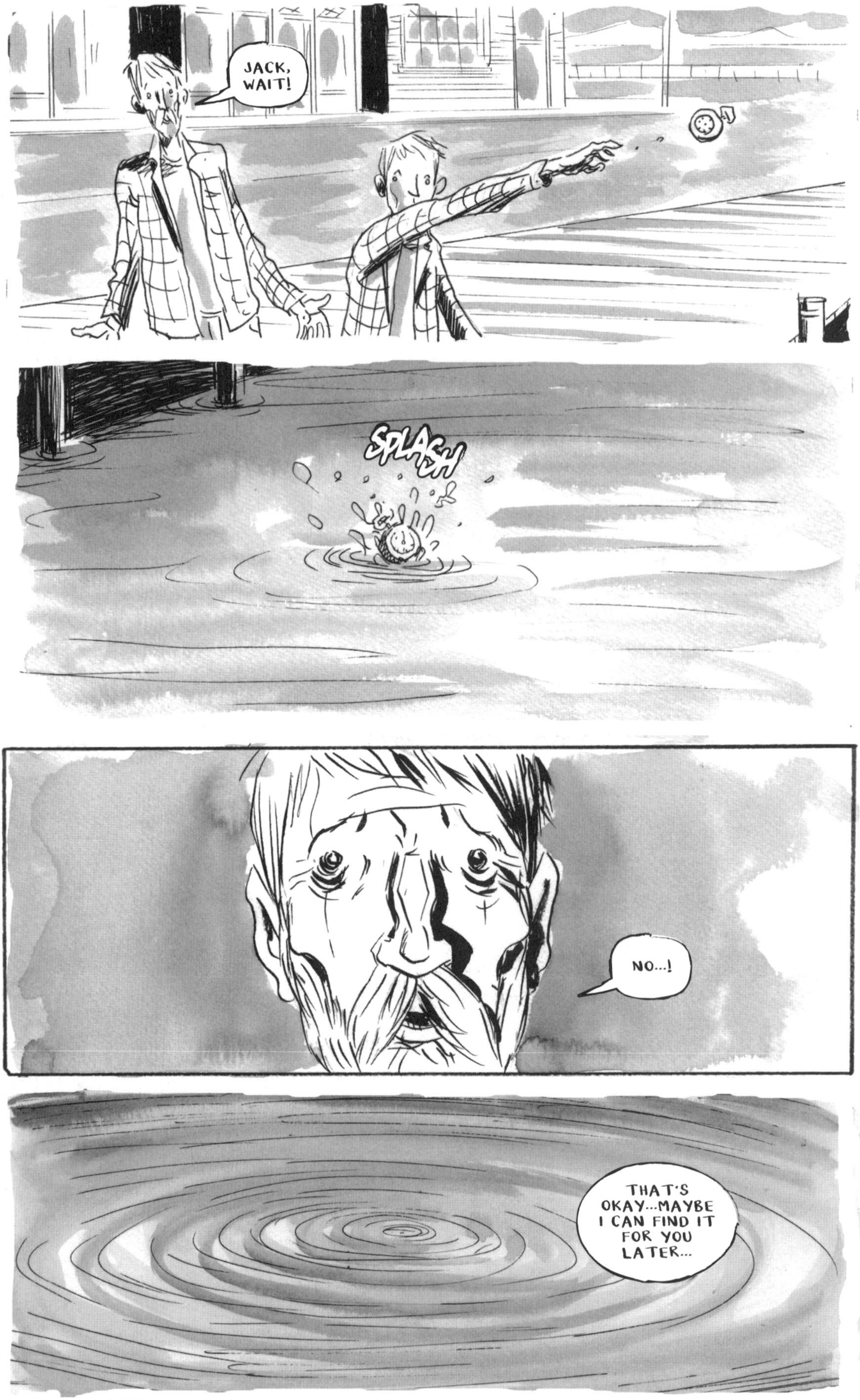
JACK, WAIT!
SPLASH
NO...!
THAT'S OKAY...MAYBE I CAN FIND IT FOR YOU LATER...

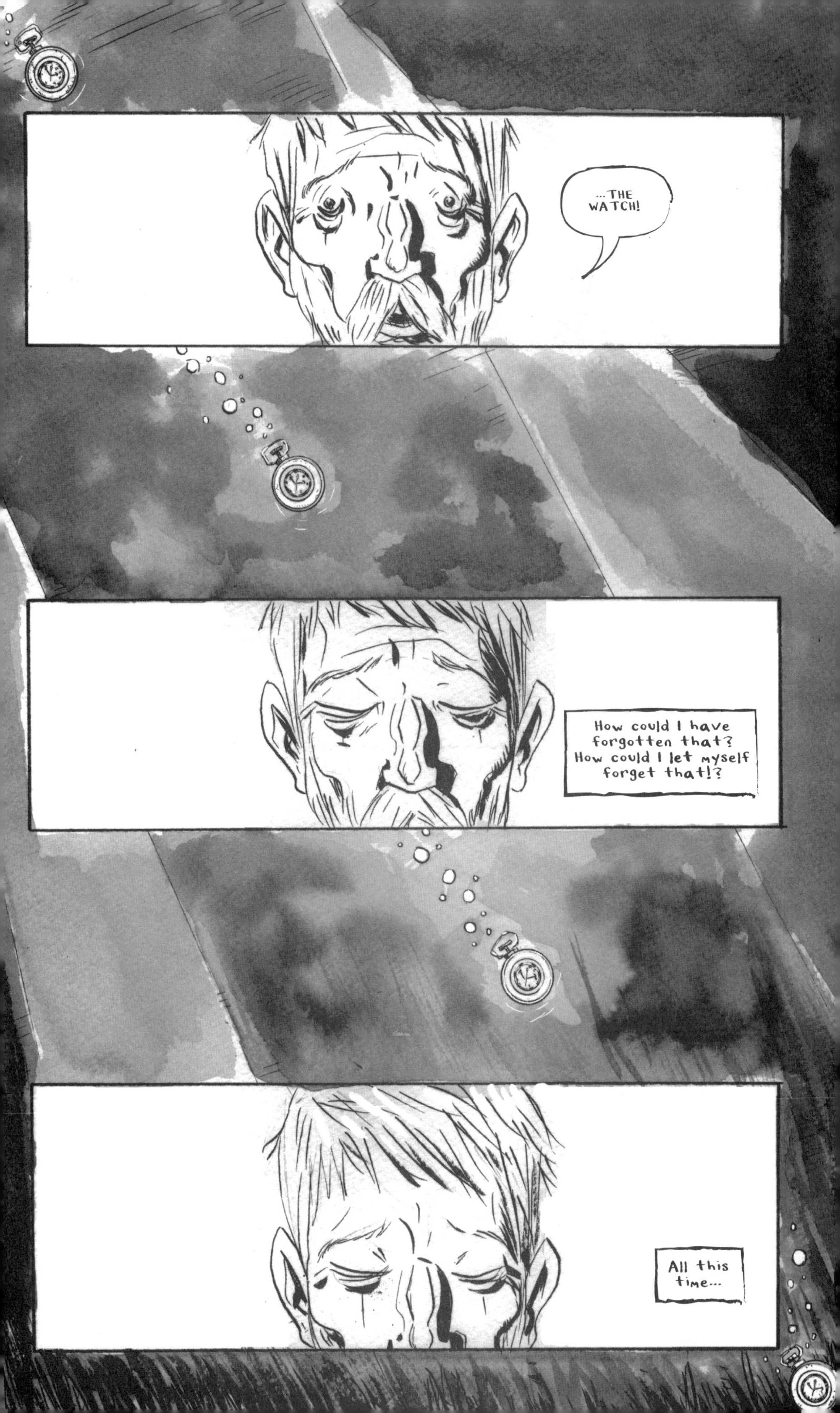
...THE WATCH!
How could I have forgotten that? How could I let myself forget that!?
All this time...

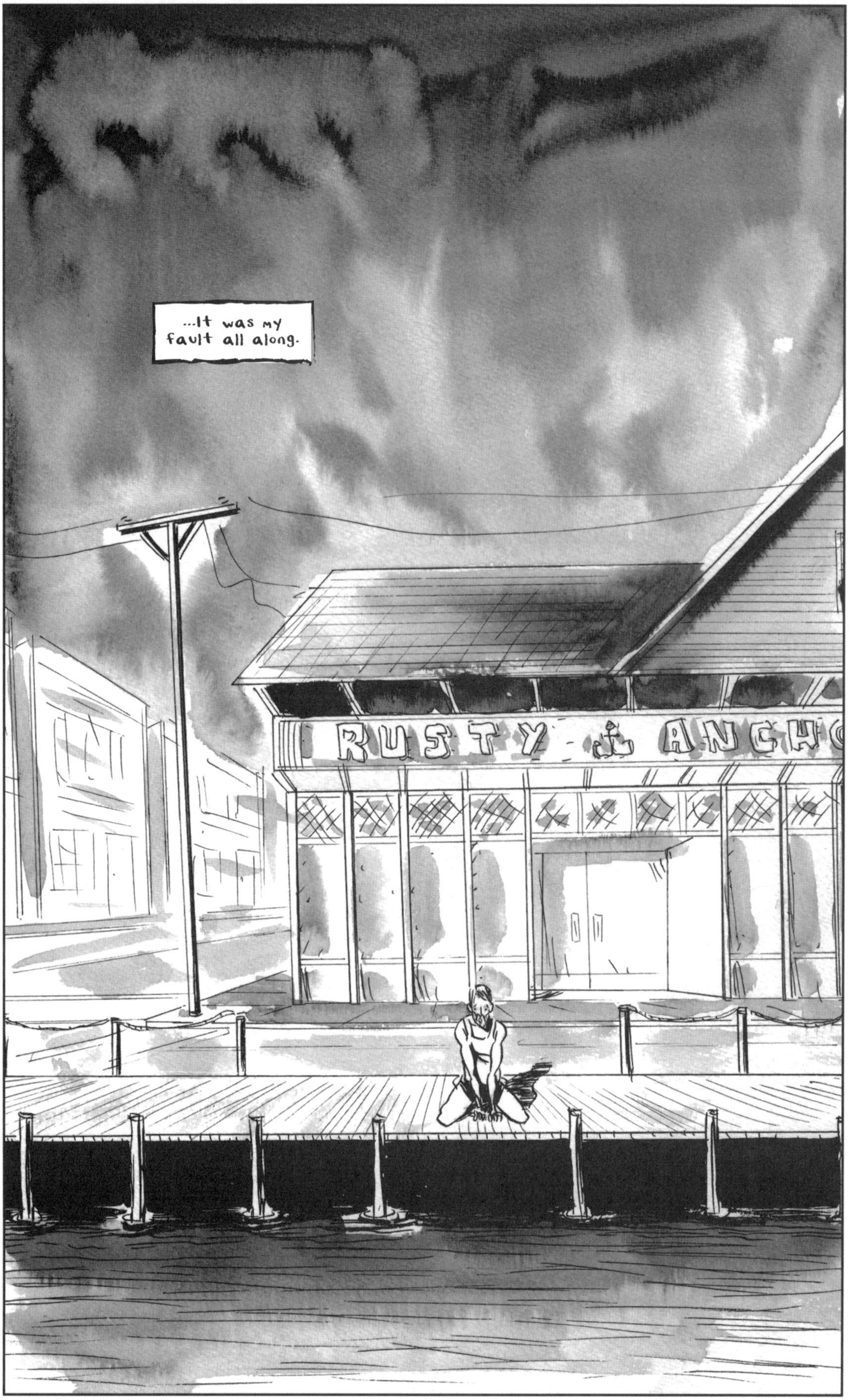
...It was my fault all along.
RUSTY ANCHO

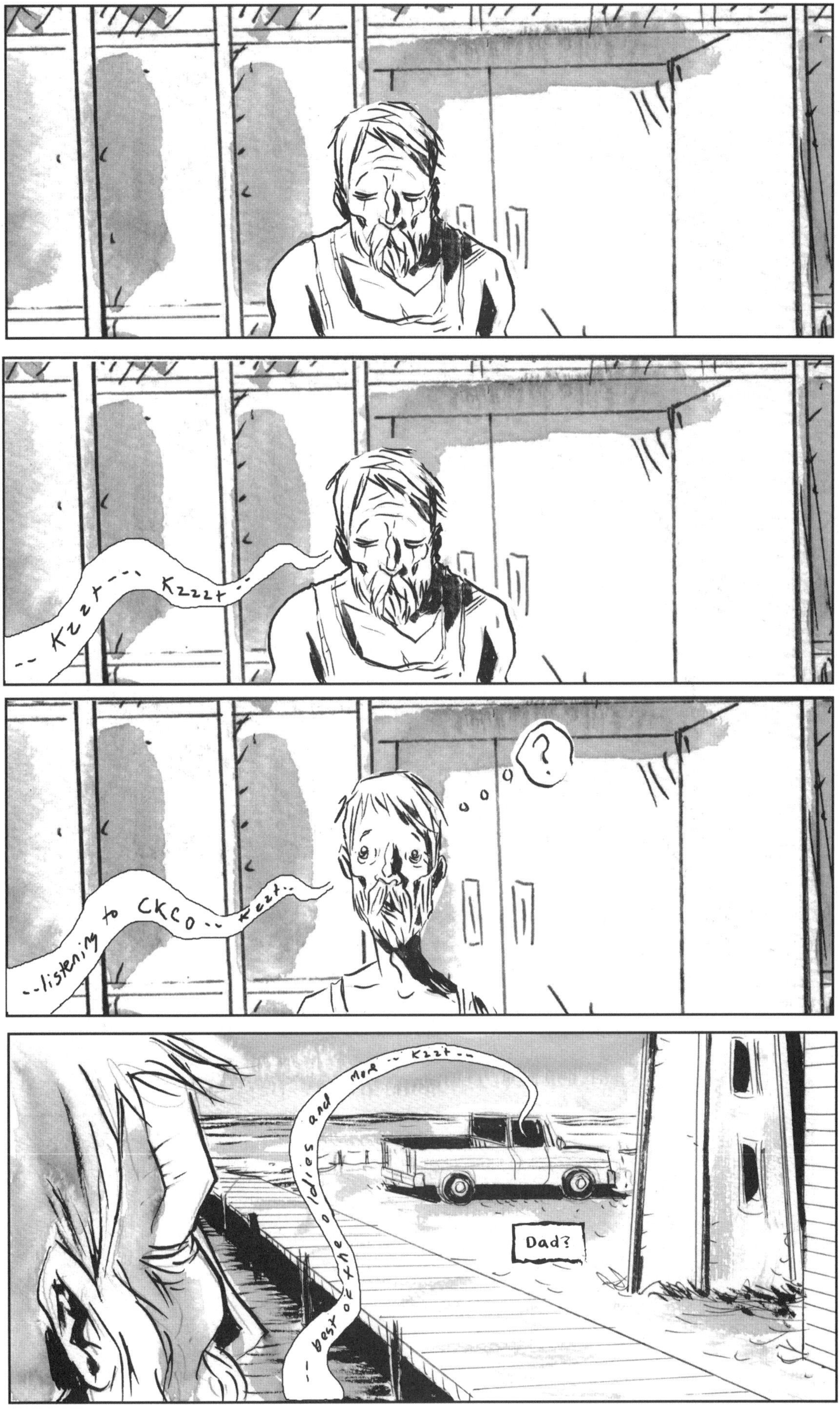
-- Kzzt --, Kzzzt --
?
--listening to CKCO -- Kzzt --
-- best of the oldies and mor -- Kzzt --
Dad?

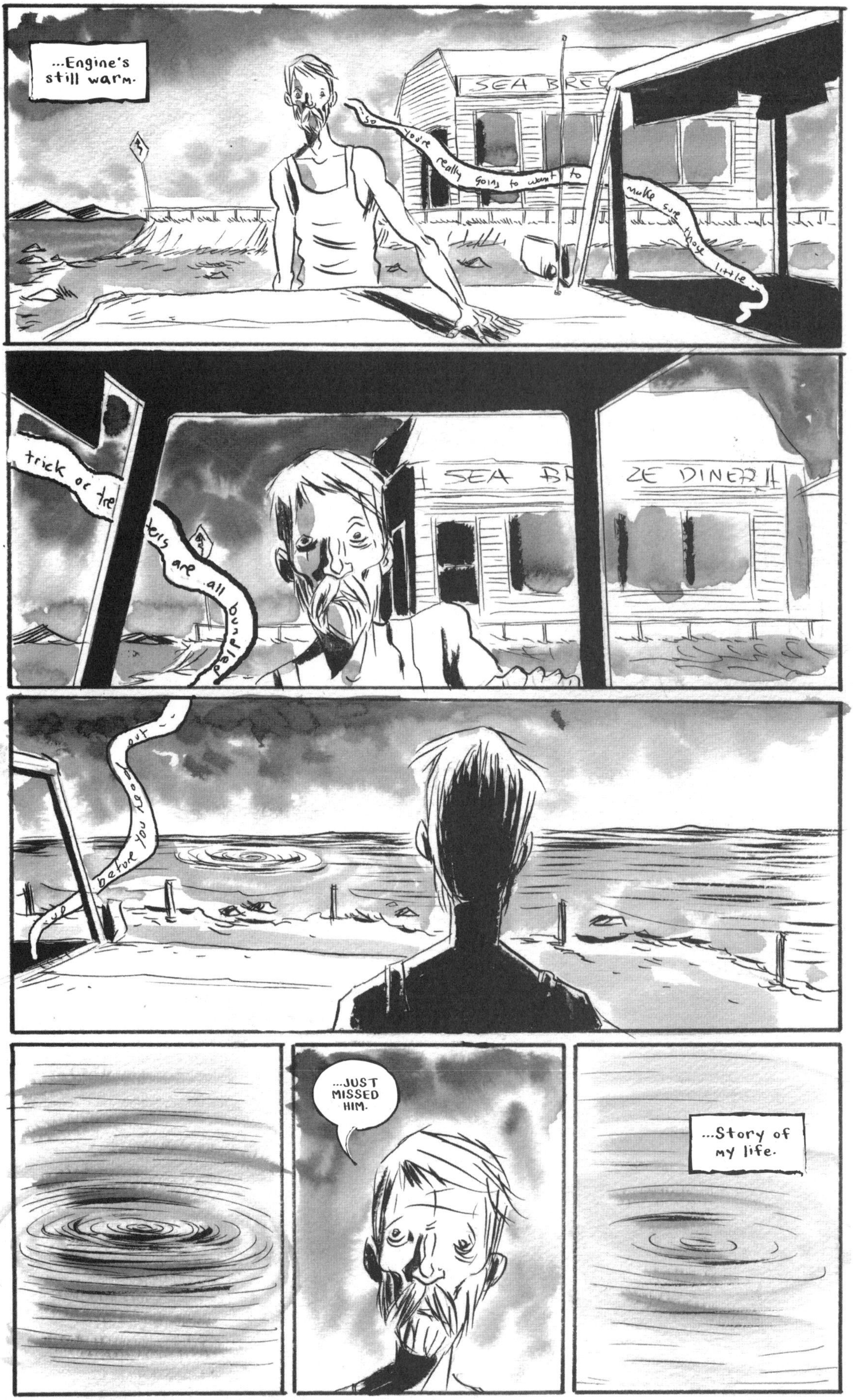
...Engine's still warm.
...so you're really going to want to make sure those little...
trick or tre
ters are all bundled
...ed before you head out
...JUST MISSED HIM.
...Story of my life.

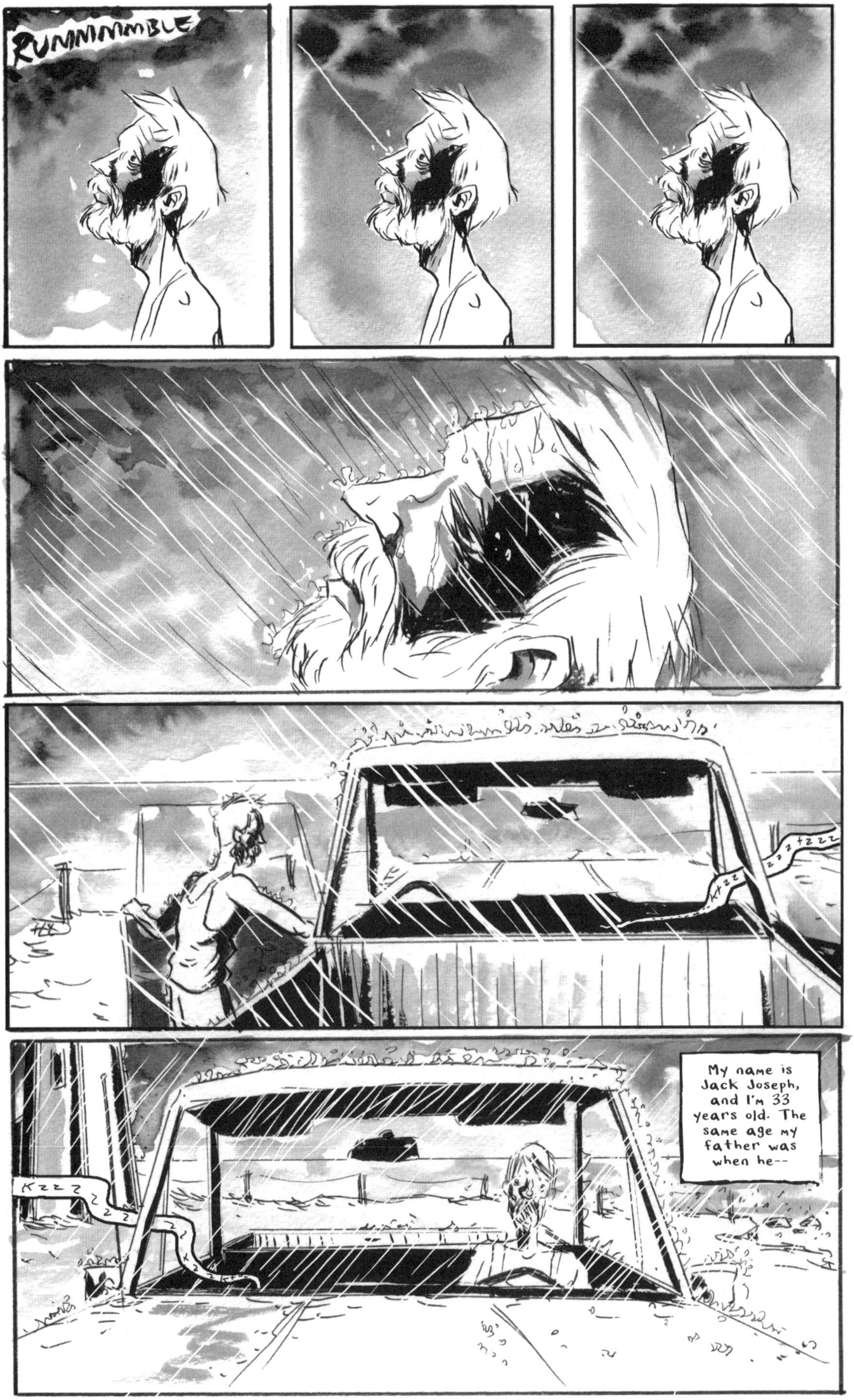
RUMMMMBLE
KZZZ
KZZZ
My name is Jack Joseph, and I'm 33 years old. The same age my father was when he--

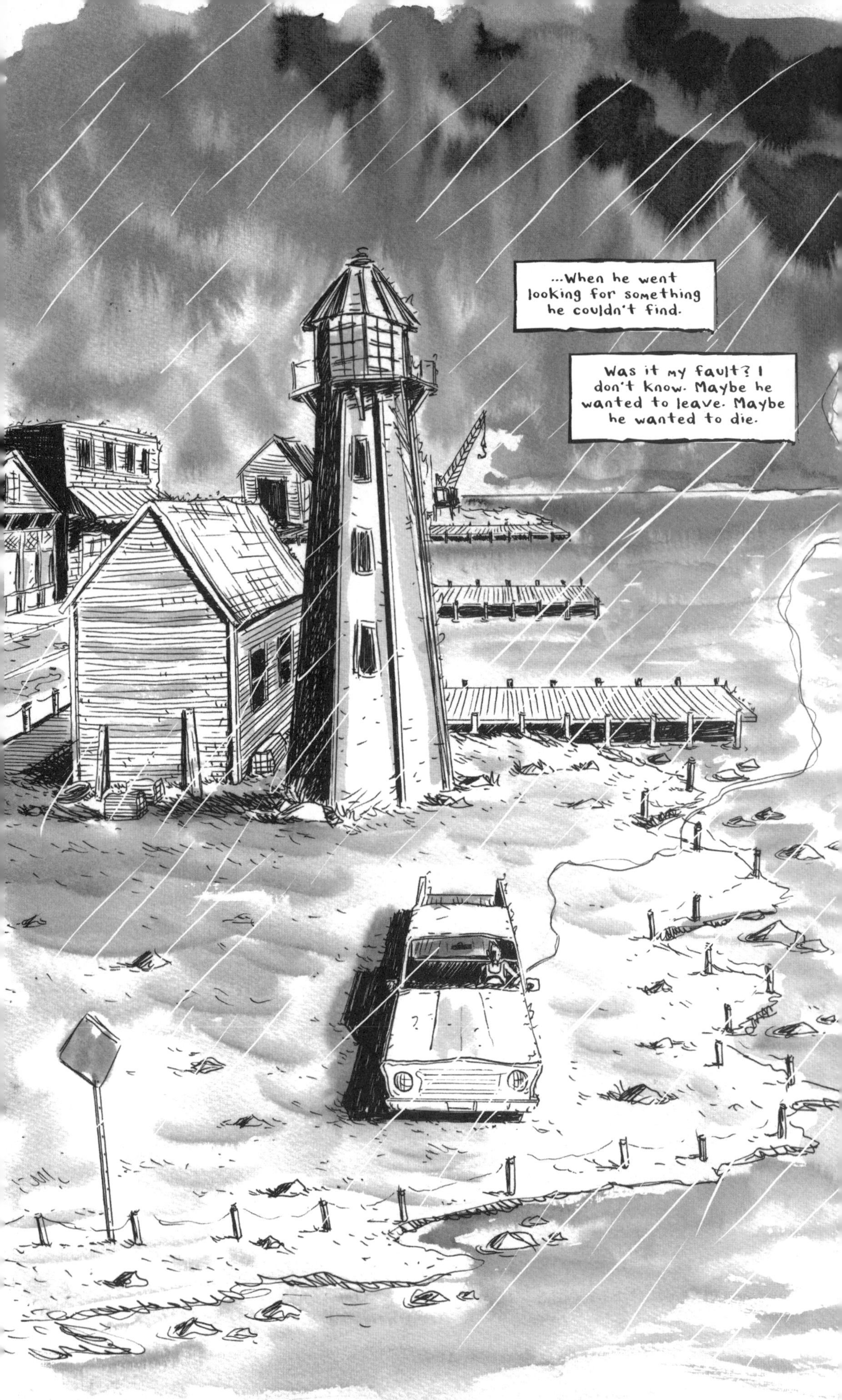
...When he went looking for something he couldn't find.
Was it my fault? I don't know. Maybe he wanted to leave. Maybe he wanted to die.

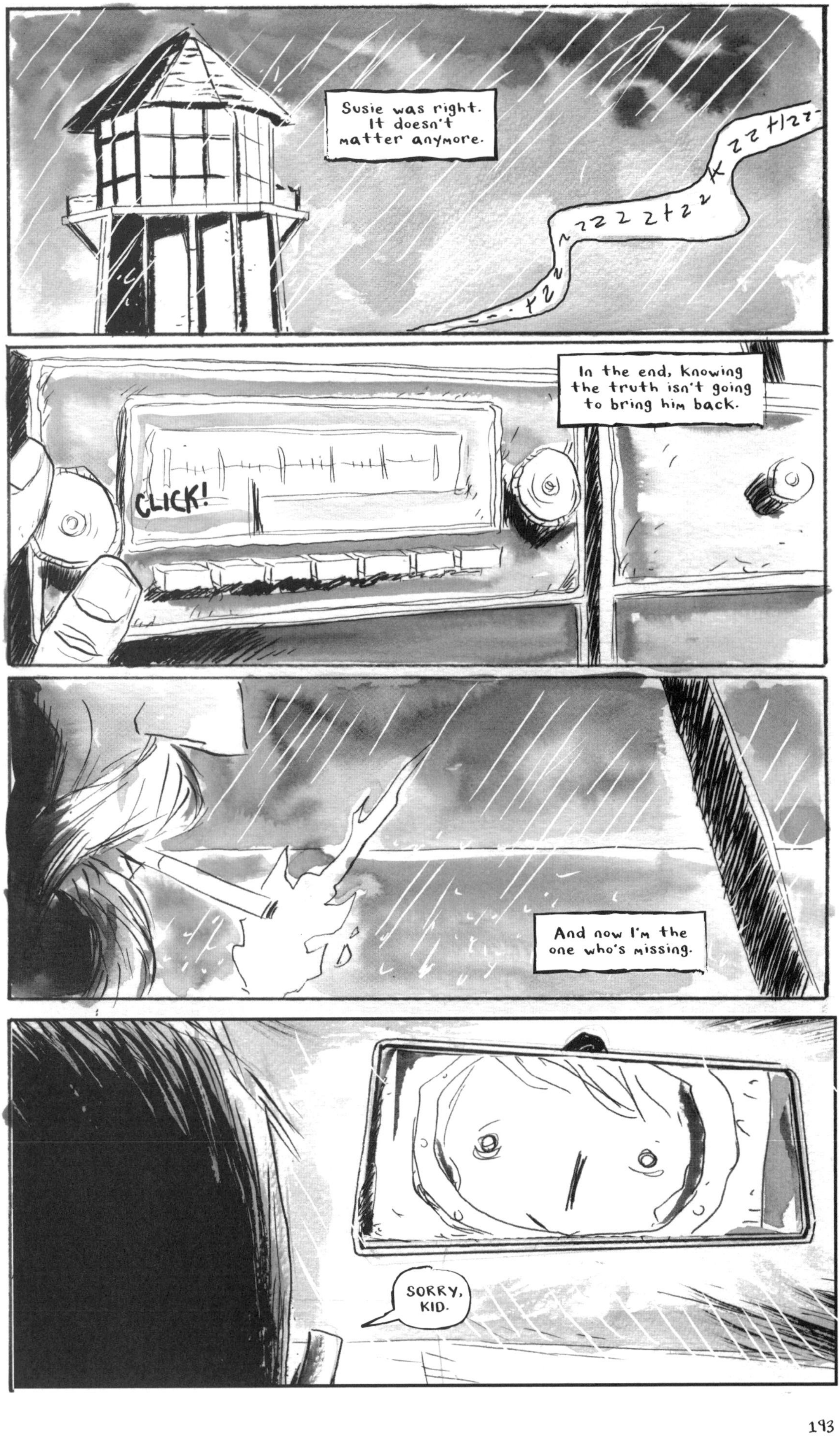
Susie was right. It doesn't matter anymore.
In the end, knowing the truth isn't going to bring him back.
CLICK!
And now I'm the one who's missing.
SORRY, KID.

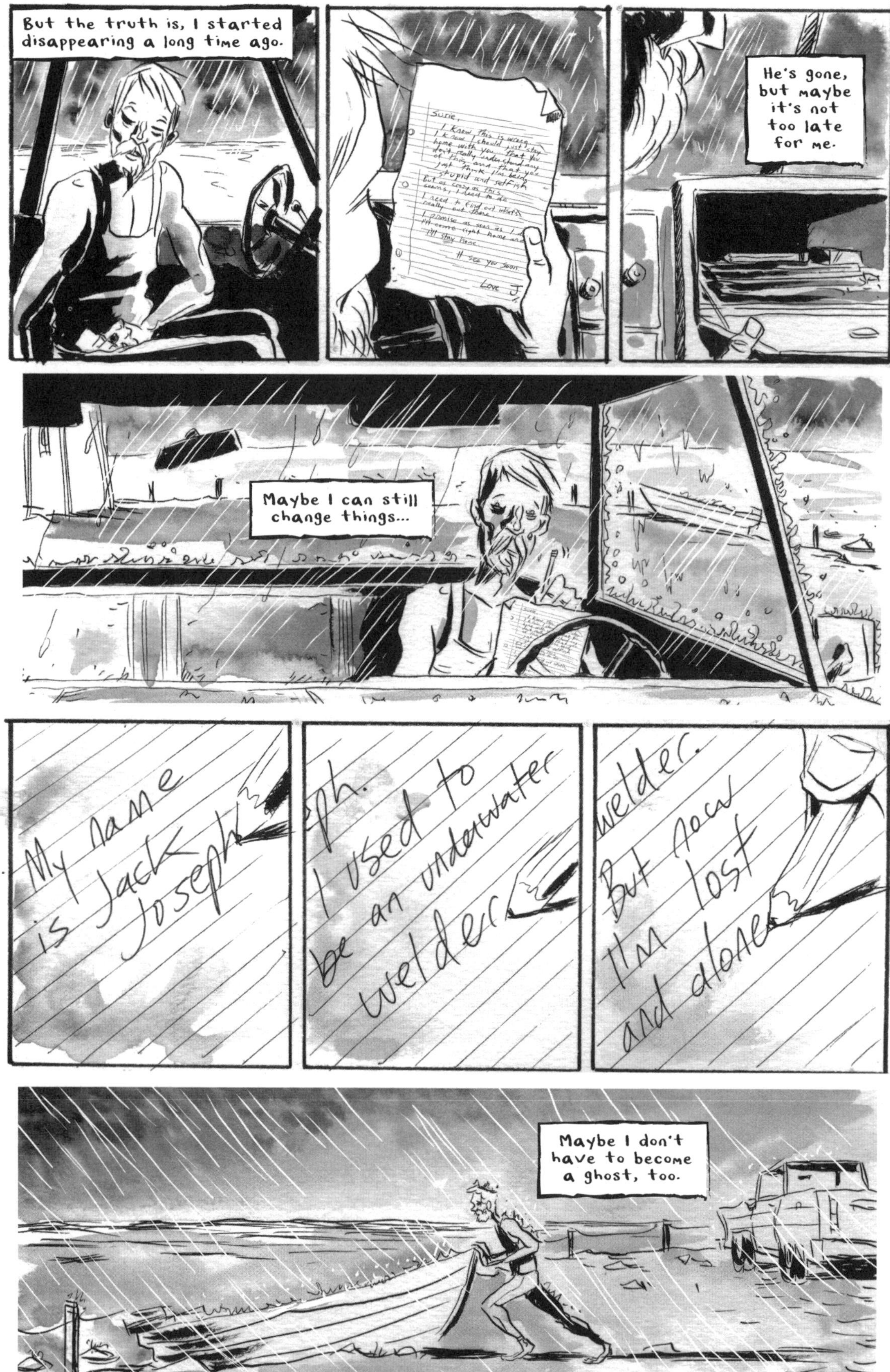
But the truth is, I started disappearing a long time ago.
Susie,
I know this is wrong.
I know I should just stay home with you. That you don't really understand any of this, and that you just think I'm being stupid and selfish.
But as crazy as this seems, I need to do
I need to find out what's really out there.
'll see you soon.
Love J
He's gone, but maybe it's not too late for me.
Maybe I can still change things...
My name is Jack Joseph.
I used to be an underwater welder.
But now I'm lost and alone
Maybe I don't have to become a ghost, too.

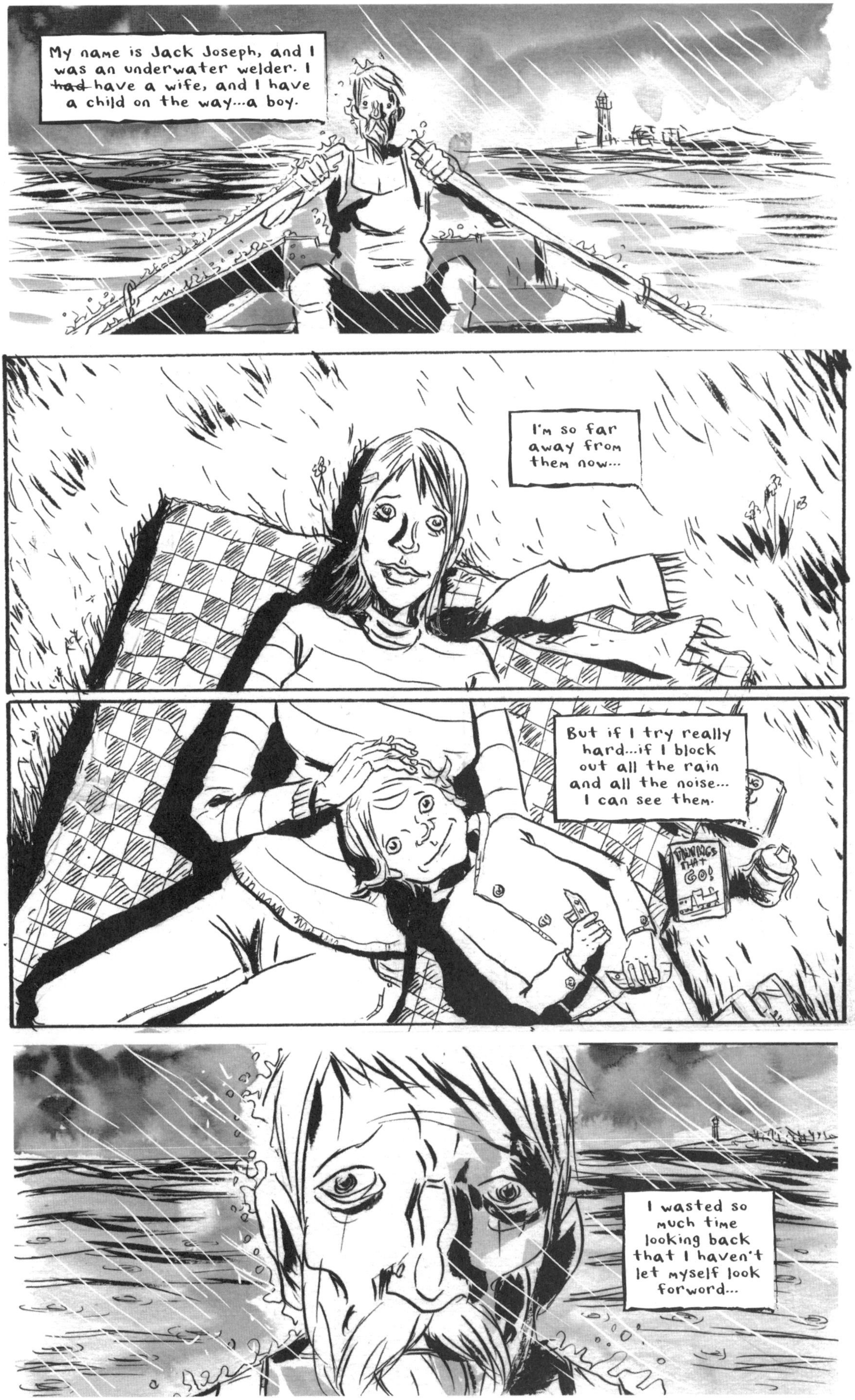
My name is Jack Joseph, and I was an underwater welder. I ~~had~~ have a wife, and I have a child on the way...a boy.
I'm so far away from them now...
But if I try really hard...if I block out all the rain and all the noise... I can see them.
THINGS THAT GO!
I wasted so much time looking back that I haven't let myself look forword...

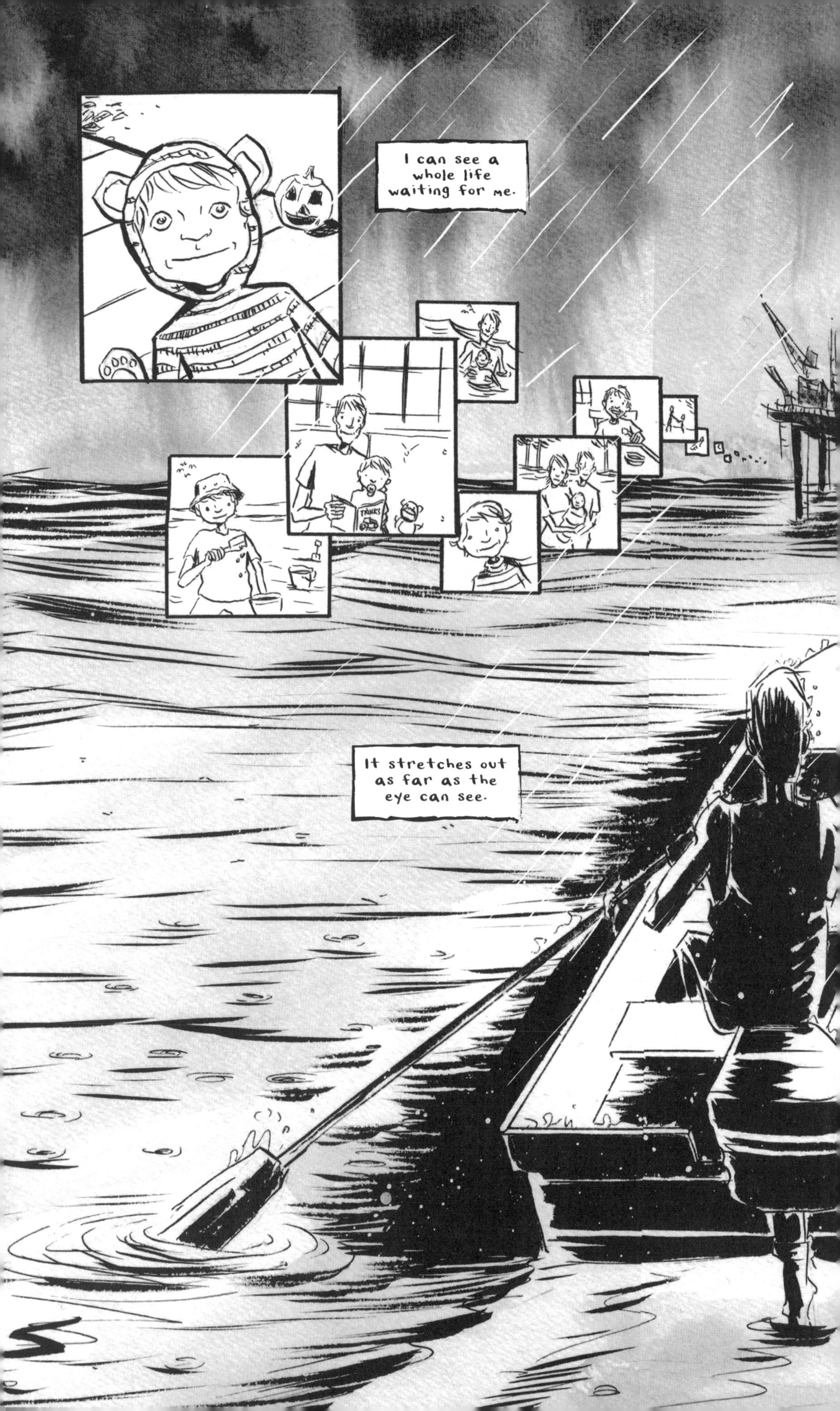
I can see a whole life waiting for me.
TRUCKS
It stretches out as far as the eye can see.

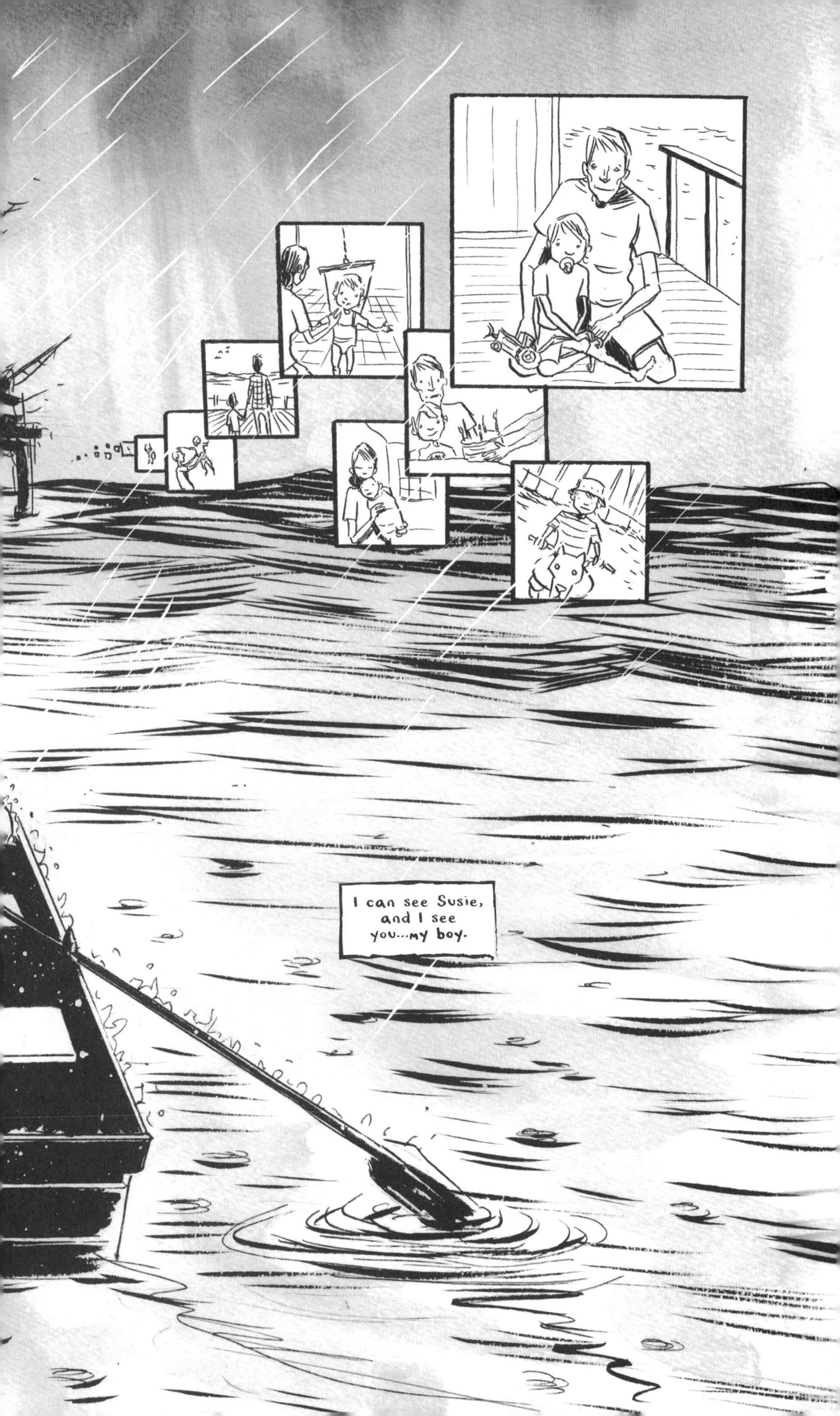
I can see Susie, and I see you...my boy.

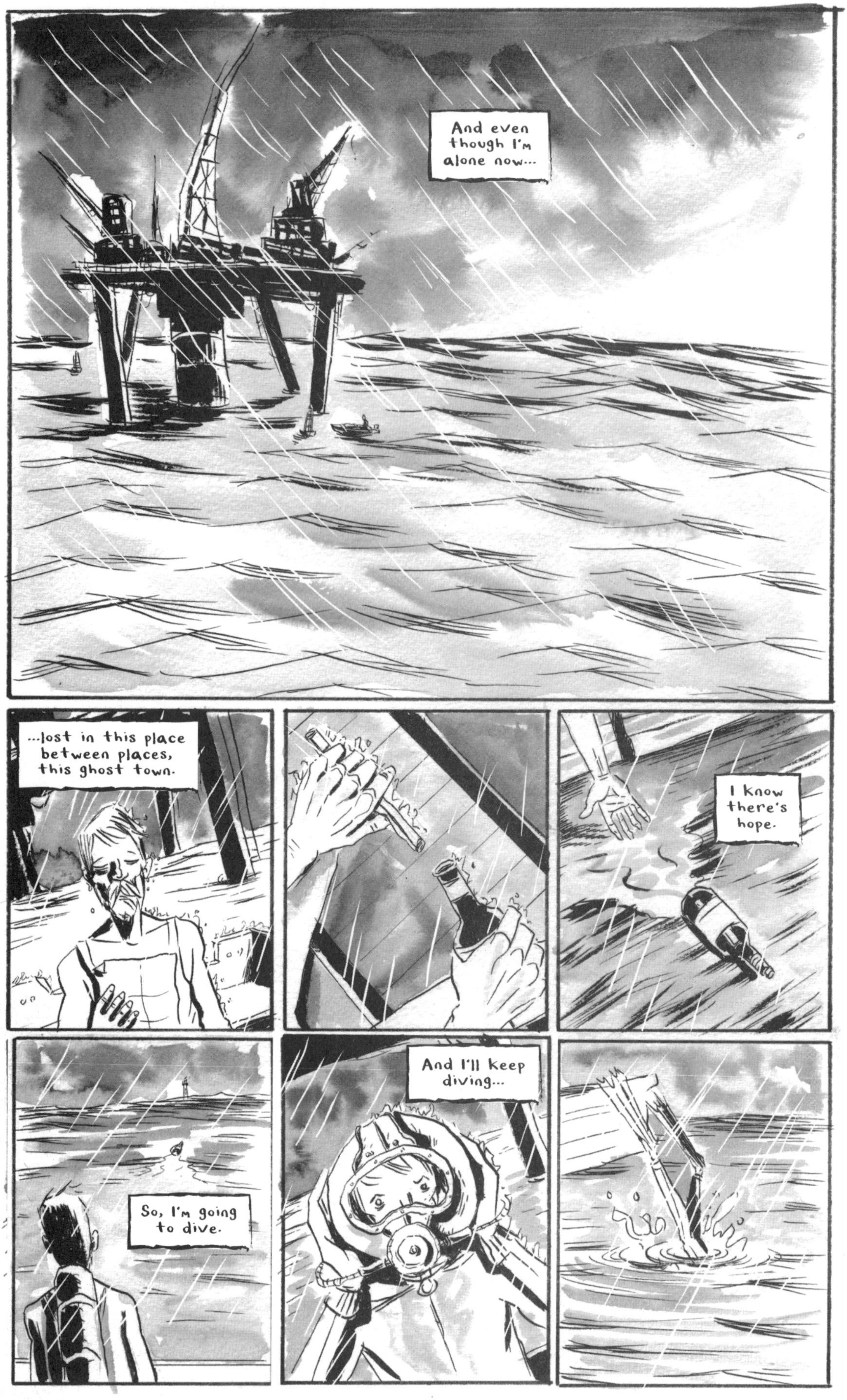

And even though I'm alone now...
...lost in this place between places, this ghost town.
I know there's hope.
So, I'm going to dive.
And I'll keep diving...

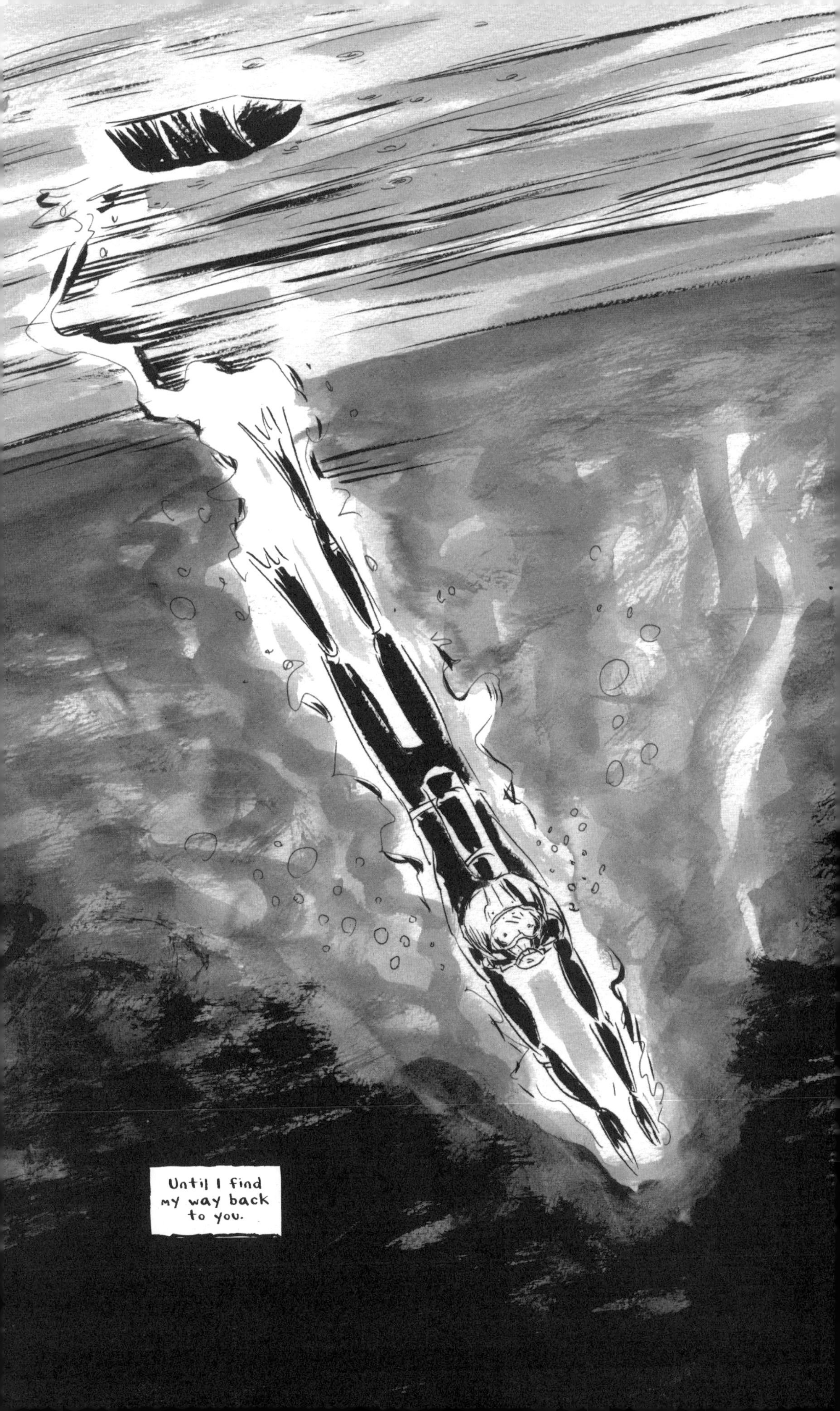
Until I find my way back to you.

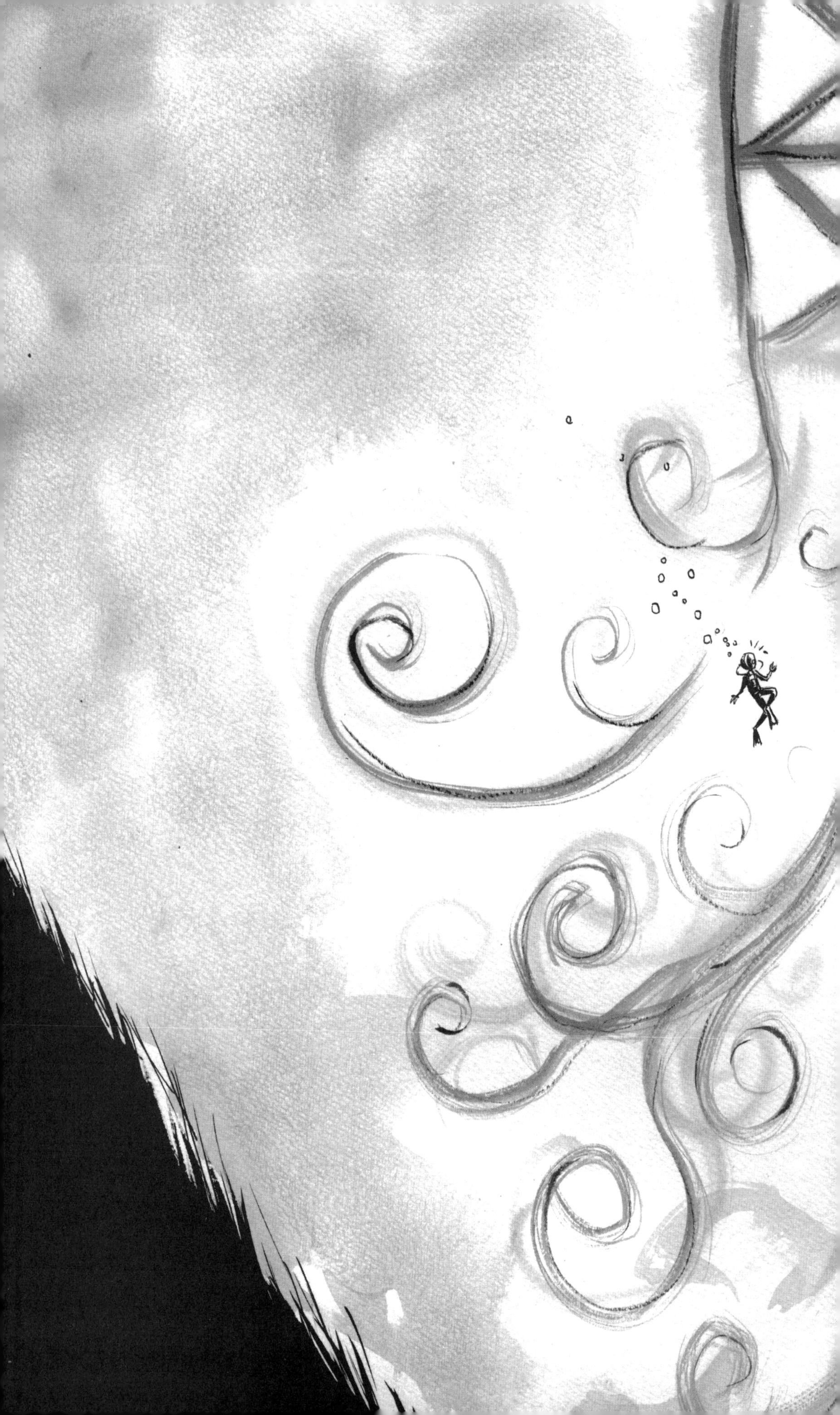

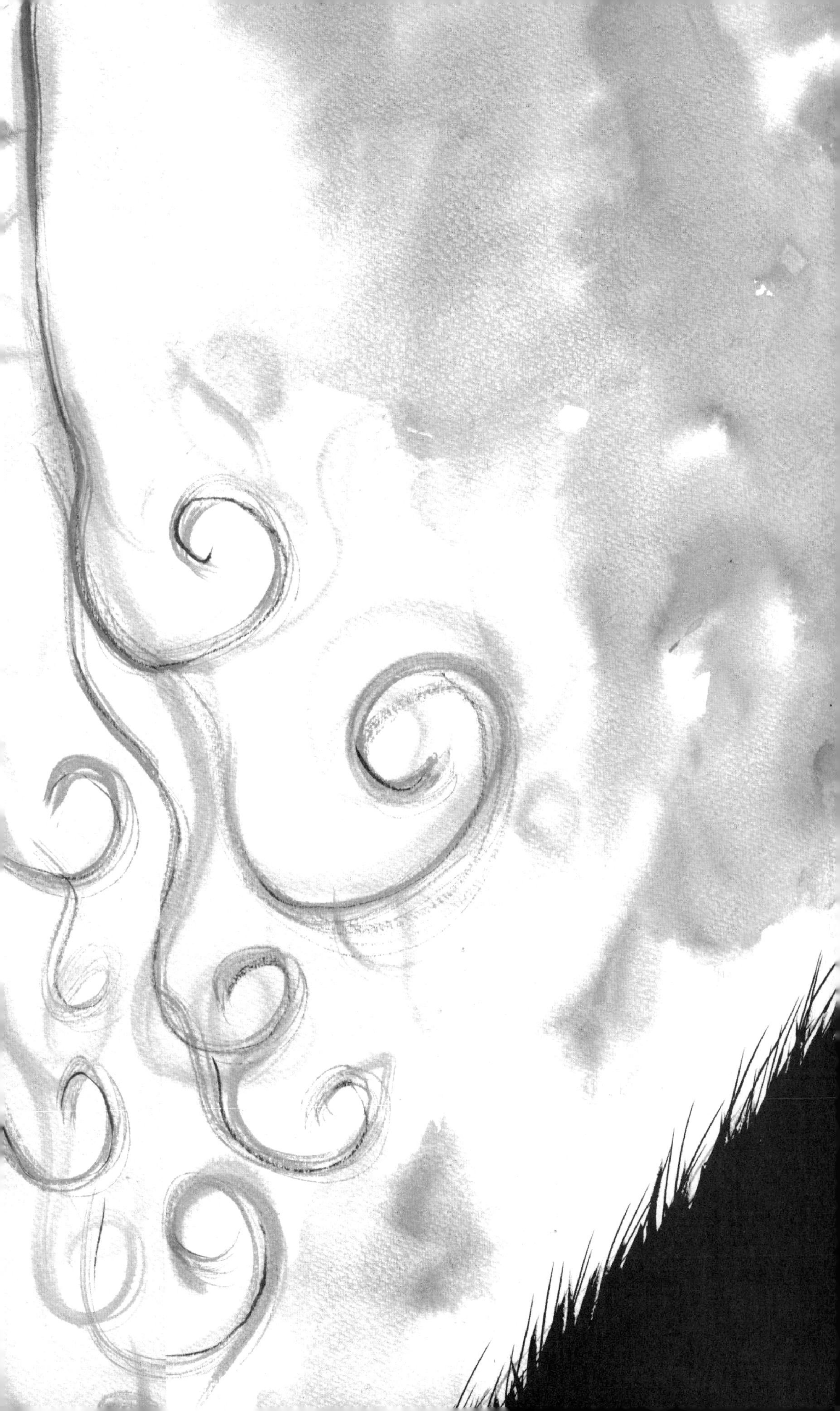

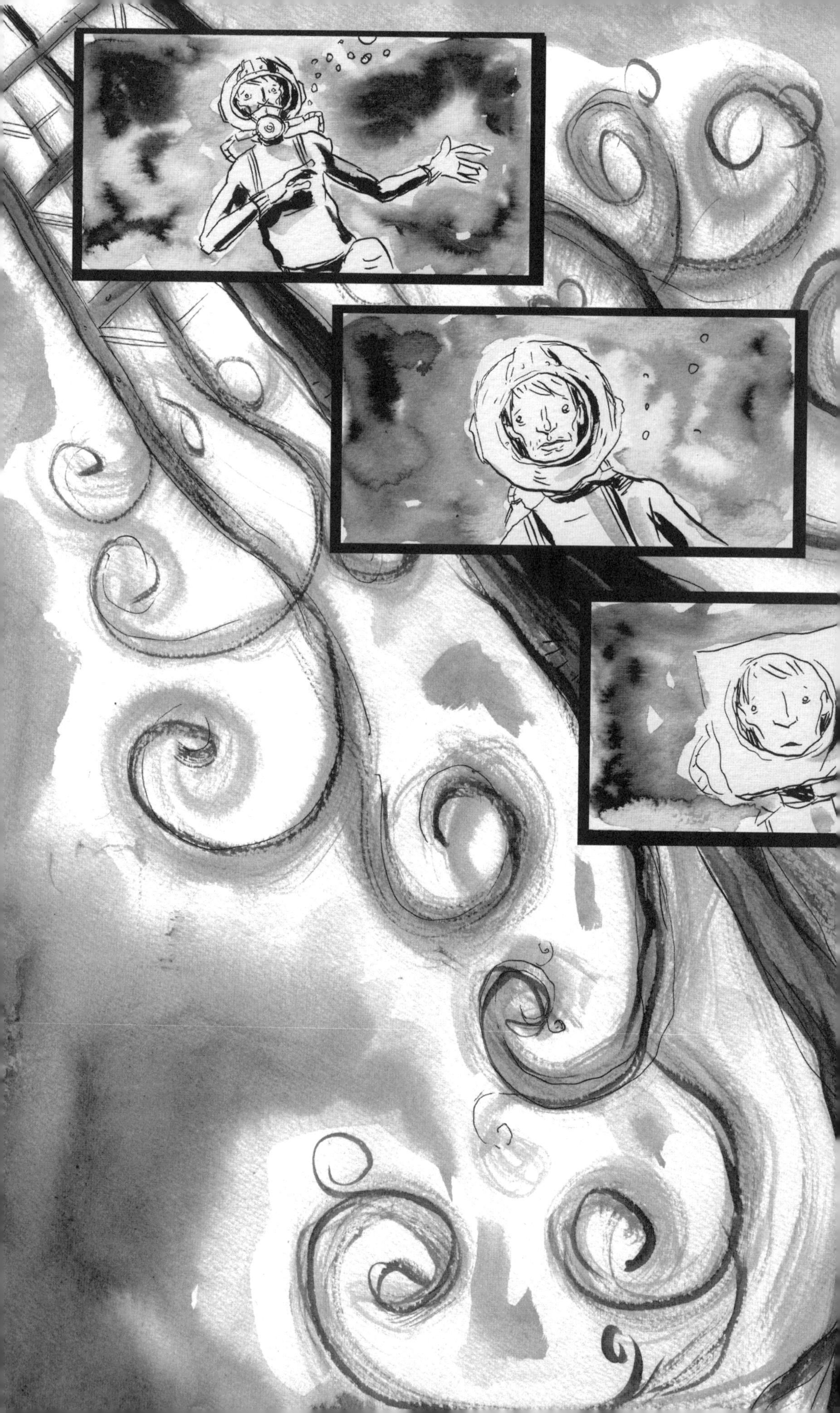

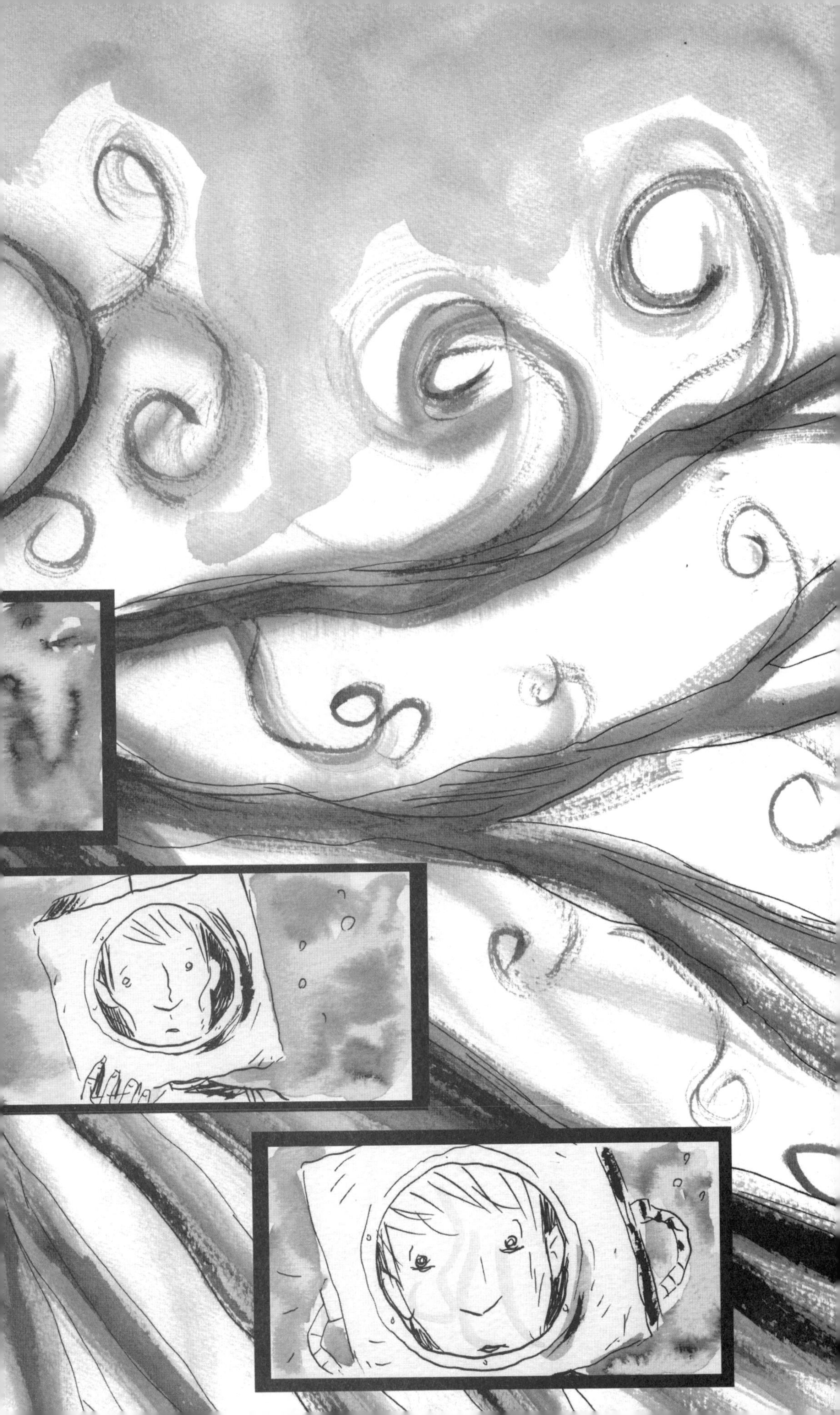

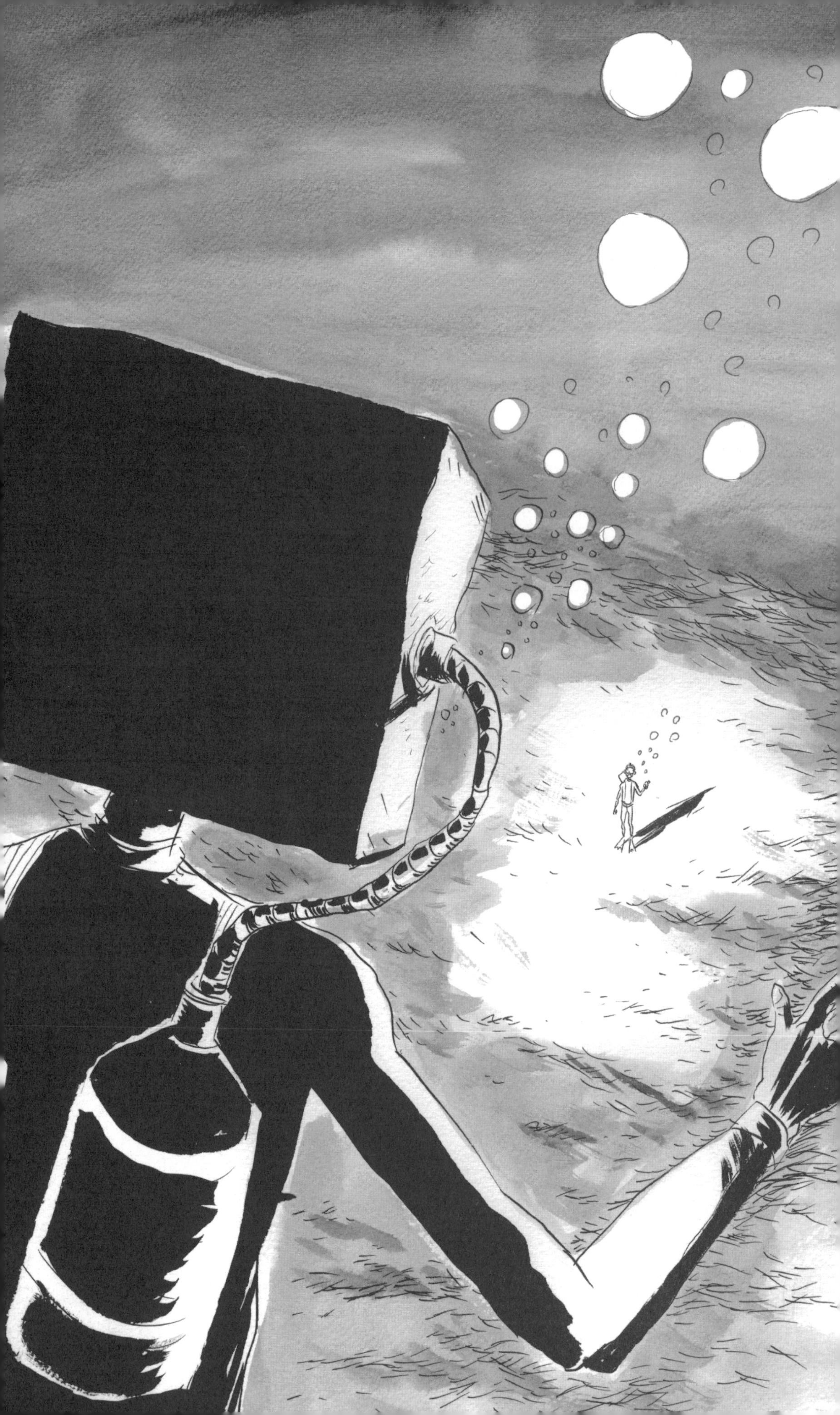

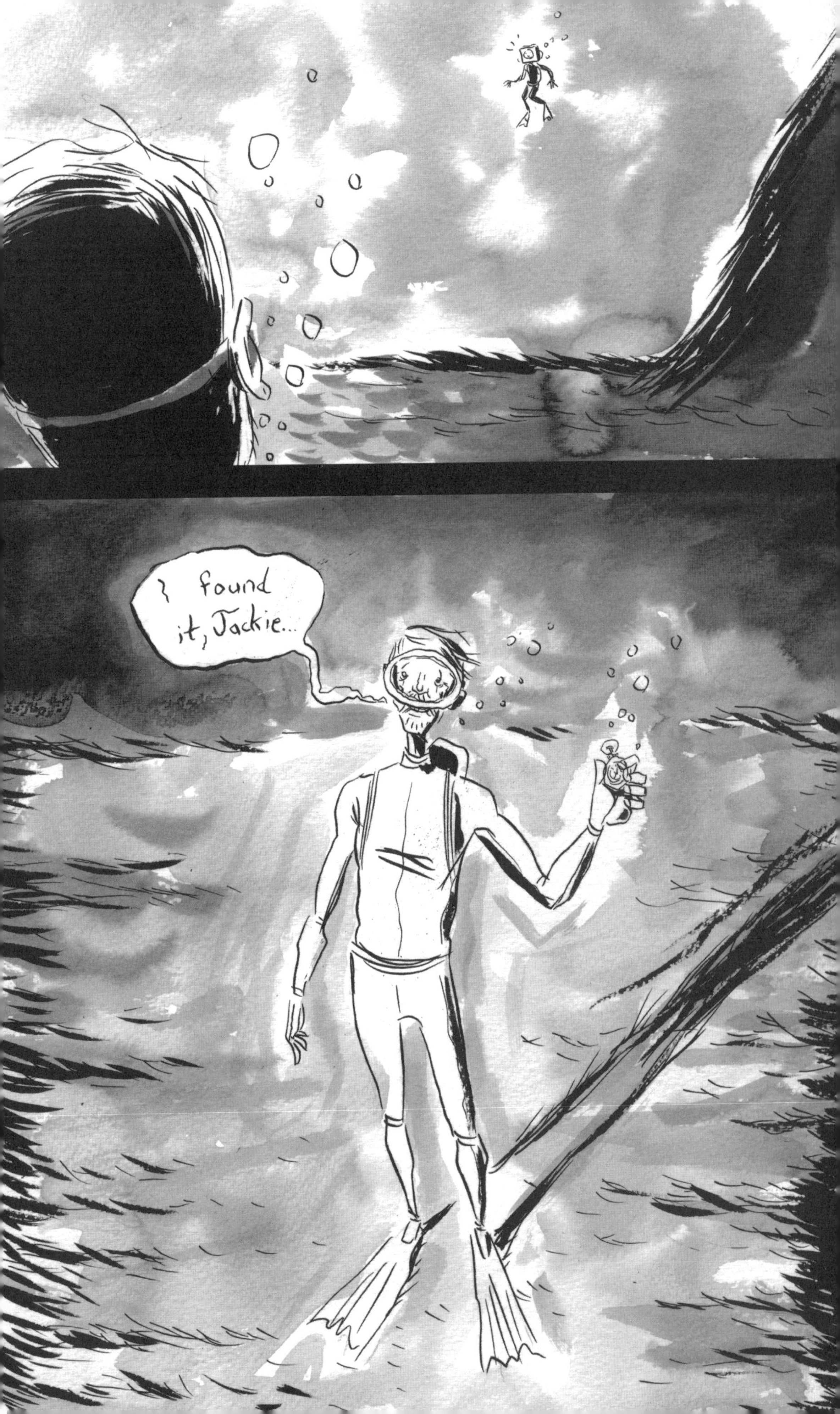
I found it, Jackie...

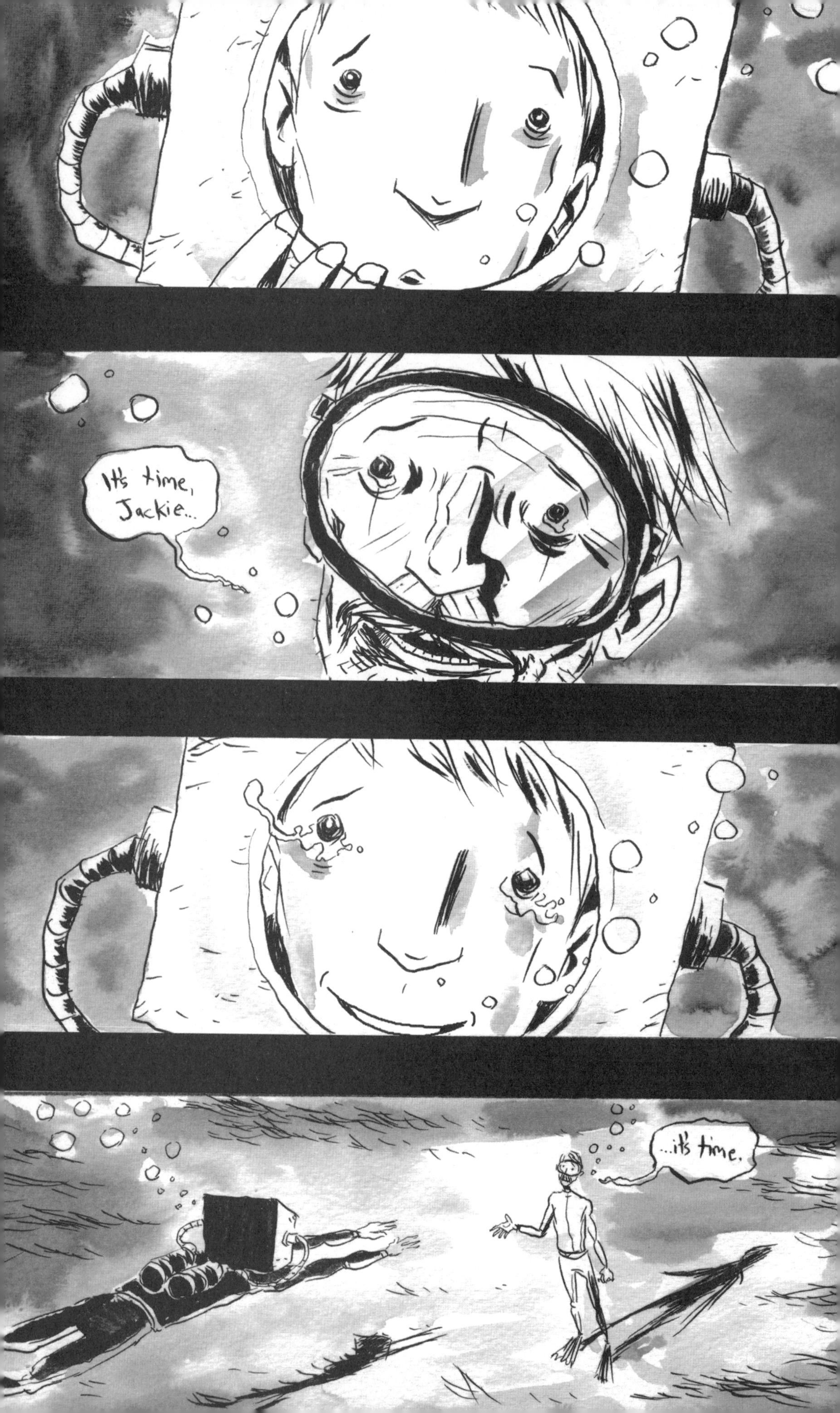
It's time, Jackie...
...it's time.

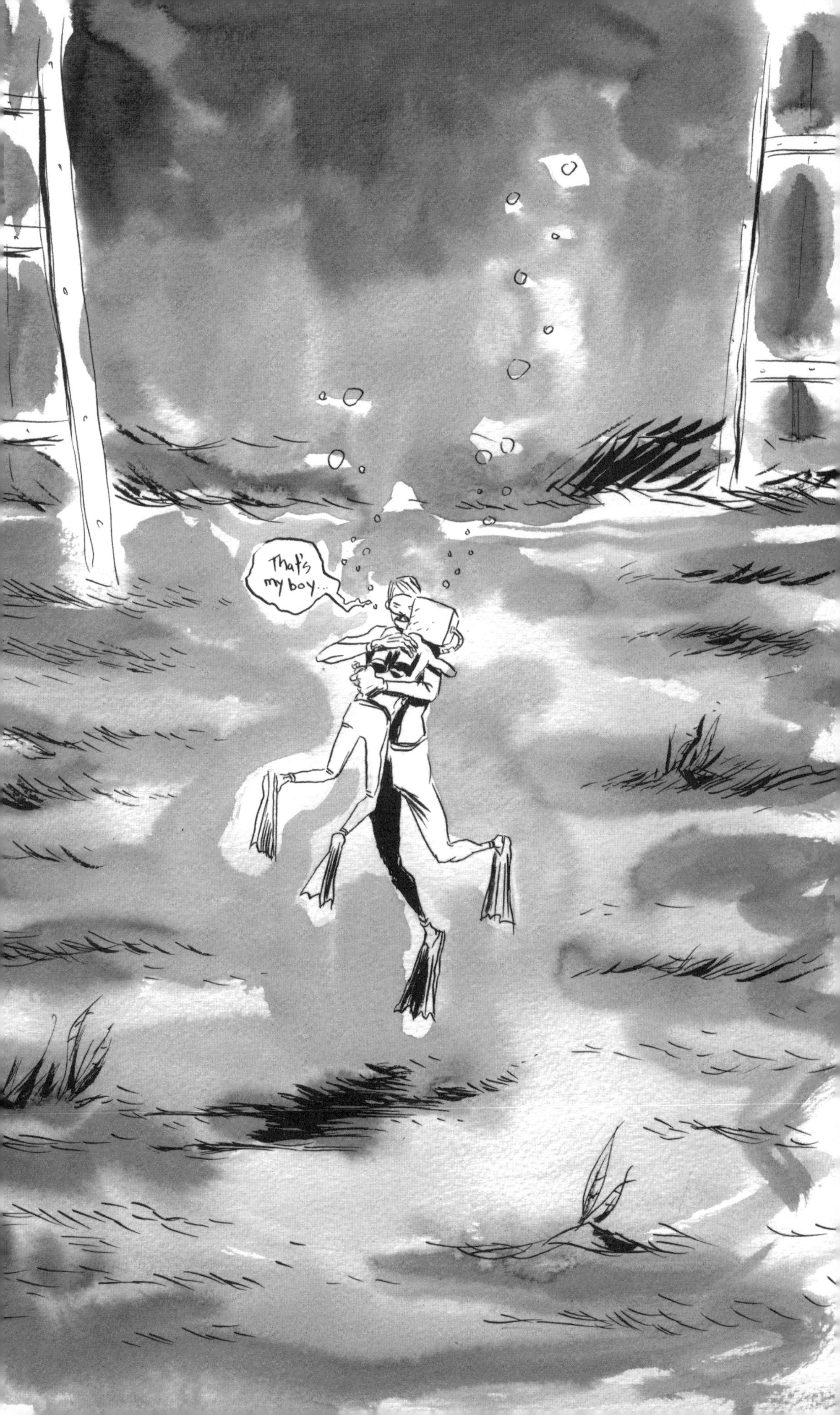
That's my boy...

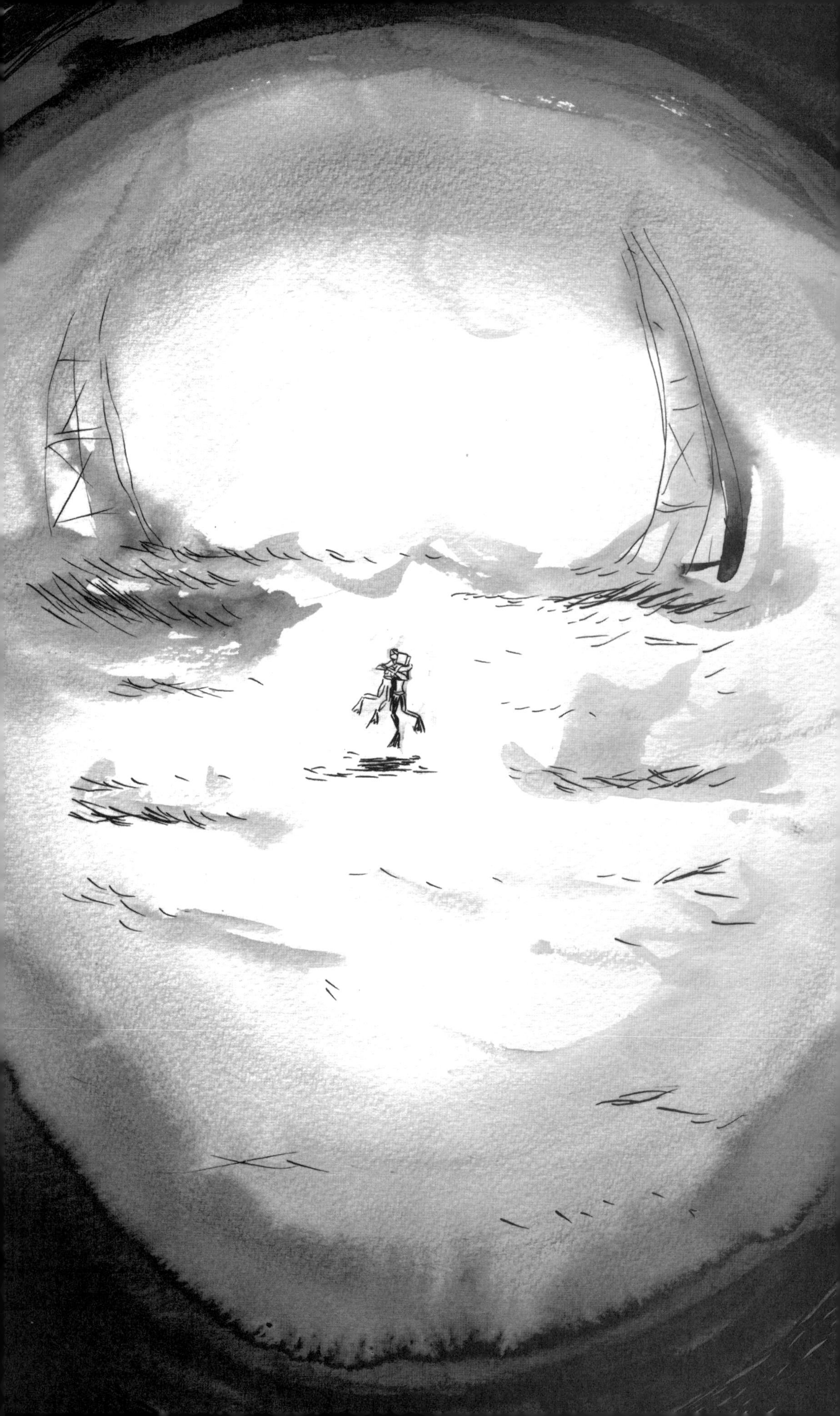

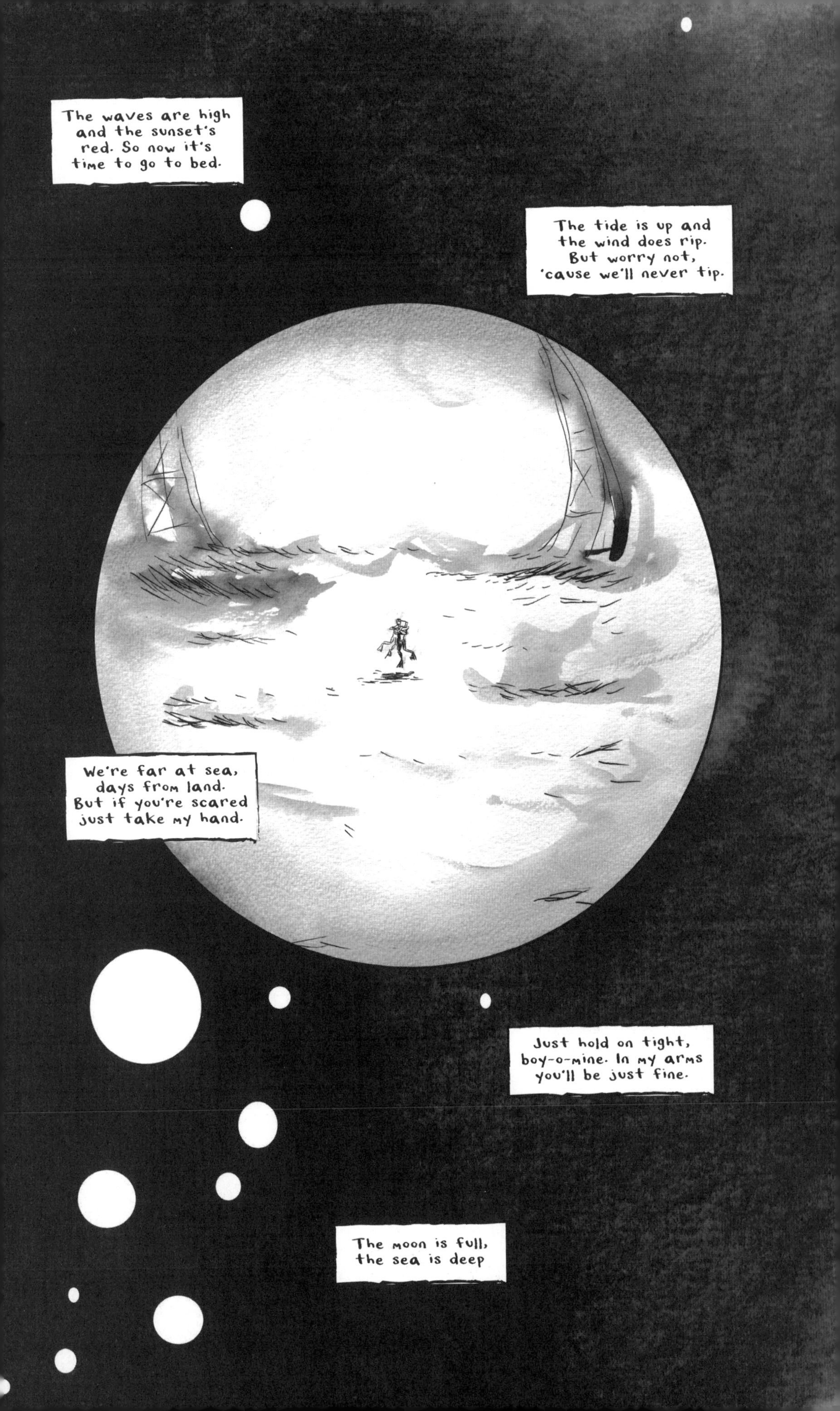
The waves are high and the sunset's red. So now it's time to go to bed.
The tide is up and the wind does rip. But worry not, 'cause we'll never tip.
We're far at sea, days from land. But if you're scared just take my hand.
Just hold on tight, boy-o-mine. In my arms you'll be just fine.
The moon is full, the sea is deep

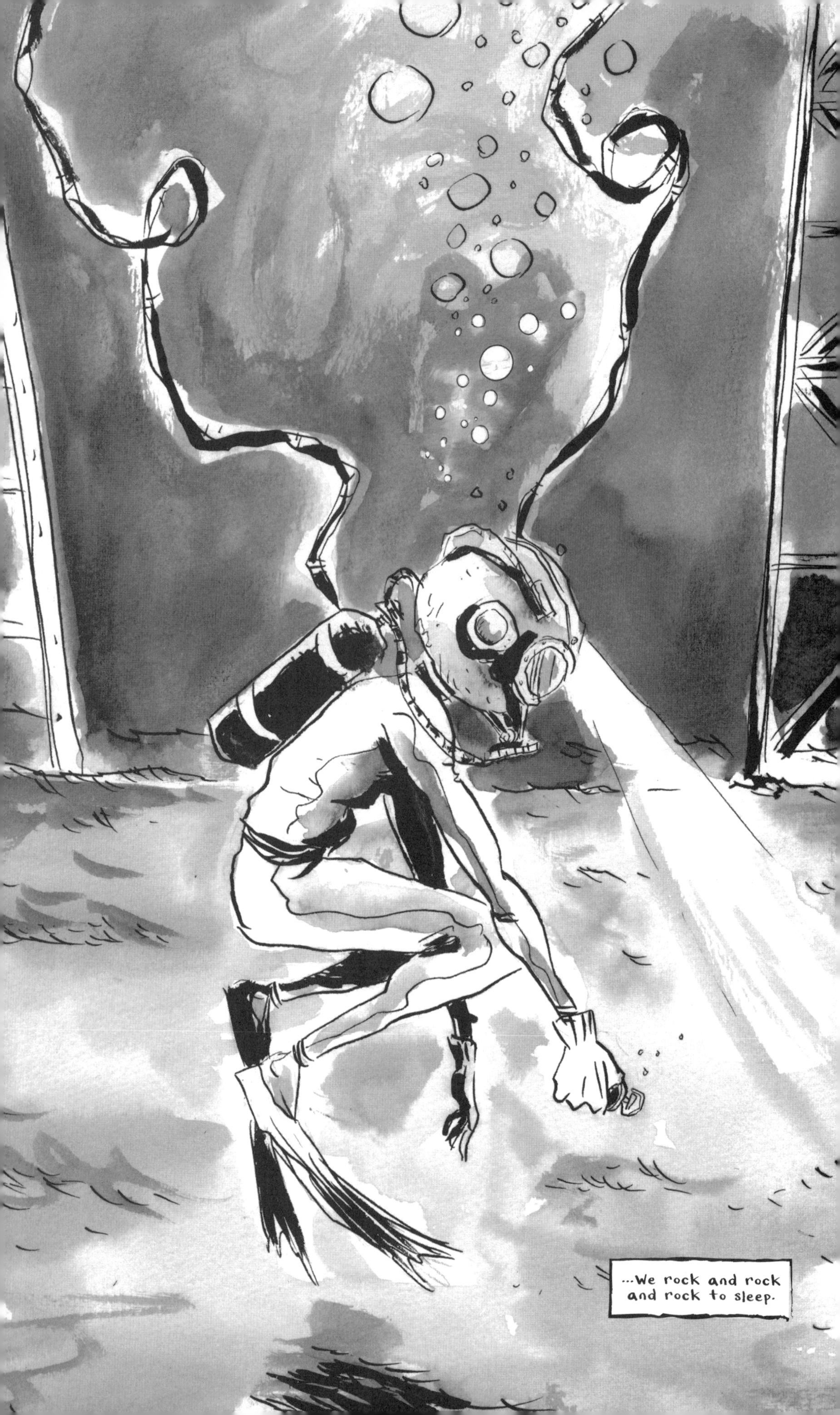
...We rock and rock and rock to sleep.

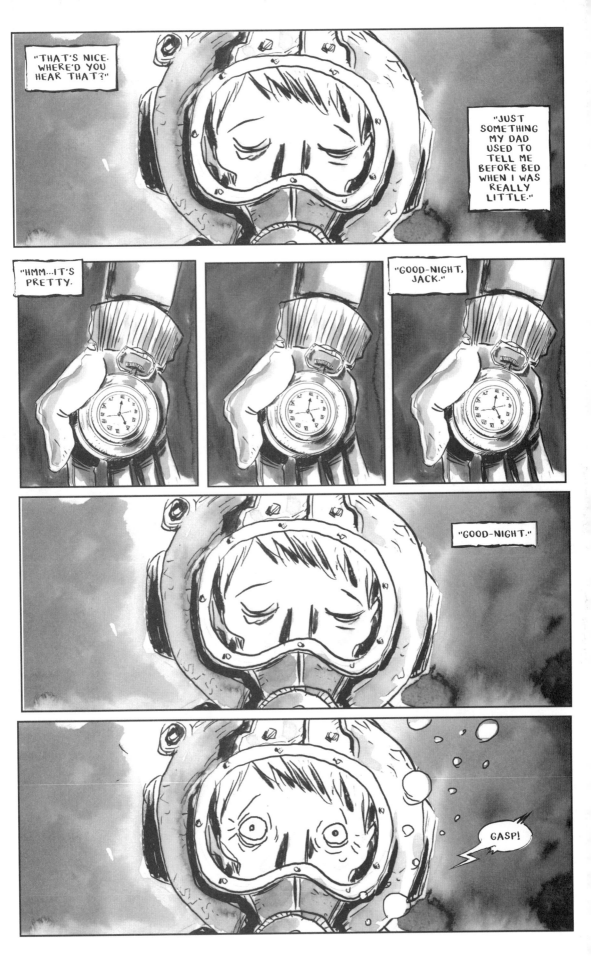

211

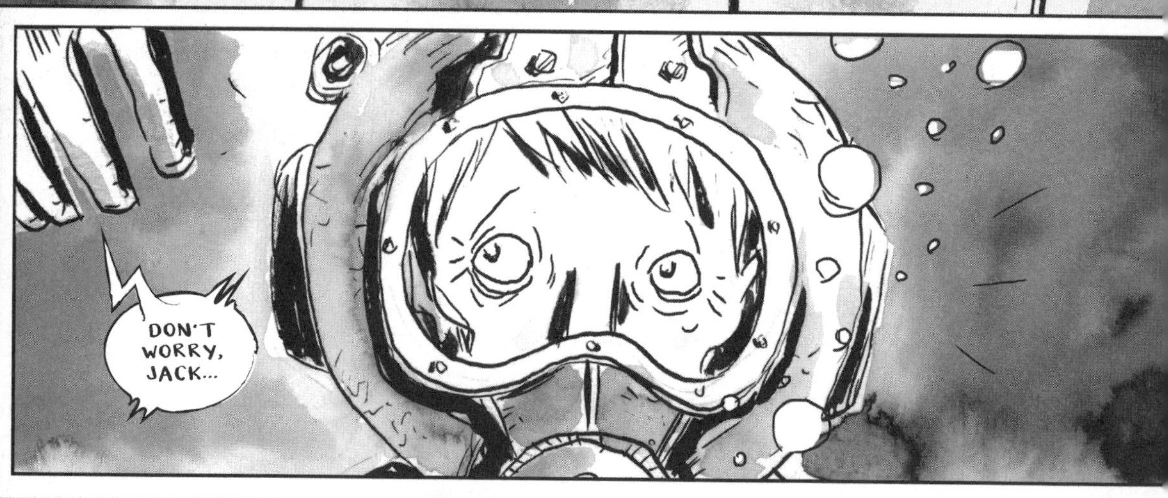
DON'T WORRY, JACK...
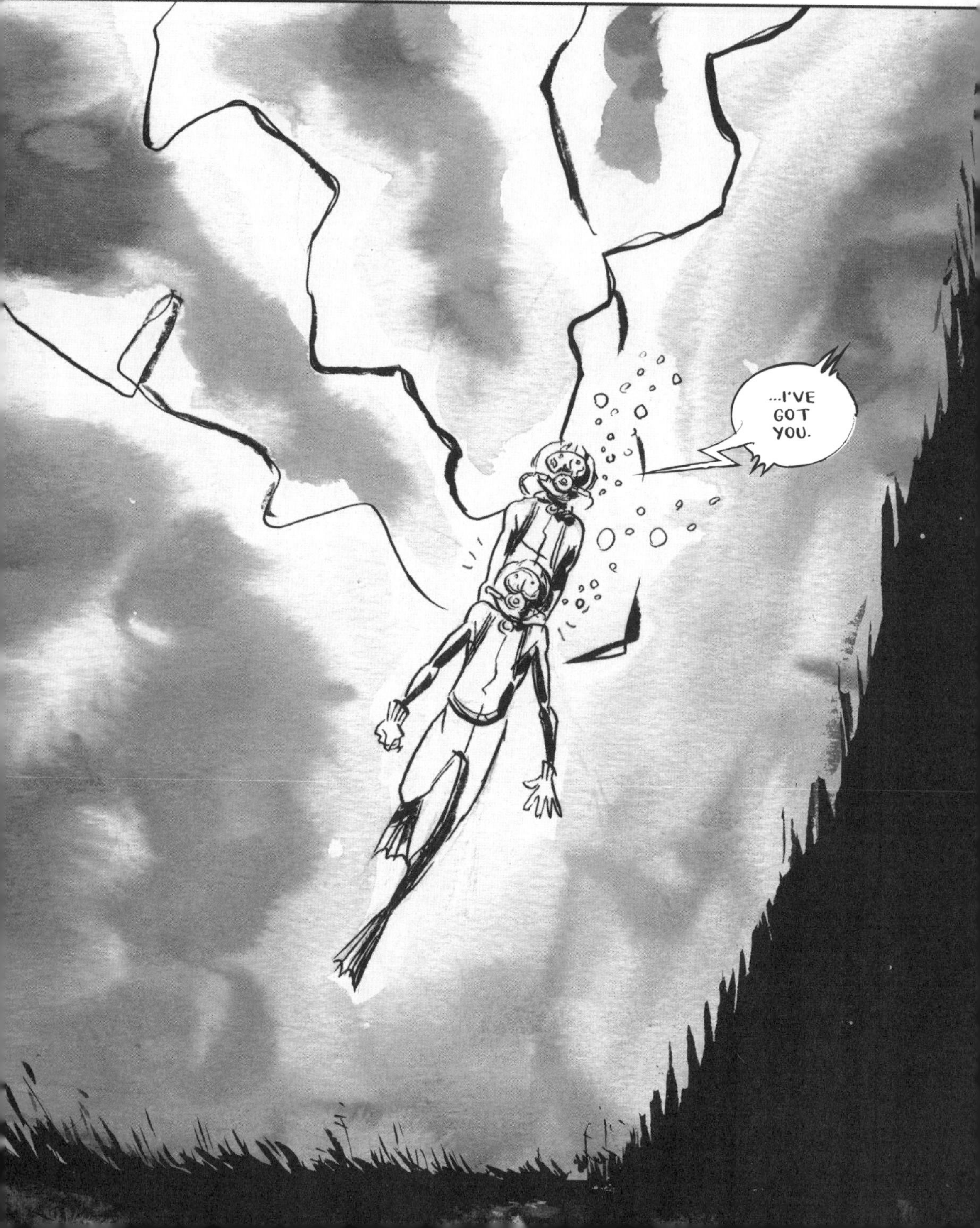
...I'VE GOT YOU.

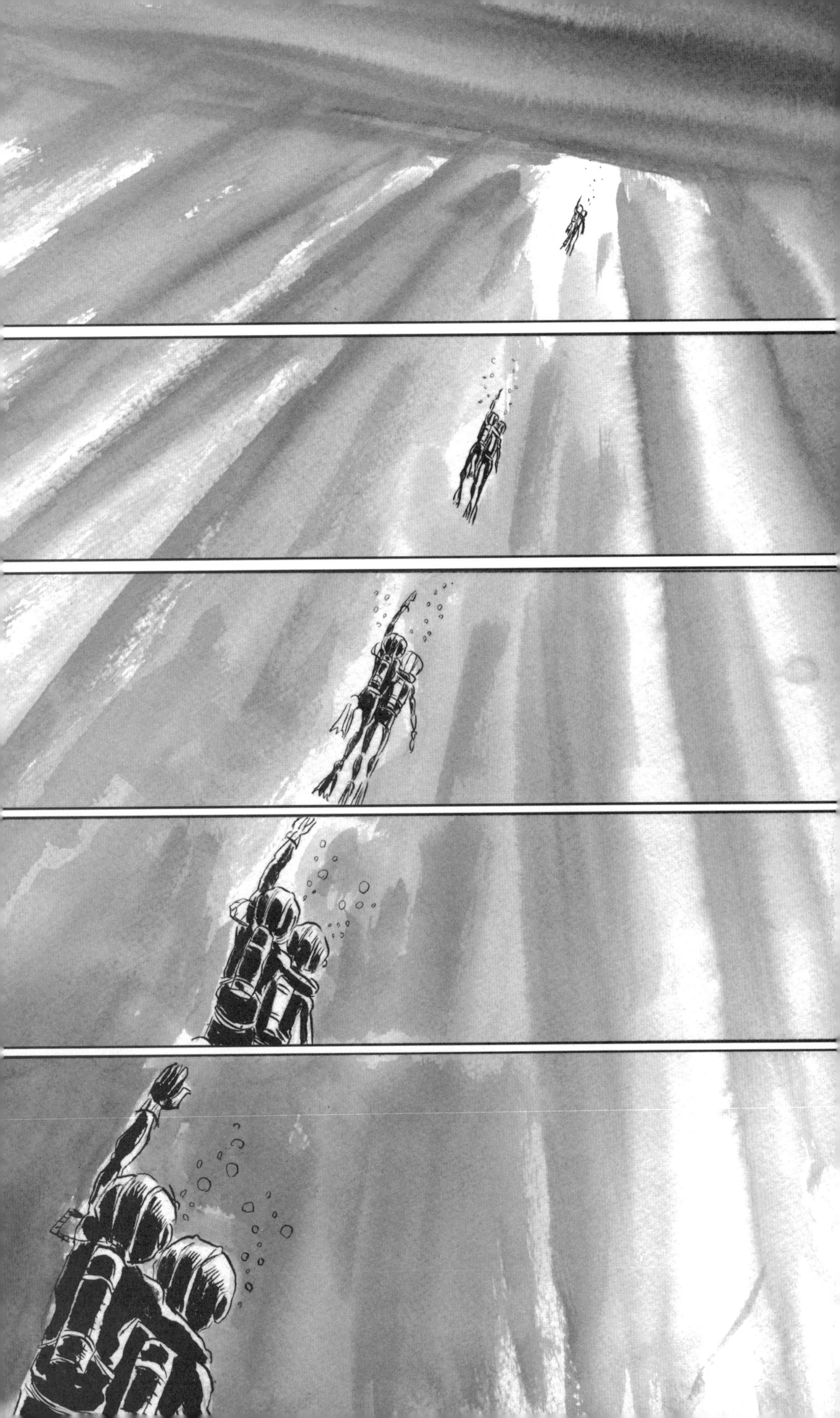

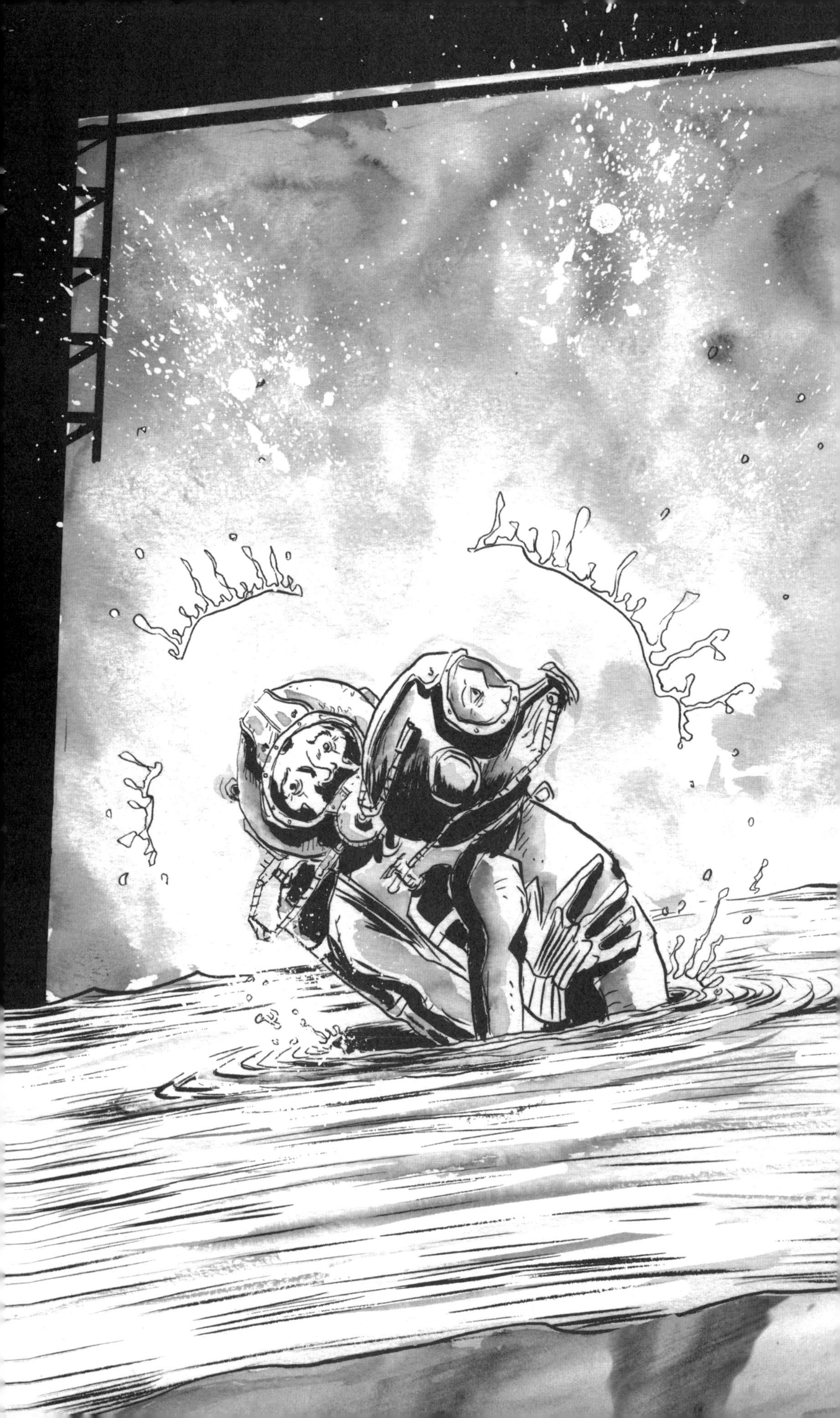

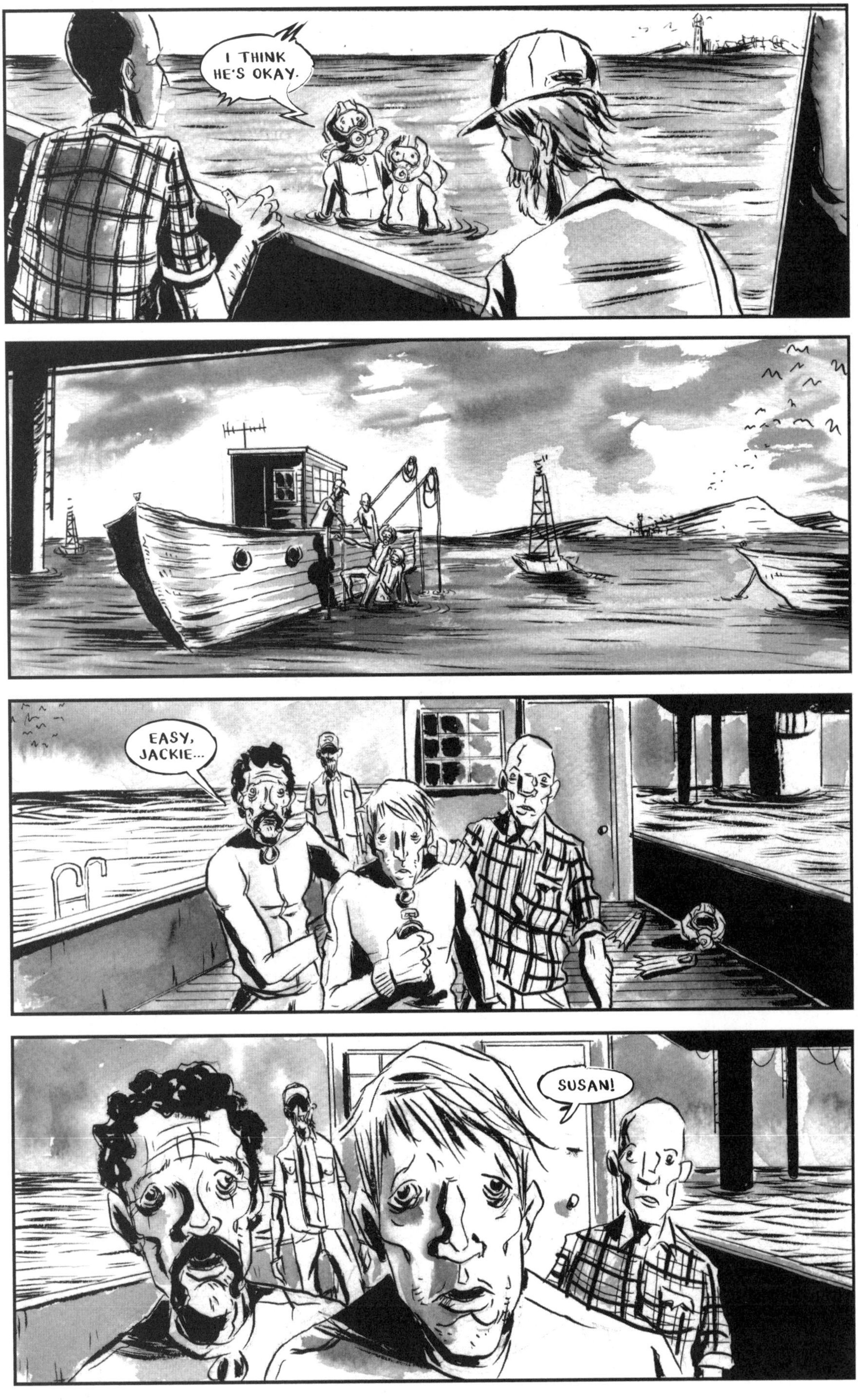
I THINK HE'S OKAY.
EASY, JACKIE...
SUSAN!

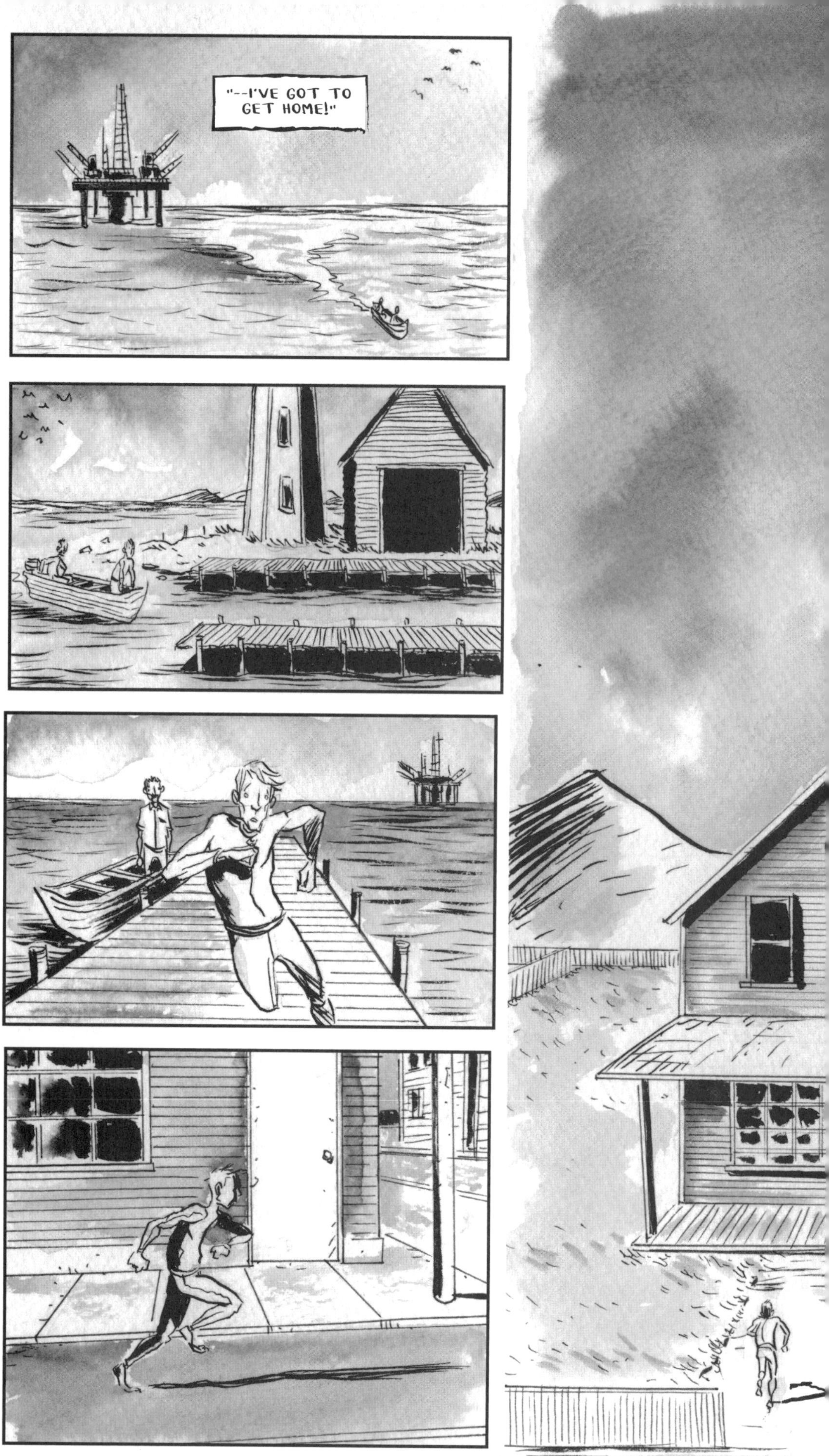
"--I'VE GOT TO GET HOME!"

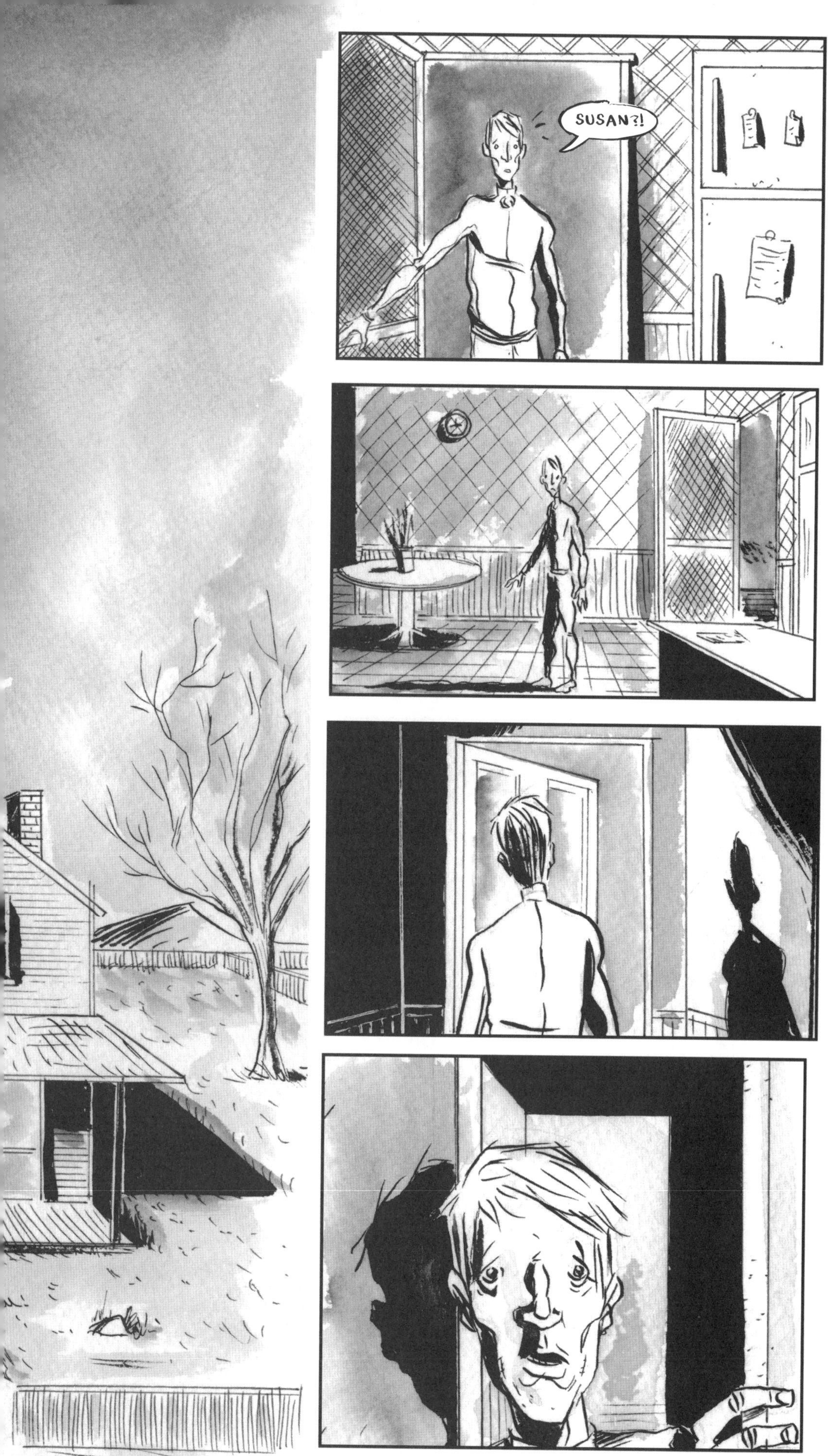
SUSAN?!

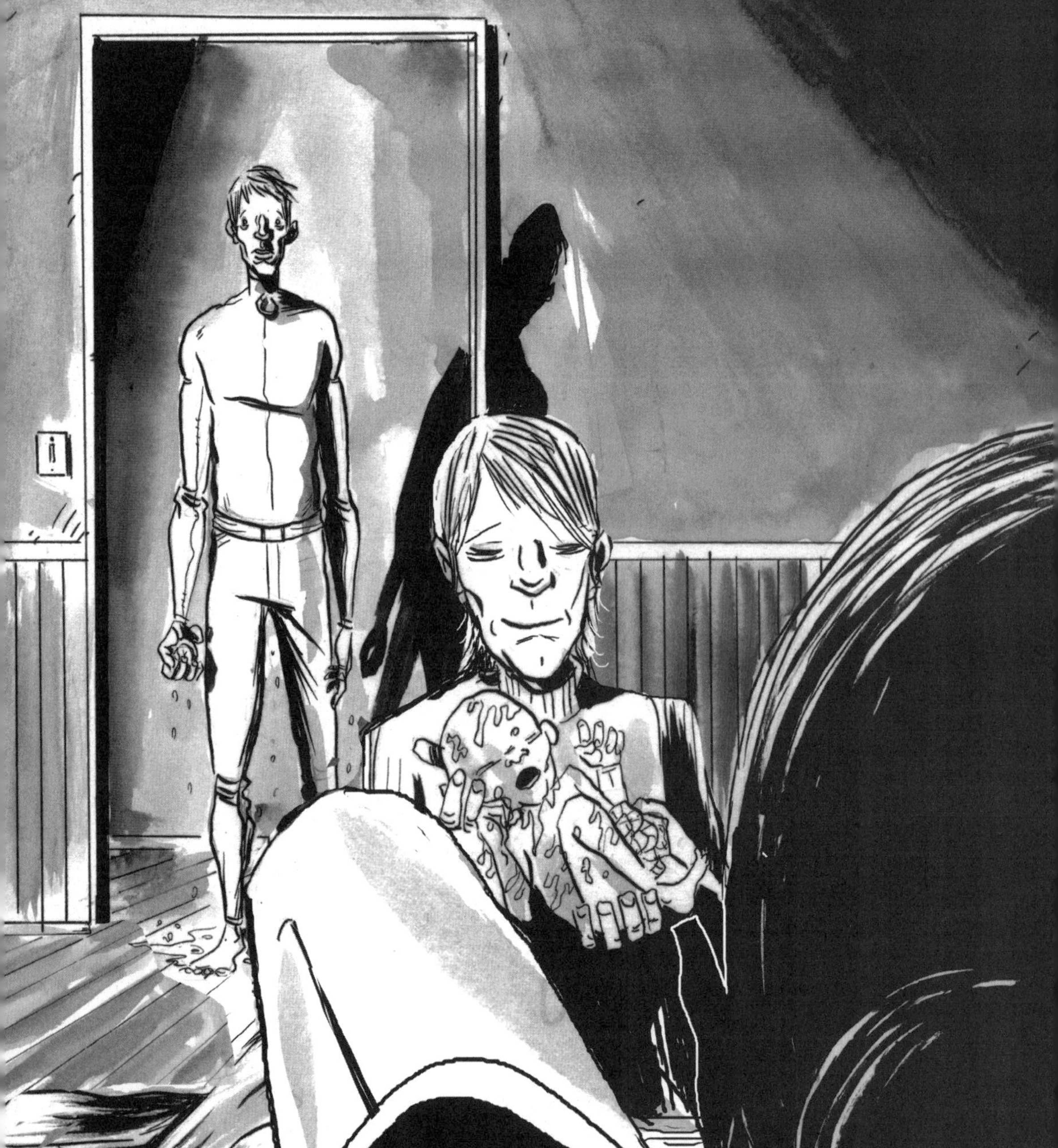
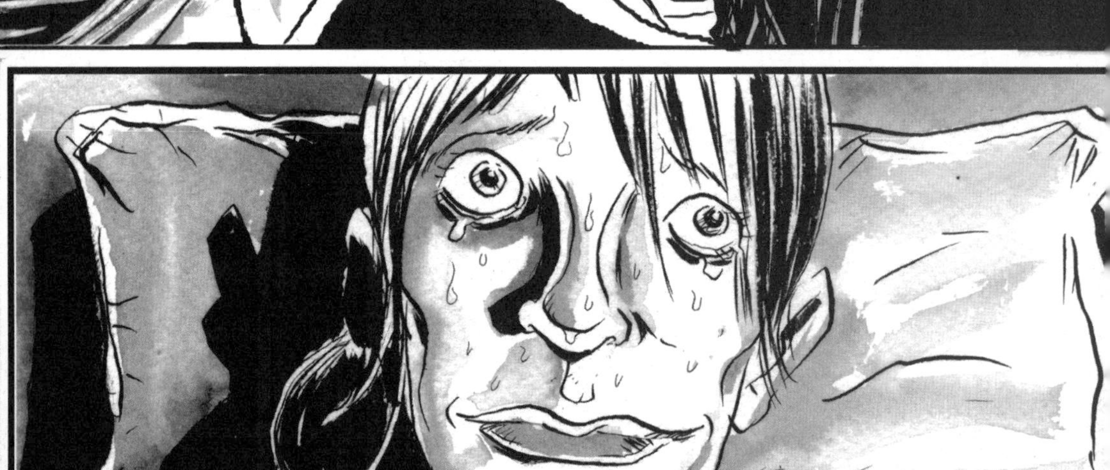

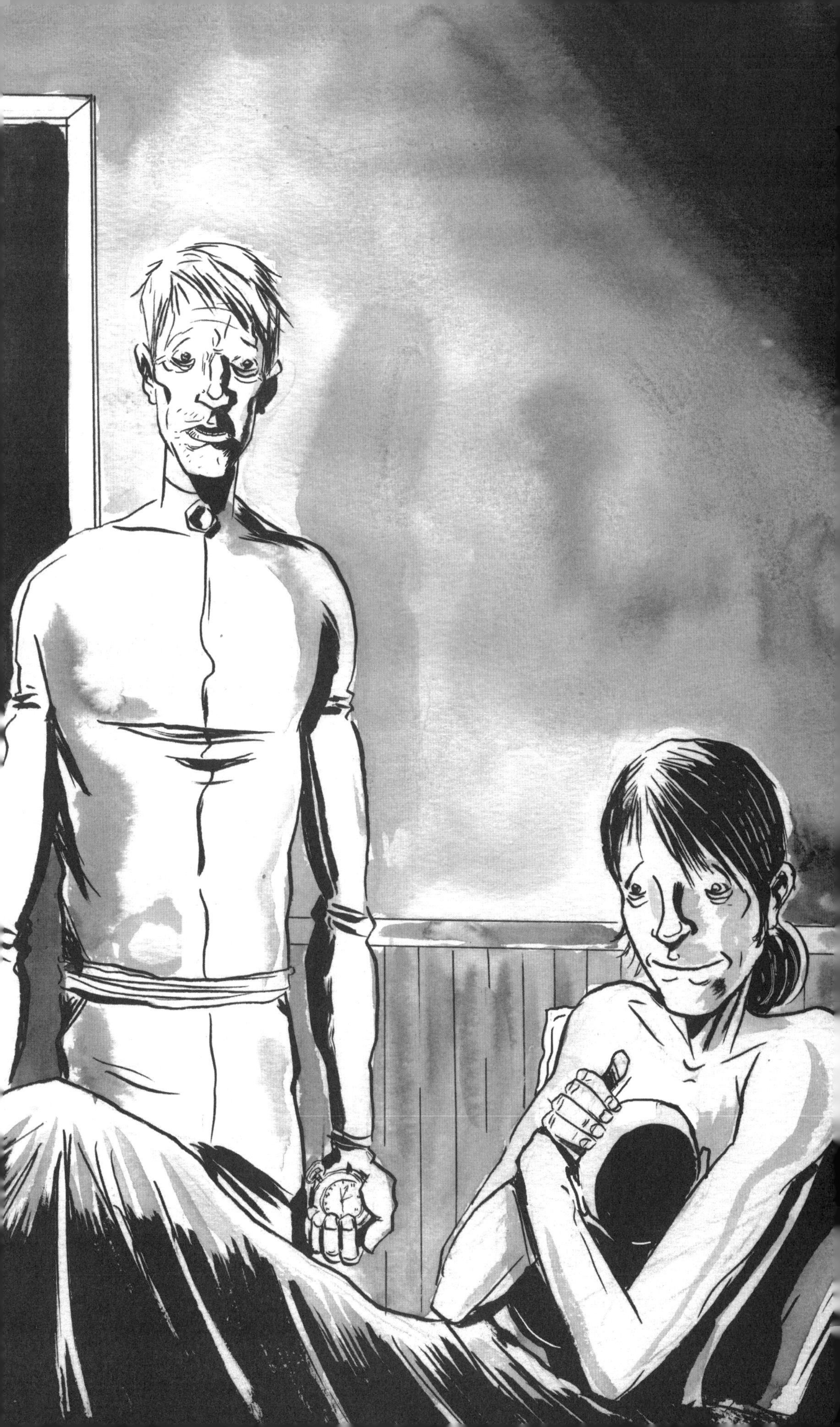

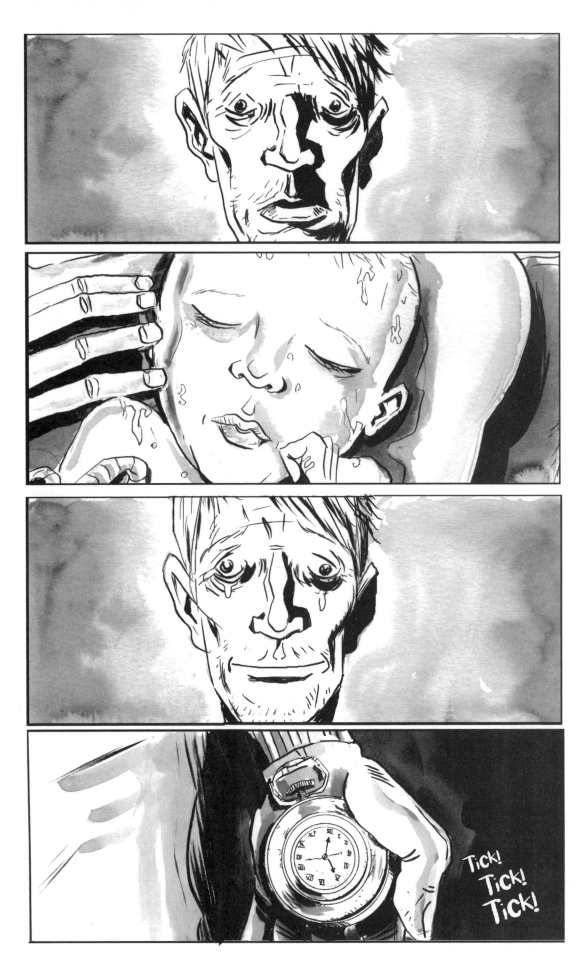

TICK!
TICK!
TICK!

220

THANK YOU

Trying to finish this book while in the midst of all my DC and Vertigo work was a real challenge, and I'd like to thank my Sweet Tooth editors past and present, Mark Doyle, Pornsak Pichetshote, and Karen Berger, for helping me find creative ways to find time to dedicate to The Welder. And on that note, a very special thanks to Matt Kindt for coming onto Sweet Tooth for three months, so I could focus on this project as it neared completion.

I'd also like to thank Chris Staros and Brett Warnock at Top Shelf for their constant support of my work and my career. I owe everything I've accomplished in comics to you guys. Thank you so much for finding a place in the Top Shelf family for this wayward Canadian. Also a big thanks to all my Top Shelf brothers and sisters and half-cousins, Nate Powell, Emi Lenox, Rob Venditti, Jeffrey Brown, Leigh Walton, Chris Ross, Andy Runton, and the rest of the gang.

I'd also like to thank the following people for invaluable advice, criticism and guidance throughout the making of this book: Dwayne Maillet, Scott Snyder, Ray Fawkes, Damon Lindelof, and Michael Sheen. Thank you all.

And finally, to Lesley-Anne for her constant support and understanding. I'm not an easy man to live with most days, but she never gives up on me. I love you, baby!

Photo by Jamie Hogge

New York Times Bestselling author Jeff Lemire is the creator of the acclaimed monthly comic book series *Sweet Tooth* published by DC/Vertigo and the award winning graphic novel *Essex County* published by Top Shelf.

Now one of DC Comics' key writers, Jeff was prominent in the publisher's recent "New 52" line-wide relaunch as the writer of *Animal Man, Frankenstein: Agent of S.H.A.D.E.,* and *Justice League Dark*. He has also written the monthly adventures of *Superboy* and *The Atom*.

In 2008, Jeff won the Schuster Award for Best Canadian Cartoonist and The Doug Wright Award for Best Emerging Talent. He also won the American Library Association's prestigious Alex Award, recognizing books for adults with specific teen appeal. He has been nominated for 6 Eisner Awards and 5 Harvey Awards.

In 2010, *Essex County* was named by the CBC's Canada Reads program as one of the five Essential Canadian Novels of the Decade.

He currently lives and works in Toronto with his wife and son.